# Toward a Vision of
# Land in 2015

*Dedicated to Roy Bahl*

# Toward a Vision of Land in 2015

*International Perspectives*

Edited by

Gary C. Cornia and Jim Riddell

**LINCOLN INSTITUTE**
OF LAND POLICY
CAMBRIDGE, MASSACHUSETTS

*Library of Congress Cataloging-in-Publication Data*

Toward a vision of land in 2015 : international perspectives /
edited by Gary C. Cornia and Jim Riddell.
     p.  cm.
   Includes index.
   ISBN 978–1–55844–174–3
   1. Land use.   2. Land tenure.   I. Cornia, Gary C.   II. Riddell, James C.
III. Lincoln Institute of Land Policy.
   HD111.T578   2008
   333.301'12—dc22        2007042172

*Designed by Walter Schwarz, Figaro*
*Cover designed by Peter Holm, Sterling Hill Productions*

Composed in Electra by Binghamton Valley Composition in Binghamton, New York.
Printed and bound by Puritan Press Incorporated in Hollis, New Hampshire.

The paper is Rolland Opaque 30, an acid-free, recycled sheet.

MANUFACTURED IN THE UNITED STATES OF AMERICA

# Contents

# Illustrations

# PART

## I

# Introduction

# 1

# Changing Views, Values, and Uses of Land

## Gary C. Cornia and Chi-Mei Lin

The decision made by the leaders of the International Center for Land Policy Studies and Training (ICLPST) to host a conference on land and land-related issues resulted from their desire to recognize the 100th international course the center had sponsored. Over the past 40 years, the center and its training programs have been a launching ground for many good ideas dealing with land and land use. The center's directors and academic and administrative leaders deemed it important that time and resources be allotted to recognize the contributions of its faculty, staff, and alumni. They also wanted to engage in a public dialogue around land and land use.

The Lincoln Institute collaborated with ICLPST to invite some of the best thinkers on land issues to prepare papers on land-related topics that would be important between the present time and the year 2015, the target date that United Nations member states have agreed to for the Millennium Development Goals. Two of the eight goals are to "ensure environmental sustainability" and to "develop a global partnership for development" (www.un.org/millenniumgoals). The assignment to identify and contact the individuals to prepare the papers was given to the academic staff at the center.[1] The ICLPST staff must be complimented for their efforts. We believe that the papers accomplished the goal of encouraging decision makers to think

---

[1] ICLPST brought the authors together for a conference held in Taipei, Taiwan, in October 2006. This conference allowed the authors to discuss their chapters with each other before making revisions to form the chapters of this book. This conference will be referred to throughout the book as the October 2006 Conference.

about land in the context of a changing world. Both the conference and this book are important, because policy makers often do not take the time or have the time to think either cautiously or creatively about land. We offer the following experience from recent history to illustrate the significance of the volume.

Only seven years ago, most of the world's population was waiting with considerable apprehension for the change in the Gregorian calendar from the year 1999 to 2000. Moving from one year to the next is a milestone that had happened thousands of times prior to 31 December 1999. However, many groups and individuals all over the world dreaded this particular change. There was a certain level of predictable alarm promoted by the advocates of a doomsday outcome. Alarming comments from such groups were expected and generally discounted as irrational.

Nevertheless, in the final few years of the twentieth century, a novel but factual fear was associated with the approaching calendar change. Interestingly, that apprehension originated with some of the most rational professionals of the twentieth century: computer software programmers and information technology specialists. One difference between this group and the doomsayers was that their alarm came from a logical and understandable source and seemed reasonable to informed individuals. Because of decisions made by software programmers in the middle of the last century, there were widespread concerns that the change in the calendar year from 1999 to 2000 could cause havoc in operational functions controlled by computers. Airlines, banking, credit cards, clocks, payroll systems, tax systems, medical records, and virtually any process that had been computerized were considered at risk when the calendar change occurred. Fortunately for humankind, by the early morning of 1 January 2000, the electronic world was perceptibly relieved that the concerns around the transition to the new century and the software itself had been successfully resolved.

What does the transition to the current century have to do with the topic of this volume—land in 2015? This historical anecdote illustrates an important point: unless a catastrophic event actually occurs or is a "near miss," societies and cultures have a propensity to overlook the cumulative importance of change. Societies also discount the importance of time, and we believe societies treat issues around changing land use in virtually the same manner. Unless there is a catastrophic event, the long-term consequences of land use decisions are ignored; yet land, like time, plays a critical role in practically every aspect of the human condition. We also ignore demographic events that have implications for land policy and land use unless a crisis is associated with the event. For example, the world has recently passed a tipping point: the population in urban areas now exceeds the population of rural areas

(World Bank 2003). This event has not received the volume of press attention associated with entering a new millennium, but the implications of an even more urbanized world for the human condition and for the role and importance of land are significant.

Thus, one purpose of this volume is to remind decision makers and policy analysts of the important background issues that surround land use and of the role these issues might play by the year 2015. The volume is not bold enough, or from our view imprudent enough, to forecast the role that land will be playing in 2015. What it does try to do is to alert policy and decision makers to the changing circumstances of how society views, values, and uses land. For example, in his chapter in this volume, Daniel Bromley reminds us that society first started thinking of land as a garden. Society then put a tractor in the garden, and some elements of society are now trying to remove the tractor from the garden. This latest view of land is referenced in this text as sustainable development.

Some of the issues addressed in this book are raised to help policy makers think about how to utilize land to help govern a community. This includes using land as a revenue source for the funding of government or as a tool in economic development. Some chapters offer insight and advice about technical and policy innovations that might improve our understanding of land use decisions, while others suggest the need for a careful reevaluation of the process of thinking about land and its fundamental importance in a society.

Together the chapters cover a wide array of topics focused around the themes of four sections: land and public finance, land in the context of economic development, institutional reforms in land management policies, and changing visions of land.

## PUBLIC FINANCE AND LAND ADMINISTRATION

Roy Bahl and Jorge Martinez-Vazquez introduce the theme of public finance in chapter 2, which concerns property taxation in developing countries. The chapter considers the revenue that is potentially available from the taxation of land and improvements to land in developing and developed countries, though the bulk of their analysis is on developing and transitional countries. The chapter focuses not only on raising revenue from property taxes, but also on the important functions that local taxes can perform if imposed on immobile factors. Such local revenue sources can enhance local autonomy and, thereby, the development of efficiencies associated with political and fiscal decentralization. The obvious, and perhaps only, candidate for such a tax is the property tax.

Bahl and Martinez-Vazquez identify a number of attributes, in addition to fiscal autonomy, that the property tax offers local governments. Those benefits include adequate and stable local revenue over economic cycles, correspondence between revenues and public expenditures, and minimal compliance costs for most property owners and taxpayers.

Bahl and Martinez-Vazquez also identify challenges that undermine the full use of the property tax. They note that it is a difficult tax to administer, especially in the less-developed regions of the world, because of inadequate information about the land market, limited financial resources, and the lack of professional talent. Making the property tax successful requires governments to commit substantial support to the functions associated with its administration. This requirement for resources leaves most governments with a dilemma: The resources they need to spend to collect revenue are just not available in many situations. There are also human resource constraints. Professionally trained appraisal cohorts do not develop overnight, and professional appraisers who do appear are likely to move from the public sector to the private sector.

Even when sound tax policy is combined with reasonable property tax administration, Bahl and Martinez-Vazquez acknowledge, serious political issues surrounding property tax remain. They note several situations in developing countries where improved administrative practices resulted in fewer revenues rather than more. Aggressive enforcement and collection procedures may result in an initial increase in the public revenues collected, but over time such actions may become ineffective by creating a political backlash or a culture of noncompliance or outright deception. Essentially, taxpayers respond to aggressive tax administration with equally aggressive noncompliant actions.

Chapter 2 offers several noteworthy observations about the future of the property tax. Among them is the authors' speculation that information technology will make property tax administration less daunting. If property tax administrators take advantage of information technology, they will have access to data on land and land improvements that could substantially improve their ability to track changes in ownership, use, and values, improving the overall accuracy of tax valuation outcomes. Information technologies may also lead to better compliance and collection outcomes.

The chapter confirms that the financial and administrative benefits that can accompany increased reliance on a local property tax have been slow in coming because use of the property tax has also been deliberate in development. In that regard, the chapter is discouraging to true believers in both the property tax and the benefits of fiscal decentralization. However, without describing the needed organizational changes, Bahl and Martinez-Vazquez illustrate how modest improvements in the key steps of administrative practices dealing with property tax have implications for substantial increases in revenue.

In chapter 3, Sally Wallace focuses on real property as a tax base. She does not consider the use of a traditional property tax, but instead examines the policy issues of applying a capital gains tax to real property. A policy that identifies, captures, and taxes capital gains from real property may seem unrealistic, but Wallace reports that such a tax does produce revenue in several countries.

Chapter 3 is not only about securing a source of increased revenue to feed the public leviathans, but also about the growing economic globalization and resulting mobility and the potential of diminishing revenue from many existing tax bases. Wallace notes that taxing mobile bases for revenue in a globalizing economy, where international boundaries are less important, is a slippery slope and that revenues from mobile tax bases are inevitably moving toward the bottom of the slope.

It is difficult to generalize as to what level of government would suffer the most harm from declining tax revenues, but we assume that in a central-versus-subcentral scheme of governing the subcentral governments are at the greatest risk of a fiscal disadvantage. The problem would be especially severe in the developing and transitional governments, where own-source revenue at the local level is already limited.

Adding to the challenges that a race to the bottom would create for fiscal decentralization are several basic questions about efficient tax policy. First is a concern that current tax schemes distort market and economic efficiency. For example, not taxing capital gains on real assets (property and improvements to property) but taxing gains on other capital assets (financial instruments) may alter the allocation of capital. The outcome could be an underinvestment in taxed productive capital goods and an overinvestment in nontaxed consumption goods.

Second, not taxing capital gains may contribute to an uneven distribution of wealth, with higher-income groups likely to benefit from a system that does not tax the capital gains on real assets. A capital gains tax would likely reduce or mitigate the financial bubbles that now confront the housing markets in the United States. In addition, while the primary focus of chapter 3 is not revenue, a substantial revenue flow is associated with a tax on the capital gains dealing with land and improvements. Wallace reports that a capital gains tax on residential housing in the United States would generate $40 billion annually.

There are economic positives associated with a capital gains tax, but there are also some important reasons a capital gains tax would prove difficult to implement, even on a partial basis. As with any new tax regime, a capital gains tax would most likely receive little political acceptance, especially if it were applied to residential land and housing. As alluded to earlier, Wallace identifies several countries where versions of a capital gains tax do exist and have been in place for a number of years: Jamaica, Korea, the Russian Federation, and the United States. None of those versions approach a true capital gains tax, however. In the United States, for example, the first $500,000 gain in the value of a residential home is exempt from the tax, which exempts most residential units.

The country that is closest to having a capital gains tax on land is Taiwan (Republic of China), which taxes capital gains on property and applies them to the gains' progressive tax rates, ranging from 20 to 40 percent on the inflation adjusted gains. Acknowledging the political challenges is important, but it is also important to realize that Taiwan's system has achieved a certain amount of success.

Wallace's chapter is important to policy makers for several reasons. It reminds readers that the world economies are globalizing and that taxes on nonmobile factors have the potential to provide governments with stable revenue sources, which seems especially important for subcentral governments interested in achieving fiscal decentralization. In addition, while there will be opposition to any new tax scheme, chapter 3 offers hope that at least a portion of that opposition can be offset by examining existing versions of a capital gains tax on land.

## LOCAL ECONOMIC DEVELOPMENT

The three chapters in this section examine the function of land policies and land use patterns in determining patterns of development, and all offer an unconventional view of land and economic development. In chapter 4, Gerrit-Jan Knaap presents a series of arguments that, when it comes to land use, the market mechanism may not achieve the most beneficial outcome. He argues that the market may actually lead to a distortion of efficient land use during periods of growth or redevelopment in a community. John Chien-Yuan Lin examines the role of land use in the context of redevelopment of urban and nonurban areas in chapter 5. He uses the example of the economic redevelopment of an island in Taiwan that would benefit from a development policy based on sustainable development. In chapter 6, Michael Luger examines in considerable detail the economic and political policies surrounding local economic development and the function that land and land policies can play in development.

Knaap's chapter questions the standard argument that market-derived land prices—and thus a market-based allocation of land—will produce an efficient outcome in land development patterns. As an economist, Knaap understands the importance of market prices in directing resource allocation, but he also realizes that there are asymmetrical outcomes in many markets, and in land markets they can result in situations where land may be misused. The neoclassical economist would recommend that the remedy for such issues is to internalize prices so that they reflect the full cost of the production factor—in this case, land—to an economy or society. Thus, an economist would add compensating taxes and fees to the market price of land and do it in a manner that would allow the market price plus the additional charges to provide the correct market signals on the consequences of land use.

Knaap also offers counterarguments to market pricing along with a series of examples to support the importance of nonmarket-driven processes that affect land use decisions. A useful illustration shows the role of public investment in infrastructures such as roads, water systems, and sewer systems in influencing land and urban development patterns. Knaap offers remarkably striking visual evidence of development patterns that appear to be strongly influenced by the patterns of public investment in infrastructure. The visuals include urban patterns from the nineteenth century and the last few decades of the twentieth century.

While many economists, including urban economists, dismiss the use of procedural rules or legislative actions to control markets, including the land market, Knaap contends that imposed policies may lead to more aesthetically appealing development patterns and more efficient housing patterns and transportation. He again offers as evidence of these assertions visual examples of housing patterns and the accompanying transportation outcomes. The term he uses to describe the improved transportation processes, including pedestrian traffic, is *network connectivity.* He concludes that a market-driven allocation of land will not achieve the most efficient network connectivity possible.

Some of Knaap's stronger arguments originate from research examining the importance of the visual aspects of neighborhood design and investigating how people value different design configurations. The chapter gives evidence that density, open space, signage, proximity to transportation nodes, and even road design are positively capitalized in land values. Moreover, Knaap asserts that those visual aspects are unlikely to develop without applying nonmarket methods to guide decision making. This chapter will be interesting to legal experts, planners, public managers, economists, and noneconomists concerned with land use.

In chapter 5, Lin focuses on the role that a land policy can have in influencing local economic development. Lin considers the possibility of using unique land configurations as engines to foster economic development. Such configurations are normally associated with naturally occurring wonders of nature, but in Lin's view unique land qualities can also be found in commercially active areas and can result from historical patterns of land use and man-made improvements to land. Lin believes that uniqueness can develop around issues such as air quality, efficient use of resources, and alternative patterns of land use. He believes that a sustainable environmental policy can contribute not only to the quality of life but also to the economic well-being of residents in a community. His views of land use correspond with at least one of the Millennium Development Goals of the United Nations: to ensure environmental sustainability (World Bank 2000). Like those of the United Nations, his views are not limited to rural or remote plots of land; he also reviews the role that unique land and improved areas can play in the sustained economic development of urban areas.

Lin's chapter will especially resonate with those interested in unconventional approaches to economic development such as tourist-led economic transformations of urban and rural areas. Under such approaches, unlike the more familiar method of establishing an economic development policy to create jobs, additional jobs are almost secondary to an improved use of the existing assets of an area. As in other chapters, a key concept in Lin's model is promotion of environmentally sustainable development.

Because Lin looks at economic development in terms of economic and environmental sustainability, his chapter is also useful for individuals and groups who support urban economic development but have seen past efforts at urban renewal fail. He offers a process that may create not only economic benefits to the participants but also political advantages as public and private partnerships are created.

In chapter 6, Luger provides a comprehensive review of the multitude of techniques used to generate economic growth and development within a community. Generally, the processes used by subcentral governments to promote economic development have been specific and direct economic incentives offered to business firms. Examples of those incentives include focused tax breaks, low-interest (subsidized) loans, and acquisition and assembly of land parcels. Of the development techniques identified, the ones most related to land are the policies that assist in the assembly of land for developers and deal with property tax breaks.

The literature and the examples reported in chapter 6 generally come from the United States, but we believe that the reported analysis also applies to developing and transitional countries. We think it quite likely that the strategic arguments and tactical steps used to encourage local governments in the United States to adopt policies that encourage economic development will become as common in the developing regions of the world. The often-referenced flattening of the world applies to virtually all economic policies, including local economic development schemes.

Luger presents a general framework that can guide decision makers during the analysis of economic development programs. His framework considers the influence of policy choices on hoped-for or intended economic and social outcomes, as well as a conceptual process that facilitates consideration of the unintended outcomes, which generally carry a negative connotation. In many situations the unintended outcomes may be positive but remain unrecognized or underreported. We believe the use of the frameworks articulated in chapter 6 will add structure and conceptual strength to the analysis of local government development policies.

Luger, along with most analysts who publish economic development literature, views the effectiveness of direct economic development incentives with considered reservation. Conversely, he believes that economic development processes are important components of a local government's success, perceived or real, in a competitive world. Like many public policy questions, those concerning the effectiveness of economic development policies have few clear answers. Luger is intrigued with the concept of using the provision of adequate public services as an indirect incentive for economic development. In the long run, for example, a quality workforce trained in demanding public schools might do more for economic development than a direct tax incentive. The author views higher education and the associated research that follows as important instruments of economic development.

Luger's review of the recent U.S. Supreme Court case *Kelo v. City of New London* on land takings is also important because it considers the political repercussions associated with that decision and reminds everyone that while policy battles are fought in the courts, policy wars are decided by elected legislative bodies. Consequently, several state governments in the United States have attempted to limit the impact of the court decision by adopting laws that minimize the ability of a government to participate in a taking.

## INSTITUTIONAL REFORM

The next three chapters cover institutional reforms associated with land and its management. Each of the reforms—estimation of the value of land and improvements to land; information technology applied to land records, land management, and land registration; and land record and titling programs—represents important yet practical challenges in land use.

In chapter 7, two real estate finance economists, Peter Colwell and Joseph Trefzger, address institutional reform, particularly the importance of accurate and reliable valuation of land and improvements. Their chapter underlines how essential it is that accurate estimates of value are used in ad valorem property taxation, financial compensation for land takings, and even arm's-length market transactions. The current processes of estimating the market value of land and improvements to land have emerged over a four-decade period, and as the technology of appraisal changed, the institutional function of appraisal also evolved.

The chapter reviews the technological advances, including software, computing capacity, and statistical innovations, now used in estimating the value of land and improvements to land, or real estate valuation. It is clear that this technical progress is revolutionizing the valuation practice and profession. The regression models and methods currently employed in real estate valuation are substantially more robust and nuanced than early models. However, the authors acknowledge that many complex valuation challenges remain to be resolved, in part because the academic community, including econometricians, statisticians, economists, and real estate economists, has not invested significant effort in resolving land and building appraisal questions.

Even with the noted shortcomings, hedonic regression models dominate valuation models. The application of regression models to valuation has benefited from the advances in computing power, including the declining cost of acquiring power. In the United States that low cost has allowed small appraisal districts the opportunity either to develop their own hedonic model or to contract for such results from commercial appraisers. While not directly discussed in the chapter, the growing affordability of computing power is one reason that an ad valorem property tax may become more realistic in developing and transitional regions.

Colwell and Trefzger observe that econometric modeling has yet to exploit the insights that spatial econometrics brings to real estate valuation. This includes developing models or employing variables that can robustly distinguish between subtle spatial characteristics. They also caution against the blanket application of spatial variables to estimate land values. Their concern is that without careful model development, regression modeling that uses spatial variables may report values but not necessarily explain the cause. They also caution against the application of geographical information systems (GIS) to valuation models. Their primary concern is the "black box" nature of the GIS, in which values are determined more on averaging processes than on econometric foundations. One intriguing observation offered in the chapter is that population characteristics (socioeconomic) may become important and accepted variables in real estate valuations.

This review of the technological applications currently used to value land and improvements to land, along with the discussions of developing technologies, is recommended to professional appraisers in the public and private sectors, as well as academics who are developing new or enhancing current econometric models to assist valuation. The chapter also offers an insightful evaluation of many emerging and still unresolved valuation questions with regard to takings, partial property rights, and the correlation of multiple appraisal methods.

In chapter 8, Ian Williamson reports on the startling increase in the application of information systems and information technology to land records and land administration processes. The image of the dust-filled land office is clearly inaccurate in most countries. The emerging technological advances that are applied to land records have transformed the land office into a dynamic and exciting center of information and policy.

The use of land records is not new; in most of the world's regions landownership documents have existed for generations. Generally, they have been formally recorded physical documents, but in some situations informal records serve similar roles. For most property records, formal or informal, the focus has been on identifying location and ownership.

Williamson describes the transformation of land records from text to digital form and highlights the resulting advantages. First, they no longer require a physical presence to access and evaluate land information. Remote site access allows a more diverse group of researchers to study land issues and analyze land use patterns. The digitization of land records is substantially more than just having easier access to land records, however, and the electronic recording of land records now extends beyond just listing location, ownership, and ownership transfers.

Where implementation has progressed, the resulting digital records now describe the associated rights of land and land use. Examples of additional dimensions of land parcels include the concepts of height and time. Examples of increased information include carbon credits, unit trusts, waste discharges, and complex commodities that are now associated with land. Williamson argues that the inclusion of information beyond ownership information is a necessary progression and relates to the complex land market emerging in developed and some of the developing regions of the world.

The use of supplementary land information, according to Williamson, will facilitate the growing desire to use land in a manner that encourages sustainable economic and environmental development. Such development is more probable when the effects of a landowner's action on other landowners are articulated before land decisions are made. With additional and readily available information, land use and land management are likely to become more comprehensive, including the consideration of partial land rights. Likewise, the development of land markets that are now trading in partial rights will become more transparent. The new markets allow such rights to resemble commodities and result in new methods leading to the securitization of those rights.

Chapter 8 highlights the growing openness of land information and land records, which are now accessible by almost anyone with access to a computer and the Internet. Data include information about the natural, built improvements and the intangible matters connected to land use. Williamson emphasizes that land markets become more efficient when information about land and land use is accessible to citizens and government policy makers.

In chapter 9, John Bruce reviews the critical role that land records play in the development of economic and property rights reform. Bruce acknowledges the contribution of economist Hernando de Soto in bringing land titles to the forefront of current development debates and practices. De Soto made the case that titling land would facilitate access to capital markets for people in poverty, because with titled land they would have an asset that could be collateralized in a mortgage process. As Bruce notes, that reasoning was not new to most international assistance organizations; for example, it is a key part of the most recent *World Development Report* (World Bank 2006). The widespread effort to title land is a significant institutional watershed in many countries, especially for the underprivileged throughout the world. (In chapter 10, Daniel Bromley raises a series of questions about the implied institutional changes associated with land titling.)

International organizations have been working for a long time to aid developing and transitional countries in their efforts to validate individual property rights. Bruce stresses that such groups are more focused on property rights now than at any other time in their history. However, the increased emphasis on land titling has been questioned. Bruce reviews several recent works that raise substantial challenges to the assertion that private ownership of land increases the productivity of land.

The World Bank, where Bruce has worked as a legal expert in land issues for several decades, is not in a position to compel countries to do much regarding land titling. What the World Bank can do—and is doing—is to create incentives that encourage changes in practices and laws. Another approach of the World Bank is policy lending, which requires the recipient government to meet certain criteria before lending takes place or all of the funds are released to the target country. In the case of titling, the release of lender funds is triggered by the actions of the government to facilitate the titling of land.

The bank uses direct investment in projects that assist in the development of land titling in Eastern Europe, East Asia, and Latin America. There has been less involvement in Africa, arguably the most challenging area of the world for economic development and land registration, due to obstacles that include the culturally and historically important role that communally held land represents there.

Bruce identifies other challenges that complicate the process of land titling, including insufficient political stability to ensure that land rights will be enforced once they are established and the sharing of land policy and administration among numerous public institutions, each of which has some control over the status of land. The problem with having numerous land authorities is that no institution sees the situation exactly like the others. No institution has the ultimate authority to act, but one institution can limit the decisions of the other institutions. Bruce describes several situations where multiple national agencies operate parallel titling functions that undermine the efforts of other agencies. He also identifies some of the technical problems of land titling.

## CHANGING VISIONS OF LAND

The study of land is the study of a dynamic factor of production. Society views land in a continuous cycle of change. The economic role of land is changing, as is the way we treat land. Chapters 10 through 13 highlight the differing and evolving views of land and its importance. In chapter 10, Daniel Bromley challenges some of the assumptions that now motivate land reform issues. An important set of themes is that land continues to matter to the human condition, but the way land is viewed has changed dramatically over the centuries, and its role in the economy will continue to change. In chapter 11, Anthony Bebbington considers the role that information plays in land use decisions. He uses a case study from Peru to describe how land use decisions are becoming international in their implications. In chapter 12, Kuo-Ching Lin describes the evolving role of land in Taiwan, which owes much of its early development to agricultural innovation in land use and land reform. The new challenge, however, is to maintain a role for land in a rapidly changing economy where the market suggests that if agricultural production is left only to the market, it will likely dramatically decline. Finally, in chapter 13, Robert Evenson reviews the role of agricultural innovation in the development of developing and transitional countries.

Bromley addresses how we think about land and how our views have had a profound effect on the development of accepted wisdom with respect to production and markets. Land has had an important role in the development and evolution of economic theories and models. Giants in the field of economics, including David Ricardo, Thomas Malthus, Karl Marx, and Henry George, have developed theoretical contributions from an analysis of land as a factor of production. Those economists viewed land and its role in a society as an asset to be managed in order to maximize production and earn an economic return.

Individuals of influence who were not trained to think as economists, like Henry David Thoreau and John Muir, also used their views of land to shape collective views. Those individuals contributed to the view of land not as a consumption asset but as an "amenity" that provides nonmarket-driven returns. Briefly, this latter set of players provided the foundation for the model of sustainable development. Bromley's quick review of the 80-year history of the journal *Land Economics* confirms the current role of land in the framework of sustainable development.

Bromley raises concerns about the standard assumption that the titling of land will benefit land occupants in some of the poorest regions of the world. He offers evidence that calls into question the robustness of some of the work he cites in support of the assertions around land titling. He suggests that the informal titling systems contribute to multiple uses of land and that formal titling might undermine the current efficiency of those uses.

Bromley concludes his chapter with a series of challenges. He argues that we need to rethink the economic development model that dominates current policies concerning land use, and he questions the benefits of land titling in some regions of the world. He also argues that the concept of land is in a constant state of flux. He states, "Land is always in the process of becoming."

Bebbington offers a partial confirmation of several of Williamson's arguments and a firsthand look at the emerging intricacies of land use decisions. He explains that the complexity surrounding land use and land use decisions is increasing. One reason is that information on land and its use is now being shared beyond local communities within a country and even beyond national borders. In the not too distant past, public and private land use and the use of resources from the land were local concerns, perhaps regional issues, but rarely countrywide issues. For example, owners of land or mineral rights could make choices and then implement those choices relatively independent of forces outside of the host community or ownership of the firm. Bebbington presents a model and some case illustrations on why that description is no longer an accurate reflection of how the process works with respect to land and land use markets.

Bebbington reviews the concept of sustainable development, the normative paradigm that argues that economic transformations and development should consider issues beyond the use, consumption, and transformation of

physical resources. That paradigm is different from past economic development practices in the following way: In the past, macro- and microeconomic
strategies were tilted toward benefiting actors who were inclined to think of
development only in terms of its effect on factors they controlled. They were
focused on the economic return on the physical asset they controlled, and
they were less likely to consider the effects of their decisions on factors beyond their own assets. Sustainable development suggests that the factors in
the calculus of analysis around land use should include human capital, social capital, physical capital, financial assets, and cultural capital.

Bebbington uses the concept of social dimensions to reconsider how resources are used in rural areas. He argues that as decisions about land use are
debated in the context of social dimensions, the scale of the discussions—and
the accompanying arguments—will go well beyond the borders of rural areas
and the boardrooms of the owners with the rights to extract natural resources
from an area. The new ease with which information about land use can be
shared is altering the land use process. Using a case from Peru, Bebbington
illustrates how citizens in a rural area were able to frame a debate on land
use, specifically mining, that went far beyond the area where the mine was
planned. The information from that debate found its way to the Internet, and
eventually even the outcome of the national election was influenced by the
questions raised over mining in the rural highlands.

Bebbington's chapter illustrates how land use decisions now go well beyond the borders of the area and even the country where land concern is
sited. We are not naive enough to argue that an inappropriate taking of land
would be reversed by adverse information blogged around the world, but the
examples of sustainable development in Bebbington's chapter do suggest that
land issues are no longer just local issues.

In chapter 12, Lin, an agricultural economist, reviews land use issues in
the host country of Taiwan, which has been historically recognized as a
leader in land reform and a country that owes much of its economic success
to innovative agricultural practices. At the same time, Taiwan is under significant pressure concerning its land use. Its population density is the third
highest in the world. Land prices are very high, and the subsequent financial
return to agricultural investment is low. The market pressure is to convert
land to activities with higher returns, which generally means conversion of
land to urban uses. The result in Taiwan is a fundamental policy issue addressing whether and how land use patterns will change.

That policy issue will not be easily resolved. Regardless of the low return
on agricultural investments and the market's demand for alternative uses of
land, the political pressure to maintain an agricultural sector in Taiwan is
strong. The ever-present agricultural lobby is a powerful political force in

most regions of the world. However, in Taiwan the constant threat of Chinese intervention creates additional political support for the security-based production of food, especially rice. The result is that some direct and indirect subsidies go to farming. Nevertheless, even that political support is shifting. For many years there was at least a political equilibrium in the governmental support of agricultural land use, but that equilibrium has shifted.

The changing political pressure is coming from several sources. Since Taiwan gained access to the World Trade Organization, it has faced countervailing pressure to curtail the support of rice farming and is now importing rice. Plans are forming to make a shift away from agricultural subsidies, but to do so slowly and to give financial protection to the displaced farmers. There is also pressure to reforest land in Taiwan due to the recent storms that caused substantial damage in many urban areas. After those storms, it was obvious that continuing to remove trees from steep hillsides or build residential or commercial buildings on floodplains without safety and financial risks was not feasible.

Lin's chapter describes the challenges that will eventually face many countries as the world economy continues to see trade barriers lowered. Subsidies to marginal agricultural operations will become more difficult to maintain. Price pressures on land, as population increases, will further reduce the return to farming. However, Lin is not certain that the market process will have the final say in land use. He recognizes the importance of nonprice or policy-directed outcomes.

Addressing the effect of technology on the production of food and fiber for human consumption and use, Evenson (chapter 13) discusses the impact of the green revolution and the gene revolution on the productivity of land and the resulting consequences for regional and country economic development and change.

A review of technological and biological breakthroughs and their consequences is important, since not all segments of society have embraced their implementation. There has always been a concern that technological advances would be available only to large farms and that small and undercapitalized farms would be left behind and further disadvantaged. Furthermore, there was a concern that the size of existing successful farming operations would increase. A related concern was that farm workers would see a reduction in real wages. Evenson thoughtfully responds to each of those major concerns.

The patterns of technological adoption have not followed the feared path of benefiting only large agricultural operations. In fact, large operations did adopt technological advances earlier than small operations, but over time the improvements in productivity have become widespread. Failure to adopt has had much more to do with country- or region-specific concerns than with the inherent size of agricultural operations. Farm size in some regions has actually declined, and the wages of farm workers have increased, as has the number of farm workers. Chapter 13 reports a variety of data showing that both revolutions have increased the return on agricultural investment across a wide spectrum.

That does not mean that the adoption of technology has not had negative consequences. The use of fertilizers, insecticides, and herbicides has increased and has had negative implications for sustainable land use. However, Evenson grades the influence of both green and gene revolutions as positive when measured by a host of socioeconomic factors. His chapter concludes with a review of the trend in the use of funds from the U.S. Agency for International Development away from support of the agricultural sector.

## CONCLUSIONS

This volume offers a review of important issues surrounding land and land use. On many dimensions, the chapters offer optimistic outlooks for the future of land. Technology is changing the way land is now managed and used; and the evidence of improvements in land records, agricultural technology, estimation of land values, and dissemination of information about land use is encouraging. The suggestions to consider land decisions without an absolute reliance on the market are worth considering, and nowhere is that notion more evident than in the frequently repeated need to consider sustainable development as an acceptable policy goal.

## REFERENCES

World Bank. 2000. *World development report: Attacking poverty.* Washington, DC: International Bank for Reconstruction and Development.
———. 2003. *World development report: Sustainable development in a dynamic world: Transforming institutions, growth and quality of life.* Washington, DC: International Bank for Reconstruction and Development.
———. 2006. *World development report: Equity and development.* Washington, DC: International Bank for Reconstruction and Development.

# Public Finance and Land Administration

# 2

## The Property Tax in Developing Countries: Current Practice and Prospects

### Roy Bahl and Jorge Martinez-Vazquez

O ver the past two decades there has been an unprecedented move toward decentralized governance all over the world. The changes have
taken on special significance in many developing and transitional countries where centralized systems were perceived to have failed to deliver improved
general welfare. The promise of political, administrative, and fiscal decentralization is that it can strengthen democratic representative institutions,
increase the overall efficiency of the public sector, and lead to improved social and economic welfare for countries that decide to adopt it. One critical
assumption behind those expectations is that decentralized governments
will generally be more accountable and responsive to citizens' needs and
preferences. At the same time, there is general agreement among experts in
decentralization that increased accountability can be ensured only when subnational governments have an adequate level of autonomy and discretion in
raising their own revenues.

Thus, if effective fiscal decentralization requires meaningful revenue autonomy at the regional and local levels of government, the question is which
taxes should be allocated at those levels. This is known in the fiscal decentralization literature as the "tax assignment problem" (see Martinez-Vazquez,
McLure, and Vaillancourt 2006). Although there is some variation in the
type of taxes recommended as desirable for providing subnational governments with revenue autonomy, virtually every student of intergovernmental
finance and a myriad of reports on fiscal decentralization design have identified the property tax as one of the best candidates for a mainstay at the subnational level, especially for local governments.

**TABLE 2.1** Property Tax Revenues as a Percent of GDP

|  | 1970s | 1980s | 1990s | 2000s |
|---|---|---|---|---|
| OECD countries | 1.24 | 1.31 | 1.44 | 2.12 |
| (number of countries) | 16 | 18 | 16 | 18 |
| Developing countries | 0.42 | 0.36 | 0.42 | 0.60 |
| (number of countries) | 20 | 27 | 23 | 29 |
| Transitional countries | 0.34 | 0.59 | 0.54 | 0.68 |
| (number of countries) | 1 | 4 | 20 | 18 |
| All countries | 0.77 | 0.73 | 0.75 | 1.04 |
| (number of countries) | 37 | 49 | 59 | 65 |

*Note:* The data for 2000s are for the years 2000 and 2001.
*Source:* International Monetary Fund, *Government Finance Statistics Yearbook*, various years.

Something else makes the property tax peculiar in the revenue assignment problem. Almost without exception, revenues from the property tax are assigned to local governments. The degree of discretion given to local governments to manipulate the tax may vary, but the thinking that it belongs to local governments seems well entrenched. That is not generally the case with other taxes that fiscal decentralization experts recommend be assigned to subnational governments—for example, motor vehicle taxes or piggyback personal income taxes.

Despite what seems to be a generally accepted argument that the property tax is local, subnational governments in developing and transitional countries make relatively little use of it. On average, the property tax revenues they raise are equivalent to only about 0.6 percent of GDP (see table 2.1).

This is a big puzzle and, in one way or another, the main subject of all the chapters in this book. There are many potential explanations of why the property tax is not used more intensively as a source of financing public services in developing and transitional countries. Not the least of these is the fact that it is a "difficult" tax, which from a rather cynical viewpoint may explain the apparent willingness or "generosity" of central authorities to hand it over to subnational governments. Rather than offering a general explanation, the more modest goal of this chapter is to examine the current practice in developing and transitional countries and identify some of the factors behind the light demand for this tax.

## ADVANTAGES AND DISADVANTAGES

As noted, there is a general presumption that the property tax is an ideal tax at the subnational government level in decentralized systems. We might challenge that view by listing the advantages and disadvantages associated with that choice.

### Advantages

The a priori case for heavier use of the property tax at the subnational level in developing and transitional countries is a strong one. There is much to recommend a greater reliance on this revenue source.

*Revenue Potential and Stability.* First, and most important, the property tax is potentially a significant revenue producer for subnational governments. In the case of Canada and the United States, property tax revenues reach between 3 and 4 percent of GDP. The value of land and improvements constitutes a broad base that is growing in virtually all countries at a fast rate, and even a modest statutory tax rate can yield significant amounts of revenue.[1] However, the realization of large amounts of revenue requires a willingness to impose the property tax at higher levels than now exist in most developing countries, plus a good valuation system and a high rate of compliance (which implies a strong program of enforcement). As we discuss below, industrialized countries have realized this revenue potential to a much greater extent than developing and transitional countries have, not only because of their valuation and enforcement systems, but also because of the extent to which they have embraced fiscal decentralization.

Another positive feature of property taxation, and one that makes it especially attractive for subnational governments, is the relative stability of its tax base. Fluctuations in the business cycle tend to have a much bigger impact on tax bases such as earned wage income and profits or even sales. However, the relatively greater stability of market values is of little consequence if they are not accurately reflected in assessed property values. As we discuss below, the valuation of property is one of the key problems with effective use of the property tax in developing and transitional countries.

---

[1]For example, Hernando de Soto (2000) estimates that the total value of Africans' informally owned houses and farmland in 1997 was roughly $1 trillion, or nearly three times sub-Saharan Africa's annual GDP. However, much of the tax base in developing countries is subject to informal property rights, which does not help with the willingness to pay taxes. As reported in *The Economist* (January 15, 2004), "In Africa . . . less than 10% of the continent's land is formally owned, and barely one African in ten lives in a house with title deeds."

*Fairness and Equity.* The property tax might be seen as a rough kind of benefit charge, and therefore not only as an efficient tax, but also as a fair tax. Businesses and some residential owners may perceive that they benefit from certain public investments approximately in proportion to the value of their properties. For example, property values may be higher, ceteris paribus, in areas where street lighting is functional, policing is better, schools are of higher quality, and so on. It follows that there is a sense in which property taxes roughly correspond to benefits received. That, of course, assumes that property is correctly valued to reflect the betterment associated with public investments and regularly provided public services, that valuations are regularly updated, that land markets function, and that benefiting properties are not routinely exempted through the political process. It also assumes that property owners and taxpayers believe that the link between tax base and benefits received is more or less accurate.

The property tax might also be seen as vertically equitable in developing and transitional countries. In fact, it can be progressive in developing countries and, therefore, can increase the overall vertical equity of the tax system (Bahl and Linn 1992; Bahl 1998; Sennoga, Sjoquist, and Wallace 2008). There are several reasons for this. Property ownership is heavily concentrated among the wealthy in developing countries, and landlords are often not reached by the income tax system. The property tax has the potential of filling the gap. On the basis of the high level of concentration of ownership, a tax on the land value base would seem to be the most progressive. At the other end of the income distribution spectrum, public housing and low-valued properties are generally not taxed at all, which also adds to the progressivity of the tax.

However, property taxes in less developed countries (LDCs) can be made regressive by exemption policies that target the well-to-do, such as policies that exempt owner-occupied properties, as practiced in some countries. Preferential assessment (or exemption) of certain commercial or industrial properties may have the same effect. The distributional effects of the property tax, then, are heavily influenced by the rate and base structure of the tax, as well as its administration. These are factors that government can control to some extent.

*Tax Exporting.* The property tax has the desirable feature that much of the tax burden is likely borne by residents in the jurisdiction where the services financed by property taxes are provided (i.e., there is a "correspondence" between the location in which the tax burdens are borne and the location in which the expenditure benefits are enjoyed). In such cases, the local governments that levy the tax are more likely to be fiscally responsible, that is, less likely to overspend on the expectation that tax exporting would allow them to pass some of the burden to residents of other jurisdictions.

The reality of the "correspondence" advantage of the property tax might be challenged. To the extent that the property tax is concentrated on nonresidential property, and improvements (versus land) are a significant component of the tax base, there is a greater potential for exporting the burden to other regions. This occurs, for example, when businesses sell outside the region and are able to pass their taxes on to consumers and when landlords are absentee owners. In countries where only industrial-commercial properties are taxed, the potential for exporting the property tax burden is greater, and the property tax is a less suitable local government levy.

*Compliance Costs.* The property tax has the advantage of imposing a relatively low compliance cost on taxpayers because taxpayer intervention in the determination of tax liability is minimal, except in the case of appeals. Most taxes are self-assessed (e.g., corporate income taxes or value-added tax), but liability to pay property taxes is determined by the tax authorities; therefore, the compliance costs are largely shifted to the government.[2] Even in cases where there has been a move to self-assessment, the argument is that compliance costs have been reduced because contact with possibly corrupt administrative and certainly bothersome administrative staff was removed. The other potential compliance cost has to do with the method of making payment, but in recent years countries have increasingly shifted to using banks as collection points (Kelly 2004).

*Tax Base Competition.* A major advantage of the property tax as a local levy is that it usually poses no significant problem of competition with the central government. The value of land and improvements is not a tax base central governments covet; hence, they often seem content to leave it to local governments.[3] As we mentioned previously, the reasons for this common behavior among central authorities are far from clear. Although central authorities may see the wisdom of assigning this tax to local governments, given the advantages discussed in this section, it could also be that their lack of interest in the property tax lies in its complexity and low revenue potential. Or it could reflect the calculus of central officials regarding revenue potential versus political cost.

---

[2]In most developing and transitional countries, property taxes are assessed by a central authority but billed and collected by local authorities.

[3]This is not always the case. For example, in China, Indonesia, and Jamaica, the property tax is a central government levy, even though local governments receive most of the revenue.

The lack of vertical tax base competition does not exclude, of course, the possibility of horizontal or interjurisdictional tax rate or base competition. Without getting into the positive and negative aspects of that type of competition, the advantage of the property tax over other potential local taxes is that interjurisdictional competition is likely to lead to fewer economic distortions and smaller excess burden losses.

*Land Use Efficiency.* Finally, a property tax might be thought of as a charge for land that can lead to significant improvements in the quality of land use. Particularly if land is taxed according to its location value in urban areas, and if assessment is at its highest and best use, a more rational allocation of land use will occur. Here the land value version of property taxation has a particular advantage. In developing countries, however, the effective rate of taxation is so low that such incentives might not be effective.

## Disadvantages

There are major drawbacks to the use of property taxes in developing and transitional countries. Administrative constraints and the perception of the tax by taxpayers go a long way toward explaining the relatively low revenue dependence on this tax.

*Administration Cost.* The major problem with the property tax is that it is generally difficult and costly to administer. Less efficient and more costly administration, in combination with low revenue yields, can make the property tax a losing proposition in terms of revenue yield per dollar of administrative cost. In most developing and transitional countries, property taxes are badly administered by any standard. As we discuss in a later section of this chapter, both assessment ratios and collection rates often are very low, which leads to unfair treatment of various categories of taxpayers and to significant revenue leakage. Property taxes are not—cannot—be self assessed; hence, a high staff cost is implied, and a great deal of record keeping is required. There also are significant administrative costs associated with collections and appeals. Compounding the problem, there is a shortage of property assessors in virtually all developing countries. Thus, even in the best of circumstances the property tax can seem a poor financing choice for local governments.

*Enforcement.* The property tax is difficult to enforce. Elected local officials are often not in a position to take actions against delinquent taxpayers, because they are not provided with the means to do so and often those who are not in compliance are leaders in the community. Potentially effective solutions—penalizing those who are out of compliance by such means as confiscation of property, for example—may be considered too extreme and generally are not feasible because of the political fallout. The special attachment to land in many developing countries raises the possibility that broad-based acceptance of a more intensively used property tax is not likely. This problem has strong similarities to that of collecting user charges for services considered to be essential to life (e.g., housing, water, electricity). Ultimately, it becomes an issue of political will, and few developing and transitional countries have been able to exercise that will. There are some exceptions. For example, South African local authorities have had mixed success with using the threat of cutting off electricity for failure to pay a property tax or utility bill.

***Taxpayer Attitudes.*** A third disadvantage is that the property tax is terribly unpopular with voters, and as a result, politicians are loathe to rely heavily on it. Per dollar of revenue raised, property taxes may generate more negative reaction than any other levy. There are several reasons for this degree of unpopularity. One is that the tax is levied on (unrealized) accretions to the wealth of an individual or a business, and those accretions do not necessarily correspond to income received. Even without increases in value, the property tax is essentially a tax on the potential income from some form of property (real estate) via the opportunity to rent or the value of using one's own home. Other forms of property—for example, stocks or other financial taxes—are taxed only upon realization. That difference creates not only special implementation problems (for example, how to treat those living on fixed incomes), but also a general hostility toward the tax. The unpopularity of the property tax is also a by-product of the judgmental approach to assessment that is taken almost everywhere. A proposed increase in the tax rate on a tax base that is determined in uncertain or even mysterious ways is bound to provoke negative reactions. Finally, the tax is unpopular in part because it is so visible. Most income tax payers are subject to withholding, but even so, may not be able to accurately report their annual payment. Consumption taxes are paid in small increments and are often obscured in the final price of the merchandise. Most people could not even estimate the annual amount of value-added tax they pay. The property tax, on the other hand, is usually billed annually or quarterly, and property owners are much more likely to know exactly what they pay.

***Elasticity.*** Government officials desire a tax that exhibits automatic revenue growth. This protects them from having to return to the voters for permission to increase the tax rate every time the demand for or cost of public services increases. The property tax is not an income-elastic tax. The basic problem is that reassessments occur only periodically; hence, year-to-year growth in revenues is mostly due to additions to the tax base through construction. When revaluation is too infrequent, say every five or ten years, it leads to large one-time increases in tax liability and to voter uproar from the shock. Countries use various means to cushion the shock, but those means often end up reducing the effective rate of property tax. Some innovations introduced internationally to deal with the low elasticity include indexation—for example, used in Jordan, Colombia, and Brazil—or the phasing-in of the reassessed values, as in the Philippines (Guevara 2004).[4]

## AN OVERVIEW OF REVENUE PERFORMANCE

Despite the a priori potential of property taxes, they are far from being a mainstay of the revenue system in developing and transitional countries. Nevertheless, the property tax can be revenue productive in, and often contribute significantly to the financing of, subnational governments in many countries. On average, as shown in table 2.1, property taxes in developing and transitional countries raise less relative to GDP than in OECD countries. In the early 2000s property taxes in OECD countries represented 2.12 percent of GDP, while for developing countries the figure was 0.6 percent and for transitional countries, 0.68 percent. It is interesting that the trend for all three categories of countries has been slightly upward since the 1970s. The data in table 2.1 strongly suggest that reliance on the property tax comes with economic development (e.g., compare OECD countries with developing countries). Some OECD countries make especially heavy use of the property tax. For example, Canada raises a revenue amount equivalent to about 4 percent of GDP, and the United States raises nearly 3 percent of GDP. The variation among countries in the intensity of use of the property tax is explored below in a more systematic way.

The figures presented in table 2.2 for the percent of total subnational expenditures financed by property taxes are particularly interesting. Developing countries may not use the property tax more intensely than OECD countries do, but they appear to rely more heavily on the property tax to finance subnational government expenditures. This gives a different perspective

---

[4]Indexation of the property tax refers to the practice of mandating an annual increase in taxes equal to some agreed-upon price index, such as the consumer price index.

**TABLE 2.2**  Property Tax Revenues as a Percent of Total Subnational Government Expenditures

|  | 1970s | 1980s | 1990s | 2000s |
|---|---|---|---|---|
| OECD countries | 9.7 | 9.88 | 13.65 | 12.40 |
| (number of countries) | 16 | 17 | 16 | 19 |
| Developing countries | 18.65 | 15.97 | 13.49 | 18.37 |
| (number of countries) | 21 | 27 | 24 | 20 |
| Transitional countries | 3.67 | 4.92 | 7.75 | 9.43 |
| (number of countries) | 1 | 4 | 18 | 20 |
| All countries | 14.49 | 12.89 | 11.63 | 13.40 |
| (number of countries) | 38 | 48 | 58 | 59 |

Note: The data for 2000s are for the five years from 2000 to 2004.
Source: Columns 2 and 3 are based on International Monetary Fund, *Government Finance Statistics Yearbook (GFS)*, 2002; columns 4 and 5 have been calculated from *GFS*.

about the importance of strengthening the practice of property taxation in developing countries. Of course, the financing of about 18 percent of subnational government spending from the property tax in developing countries is also a reflection of relatively lower subnational government expenditures and generally fewer options for local taxes. For example, income taxes are much more common at the subnational level in OECD countries.

The average figures in tables 2.1 and 2.2 hide considerable levels of variation in the use of property taxes within each of the three categories of countries represented.[5] What we want to ask next is, besides the level of economic development, what other external and institutional factors may help explain variations in the use of property taxes?

## FISCAL DECENTRALIZATION AND THE PROPERTY TAX

Although many factors affect the use of property taxes, a useful approach to explaining the relative demand for property taxation in a country is to

---

[5]See Bird and Slack (2004) and Malme and Youngman (2001) for descriptions of individual country property taxes.

view it as derived from the national electorate's demand for fiscal decentralization. A reasonable working hypothesis is that countries that seek greater fiscal decentralization will rely more heavily on property taxation. To be truly effective, fiscal decentralization requires autonomous subnational government taxes, and property taxes are a logical choice. Consider the following:

- A good local tax features a correspondence between the boundaries within which the expenditure benefits are received, and the boundaries within which the tax burden falls. The property tax comes close to satisfying that condition for both second- and third-tier governments.
- Under a good administration, with a commitment to provide important services, the property tax can be a significant source of revenue for subnational governments. With an efficient administration and with commitment to enforcement, the property tax base can be large and income elastic.
- Subnational governments, particularly third-tier local governments, may have a comparative advantage in assessing the property tax base because of their familiarity with the local economy and its land use patterns.
- Higher-level governments are not likely to aggressively compete for the right to levy property taxes, because it is a high-cost method of raising revenue, it is politically unpopular, and central governments do not have a comparative advantage in assessing the base.

In this section, with the help of a multicountry panel data set drawn from the Government Finance Statistics (GFS) of the International Monetary Fund (IMF) and from several other sources, we test the hypothesis that fiscal decentralization drives the intensity of property tax use. We measure fiscal decentralization as subnational government expenditures as a percent of total government expenditures. In order to test the role of fiscal decentralization on the relative use of property taxation, we need to control for other variables that are expected to affect the dependent variable. In particular, we expect that reliance on property taxation may be higher across countries and over time the greater the degree of urbanization. Both land values and improvement values tend to increase significantly in urban centers, and with that, property taxation becomes more attractive. Besides degree of urbanization, in the regression analysis we control for GDP per capita, because we have seen that for a variety of institutional reasons richer countries tend to make higher use of property taxation. Transitional countries are identified by a dummy variable; even controlling for differences in income per capita, transitional countries present distinct institutional peculiarities, such as titling and history of land ownership, that may affect the relative use of property taxation. We also control for population size and the rate of population growth.

The estimation is based on a panel of 70 countries for three years, 1990, 1995, and 2000. Although data for many of the variables are available on an annual basis, the restriction to three years is imposed by the data availability for the urban population ratio. Besides the GFS, we use data from the World Resources Institute (www.wri.org) for GDP per capita, population, and population growth rate. The data for urbanization are from the United Nations Secretariat (2004).

Before we discuss the regression results, we need to address several econometric issues. Because of the possible nonlinear effects of population and GDP per capita, those two variables are entered in the regression in logarithms. Given the cross-country nature of the data set, there were potentially issues specific to each of the countries for which we could not control that might have an impact on the behavior of the dependent variable (property taxes relative to GDP). That might seem to indicate that the appropriate approach was fixed or random effects estimation. However, because we were restricted to three years and because of missing data for some of the variables, we had an unbalanced panel data set with 107 observations, which did not support a fixed effects estimation approach for 70 different countries. Instead, we used ordinary least squares regression and allowed for time effects by using dummy variables for 1990 and 1995.

In table 2.3 we present the ordinary least squares (OLS) results and in table 2.4 two-stage least squares (TSLS) results. The need for TSLS arises from the potential endogeneity of the main control variable of interest, the level of fiscal decentralization. It may be not only that decentralization affects the relative use of property taxation, as hypothesized, but also, in a reverse causation, that the presence or relative ease of property taxation affects the extent of decentralization. In fact, the Hausman test for endogeneity shows that we could not reject the possibility that the decentralization variable was indeed endogenous. For that reason we ran TSLS as an alternative and in the first stage used as instruments for decentralization a dummy variable denoting whether the country is an ex-British colony,[6] and population growth rates.

Results from both the OLS and TSLS estimations show that the coefficient

---

[6]This includes Canada and the United States. This variable may not be the ideal instrument because it may be correlated with the errors in the OLS regression, but finding a good alternative instrument for decentralization is a notoriously difficult problem in the entire fiscal decentralization literature.

**TABLE 2.3**    Determinants of the Relative Use of Property Taxation: OLS Estimation (Dependent variable: property tax revenues to GDP)

| Variables | Coefficient estimate | T-stat | Probability $> t$ |
|-----------|---------------------|--------|-------------------|
| Constant | −2.012 | −3.80 | 0.000 |
| lgdpcap | 0.322 | 5.11 | 0.000 |
| lpop | −0.069 | −1.85 | 0.068 |
| decent | 1.496 | 3.25 | 0.002 |
| urbanpct | 0.855 | 1.77 | 0.080 |
| pgr | 24.43 | 3.32 | 0.001 |
| transition | −0.102 | −0.48 | 0.630 |
| dy90 | −0.132 | −0.70 | 0.485 |
| dy95 | −0.223 | −1.27 | 0.208 |

| | |
|---|---|
| Number of observations | 107 |
| $F(8,98)$ | 13.09 |
| R-squared | 0.5166 |
| Adjusted R-squared | 0.4772 |
| Root Mean Square Error | 0.7005 |

*Notes on variables:* lgdpcap=logarithm of GDP per capita; lpop=logarithm of population amount; decent=decentralization, measured as subnational revenue as a percent of national revenue; urbanpct=percent of urban population to total population; pgr=average of population growth rate; transition=dummy of countries in transition; dy90=dummy of year 1990; dy95=dummy of year 1995.

for fiscal decentralization is positive and statistically significant, being much larger in the second case. This fundamentally supports the hypothesis that demand for the use of property taxation derives in part from the level of decentralization. The degree of urbanization, as expected, takes a positive and statistically significant coefficient in the TSLS estimation. The log of per capita income is positive and highly significant in both equations. The dummy year variables and the dummy for transitional countries are not statistically significant, while the log of population is negative and significant and the population growth rate is positive and significant.

We may use these findings to help explain the slow growth of the property tax in developing countries, as reported in table 2.1. As we show in table 2.5,

**TABLE 2.4** Determinants of the Relative Use of Property Taxation: TSLS Estimation (Dependent variable: property tax revenues to GDP)

| Variables | Coefficient estimate | T-stat | Probability > $t$ |
|---|---|---|---|
| Constant | −6.487 | −4.47 | 0.007 |
| lgdpcap | 0.362 | 5.87 | 0.000 |
| lpop | −0.042 | −1.16 | 0.864 |
| decent | 12.766 | 3.00 | 0.013 |
| urbanpct | 1.226 | 2.52 | 0.014 |
| pgr | 78.942 | 3.78 | 0.589 |
| transition | 0.015 | 0.07 | 0.754 |
| dy90 | −0.2329 | −1.25 | 0.707 |
| dy95 | −0.3109 | −1.76 | 0.157 |

| | |
|---|---|
| Number of observations | 107 |
| $F$ (8,98) | 12.72 |
| R-squared | 0.5093 |
| Adjusted R-squared | 0.4693 |
| Root Mean Square Error | 0.7058 |

*Notes on variables:* lgdpcap = logarithm of GDP per capita; lpop = logarithm of population amount; decent = decentralization, measured as subnational revenue as a percent of national revenue; urbanpct = percent of urban population to total population; pgr = average of population growth rate; transition = dummy of countries in transition; dy90 = dummy of year 1990; dy95 = dummy of year 1995.

there has been little growth in the fiscal decentralization ratio for three decades. For developing countries, the level of fiscal decentralization, measured by subnational government expenditures as a share of total government expenditure, was about 13 percent, on average, in the 1970s, and was marginally lower in the 1990s and 2000s. Based on the estimated coefficient for decentralization in table 2.4, we can say that, other things being equal, if the decentralization ratio had increased by 5 percent for developing countries in the 1990s, the ratio of property tax revenue to GDP in that decade would, on average, have been close to 0.6, or the average level reached in the 2000s by that group of countries.

With an adjusted R-square of 0.47 for the regression in table 2.4, we

**TABLE 2.5** Fiscal Decentralization Indicators (Percent)

| | 1970s | | 1980s | | 1990s–2000s | | |
|---|---|---|---|---|---|---|---|
| | Developing countries | OECD countries | Developing countries | OECD countries | Developing countries | OECD countries | Transitional countries |
| Subnational government tax as a share of total government tax | 10.68 (43) | 17.91 (24) | 8.87 (33) | 18.18 (23) | 10.61 (28) | 18.39 (21) | 22.41 (23) |
| Subnational government expenditure as a share of total government expenditure | 13.42 (45) | 33.68 (23) | 12.09 (41) | 31.97 (24) | 12.97 (54) | 32.68 (24) | 30.32 (24) |

*Note:* Sample sizes are in parentheses.
*Source:* International Monetary Fund, *Government Finance Statistics Yearbook*, various years.

**TABLE 2.6** Ratio of Third-Tier Government Expenditures to Total
Subnational Government Expenditures, Selected Countries (Percent)

|  | 1990s | 2000s |
|---|---|---|
| OECD countries | 53.91 | 46.89 |
| (number of countries) | 10 | 10 |
| Developing countries | 40.97 | 40.63 |
| (number of countries) | 8 | 8 |
| All countries | 47.44 | 29.17 |
| (number of countries) | 18 | 18 |

*Notes:* The table excludes countries with 100 percent of subnational expenditures at the local level (that is, those countries without intermediate regional or provincial governments). The data for 2000s are for the five years from 2000 to 2004.
*Source:* International Monetary Fund, *Government Finance Statistics Yearbook*, various years.

are far from explaining satisfactorily what goes into determining the intensity of property tax use. The lack of consistent data is a major difficulty. For example, the arguments for property taxation are that it is the most suitable tax for third-tier local governments—that is, city and municipal governments that are small enough to have the advantage of familiarity in setting tax rates that reflect voter preferences for financing local services and in assessing property. Thus, a reasonable additional hypothesis would be that the greater the importance of local governments in the subnational government sector (local plus regional), the higher the intensity of property tax use.[7] Unfortunately, because the GFS does not consistently show that breakdown, we cannot introduce that type of variable in the regressions in tables 2.3 and 2.4. In table 2.6 we use available data to describe the importance of third-tier governments in fiscal decentralization in recent years. One can intuit from table 2.6 that even if the additional hypothesis were correct, little change in the intensity of use of the property tax should have been expected because, if anything, the relative importance of local governments in the subnational sector has slightly decreased in recent years.

---

[7] A corollary of this reasoning is that other taxes, such as personal income and consumption taxes, are more easily applicable at the regional level, so that the greater the importance of intermediate-level governments in the subnational government sector, the lower the relative use of property taxation vis-à-vis other taxes.

## HOW TO STRENGTHEN REVENUE PERFORMANCE

As shown in table 2.1, the property tax share of GDP has not increased significantly over the past 30 years. In the previous section of this chapter we identified several "external" institutional reasons for that, such as the lack of an increase in fiscal decentralization. There are other, "internal" institutional reasons—having to do with how property taxes are structured and administered—that no doubt contribute to the overall lackluster performance of property taxation. Those factors are especially relevant in the developing world. Data are not available for us to analyze those internal determinants of revenue growth on a country-by-country basis. However, we might use a priori reasoning to speculate on what has gone wrong and then try to illustrate those conjectures with examples and information from selected countries.

The following identity describes the components or steps that go into identifying the ratio of property tax revenues to GDP in any particular country.

$$\frac{T_C}{y} = \left(\frac{T_C}{T_L}\right)\left(\frac{T_L}{AV}\right)\left(\frac{AV}{TMV}\right)\left(\frac{TMV}{MV}\right)\left(\frac{MV}{y}\right)$$

where

| | | |
|---|---|---|
| $T_C$ | = | property tax revenue collections |
| $y$ | = | GDP |
| $T_L$ | = | property tax liability |
| AV | = | taxable assessed value |
| TMV | = | taxable market value |
| MV | = | full market value |

The term on the left of the identity is the ratio of property tax revenue collections to GDP. It is the wide variation in this ratio (reported in table 2.1) that we would like to explain. Why do some countries realize a much higher effective property tax rate than others? Our focus here is on the components of the tax structure and its implementation, particularly assessment and collection.

The first term on the right is the collection ratio—that is, the percent of true liability that is collected. In developing countries, where enforcement is often lax, collection rates as low as 50 percent are not unusual. The examples presented in table 2.7 support this point.[8] Even the low collection rates re-

---

[8]There are numerous other examples of low collection rates. For example, Iregui, Melo, and Ramos (2004) report effective collection rates of 80 percent for a large sample of Colombian municipalities in the 1999–2002 period; Kim (1993) reports a collection efficiency in Indonesia of 65 percent.

**TABLE 2.7** Selected Measures of Property Tax Administration

| Country | Collection rate | Assessment ratio | Selected exemptions (partial or total) |
|---------|-----------------|------------------|----------------------------------------|
| Philippines (Rosengard 1998; Guevara 2004) | 50–60 percent of current billings in 1990 | Legal assessment ratios vary from 15 percent to 80 percent | Assessment ratios vary by value class and by property use |
| Jamaica (Sjoquist 2004) | 40 percent in 2004 | The median assessment ratio was 11 percent between the general revaluations | Certain agricultural properties |
| Chile (Rosengard 1998) | 73 percent in 1990 | — | Two-thirds of all property is exempt |
| Indonesia (Rosengard 1998) | 80 percent in 1990 | Legal assessment rates of 20 percent | — |
| Kenya (Kelly 2004) | 10–60 percent | Actual rates vary between 20 percent and 70 percent | — |
| Colombia (Iregui et. al. 2004; Bird 2004) | 80 percent | 70 percent in Bogota, 85 percent in Medillin | — |

*Source*: Various works cited in the table.

ported in the table may be overestimates, because in some cases they include collections of arrears in the numerator and only current-year liabilities in the denominator.

The second term, the ratio of tax liability to assessed value, describes the tax rate. The higher the legal tax rates, the higher the value of this term. Governments in all countries face great pressure to keep the nominal rates low, because of the unpopularity of the property tax. A typical range for tax rates may be between 0.5 percent and 1.0 percent for countries using a capital value system.

The third term is the ratio of assessed value to taxable market value. This describes the efficiency of the valuation process and also discretionary decisions to reduce the base offered by the taxable market value by applying an assessment ratio that is less than 1.0. If no discretionary assessment ratios were applied, and all properties on the roll were valued at 100 percent of full market value, this ratio would be 1.0. In practice, valuation rates can be as low as 20 percent. As mentioned, assessed values are sometimes low because legally they are set at something less than full market value. The overwhelming evidence from developing countries is that properties are dramatically underassessed. Some evidence on assessment ratios is given in table 2.7.

The ratio of taxable market value to total market value gives an indication of the impact of exemptions and preferential treatments on the property tax base. In many countries, sizable exemptions have been provided, depleting the tax base. The exemptions range from preferential treatment for homeowners to property tax holidays for new businesses. Another important reason the taxable market value may be much lower than full market value is that many properties are not valued at all. Again, some evidence is presented in table 2.7. For example, in the case of Chile, two-thirds of all property is reported to be exempt. Another cause for the divergence between taxable market value and total market value is the failure to incorporate new construction in the tax rolls.

Finally, the ratio of market value of real property to GDP tells us how property values compare to total output in the economy. For example, in an urbanized country, one might expect a higher (and growing) ratio of market value of property to total GDP. Local governments can exert little control over this component of revenue performance. We have no evidence on this last term and treat it simply as a residual to complete the identity.

In sum, what this identity tells us is that administrative and policy reasons for the poor revenue performance of the property tax in developing countries are numerous, but are largely within the control of the local governments.

The importance of this point can easily be illustrated by running a simple simulation to identify the potential revenue impacts of local government administrative reform, as shown in table 2.8. In the columns of the table we show the components of the property tax identity presented above—for example, column 1 shows the ratio of property tax to GDP; column 2 shows the collection rate. The first row of the table shows the baseline simulation, where the values of all the parameters are reasonably chosen so that the resulting property tax effort is 0.6 percent of GDP, the international average for developing countries, as we saw in table 2.1. The parameters of concern are the collection rate, the assessment ratio, and the exemption policy, and for those we have chosen values that seem more or less reflective of the actual practice. A statutory tax rate of about 0.5 percent seems a reasonable assumption, though we will not vary this component of the simulation. The ratio of market value to GDP (which may hold many other factors) is calculated as a residual to satisfy the identity.

**TABLE 2.8** Simulated Impacts of Alternative Property Tax Administration Reform

| Simulation | $\left(\frac{T_c}{y}\right)=$ | $\left(\frac{T_c}{T_L}\right)$ | $\left(\frac{T_L}{AV}\right)$ | $\left(\frac{AV}{TMV}\right)$ | $\left(\frac{TMV}{MV}\right)$ | $\left(\frac{MV}{y}\right)$ |
|---|---|---|---|---|---|---|
| Baseline | 0.6 | 0.5 | 0.05 | 0.5 | 0.8 | 60 |
| Scenario 1 | 0.84 | **0.7** | 0.05 | 0.5 | 0.8 | 60 |
| Scenario 2 | 0.90 | 0.5 | 0.05 | **0.75** | 0.8 | 60 |
| Scenario 3 | 0.75 | 0.5 | 0.05 | 0.5 | **1.0** | 60 |
| Scenario 4 | 1.58 | **0.7** | 0.05 | **0.75** | **1.0** | 60 |

Note: **Bold** figures indicate parameter deviations from baseline values.

The results of the simple simulation show the following:

- In row two we vary only the collection rate, from 50 percent to 70 percent. The result is that the property tax share of GDP increases from 0.6 percent to 0.84 percent, or by about one-third.
- In row three we vary only the assessment ratio, from 50 percent to 75 percent. The result is that the property tax share of GDP rises to 0.9, an increase of nearly 50 percent.
- In row four we eliminate exemptions and do not change anything else. The result is that the property tax share of GDP rises to 0.75, an increase of about one-fourth.
- In row five we vary all three of these factors together and more than double the property tax share of GDP.

In summary, this simple simulation illustrates that quite plausible improvements in government administrative and design practices can move the property tax to a much more significant place in the revenue system of developing countries. Getting property taxes to rise by 1 percent of GDP will generally imply a significant jump in the financing capacity of local governments in many countries around the world. In table 2.9 we perform an additional simple simulation to illustrate that point. If, for the sample of countries in our data set (used to run the regressions in tables 2.3 and 2.4), we first select those countries that collect less than 1 percent of GDP in property taxes and then allow those countries to collect 1 percent of GDP in property taxes, the average increase in subnational government revenues would be around one-third.

**TABLE 2.9**  Simulations of Revenue Implications of Property Taxes Representing 1 Percent of GDP in the Year 2000 (21 Countries)

| Selected countries | Property tax as a percent of GDP | Resulting percent increase of subnational government revenues when property tax is equal to 1 percent of GDP |
|---|---|---|
| Austria | 0.1 | 4.7 |
| Bulgaria | 0.3 | 9.2 |
| Chile | 0.7 | 13.1 |
| Croatia | 0.5 | 9.2 |
| Czech Republic | 0.5 | 1.4 |
| Estonia | 0.5 | 7.7 |
| Ethiopia | 0.2 | 7.0 |
| Hungary | 0.7 | 2.2 |
| Indonesia | 0.1 | 66.0 |
| Iran | 0.2 | 45.5 |
| Italy | 0.9 | 0.6 |
| Jamaica | 0.2 | 141.9 |
| Lithuania | 0.6 | 6.0 |
| Romania | 0.5 | 11.5 |
| Slovak Republic | 0.6 | 17.8 |
| Slovenia | 0.7 | 3.9 |
| Sri Lanka | 0.7 | 79.9 |
| Swaziland | 0.1 | 130.0 |
| Thailand | 0.3 | 34.5 |
| Uganda | 0.1 | 20.1 |
| Ukraine | 0.0 | 9.2 |
| Mean values | 0.4 | 29.6 |

Of course, we remain aware that even small improvements in some of these parameters can be hard to produce. What is worse, big efforts are often put together to improve one or two critical parameters just to see the deterioration of other parameters, thus with little overall impact on actual revenue collections. For example, Dillinger (1988) reports how the Philippines' Property Tax Administration Project was successful in producing tax maps and updated property assessments, but never yielded a substantial increase in revenue because the problem of poor collection practices was never addressed. Even though valuations increased by 37.5 percent and collectibles by 13.6 percent, actual tax revenues increased by only 1.1 percent. In contrast, as Kelly (1993) reports, the Indonesian reform was more successful. By focusing on improved collection efficiency and improved valuation and assessment, property tax collection efficiency rose from 65 to 79 percent, and the share of property tax revenue in total own source revenue almost doubled between 1990 and 1991.

## THE FUTURE OF THE PROPERTY TAX IN DEVELOPING COUNTRIES

Making property taxes work more effectively in developing and transitional countries is a complex challenge. Although many internal and external factors are involved, we speculate that the future of the property tax in such countries is mainly dependent on four factors: (1) the pace of decentralization; (2) the efficacy of shortcuts to valuation of property; (3) technology catch-up; and (4) the willingness of central governments to give local governments access to other productive tax bases.

### Factor 1: The Pace of Decentralization

Despite being one of the most talked about development strategies in the past two decades, decentralization has hardly taken off. Although there are now many decentralized and decentralizing developing countries, the average expenditure share of subnational governments in total government spending is considerably less than in developed countries and has barely budged from its 15 percent level in the 1970s. However, more elected officials are bringing pressure, there is a continuing reaction against central governments that have become too controlling, and there is a political strategy to promote bringing governments closer to people. All of this could lead to increased decentralization. As decentralizing countries turn to the job of identifying revenue sources for local governments, an expanded property tax will be an obvious choice.

## Factor 2: The Efficacy of Shortcuts

Administrative cost is arguably the biggest constraint to the growth of the property tax. It is just too expensive and too hard to properly levy and enforce. Countries are turning increasingly to "shortcuts" to address this problem. The introduction of notional valuation based on location and area, self-assessment, indexing between valuation periods, and the exemption of "hard to tax" properties are all examples of such shortcuts. Will these innovations save the property tax or destroy it?

The approach that is gaining currency in developing countries appears to be area-based assessment. This is both inexpensive and simple enough to be acceptable to taxpayers. However, at base it requires a judgmental assessment of value per square meter in each of the valuation zones prescribed by the regional or local government. These notional values will require adjustment each year in order to build elasticity into the property tax. Moreover, the idea that all properties in a zone can be subjected to the same notional valuation per area unit may turn out to be an enemy of fairness in property taxation. Area-based assessments are likely to improve the revenue yield of the tax and give a better ratio of administrative cost to collections, but local governments are not likely to move to a higher intensity of property tax use with this approach to valuation.

## Factor 3: Technology Catch-Up

Will technology save property tax administration in developing countries? In general, developing countries appear to be closing the technology gap at a much faster rate than they are closing the income gap. Can new technologies such as computerized mass appraisal, satellite-aided mapping, and cross-referencing circumvent the high costs and time delays associated with the valuation process?[9] Will it soon be possible for local governments to keep up-to-date records of land characteristics and ownership? If new technologies in property tax assessment, collection, and record keeping do catch on, they could minimize much of the current problem with the property tax in developing nations.

## Factor 4: The Willingness of Central Governments

Will central governments release other productive revenue sources to local governments? Examples are the right to tax payrolls, piggyback personal in-

---

[9]Dillinger (1989) describes the successful practice in some Brazilian municipalities of using data provided by other agencies to flag changes in the tax base.

come taxes and excises, business taxes, and taxes on the use and ownership of motor vehicles. To the extent these "easier" tax sources are available to local governments, the property tax might be minimized as a subnational government revenue source.

In sum, property taxation still has great potential but also great uncertainty as an instrument for bringing revenues and accountability to subnational governments in developing and transitional countries around the world.

## REFERENCES

Bahl, R. 1998. Land value taxation in third world and transition countries. In *Land value taxation in contemporary societies*. D. Netzer, ed., 131–171. Cambridge, MA: Lincoln Institute of Land Policy.

Bahl, R., and J. F. Linn. 1992. *Urban public finance in developing countries*. Washington, DC: Oxford University Press.

Bahl, R., and S. Wallace. 2003. Fiscal decentralization: The provincial-local dimension. In *Public finance in developing and transition countries*. J. Alm and J. Martinez-Vazquez, eds., 5–33. Northampton, MA: Edward Elgar.

Bird, R. 2004. Land taxes in Colombia. In *International handbook of land and property taxation*. R. Bird and E. Slack, eds., 265–280. Northampton, MA: Edward Elgar.

Bird, R., and E. Slack, eds. 2004. *International handbook of land and property taxation*. Northampton, MA: Edward Elgar.

de Soto, H. 2000. *The mystery of capital: Why capitalism triumphs in the west and fails everywhere else*. New York: Basic Books.

Dillinger, W. 1988. Urban property tax reform: The case of the Philippines' Real Property Tax Administration Project. World Bank Discussion Paper, Report INU 16. Washington, DC: World Bank.

———. 1989. Urban property taxation: Lessons from Brazil. World Bank Discussion Paper, Report INU 27. Washington, DC: World Bank.

Guevara, M. 2004. Real property taxation in the Philippines. In *International handbook of land and property taxation*. R. Bird and E. Slack, eds., 152–158. Northampton, MA: Edward Elgar.

Iregui, A. M., L. Melo, and J. Ramos. 2004. Property tax in Colombia: Recent behavior, tariffs, and potential tax revenues. *Revista ESPE*, no. 46-II (special edition).

Kelly, R. 1993. Property tax reform in Indonesia: Applying a collection-led implementation strategy. *Bulletin of Indonesian Economic Studies* 29(1):85–104.

———. 2004. Property taxation in Indonesia. In *International handbook of land and property taxation*. R. Bird and E. Slack, eds., 117–128. Northampton, MA: Edward Elgar.

Kim, K-H. 1993. *Urban finance in selected Asian countries: A case study of Thailand, Indonesia, the Philippines and India*. Nairobi, Kenya: UN Centre for Human Settlements.

Malme, J. H., and J. M. Youngman. 2001. *The development of the property tax in economies in transition.* Washington, DC: World Bank.

Martinez-Vazquez, J., C. McLure, and F. Vaillancourt. 2006. Revenues and expenditures in an intergovernmental framework. In *Perspectives on fiscal federalism.* R. M. Bird and F. Vaillancourt, eds., 15–34. Washington, DC: World Bank Institute.

Rosengard, J. K. 1998. *Property tax reform in developing countries.* Norwell, MA: Kluwer Academic Publishers.

Sennoga, E., D. Sjoquist, and S. Wallace. 2008. Incidence and economic impacts of property taxes in developing and transitional countries. In *Making the property tax work: Experience in developing and transitional countries.* R. Bahl, J. Martinez-Vazquez, and J. Youngman, eds., 63–102. Cambridge, MA: Lincoln Institute of Land Policy.

Sjoquist, D. 2004. The land value tax in Jamaica: An analysis and options for reform. Working Paper 04-26. Atlanta: Andrew Young School of Policy Studies, Georgia State University.

United Nations Secretariat. 2004. *The world urbanization prospects: The 2003 revision.* New York: UN Department of Economic and Social Affairs, Population Division.

# 3

## Property Taxation in a Global Economy: Is a Capital Gains Tax on Real Property a Good Idea?

### Sally Wallace

The concept of globalization has become an increasing concern of public finance scholars around the globe. As capital becomes more mobile and barriers to its entry and exit fall, we expect it to migrate among sectors of the economy and among countries seeking out the highest rate of return. Competition for capital may therefore be affecting tax policies from corporate income taxes to property taxes. Some believe that tax policy is in a race to the bottom, where systems will become more and more homogenous among countries—developed and developing alike.

There continues to be much debate about the globalization of tax bases. Aizenman and Jinjarak (2006) test the hypothesis that globalization forces countries to move from easy-to-tax bases (trade taxes, seigniorage) to bases that are more difficult to tax (value-added tax and income tax, for example). They find evidence of this type of change in countries increasing their share of hard-to-tax bases between the early 1980s and the late 1990s. Other studies have not found as much evidence. For example, Alm, Chen, and Wallace (2002) analyzed the composition of taxes in the United States under the hypothesis that mobile taxes such as state and local taxes on capital would decline. They could not find conclusive evidence of such a trend.

The relative mix of taxes among countries and the differences in tax administration may be reasons for the lack of consensus regarding the empirical impact of globalization on taxes. Developed countries tend to have better-funded tax administrations, which may make them more able to adapt to changes in the tax base due to globalization. Countries with a large use of trade taxes may be particularly vulnerable to the impact of globalization. The type of central-state-local revenue assignment used in various countries may also increase the impact of globalization. We might think that in cases of significant decentralization of revenue authority, there would be more pressure to integrate tax bases due to competitive pressures associated with globalization.

The property tax is a bit unusual in terms of its role in the globalization debate. On one hand, as a benefits tax, it should be only partially affected by the pressures of worldwide competition for capital. In a world where individuals are mobile and can vote with their feet, the property tax is akin to a lump-sum tax and is nondistortionary in its impact on the allocation of capital. On the other hand, the new view of the property tax holds that it is a distortionary tax on capital and that differentials in the effective property tax rate can affect the migration of capital among jurisdictions. In that world, with the increased ease of capital migration due to globalization, the property tax might be viewed as an endangered species.[1]

The property tax has a number of dimensions. In this chapter, we focus on the growth in the value of real property—itself a product of globalization, and the possibility of integrating a tax on capital gains on real property into the tax mix. While some countries tax capital gains in real property, few do it well, and others rely on other taxes to do the job of a capital gains tax. We suggest that those are not good imposters and that there may be room to integrate a real capital gains tax in some developing countries.

## GLOBALIZATION AND REAL PROPERTY VALUES

Globalization continues to be difficult to define but easy to point out. Increased access to international markets, outsourcing of work, Internet communication and sales, and more are evidence of globalization. The economics of globalization and its impact on property is, in theory, fairly clear cut. Mobile capital will seek the highest rate of return. As the barriers to mobility fall (for example, financial markets open up, transportation becomes cheaper, tariffs and other taxes fall), capital moves more easily among countries. This mobility of capital has been hailed as one of the driving factors in the potential "race to the bottom" of taxes worldwide, since, under certain conditions, taxes will lower the rate of return to capital.[2] Countries with high taxes on capital will be at a competitive disadvantage vis-à-vis other countries, so there is pressure to bring tax rates on mobile capital down to match those of other countries.

---

[1]There are many good discussions of the benefits view versus the capital tax view of the property tax. See, for example, Zodrow (2001) and Fischel (2001).
[2]See, for example, Alm, Chen, and Wallace (2002) and Neumann, Holman, and Alm (2002).

**Figure 3.1:** FDI Inflows, 2000–2004

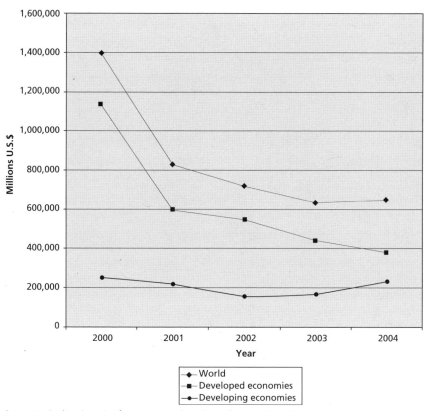

Source: United Nations Conference on Trade and Development (2006).

Increased capital flows can increase productivity, leading to higher levels of economic growth. Increased investment, expanding businesses, and increased employment will boost the demand for real property, thereby putting pressure on the prices of land and structure. Thus, we might expect the march of globalization to yield significant gains in property values.

Evidence on the progress of globalization and investment can be found by studying the flow of foreign direct investment (FDI) around the world. The United Nations Conference on Trade and Development (UNCTAD; 2006) produces FDI flows for most countries in the world. In figure 3.1, we see that in the post-2000 boom-to-bust period, FDI dropped substantially between 2000 and 2001. By 2004, we see some recovery of investment—with most of the growth occurring in the developing countries. As a frame of reference, in 2004, FDI inflows worldwide were over three times what they were in 1990. In developing economies, they were over six times as great as 1990 levels.

**Figure 3.2:** Residential Fixed Investment as a Share of GDP, United States, 1980–2005

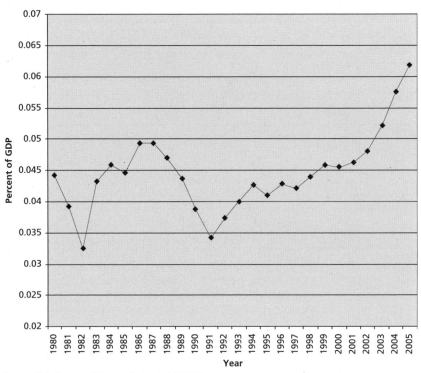

*Source*: U.S. Bureau of Economic Analysis (2006).

Has the flow of capital had an impact on the price of real property?[3] There is much anecdotal evidence that property values have increased in many parts of the world. It is more difficult to find comparable empirical evidence regarding the value of real property. Gravelle (1994) reports that in the United States net gains on personal residences accounted for 25.3 percent of all capital gains in the early 1980s, putting the total gain on residences at approximately $27 billion. That amount increased over time, and by 1990, the total level of capital gains was $145 billion. If housing had retained its 25.3 percent share, the level of capital gains in real property would have increased more than 30 percent in eight years.

---

[3]It would be interesting to analyze this question empirically by estimating whether urbanization, for example, is affected by flows of FDI. A positive correlation between FDI and urbanization would suggest that increased FDI increases the demand for housing and land. There may also be a longer-term impact whereby increases in the value of real property reduce the growth of further FDI. If that is the case, property values may naturally stabilize or even fall after a big run up in gains fueled by FDI. The analysis is not done here.

**Figure 3.3:** Private Residential Fixed Assets as a Share of GDP, United States, 1980–2005

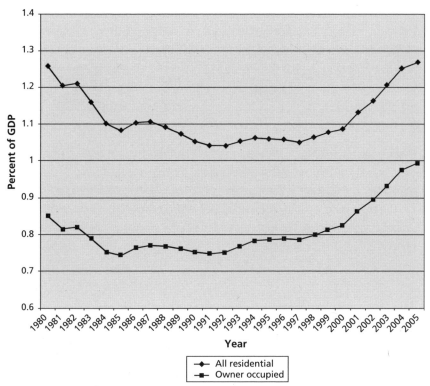

*Source*: U.S. Bureau of Economic Analysis (2006).

In 2004–2005 concerns over the potential bursting of the "housing bubbles" in the United States and the United Kingdom provided some evidence that there are significant gains on real property.[4] The United Nations (2005) reports that rising housing prices in developing economies may lead to risky housing price bubbles in those countries as well.

In the United States, we can identify more specific data to analyze the trend in gains to real property. We use the ratio of residential fixed investment as a share of GDP and the stock of residential property as a share of GDP as rough measures of evidence of capital gains. Figures 3.2 and 3.3 demonstrate the growth in both of these indicators. In figure 3.2, we see that as a share of

---

[4]Many popular outlets have published "bubble" stories. *Business Week* (2005) reported that the chief economists for Freddie Mac found rational reasoning (job and income growth) behind the double-digit growth in home values in some large U.S. markets. BBC News (2006) reported strong gains for housing in the United Kingdom over several previous years.

**BOX 3.1 Globalization in Ghana**

There are many specific examples of globalization around the world. In Ghana, recent interviews with industry officials provide some insight into the impact of globalization on a developing economy. In the Ghanaian cigarette industry, the only domestic producer has recently decided to close its production line and become an importer of cigarettes. Economics was the driving reason—the marginal cost of production including transportation costs was significantly lower in other countries in Africa.

Another example comes in the case of a local alcohol producer. Facing large costs of importing new machinery from the United Kingdom and the United States to replace antiquated capital, the company searched for alternatives in Europe but felt the costs were too high. The managers eventually looked to China, which they claim has become an easier exporter, and are in the process of finalizing a deal to bring in the machinery from there.

GDP, residential fixed investment has grown steadily since 1991. The values of capital stock of all residential property and owner-occupied property as a share of GDP (figure 3.3) have also shown consistent growth since 1991–1992. Neither of these ratios is a perfect measure of the growth of net capital gains in real property, but they provide some evidence of growth in capital gains on real property.[5]

At the very least, these data provide some circumstantial evidence on the globalization–FDI–property value link. A structural model of globalization, investment, and property values could be developed and tested if data were available. However, the pattern of strong FDI (with expected downturns during recessionary periods) and evidence of housing price increases provide some support for the intuitive notion that globalization, increased flows of investment, and housing prices are related.

---

[5]The national income accounts do not include capital gains because capital gains do not represent an addition to investment in the economy. In the United States the near elimination of capital gains on owner-occupied housing reduces the usefulness of IRS data on capital gains on real property.

**TABLE 3.1** Property Tax as a Percent of GDP

|  | 2000 | 2001 | 2002 | 2003 | 2004 |
|---|---|---|---|---|---|
| **OECD countries** | | | | | |
| Observations | 18 | 18 | 17 | 16 | 12 |
| Average | 2.17 | 2.06 | 2.10 | 2.01 | 2.16 |
| **Developing countries** | | | | | |
| Observations | 40 | 30 | 4 | 2 | 1 |
| Average | 0.57 | 0.54 | 0.62 | 1.14 | 1.63 |
| **Transitional countries** | | | | | |
| Observations | 20 | 18 | 11 | 14 | 10 |
| Average | 0.65 | 0.64 | 0.79 | 0.77 | 0.79 |

*Source*: International Monetary Fund (2006); also reported in Bahl and Martinez-Vazquez (2006).

## CAPITAL GAINS TAX ON REAL PROPERTY

As a tax on real property, a capital gains tax on land and structures is related in some ways to "traditional" property taxes. The property tax, despite its merits as a local tax, is not heavily used in many developing and transitional countries. Table 3.1 demonstrates the recent trends in property tax relative to GDP. Our data for developing countries is too sparse in 2002–2004 to provide a meaningful comparison, so we compare 2000 and 2001 among countries. In OECD countries, the average is just slightly over 2 percent, while in developing and transitional countries, it is much lower and averages around 0.59 percent of GDP. Earlier estimates from Bahl (2001) suggest that those ratios have increased only gradually since the 1980s for a variety of reasons including valuation, pressure to keep rates low, collection, and compliance.

A capital gains tax on real property could increase the effective rate of taxation on property in developed, developing, and transitional countries. A real capital gains tax would tax the change in *real* value of the property. The tax base is the sales price minus the real purchase price minus the real value of improvements.[6] In this chapter, we focus on taxing realized capital gains. While a tax on unrealized gains may be preferable from a Haig-Simons perspective, the administration of an annual tax on unrealized gains could be unwieldy.

---

[6]To be consistent, real losses on property should be deductible under an integrated income tax system. For purposes of this chapter, we can implicitly assume the symmetric treatment of gains and losses.

## Arguments in Favor

There are numerous arguments in support of a capital gains tax on real property, and they focus on equity and efficiency issues. The first issue is that many countries tax a variety of assets, but relatively few tax real capital gains on real property. There are situations, as in the case of the United States, where nominal gain on corporate stocks is taxed, but the gain to residential property is effectively exempt.[7] That difference in treatment of assets may redirect investment in ways that are not anticipated—potentially lowering the price of real assets relative to other capital assets and fueling increased prices in housing. That may not be as much of an issue in developing countries as in developed countries. Or it may be an issue for urban areas in developing countries, but not so much for rural areas.

Second is the important issue of vertical equity. The distribution of wealth around the world continues to show patterns of heavy concentration in the upper-income deciles in all countries. The World Bank (2005) reports that the level of poverty and the distribution of income or consumption have shown improvement in some countries, but have changed very little, or even gotten worse, in other countries (countries of sub-Saharan Africa having some of the most disparate distributions). While data on the distribution of capital assets are not readily available for most countries, we expect that the ownership of real assets is concentrated in higher-income groups. On grounds of vertical equity, a capital gains tax on real property could therefore rate quite high.

Third, the revenue from a real capital gains tax could be significant. Of course, this is a big "could." Tax administration plays a critical role in instituting a tax on capital gains. Lax enforcement of taxes in many countries calls into question the ability of a tax on capital gains to yield significant revenue.

How much revenue is possible? In the United States, for example, the estimate of the tax expenditure associated with the exclusion of capital gains on housing is upward of $40 billion. This means that, based on available data, if residential properties were subject to the capital gains tax, receipts would be $40 billion higher. In Jamaica, which has no tax on capital gains, it has been estimated that a tax on real property and financial assets could raise as much as $J1 billion (Wallace and Alm 2004). Bahl (2004) estimates that the real property portion of a capital gains tax in Jamaica could be $J200 million.

Increased property values may be viewed as a monetary gain that property owners get from general government expenditures on infrastructure and other

---

[7]In the United States, an individual can exempt up to $250,000 of capital gains, and a married couple can exempt up to $500,000 of gains on the sale of a primary residence.

general public goods. From that perspective, it is only fair that government should receive a share of that benefit via a capital gains tax (Bahl 2004).

The imposition of a property tax and a capital gains tax does not mean that real assets are the subject of "double taxation." Under the benefits view of tax incidence, the property tax is a payment for local government services. If the tax is fully capitalized, property values decrease to the extent of the tax. If benefits are also capitalized, property values may increase due to the value of the benefits. The property tax–benefits impact could net out, so that there would be no change in the value of property (or even a reduction in the value of property if tax capitalization were more than capitalization of the benefits). A capital gains tax would tax real *appreciation* in the value of real property—which comes due to such factors as increased demand for housing, better living conditions in a particular area, and externalities associated with the specific benefits. If there were no appreciation in assets, there would be no capital gains tax to levy.

From the new view, or capital tax view, differentials in property tax rates lead to migration of capital to lower-taxed jurisdictions. Globalization may enhance that movement. For jurisdictions with higher than average property taxes, the gross price of property increases, but the net price in the entire market (province, state, country, worldwide market) would fall. A capital gains tax in that world would be based on a higher gross price in the higher-taxed jurisdiction. In all other jurisdictions, once again, a capital gains tax would be due only if the value of the property appreciates. Double taxation would become even less of an issue if a national capital gains tax were proposed or if the gain to the value of land alone were the subject of taxation.

A tax on real capital gains could discourage speculation by reducing the after-tax rate of return on real property. This could have the effect of smoothing the returns to real property and reducing the chance for bubble phenomena. However, if the capital gains tax allowed full-loss offset in the case of real losses on property, the government would share both the risk and the yield of the assets, which might in fact increase the incentive for individuals to take on a slightly riskier set of real estate investments.

Finally, there is a possible self-policing aspect of a capital gains tax that could be attractive to the tax administrations of developing countries. Currently, in the case of most property transfer tax systems, both seller and buyer have an incentive to underreport the value of the transaction. In the case of a capital gains tax, the seller might want to underreport the value of the sale (to reduce his capital gain), but the buyer wants her basis to be as high as possible—so she would want the sale reported at the highest possible price (barring any other taxes or fees). Self-interest is likely to push both parties toward reporting a transaction value that is more in line with the actual value than is currently the practice in many countries.

## Arguments Against

Just as there are proponents of taxing real gains to real property, there are solid arguments against such taxation. The lock-in effect of capital gains taxation is one problem that has received much attention in the literature, which covers real property as well as other capital assets, like corporate stocks. The lock-in effect in the case of real property means that imposition of a capital gains tax (or an increase in the tax rate) increases the cost of selling a house. If, in the absence of the tax, an individual would sell the house and move, the lock-in effect reduces utility. The economy as a whole suffers an efficiency loss, as capital may be misallocated and thus not be put into its most productive use. That effect is similar to the lock-in effect attributed to acquisition-value property taxes, whereby houses are revalued for property tax purposes only when sold (O'Sullivan, Sexton, and Sheffrin 1995).[8]

Administration of a capital gains tax is difficult. To be true to the base of "real capital gains" administrators must have documented evidence of the sales or purchase price, as well as the timing and cost of improvements. That type of documentation is standard in some countries, but not in most developing nations. Indexation is less of a problem. Although not perfect, an annual inflation adjustment could be based on the consumer price index over a calendar year. Another administrative issue is the treatment of interfamily transactions. There is a tendency to allow those types of transfers to be tax free, but the potential for tax evasion is significant. For example, an individual who wants to buy a property may bankroll someone related to the owner to purchase the property. The financier then could rent back the property for no cost. This is risky for the financier, but in certain markets, escalating rental prices could make the risk worthwhile.

A capital gains tax, even if it is a substitute for another tax, is likely to be politically unpopular. It would be very transparent, as it is a big-ticket item when real property is sold.

In addition, capital gains tax revenue flows can be erratic, although most empirical evidence on their stability covers taxes on financial assets (Sjoquist and Wallace 2003). Housing values have grown in many countries over the last decade, but not all areas have experienced growth; and in the case of developed nations, there is documented evidence of declines in the value of real property.

---

[8]The lock-in effect for capital assets such as stocks has been heavily researched, without a definitive answer regarding the impact of capital gains taxes on the long-run lock-in effect. See, for example, Gravelle (1994), Burman and Randolph (1994), and Auerbach (1989).

There are also arguments that preferential treatment for capital (in the form of lower or no taxes on capital gains) is needed to encourage investment and entrepreneurship and to increase the incentive for individuals to own their own homes. Higher capital gains taxes increase the price of home ownership and may therefore reduce ability to purchase a home.

To summarize, there are good and bad points to a capital gains tax. A proponent of a tax on real capital gains would emphasize that such a tax could raise significant amounts of revenue, reduce disparities among treatment of capital assets, and enhance vertical equity; and that it could be self-policing, thus reducing evasion. Opponents of such a tax might emphasize that it could be difficult to administer, especially for local governments, could create a lock-in effect and reduce the mobility of individuals and companies, and might be too burdensome. Both sides have valid arguments, as is the case in most tax policy debates. In the next section, we turn to reviewing capital gains–like taxes that already exist and rate them and a tax on real capital gains on a number of economic and administrative issues.

## DO CAPITAL GAINS TAXES ON REAL PROPERTY EXIST?

There are taxes that may look like capital gains taxes but fall short of taxing capital gains on real property for a variety of reasons. These include stamp duties, property transfer taxes, gift taxes, betterment levies, and land value increment taxes. The value-added tax (VAT) might also be considered a capital gains–type tax.[9] There are also some examples of real capital gains taxes. Recall that we define a capital gains tax as one that taxes real returns to real property. We might evaluate potential capital gains tax "imposters" by considering the following issues:

- Does it tax real capital gains?
- Are improvements accounted for?
- Does it raise significant revenue?
- What is the distributional impact?
- Does it induce "bad" behavior, such as evasion or lock-in effects?
- Is the administration clear or arbitrary?

To evaluate whether there are many true capital gains taxes on real property out there, we first take a look at the types of capital gains (and other) taxes used in a small sample of countries. The experiences of various countries

---

[9]The VAT typically taxes the value of the transaction, so it is not a tax on real capital gains in most countries.

**TABLE 3.2**  Examples of Property-Related Taxes in Select Countries

| Country | Tax | Base | Rate | Other issues |
|---------|-----|------|------|--------------|
| Jamaica | Property transfer tax | Nominal transaction value | 7.5% | Rate is coupled with a stamp duty of 5.5% |
| Taiwan | Land value increment tax | Total increment amount of land value | Progressive rates from 20% to 40% | Adjusts for improvements and inflation |
| Korea | Land value increment tax (1990s) | Unrealized gains | 50% of excess profits | Basic value increase is exempt; not all property is taxed |
| Russian Federation | Estate and gift taxes, capital gains tax | Self-reported nominal value of transfer | Individual income tax rate (13% flat rate) | System of a market-based property tax is in development |
| United States | Capital gains tax | Nominal capital gain | Individual income tax rate | $500,000 exemption for married filers, $250,000 for single |

are summarized by the information in table 3.2, and then in table 3.3 we evaluate those examples according to the criteria listed above. Of course, the countries listed in the tables are only illustrative. More detailed summaries of property taxes, other taxes on property, and capital gains taxes are reported by Bird and Slack (2002), Youngman and Malme (1994), Almy (2001), and Franzsen and McCluskey (2005).

Jamaica imposes a property transfer tax and a stamp duty tax. Bahl (2004) evaluates both and finds them to be unconvincing capital gains–like taxes. The stamp duty is charged on transactions and a few types of sales (airline tickets, for example). The property transfer tax is levied on the transaction value of real property. As noted by Bahl (2004), there is an incentive to underreport the value of transactions in Jamaica's property transfer tax system. Little effort is expended in the administration of those taxes, so the undervaluation problem has been an issue for much of their history.

The property transfer tax in Jamaica is sometimes referred to as a substitute for a capital gains tax, but it is not a good substitute. Its base is not the real capital gain. There is no inflation adjustment or accounting for original sales price or improvements, and the reported transaction value is universally below the actual sales price. The tax does not reach the realized value of real property in Jamaica.

**TABLE 3.3** Survey of Taxes Similar to Capital Gains

| Country | Tax | Are capital gains taxed? | Inflation adjustment? | Revenue? | Bad behavior and economic costs |
|---|---|---|---|---|---|
| "Ideal case" | Capital gains tax on real property | Yes, on land and structures | Yes | Could be significant | Self-policing ("good behavioral effect"), lock-in possible |
| Jamaica | Property transfer tax, stamp duty | No | No | Small | Under declaration |
| Taiwan | Land value increment tax | Yes, on land, realized | Yes | Substantial amount for subnational government | Lock-in effect; local governments must revalue the tax base regularly |
| Korea | Land value increment tax | Yes, on land, unrealized | No | Small due to political pressures and definition of taxable property | Tax avoidance can be achieved by constructing improvements, which may or may not be finished |
| Russian Federation | Capital gains tax | Residential property largely exempt | No | Small | If enforced, it could induce a lock-in effect |
| United States | Capital gains tax | Residential property largely exempt | No | Relatively small | Nonbinding for most homeowners, so it has little impact |

There are numerous other examples of capital gains–type taxes levied on real property. Youngman and Malme (1994) summarize the state of other taxes on immovable property in the early 1990s. At that time, of the 14 surveyed countries for which information is reported (largely OECD countries, with the addition of South Korea, Chile, Israel, and Indonesia), all but one report some type of tax on gains to immovable property. Most often, the tax on capital gains is a combination of transfer tax and capital gains tax.

Franzsen and McCluskey (2005) provide a comprehensive list of countries with property transfer taxes and capital gains taxes. Almy (2001) also surveys a number of countries and reports "other property-related taxes" for transitional countries—mostly transfer, gift, and inheritance types of taxes, with the exception of Estonia's land use fees.

Nuances of capital gains and other property-related taxes are reported in the studies of Youngman and Malme (1994), Franzsen and McCluskey (2005), and Almy (2001). The details for a handful of countries suggest that their taxes are not taxes on real capital gains, and their property-related taxes are not good approximations of a capital gains tax. For example, we find that in Malaysia, the capital gains tax on real property for individuals falls to zero when assets are held for five or more years. There is, in fact, a sliding scale for all property owners, according to which the tax rate falls as the holding period increases. This may be intended as a rough adjustment for inflation (which is not explicitly accounted for in the definition of the tax base).

In Ghana, the capital gains tax base is basically on transactions rather than the increase in value of real property. In the United Kingdom, realized capital gains on residential property are exempt. These cases provide some evidence that countries' "capital gains taxes" may not be the real thing.

Another example of incomplete capital gains taxation is provided by the Russian Federation, where the tax base of gift and transfer taxes is based on the self-reported value of the transaction, not appreciation in the value of the asset (Martinez-Vazquez, Rider, and Wallace 2006). It is likely that similar treatment is found in other transitional countries as well. The capital gains tax in Russia exempts residential property, but transfers of real property are subject to the VAT.

Korea and Taiwan provide examples of a tax that is more like a real capital gains tax on real property. Taiwan's land value increment tax (LVIT) taxes the real return to land and makes allowances for inflation and the costs of improvements and fees ("costs" of owning land). The tax is levied using a progressive rate structure. There are some exemptions, including transfers that occur as inheritances (Tsui 1998).

Korea's LVIT is a tax on unrealized capital gains on unimproved land held by companies and excess residential land (Lee 2000). The definition of *idle land* led to a means for tax evasion. Lee (2000) points out that property owners could construct cheap improvements to the land to avoid taxes. Challenges to the tax in 1995 reduced its usefulness as a tax on capital gains from real property.

This brief survey of taxes on property is summarized by the information in table 3.2. Taiwan's and Korea's LVITs come closest to a tax on real capital gains. Korea's tax faced stiff resistance by taxpayers.

Table 3.3 shows the similarities and differences between the taxes listed in table 3.2 and a real capital gains tax (on real property). A capital gains tax, with a strong tax administration component, could be a significant revenue producer, as noted earlier. It could also induce some bad behavior via the lock-in effect. Of the small sample of other taxes that are listed in tables 3.2 and 3.3, the LVITs of Taiwan and Korea come closest to the capital gains tax in terms of impacts and revenue potential—at least in theory. Korea's LVIT is a good case study in the politics of that type of tax. However, in Korea, the tax rate on gains was 50 percent—high by most standards for any tax. An additional lesson that could be taken from Korea's case is that the tax rate matters to the taxpayer. Introducing a new capital gains tax at a relatively low rate probably has a better chance of success than one that is enacted with a high tax rate.

## DESIGN AND ADMINISTRATIVE ISSUES: CAN THEY BE OVERCOME?

The demands for information, reporting, record keeping, and the like could prevent any developing nation (or developed one) from seriously considering a significant capital gains tax on real property. However, there are cases in which a basis exists for implementing a real capital gains tax on real property. Dasgupta (2002) reports on the administrative structure of transfer and property taxes in Uttar Pradesh, a state in India. Much effort has been put into developing a baseline value for properties there. Cost-based norms are used to regularly adjust the values for buildings. The adjusted baselines can be compared against self-reported values. If an inflation adjustment were included, that type of valuation could be used to implement a capital gains tax on real property.

Bahl (2004, 53) describes an approach to levy a land-based capital gains tax in Jamaica. The estimation of liability is carried out in six steps:

1. land value at time of sale;
2. minus land value at purchase, net of costs of improvements, adjusted for inflation over the period;
3. minus allowable exemption status;
4. equals taxable realized capital gain;
5. times tax rate;
6. equals tax due.

A method similar to that used in Uttar Pradesh could be used to estimate 1 and 2. Exemption status is specified in law (exemptions may include low-valued homes, for example). The greater administrative costs and difficulties come from the inclusion of improvements.

If a capital gains tax were feasible, could it coexist with a property tax in our globalized world? Property taxes vary among countries due to their structure and administration. This makes it difficult to make general statements about the potential coexistence of a capital gains tax and a property tax. However, as explained earlier, a real capital gains tax is not a double tax in the sense of a "tax on tax." Capital gains taxes may be a better way to address vertical equity and to repay government for the general benefits of increased infrastructure and an atmosphere that promotes foreign direct investment and growth in real estate markets. With the pressures of increased capital mobility within and among countries, a capital gains tax on all real property (even properly administered) could exacerbate capital outflows. A more reasonable alternative might be to focus on development of a capital gains tax on land. With some work on developing a baseline that could take advantage of the tax administration infrastructure of the property tax, a real capital gains tax on land might be a viable alternative in countries where it is not yet used.

## CONCLUSIONS

Globalization is changing the structure of the worldwide economy. The easing of the flow of capital, labor, and goods among countries produces changes in the distribution of resources among countries and also possibly within countries. In this chapter, we have appealed to the notion that globalization has increased the movement of capital and that the increase in investment across the globe has produced upward pressure in the value of real property. Of course, not all countries are necessarily winners in the capital mobility game — even within countries, urbanized areas may see large increases in real values of property, while rural areas witness a decline.

The growth in the value of real property may provide an important tax base for developing countries. A brief survey of tax treatment of property suggests that while a number of countries report capital gains or capital gains–like taxes, the reality is that real capital gains are probably not taxed in many countries. Issues of equity (vertical equity, as well as reasonable contributions for general benefits from public goods), potential revenue generation, and the possible tie-in with property tax administration may be intriguing enough for countries to further explore a capital gains tax on real property. Since globalization makes the taxation of capital more difficult, a capital gains tax on real increases in the value of land may be a more appropriate concept to explore in more detail.

# REFERENCES

Aizenman, J., and Y. Jinjarak. 2006. Globalization and developing countries: A shrinking tax base? Working Paper 11933. Cambridge, MA: National Bureau of Economic Research.

Alm, J., S. Chen, and S. Wallace. 2002. Globalization and state-local finances. In *Proceedings of the 95th Annual National Tax Association Conference*, 155–164. Orlando, FL: National Tax Association.

Almy, R. 2001. A survey of property tax systems in Europe. Prepared for the Department of Taxes and Customs, Ministry of Finance, Republic of Slovenia. http://www.agjd.com/EuropeanPropertyTaxSystems.pdf.

Auerbach, A. 1989. Capital gains taxation and tax reform. *National Tax Journal* 42:1–36.

Bahl, R. 2001. The property tax in developing countries: Where are we in 2002? Lecture at the Lincoln Institute of Land Policy, Cambridge, MA, October 23.

———. 2004. Property transfer tax and stamp duty. International Studies Program Working Paper. Atlanta: Andrew Young School of Policy Studies, Georgia State University.

Bahl, R., and J. Martinez-Vazquez. 2006. Property taxation. Prepared for conference, Lincoln Institute of Land Policy and International Studies Program, Andrew Young School of Policy Studies, Georgia State University, Atlanta, October.

BBC News. 2006. Will house prices boom again? http://news.bbc.co.uk/1/hi/business/4972220.stm.

Bird, R., and E. Slack. 2002. Land and property tax: A review. *Journal of Property Tax Assessment and Administration* 7(3):31–89.

Burman, L., and W. Randolph. 1994. Measuring permanent responses to capital gains tax changes in panel data. *American Economic Review* 84(4):794–809.

*Business Week*. 2005. Housing bubble—Or bunk? http://www.businessweek.com/bwdaily/dnflash/jun2005/nf20050622_9404_db008.htm.

Dasgupta, A. 2002. *India: Uttar Pradesh policy notes: UP's own revenue system: Assessment and reform suggestions*. Washington, DC: World Bank.

Fischel, W. 2001. Municipal corporations, homeowners and the benefit view of the property tax. In *Property taxation and local government finance*. W. E. Oates, ed., 33–77. Cambridge MA: Lincoln Institute of Land Policy

Franzsen, R. C. D., and W. J. McCluskey. 2005. An exploratory overview of property taxation in the Commonwealth of Nations. Working Paper WP05RF1. Cambridge, MA: Lincoln Institute of Land Policy.

Globe Africa. 2003. Namibia investment policy. http://www.globeafrica.com/Namibia/namibia2.htm.

Gravelle, J. 1994. *The economic effects of taxing capital income*. Cambridge, MA: MIT Press.

Invest in Taiwan, Department of Investment Services. 2006. Real property taxes: Land value tax. http://investintaiwan.nat.gov.tw/en/env/guide/tax/land_value.html.

Kelly, R. 2002. Designing a property tax reform strategy for sub-Saharan Africa: An analytical framework applied to Kenya. *Public Budgeting and Finance* 20:36.

Lee, T-I. 2000. Republic of Korea (South Korea). In *Land value taxation around the world.* R. V. Andelson, ed. Malden, MA: Blackwell.

Martinez-Vazquez, J., M. Rider, and S. Wallace. 2006. Russia's tax reform. Draft manuscript, Andrew Young School of Policy Studies, Georgia State University.

Neumann, R., J. Holman, and J. Alm. 2002. Globalization and tax policy. Working paper. Madison: University of Wisconsin.

O'Sullivan, A., T. A. Sexton, and S. M. Sheffrin. 1995. *Property taxes and tax revolts: The legacy of Proposition 13.* Cambridge: Cambridge University Press.

Sjoquist, D., and S. Wallace. 2003. Capital gains: Its recent, varied, and growing (?) impact on state revenues. Paper presented at the State Fiscal Crises: Causes, Consequences, and Solutions conference, Urban Institute, Washington, DC (reprinted in *State Tax Notes,* August 2003).

Tsui, S. 1998. Land value increment tax for redistribution and efficiency in Taiwan, ROC. Paper presented at the International Seminar on Land Policy and Economic Development, November 16–17, Taipei, Taiwan, Republic of China.

United Nations. 2005. Sustained economic growth in developing regions opens window of opportunity for development goals. Press release. http://www.un.org/News/Press/docs/2005/eco90.doc.htm.

United Nations Conference on Trade and Development. 2006. Foreign direct investment database. http://www.unctad.org/Templates/Page.asp?intItemID=3199&lang=1.

U.S. Bureau of Economic Analysis. 2006. National Income Accounts database. www.bea.gov.

U.S. Office of Management and Budget. 2006. Analytical perspectives. In *Budget of the United States Government.* Washington, DC: U.S. Office of Management and Budget. http://www.whitehouse.gov/omb/budget/fy2006/pdf/spec.pdf#search=%22tax%20expenditures%20in%20US%20budget%22.

Wallace, S., and J. Alm. 2004. The Jamaican individual income tax. International Studies Program Working Paper. Atlanta: Andrew Young School of Policy Studies, Georgia State University.

World Bank. 2005. *World development indicators.* Washington, DC: World Bank.

Youngman, J., and J. Malme. 1994. *An international survey of taxes on land and buildings.* Deventer, The Netherlands: Kluwer Law and Taxation Publishers.

Zodrow, G. 2001. Reflections on the new view and the benefit view of the property tax. In *Property taxation and local government finance.* W. E. Oates, ed., 79–111. Cambridge MA: Lincoln Institute of Land Policy.

# Local Economic Development

# 4

# The Sprawl of Economics: A Response to Jan Brueckner

## Gerrit-Jan Knaap

Under a variety of labels, smart growth has risen rapidly in popularity in the United States. The reasons for this rapid ascendance are multiple—increasing traffic congestion, rising property taxes, continued loss of farmland and open space. But a significant contributor to the growing popularity of smart growth has been the work of an active and vocal set of interest groups, including Smart Growth America, the Smart Growth Network, the Congress for New Urbanism, and many others.[1] The remarkable success of smart growth advocates, however, has not gone unnoticed by interest groups with opposing points of view. Such interest groups contend that urban sprawl is simply the result of "natural" market forces and that the remedies to sprawl offered by smart growth advocates are certain to do more harm than good. Proponents of that point of view include the Reason Foundation, the Heritage Foundation, and the Thoreau Institute.[2]

Until fairly recently, academic economists had written little on this subject. According to Edwin Mills (1999),

> Academic economists have weighed in on issues relating to suburbanization. Their most important contributions have been in the areas of metropolitan location and spatial analysis, local government tax and expenditure analysis, and the analysis of interactions between metropolitan transportation and spatial issues. Yet, remarkably, academic economists have written

[1]See http://www.smartgrowthamerica.org; http://www.smartgrowth.org; http://cnu.org.
[2]See http://www.reason.org; http://www.heritage.org; http://ti.org.

almost nothing on the general government policy issue of allegedly excessive metropolitan suburbanization.

In recent years, that has changed; and for the most part, economists have joined the chorus of voices opposed to smart growth. Most economists contend that if urban growth is excessive, the best way to attack the problem is to use various forms of prices, taxes, and fees to discourage it (Brueckner 2000; Mills 1999).

In this chapter, I respond to economists critical of smart growth and challenge the suggestion that prices, taxes, and fees are sufficient for addressing the problem of urban sprawl. I begin by presenting the conventional view of economists, drawing primarily on a paper by Jan Brueckner. I then critique the "pricing" approach by making three arguments. First, if urban expansion, or falling urban densities, is the primary problem, there is no theoretical reason why pricing is necessarily a superior approach to direct control. Economists who have looked closely at this question in other contexts conclude that the optimal approach depends critically on the institutional aspects of the problem. Second, I argue that the problem of urban sprawl involves much more than urban expansion or falling urban densities. A burgeoning literature now demonstrates that social welfare is a function of many attributes of urban form. Third, much of the character of urban growth is shaped by public investments in road networks, sewer systems, and public parks. These public investments—especially the critical elements of their design—are largely unaffected by the price system. I conclude by asserting that the pricing approach to urban sprawl is a necessary but not sufficient approach to the problem. Clearly it is important to get prices right and to use economic incentives when appropriate. But getting the prices right will never adequately address some of the most critical elements of the urban form. A comprehensive, and less ideological, approach to urban sprawl will require the use of prices, taxes, fees, public investments, public-private partnerships, planning, *and* land use regulation.

## ECONOMISTS ON URBAN SPRAWL

In an early and widely read paper, Wilbur Thompson (1968) characterized the city as a "distorted price system." He argued that many urban problems stem from imperfect or nonexistent prices and that greater use of the price system would "ration existing facilities," "guide the distribution of income," and "increase the range of choice." Imposing a toll during peak hours,

Thompson suggested, is one example of how prices can enlarge the range of choice.

Jan Brueckner (2000) offers a classic statement on the economics of urban sprawl, making several points. First, he contends that urban expansion, or falling urban densities, has been occurring for many years all over the world and is primarily the result of three "natural" market forces: population growth, rising incomes, and falling transportation costs. Rising populations cause urban areas to expand to accommodate more residents. Rising incomes, with positive income elasticities of demand for space, cause residents to demand more urban space per person. Falling transportation costs enable residents to live at greater distances without increases in expenditures. If urban areas expand largely for those three reasons, he argues, there is no compelling need to contain urban growth.

Brueckner then claims that urban expansion can be excessive for at least three reasons. First, undeveloped land may be underpriced. That is, land used for forests, farming, or other unimproved uses may provide benefits to urban residents that are not captured by the owner of the land. If so, the owner of undeveloped land may sell or develop land for urban uses even though the social value of the land is greater in its undeveloped state than in a developed state. Under those conditions, too much land will be developed for urban use. The appropriate policy response to that problem, according to Brueckner, is imposition of a development tax that lowers the value of the land for urban development to a more appropriate level.

Second, Brueckner argues, automobile travel may be underpriced. When highways are congested, motorists impose costs on other motorists. As a result, the marginal cost of an additional motorist exceeds the average cost of that motorist—the price actually paid—and from a social welfare perspective, too many motorists travel too far for too long. The appropriate policy response to this problem, according to Brueckner, is imposition of a congestion fee that raises the cost of travel to its true social cost. In a similar, though less widely cited article, Mills (1999) argues that automobiles impose more general environmental externalities (i.e., the more general environmental effects, such as exhaust emissions, and adverse effects of paved roads and parking lots), and therefore gas should be taxed by an amount that equals those external costs. Although their diagnoses of the problem and their policy recommendations are slightly different, Mills and Brueckner agree that urban sprawl should be addressed by increasing the cost of automobility.

Third, Brueckner argues, other forms of public infrastructure—such as schools, sewer services, police and fire protection—may also be underpriced.

If, as in the case of highways, these other forms of public infrastructure are congested, the marginal capital cost of an additional resident exceeds the average cost of existing residents. In that case, property taxes, which generally equal the average cost of public infrastructure, are too low, and urban areas expand to include too many residents. The appropriate response to the problem, Brueckner argues, is imposition of impact fees that equal the marginal cost of public infrastructure. In an extension of that argument, Knaap, Ding, and Hopkins (2001b) demonstrate how such optimal impact fees should increase over time as congestion increases and should fall abruptly after new investments in public infrastructure are made.

In sum, Brueckner argues that much of what constitutes urban sprawl is the result of natural market forces. He believes that excessive urban growth, however, is caused by imperfect pricing and should be addressed by correcting those prices. Addressing such problems by directly restricting the growth of urban areas—via zoning or urban growth boundaries (UGBs)—he suggests, could have "draconian" effects.

## IS PRICING THE SOLUTION?

While Brueckner's analysis of urban growth is sound, his case for using prices over land use controls is weak. His case for prices is based on two propositions: (1) congestion costs and impact fees are relatively easy to estimate; and (2) land use controls such as UGBs can have draconian effects. While excessively tight UGBs can indeed have draconian effects, so can excessively high taxes or impact fees. In general, whether it is better to impose fees or direct controls depends on the relative difficulty of estimating appropriate fees or quantities, the risk of error in their estimation, and the likelihood that local governments will impose either at the appropriate level. These are all complicated issues.

Although Brueckner suggests that congestion costs and impact fees are relatively easy to calculate, the difference in recommendations for pricing automobility between Brueckner and Mills suggests that the pricing task is not all that simple. Is it better to price congestion on specific highways or to impose higher taxes on gasoline? Should congestion fees be higher during peak-hour traffic and lower for carpools? Should gasoline taxes be higher in cities with stagnant air sheds where emissions do more damage? If local governments choose to impose impact fees, how do they estimate marginal capital costs of infrastructure when public infrastructure is expanded in large lumpy investments? Should impact fees vary with the size and location of the housing unit and the level of school congestion at the time the unit is built? If local governments impose open-space development fees, should such fees vary by the type and location of open space as well as by the amount of open space that already exists? In short, is it any easier getting prices right than it is to get quantities right?

Whether prices or direct controls is the chosen approach, the level of fees or size of the urban area will be a political decision. Is there reason to believe that local governments are more likely to impose optimal fees or optimal growth areas if both such optimal levels could be determined? There is an extensive literature that suggests local governments use land use controls to exclude low-income residents and constrain growth. But there is also growing evidence that local governments use impact fees and exactions to do the same (Altshuler and Gomez-Ibanez 1993).

## IS SPRAWL PRIMARILY A MATTER OF DENSITY?

Sprawl has many defining characteristics, including low-density development. While most economists still define sprawl in terms of density or rent gradients, Malpezzi (1999) defines and computes 10 measures of sprawl based on U.S. Census data on household and employment location. Where metropolitan areas rank on Malpezzi's sprawl indexes varies extensively, depending on the measure used. Using similar data and more complex methods, Galster et al. (2001) compute a number of additional measures of urban sprawl, including density, contiguity, and centeredness. Ewing, Pendall, and Chen (2002) compute an aggregate sprawl index based on several measures of urban form.

The limitations of density as a measure of urban form are cleverly illustrated by Duany and Plater-Zyberk (1992) in figure 4.1. The top half of the figure illustrates a typical suburban neighborhood design, while the bottom half illustrates a traditional or new urbanist neighborhood. The density of development in the two halves of the figure is the same, however. The primary difference between the two development types is the mixture of uses and the connectivity of the road network. In the typical suburban neighborhood, where uses are separated and roads are poorly connected, it is impossible to travel from one use to another without using the arterial road. This has several potentially adverse effects:

- The arterial will have more traffic
- Children in the low-density housing are less likely to play with children in the high-density housing
- Few residents, if any, will walk or bicycle to the mall
- Few children, if any, will walk or bicycle to school
- Both the school and the mall will need bigger parking lots

**Figure 4.1:** Map of Population Density, Comparing Suburban Sprawl and Traditional Neighborhoods

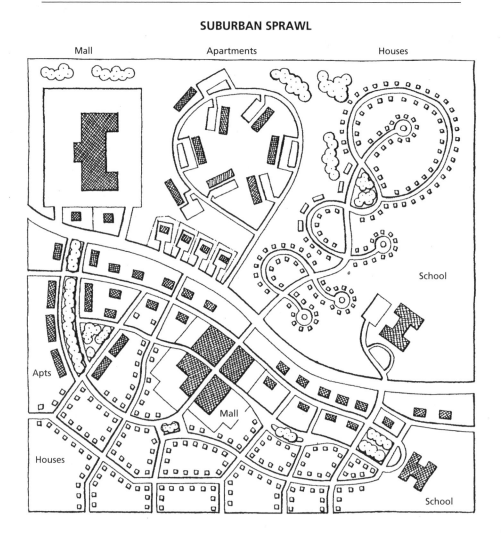

## SUBURBAN SRAWL

Mall     Apartments     Houses

## TRADITIONAL NEIGHBORHOOD

*Source:* Duany and Plater-Zyberk (1992).

- More driving, larger parking lots, and greater income separation can have adverse health, environmental, and social impacts

To be fair, neighborhood design cannot solve every urban health, environmental, and social problem. Economies of scale in education and retailing will require students and customers to travel on the arterial from other parts of the metropolitan area. The majority of residents of both neighborhoods will likely work in other parts of the metropolitan area as well. Finally, the benefit of greater internal accessibility in the traditional neighborhood comes at the cost of greater internal traffic exposure. Some of the trade-offs can be confronted in a competitive market of subdivision design, but at the larger scale, the design of cities is determined by public policy.

In a lengthy survey of literature across several disciplines, Knaap et al. (2004) demonstrate that measures of form vary widely across disciplines. In general, economists focus on spatial patterns of populations and employment over entire metropolitan areas; transportation planners tend to focus on distances between origins and destinations within metropolitan areas; planners tend to focus on spatial patterns of developments within parts of metropolitan areas; natural scientists focus on the spatial patterns of patches outside metropolitan areas; and urban designers focus on streets, facades, and building design.

These multiple measures of urban form would not be relevant to economists if they had no impact on utility or social welfare, but ample evidence suggests that they do. Visual preference surveys reveal that individuals have clear and consistent preferences regarding neighborhood design (Nelessen 1994). Conjoint analysis of those preferences reveals that individuals are able to trade certain features against others in a consistent fashion. Further, many measures of urban sprawl are capitalized into land values. Song and Knaap (2003) showed that individual measures of urban form, such as density, distance from open space, and distance from transit stations, had adverse effects on property values, while commercial accessibility, internal connectivity, and external disconnectivity have favorable effects on property values. Those findings have two important implications. First, many of the attributes that define urban form—besides density—have impacts on household utility and thus social welfare. Second, a comprehensive pricing approach to urban sprawl requires that the prices of all of those attributes must be right as well.

## PUBLIC DETERMINANTS OF URBAN FORM

Given that urban form has multiple dimensions, it is reasonable to ask what the primary determinants of urban form are. Clearly, density is a critical factor; and density is primarily a function of lot size and the price of land. But at least three major determinants of urban form are directly shaped by public policy with little or no direct influence by prices or market forces. They include the networks of highways, roads, sidewalks, bike paths, and transit service; networks of sewage treatment plants and pipes; and, increasingly, networked parks, greenways, and natural areas.

## Transportation Networks

It is difficult to dispute that transportation networks have great influence on urban form. Every urban economics text explains the structure of the city in terms of a trade-off between land prices and accessibility to jobs. It takes only a marginal extension of that logic to understand that urban form is largely shaped by transportation infrastructure. Strong empirical evidence that highways shape urban development patterns is offered, for example, by Boarnet and Haughwout (2000).

At the neighborhood scale, urban form is also strongly shaped by transportation infrastructure. According to Southworth and Owens (1993),

> Street patterns are one of the primary design elements at the community scale. They invariably constitute the first marks of settlement on the undeveloped landscape at the fringe. As the basic skeletal structure of communities, streets both divide and connect urban space. They affect environmental interaction by dictating the means of access between home and other places. They determine where residents can go and what they observe and interact with along the way, providing, in a sense, public windows to a shared world.

Examples of the powerful influence of transportation networks on urban form are offered in figures 4.2 through 4.4. Figure 4.2 illustrates the grid pattern of Philadelphia, as originally designed in the seventeenth century by William Penn. Penn desired a city with large open spaces and shaded avenues oriented to the Delaware River. As the population increased, row houses replaced single-family structures, and large blocks were divided into smaller rectangles. The basic structure of the original grid layout, however, remains to this day.

Figure 4.3 illustrates the urban form of central Amsterdam. As shown, three canals and the dammed river in the center of the city shaped the pattern of urban growth for centuries. Rings of canals surround the city center with larger basins and docks. To circulate land traffic, roads were built along dikes. People and goods were transported along both roads and dikes, and buildings were designed accordingly.

**Figure 4.2:** Grid Pattern of Philadelphia

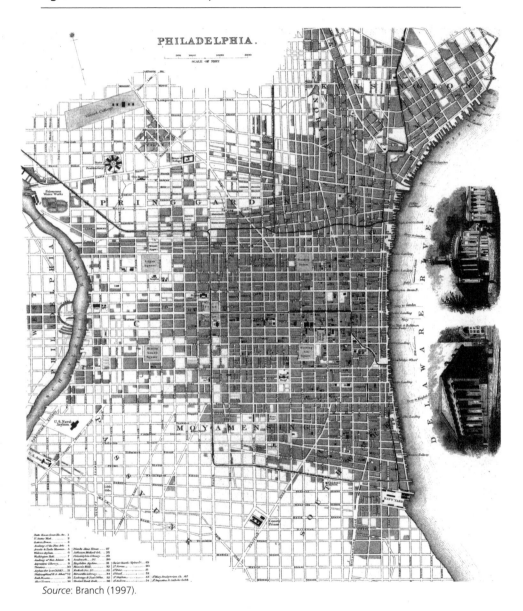

*Source*: Branch (1997).

**Figure 4.3:** Urban Form of Central Amsterdam

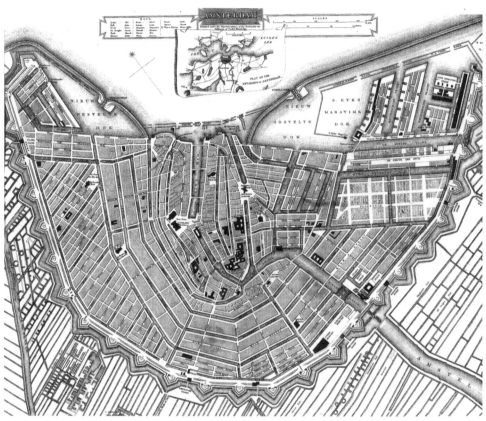

*Source*: Branch (1997).

Figure 4.4 illustrates the urban form of Calcutta. As shown, growth was intended to follow a gridiron plan, though the irregularity in size, shape, form, and placement of structures leaves little evidence of that. There are three throughways running north-south and seven running east-west, in addition to circular roads. Plagued by explosive population growth and wrought with drainage and sanitation engineering problems, the city has been prone to epidemics and cholera.

In sum, transportation infrastructure is clearly a major determinant of urban form. It shapes the character of neighborhoods and the relationship between neighborhoods. And while it might be advantageous to ration the capacity of transportation infrastructure using gas taxes, congestion fees, and tolls, it is hard to imagine that such pricing instruments could have much of an effect on street network design.

**Figure 4.4:** Urban Form of Central Calcutta

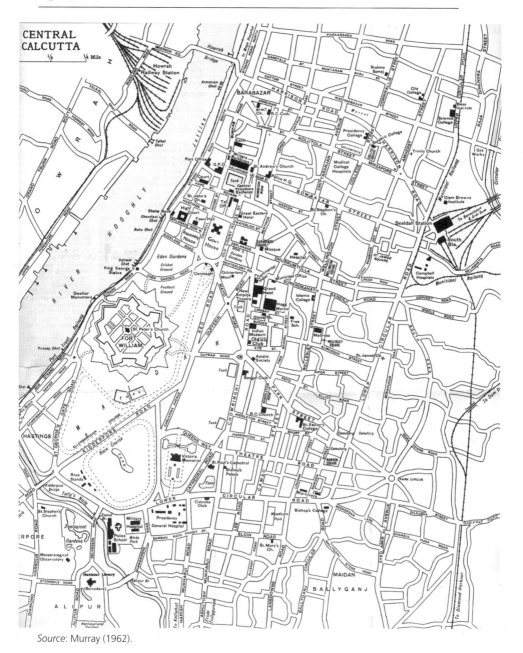

*Source*: Murray (1962).

## Sewer Service Networks

Another major determinant of urban form is wastewater service networks. According to Tabors, Shapiro, and Rogers (1976, 3),

> Because of the fragmented and uneven manner in which zoning policies have been applied, they have not been the sole or even the major factors in determining land use patterns in the United States. In many areas location of major public facilities tends to be far more significant in determining actual land use patterns than zoning. There can be no doubt that the federal highway program, in particular, has had a significant impact on where Americans live and work. More recently, it has been recognized that the provision of public sewerage is having a similar secondary impact on land use development.

Recent empirical evidence on the influence of sewer service networks on urban development patterns is offered by Hanley and Hopkins (2007). Using dynamic game theory, they demonstrate that development closely follows investments in sewer service infrastructure.

Hopkins (n.d.) offers a further illustration of the importance of sewer networks in figure 4.5, which illustrates the sewer network annotated with pipe design capacities for Urbana, Illinois. As shown, the entire network flows to a treatment plant in the east-central part of town. Treatment capacity diminishes in pipes upstream from the treatment plant. Flow capacity is also constrained at several lift stations. A brief consideration of this illustration reveals several insights. First, private development at all levels of density must be coordinated with the distribution and treatment capacity of the sewer network. Poor coordination could have terrible environmental or fiscal impacts. Second, the layout of primary sewer interceptors must have large-scale and long-term impacts on development patterns. Thus, it would be difficult to underestimate the effects of sewer system design on urban form. Finally, it is hard to imagine a system of taxes or fees that would be capable of efficiently allocating sewer service capacity over time and space without complementary land use planning and regulations.

## Public Parks and Open Spaces

Although perhaps less influential than networks of roads and sewer pipes, networks of parks and open spaces also have a powerful and perhaps increasing influence on urban form. Figure 4.6 illustrates the variation in property values on Manhattan in relation to Central Park, for example. From the figure one can clearly see how property values are higher near the park, especially on the eastern edge. Similar effects have been confirmed by a large

**Figure 4.5:** Flow and Treatment Capacity in a Sewer Network

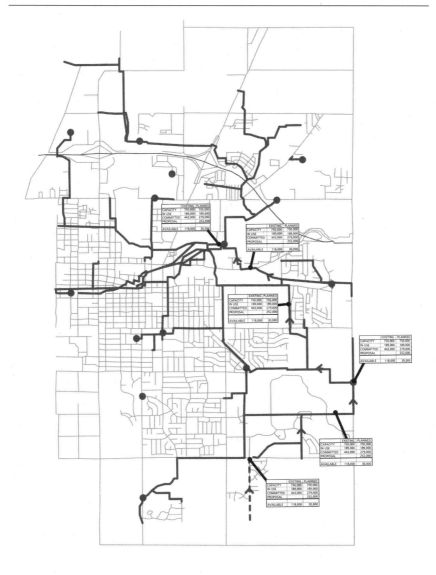

| | EXISTING | PLANNED |
|---|---|---|
| Capacity | 750,000 | 750,000 |
| In Use | 189,000 | 189,000 |
| Committed | 443,000 | |
| Projected | | 531,000 |
| | | |
| Available | 118,000 | 30,000 |
| Units in gallons per day | | |

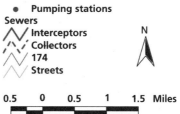

● **Pumping stations**

**Sewers**
  **Interceptors**
  **Collectors**
  **174**
  **Streets**

N

0.5   0   0.5   1   1.5 Miles

*Source*: Hopkins (n.d.).

79

**Figure 4.6:** Median Owner-Occupied Housing Value by Census Tract, New York City, 1999

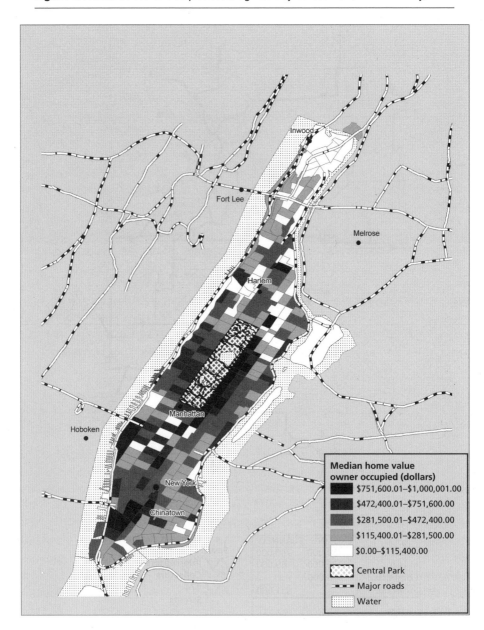

literature in economics on the subject (Crompton 2001). Figure 4.7 illustrates the variation in household income in Washington, D.C., relative to Rock Creek Park. Although it is not clear that Rock Creek Park is the cause of the social division (Brookings Institution 1999), it would be hard to deny that the park helps sustain the division. Both cases illustrate that the location of parks — by local governments — have had major and longstanding effects on urban form.

## PRICES, REGULATIONS, OR SOMETHING ELSE?

The analysis above suggests that urban form is defined by multiple attributes only some of which are determined in markets. If that is true, a pure pricing approach to urban sprawl is surely inadequate. Thus, both pricing and regulatory tools are needed. Recognizing this, Brueckner (2000) states the following:

> Because the stakes are high in the debate on sprawl, it is important to gain an understanding of the forces that might lead to excessive spatial growth of cities and to understand the nature of appropriate remedies. In working toward this understanding, the ensuing discussion does not address an issue frequently raised in criticisms of urban sprawl, namely, the proliferation of unattractive land uses such as strip malls and fast food outlets. Because this complaint concerns the character of development rather than its spatial extent, it lies outside the definition of urban sprawl used here. Although ugly development cannot be banned, a remedy for this problem lies in the use of zoning regulations and other tools of urban planning, which allow land use to be channeled toward more aesthetic outcomes. These tools can complement the policies discussed below, which are designed to limit the extent, rather than the character, of development.

But as the discussion above makes clear, the problem of urban sprawl extends beyond density, ugly strip malls, and fast-food outlets. It involves the complicated problem of coordinating private investments in residential neighborhoods, industrial parks, and commercial centers with public investments in roads, sewer lines, and parks. Brueckner recommends that local governments plan for investments in public infrastructure but use taxes and fees to guide the developments that infrastructure serves. Holcombe (2001, 150) offers more specific recommendations:

> The first step in the process would be to map out the area's major transportation corridors. In a growing area, this may mean determining where major thoroughfares will go in areas that are now primarily rural in character. The second step is to secure the right-of-way in undeveloped areas;

**Figure 4.7:** Median Household Income by Census Tract, Rock Creek Park, 2000

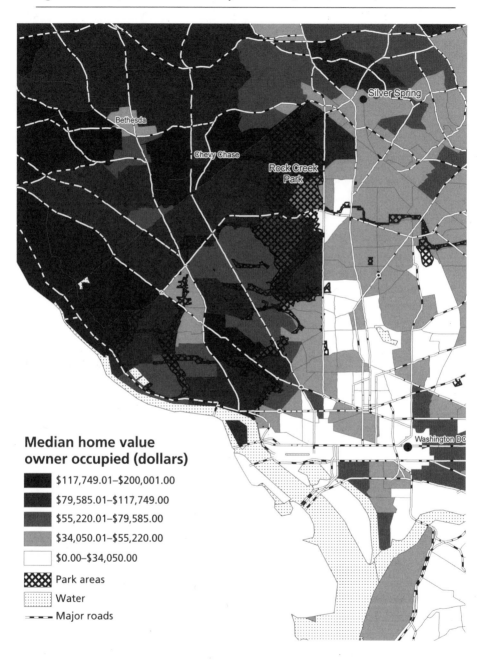

Median home value
owner occupied (dollars)

| | |
|---|---|
| ▓ | $117,749.01–$200,001.00 |
| ▓ | $79,585.01–$117,749.00 |
| ▓ | $55,220.01–$79,585.00 |
| ▓ | $34,050.01–$55,220.00 |
| ☐ | $0.00–$34,050.00 |
| ▓ | Park areas |
| ░ | Water |
| ▬▬ | Major roads |

this will be cheaper than trying to buy up land in already-developed areas.... When the right of way is secured, it must be adequate for its future purpose, and thus be wide enough to accommodate limited access divided highways, perhaps a rail line, interchanges at points where major thoroughfares will meet, and access roads so that local traffic will not be congesting major traffic thoroughfares. . . . Once the right of way is secured, the next step is to build the roads. However, while the right of way to accommodate the future traffic must be secured, roads only need to be built to accommodate the current level of traffic. . . . If transportation arteries are built in this way, and if the right of way is secured and two-lane roads are built until more capacity is needed, land use patterns will evolve efficiently without any government planning for private land use.

In Holcombe's conceptualization, urban development is a recursive process in which local governments first ascertain and build desired, if not optimal, road networks; based on those networks, private developers and landowners build neighborhoods and commercial centers. Knaap, Hopkins, and Donaghy (1998) offer a more formal version of this conceptualization, in which local governments signal their investment intentions in transportation plans. In that way, the market captures the expected impact of road investments, and development decisions are adjusted accordingly. Knaap, Ding, and Hopkins (2001a) offer empirical evidence that signals provided in transportation plans are indeed capitalized into land values and development decisions.

Even if plans for transportation investments are credible and clear, there will be variation in response to any government plan. And stochasticity in the timing and density of development is disadvantageous to maximizing efficiency in the utilization of public infrastructure. Road networks, sewer pipes, and to some extent even public parks are designed to meet specific traffic, wastewater, and population standards. And, from an infrastructure perspective, it is most efficient to have traffic, wastewater loadings, and urban populations rapidly reach and closely match design capacity.

Thus, any gains in private flexibility and freedom realized via a pricing approach might be lost in the variable and hence inefficient utilization of public facilities. Further, as Holcombe's illustration makes clear, investment decisions in public infrastructure and private buildings and improvements are interdependent, not dependent. That is, optimal investments in transportation—and other forms of public infrastructure—are dependent on the extent of private investments, just as the other way around. When development decisions are interdependent, optimality can be achieved via a variety of institutional approaches, but signaling through prices and plans is not likely to be most effective (Hopkins 2001).

**Figure 4.8:** Typical Development in the United States

*Source*: www.urban-advantage.com.

In a widely distributed PowerPoint presentation produced by Smart Growth America (n.d.), the case for smart growth is made using a sequence of three illustrations. Figure 4.8 is presented as a "typical" development in the United States while figures 4.9 and 4.10 are presented as successively "smarter" forms of development. While perhaps not everyone would prefer to live in the development shown in figure 4.9, a large number of citizens probably would—and would pay a price premium to do so. Suppose then, for the sake of illustration, that a sufficiently large segment of the population would prefer to live in the figure 4.10 development. Could that type of development occur if the local government simply built the road, charged a congestion toll, assessed an impact fee, and imposed a development tax? It seems highly unlikely. If not, then a potentially large segment of the population is disserved by the standard economic prescription.

Because the illustration is hypothetical, the institutional arrangements that could create the development in the third frame are unknown. But in most parts of the United States, it would probably require extensive interaction between residential developers, commercial developers, the state highway administration, the municipal government, the regional transit district, the Federal Transit Administration, and perhaps hundreds of condominium owners. It is possible that the development in the third frame could occur through a series of arm's-length market transactions following the construction of the highway and transit line. But more likely, the development would

**Figure 4.9:** Smarter Forms of Development I

*Source*: www.urban-advantage.com.

**Figure 4.10:** Smarter Forms of Development II

*Source*: www.urban-advantage.com.

require extensive planning, communication, negotiation, and public-private partnerships between the city and the developers. Also likely are intergovernmental agreements between the state, the municipality, and the regional transit agency and many negotiated leases between landowners, building owners, and occupants. In short, producing richly complex and smart growth developments is likely to require a similarly rich and smart set of tools and institutional arrangements.

## CONCLUSIONS

The superiority of prices over regulations as an instrument for addressing the problem of urban sprawl has both intuitive and political appeal. But the proposition has yet to be proven either in theory or in practice. As stated by Bohm and Russell (1985), in a detailed analysis of effluent fees as an instrument of pollution control,

> The message [of this assessment of effluent fees] may be seen as positive or negative depending on the perspective of the reader. The negative version is that no general statements can be made about the relative desirability of alternative policy instruments once we consider such practical complications as that location matters, that monitoring is costly, and that exogenous change occurs in technology, regional economies, and natural environmental systems. The positive way of stating this is to stress that all the alternatives are promising in some situation. . . . If the classic case for the absolute superiority of effluent fees is flawed by the simplicity of the necessary assumptions, the arguments for the superiority of rigid forms of regulation suffer equally from unstated assumptions and static views of the world. There is no substitute for careful analysis of the available alternatives in the specific policy context at issue.

In the case of prices as instruments to address urban sprawl, such careful analysis has yet to be conducted. And though economists have greatly enhanced our understanding of urban spatial structure, their advice on smart growth has sprawled beyond the extent of compelling theoretical or empirical support.

## REFERENCES

Altshuler, A., and J. A. Gomez-Ibanez, with A. M. Howitt. 1993. *Regulation for revenue: The political economy of land use regulation.* Washington, DC: Brookings Institution.

Boarnet, M. G., and A. F. Haughwout. 2000. *Do highways matter? Evidence and policy implications of highways' influence on metropolitan development*. Washington, DC: Brookings Institution Center on Urban and Metropolitan Policy.

Bohm, P., and C. S. Russell. 1985. Comparative analysis of alternative policy instruments. In *Handbook of natural resource and energy economics*. A. V. Knees and J. L. Sweeney, eds. Amsterdam: North-Holland.

Branch, M. C. 1997. *An atlas of rare city maps: Comparative urban design, 1830–1842*. New York: Princeton Architectural Press.

Brookings Institution. 1999. A region divided: The state of growth in Greater Washington, DC. Washington, DC: Brookings Institution.

Brueckner, J. 2000. Urban sprawl: Diagnosis and remedies. *International Regional Science Review* 23(2):160–171.

Crompton, J. L. 2001. The impact of parks on property values: A review of the empirical evidence. *Journal of Leisure Research* 33(1):1–31.

Duany, A., and E. Plater-Zyberk. 1992. The second coming of the American small town. *Wilson Quarterly* (Winter):19–50.

Ewing, R., R. Pendall, and D. Chen. 2002. *Measuring sprawl and its impact*. Washington, DC: Smart Growth America.

Galster, G., R. Hanson, M. R. Ratcliffe, H. Wolman, S. Coleman, and J. Freihage. 2001. Wrestling sprawl to the ground: Defining and measuring an elusive concept. *Housing Policy Debate* 12:681–717.

Hanley, P. F., and L. D. Hopkins. 2007. Do sewer extension plans affect urban development? A multiagent simulation. *Environment and Planning B: Planning and Design* 34(1):6–27.

Holcombe, R. 2001. Growth management in action: The case of Florida. In *Smarter growth: Market-based strategies for land use planning in the 21st century*. S. R. Staley and R. G. Holcombe, eds. Westport, CT: Greenwood Press.

Hopkins, L. n.d. Using and making systems of plans. PowerPoint presentation, University of Illinois at Urbana–Champaign.

Hopkins, L. D. 2001. *Urban development: The logic of making plans*. Washington, DC: Island Press.

Knaap, G. J., C. Ding, and L. Hopkins. 2001a. Do plans matter? The effects of light rail plans on land values in station areas. *Journal of Planning, Education and Research* 21(1):32–39.

———. 2001b. Managing urban growth for the efficient use of public infrastructure: Towards a theory of concurrency. *International Regional Science Review* 24(3):328–343.

Knaap, G. J., L. Hopkins, and K. Donaghy. 1998. Do plans matter? A game-theoretic model for examining the logic and effects of land use planning. *Journal of Planning Education and Research* 18(1):25–34.

Knaap, G. J., Y. Song, R. Ewing, and K. Clifton. 2004. Seeing the elephant: Multidisciplinary measures of urban sprawl. http://www.smartgrowth.umd.edu/research/pdf/KnaapSongEwingEtAl_Elephant_022305.pdf.

Malpezzi, S. 1999. *Estimates of the measurement and determinants of urban sprawl in U.S. metropolitan areas*. Madison, WI: Center for Urban Land Economics Research.

McDonald, J. F. 1989. Econometric studies of urban population density: A survey. *Journal of Urban Economics* 26:361–385.

Mills, E. S. 1999. Truly smart "smart growth." *Illinois Real Estate Newsletter* 13(3):1–7.

Murray, J. 1962. *A handbook for travellers in India, Pakistan, Burma, and Ceylon.* London: John Murray.

Nelessen, A. C. 1994. *Visions for a new American dream.* Chicago: American Planning Association.

Smart Growth America. n.d. Smart growth: Better choices for our communities. CD-ROM. https://secure2.convio.net/sgusa/site/Ecommerce?ecommerce=store_list&ts=1126038417679&store_id=1161&JServSessionIdr012=uf93p8yy51.app5a.

Song, Y., and G-J. Knaap. 2003. New urbanism and housing values: A disaggregate assessment. *Journal of Urban Economics* 54:218–238.

Southworth, M., and P. M. Owens. 1993. The evolving metropolis. *Journal of the American Planning Association* 59(3):271–288.

Tabors, R. D., M. H. Shapiro, and P. P. Rogers. 1976. *Land use and the pipe.* Lanham, MD: Lexington Books.

Thompson, W. 1968. The city as a distorted price system. *Psychology Today* (August).

# 5

# Urban Regeneration and Sustainable Environment: A Nature Conservation–Based Approach for the Green Island of Taiwan

## John Chien-Yuan Lin

More and more cities claim to be aiming at sustainable development, although politicians and scholars often have different interpretations. The World Commission on Environment and Development (WCED; 1987), also known as the Brundtland Commission, defined sustainable development as "development that meets the needs of the present without compromising the ability of future generations to meet their own needs." Whereas that widely cited definition is couched in terms of intergeneration equity, today the context of sustainable development has been expanded and is interpreted in terms of ecology, economy, and sociology. Among various applications of the concept, the eco-city represents the ideal model of future sustainable urban development.

Based on the design principles of the eco-city summarized by Register (2002), urban regeneration is an effective instrument for the development of sustainable environments. Urban regeneration contributes to sustainable development through the recycling of derelict land and buildings, reducing demand for peripheral development and facilitating the development of more compact cities (Couch and Dennemann 2000). In other words, a successful urban regeneration project will not only solve problems of economic decline in the inner city, contributing to economic development and social equity, it can also reduce the pressure of urban sprawl in suburban greenfields.

In addition to the conservation of open green space, urban regeneration can make a contribution to the global environment. Environmental concerns at the global scale include the efficient use of resources, biodiversity, air quality, depletion of the ozone layer, and global warming. Urban areas play a key role in tackling those global issues. Based on the idea of the compact city, urban regeneration could reduce the need for commuting (e.g., by combining higher urban densities and mixed-use developments in city centers).

Urban areas decline for different reasons. Some small cities with a single industrial base decline because of resource depletion or a weakening market (e.g., in the mining or logging industries). Some old central business districts (CBDs) are unable to compete with suburban shopping malls because of inadequate parking facilities and transportation service. In some communities a decline in infrastructure and public service downgrades environmental quality, and only low-income residents will stay because they are unable to move to a better place. Today, more and more urban and rural areas decline because of economic globalization. As Peter Hall (1991) argues, traditional location theory no longer accounts for the location of high-tech and producer services. Places are now competing in a global context, and more and more local areas decline because of the new international labor division. This is particularly true for many cities in Taiwan, because of the impact from China and other less developed countries in Asia. To deal with decline that results from industrial restructuring, traditional property-based urban redevelopment is not effective enough. In addition to improving the physical environment, urban regeneration is critically needed to establish social and economic incentives.

To address the interconnected problems in many urban areas, a strategic framework for urban regeneration needs to be developed at the city level. Successful urban regeneration requires a strategically designed, locally based, multisector, multiagency, partnership approach (Cater 2000). The emerging trend of urban regeneration can be seen as a response and challenge to the rapid and fundamental social, economic, and institutional changes that society has witnessed over the past few decades.

To appropriately and effectively solve the problems of different areas, different approaches of urban regeneration will be needed. Essentially, urban regeneration can be promoted in either a redevelopment-based approach or a conservation-based approach. This chapter argues that a nature conservation–based approach of urban regeneration is most important for those areas where local economic development relies heavily on the quality and preservation of the natural environment. An urban regeneration strategy based on the nature conservation–based approach is here formulated for a case study of Green Island in Taiwan.

## CONTEXT AND EVOLUTION OF URBAN REGENERATION

Although urban regeneration has been widely discussed, no definition has been universally accepted. Shutt (2000) concluded that it is difficult to generalize about urban regeneration. The United States and the United Kingdom have a long experience of transatlantic policy exchange and political parties, and academics and policy makers have regularly discussed policies for reviving urban economics with similar policy initiatives on both sides of the Atlantic, but the same terms operate in different contexts in the two countries. Shutt further concluded that in the United States there is little evidence of a strong, coherent, and integrated federal, state, and local government approach to urban regeneration, one that tackles the underlying structural issues that are forcing American cities into decline. Most literature about urban regeneration is related to European experiences.

Roberts (2000, 17) has defined urban regeneration as "comprehensive and integrated vision and action which leads to the resolution of urban problems and which seeks to bring about a lasting improvement in the economic, physical, social and environmental condition of an area that has been subject to change." Compared to traditional concepts of urban redevelopment, urban renewal, and urban revival, the concept of *urban regeneration* deals with urban problems in a more comprehensive and strategic way. Roberts traces the major changes that have occurred in the approach and content of urban policy and practice from the 1950s to the present day and summarizes the key features in different stages of the evolution of urban regeneration. Parts of the summary are revised and listed in table 5.1.

Urban development is a complicated and dynamic process. The current status of a city is the result of interplay among different driving forces. Without government intervention, cities are shaped through the market mechanism within the physical constraints of the natural environment. As a government action, the purpose of urban regeneration is to harness and direct those driving forces toward a so-called sustainable environment. Other than the basic forces of the market mechanism and government intervention, three main factors have been identified by the Urban Task Force (2002) that are central to the process of urban change:

- The technical revolution—centered on information technology and the establishment of new networks connecting people from the local to the global level
- The ecological threat—greater understanding of the global implications of humankind's consumption of natural resources and the importance of sustainable development
- The social transformation—changing life patterns to reflect increasing life expectancy and the development of new lifestyle choices

These forces are changing the way that cities are developed and shaped.

**TABLE 5.1**    The Evolution of Urban Regeneration

| Period<br><br>Policy type | 1950s<br><br>Reconstruction | 1960s<br><br>Revitalization | 1970s<br><br>Renewal | 1980s<br><br>Redevelopment | 1990s<br><br>Regeneration |
|---|---|---|---|---|---|
| Major strategy and orientation | Reconstruction and extension of older areas of cities, often based on a "master plan" | Continuation of 1950s theme; suburban and peripheral growth; some early attempts at rehabilitation | Focus on in-situ renewal and neighborhood schemes; still development at periphery | Many major schemes of development and redevelopment; flagship projects, out-of-town projects | More comprehensive form of policy and practice; more emphasis on integrated treatments |
| Economic focus | Public sector investment with some private involvement | Continuing from 1950s with growing influence of private investment | Constraints in public sector and growth of private investment | Private sector dominant with selective public funds | Greater balance between public, private, and voluntary funds |
| Social content | Improvement of housing and living standards | Social and welfare improvement | Community-based action and greater empowerment | Community self-help with selective state support | Emphasis on the role of community |
| Physical emphasis | Replacement of inner areas and peripherals | Some continuation from 1950s with parallel rehabilitation of existing areas | More extensive renewal of older urban areas | Major schemes of replacement and new development | More modest than 1980s; heritage and retention |
| Environmental approach | Landscaping and some greening | Selective improvements | Environmental improvement with some innovations | Growth of concern for wider approach to environment | Introduction of broader idea of environmental sustainability |

Source: Adapted from Roberts (2000), p. 14. Reproduced by permission of Sage Publications, London, Los Angeles, New Delhi and Singapore, from Roberts & Sykes, *Urban Regeneration: A Handbook,* © Peter Roberts, 2000.

Based on the operation of the market mechanism and government management, urban regeneration combines these three drivers to push the course of urban development toward sustainable environment. It should be noted that urban regeneration is also different from traditional redevelopment in terms of public involvement. Urban regeneration aims to change the decision-making process from the top-down model of governance to a less confrontational, more open and flexible democratic framework, based upon public participation and public involvement.

## THE REDEVELOPMENT-BASED APPROACH

Essentially, urban regeneration can be roughly divided into two approaches, the redevelopment-based approach and the conservation-based approach. The redevelopment-based approach tends to clean up existing buildings and replace them with new construction to stimulate further investments. That approach is based on traditional urban renewal or urban redevelopment, except that more incentives for economic revival are incorporated. Most reported case studies of urban regeneration in big cities are based on the redevelopment-based approach.

Redevelopment in old inner-city areas is less attractive to private developers than new development in suburban areas for many reasons:

- *Difficulty of assembling land.* When developing agricultural land into urban land uses, the number of landowners is usually small and it is much less difficult to assemble land ownerships than redevelopment of old communities in inner-city areas, where the transactions for acquiring land can be a long process with many uncertainties and difficulties.
- *Disadvantage in highway transportation.* Suburban communities usually enjoy better accessibility to freeway service and parking convenience, whereas most inner-city communities suffer from traffic congestion and parking difficulty.
- *Poor condition of infrastructure.* The quality of the infrastructure in inner cities is poor not simply because of age, but also because technological progress makes the old facilities less useful to meet new demands.
- *High cost of reconstruction.* Reconstruction is more expensive than new development. Demolition and disposal of existing buildings add cost to a reconstruction project. Redevelopment projects on brownfields, where contaminated land has to be cleaned up for reuse, are especially expensive.
- *Additional costs and factory relocation.* Additional costs and uncertainties will also discourage developers from those areas where they have to deal with the relocation of factories in operation or houses for low-income residents because they are unable to move without assistance.
- *Uncertainty of market response.* It is always safer to invest in a growing market than a declining market. That is also true of investing in estate development. Given the trend of suburbanization, the market response in an old inner city will be much less certain than in a new suburban development.

Because of the above factors, without government intervention, urban redevelopment by the private sector will be impossible in most cases, which is an example of a market failure in the urban development process. Development projects with high social benefits are not carried out because of low market values. Many policy instruments and incentive programs have been proposed and experienced in different countries for development of a sustainable urban environment. The most frequently offered incentives to stimulate urban redevelopment include the bonus of more floor area for building permission, land use rezoning for higher intensity and market value, and transferable development rights.

Over the past three decades, economic regeneration has responded to and been influenced by a wide range of economic, political, and social factors. Policy initiatives developed out of a strong economic rationale that, in the 1960s and 1970s, urban areas were facing the prospect of continuous decline in the absence of major injections of public funds. Many initiatives were designed to overcome the inner-city disadvantages of accessibility, environmental quality, and relative cost of land development compared with greenfield sites.

In the redevelopment-based approach, major financial support is usually required to support construction. The property requirements of the types of firms to be attracted must be understood to avoid the risks of the property market, given its increasing differentiation and segmentation. For urban regeneration strategies, it is important to first conduct a feasibility study. To make strategic assessments of land and building supply-and-demand characteristics, the following factors have to be identified: the quality of existing stock; the sources of future demand by the industrial sector; and trends in terms of location and type of premises.

Redevelopment in the business district should be distinguished from redevelopment projects of public housing. Redevelopment of the physical environment does not ensure the success of economic regeneration. Investors do not choose a place to operate a business simply because the buildings are newly constructed. They invest in a particular area because it offers the potential for making a profit on their investment. In order to successfully promote a redevelopment-based regeneration project, incentives should be offered to both land developers and industrial investors.

Taking the United Kingdom as an example, the following are well-known incentive programs for urban regeneration (Noon, Smith-Canham, and Eagland 2000):

- *Grant support.* Land grant supports are essentially used to lower the entry threshold for the private sector in order to induce significant investment. Derelict Land Grants (DLGs) were initiated in the 1960s; Urban Development Grants (UDGs) were established in 1982; and Urban Regeneration Grants (URGs) were launched in 1987. Both UDGs and URGs were replaced by City Grants in 1988.

- *Relaxation of regulations.* Enterprise zones were established in 1981 based on the principle of removing the "burden on business" through relaxing planning controls and providing tax benefits. The benefits currently available to businesses situated in those zones include tax exemption from nondomestic rates; 100 percent allowances for corporation and income tax purposes for capital expenditure on industrial and commercial buildings; a simplified planning system to reduce time, cost, and uncertainty in the application of development permission; and a reduction in government requests for statistical information. With simplified zoning, building permission can be directly applied without development permission.

- *Urban development agencies.* The Local Government, Planning and Land Act of 1980 gave the government the power to create Urban Development Corporations (UDCs). London Docklands redevelopment was the typical project conducted by the London Docklands Development Corporation. English Partnerships was set up in 1993 to replace UDC.

- *Coordination units.* In response to the need for a more holistic approach to be applied across a local area and in recognition of the importance of local community input, City Action teams were created to help the integration and coordination of urban policies and initiatives in 1981. Task forces were launched in 1986 to better coordinate the efforts of government departments, local governments, the private sector, and the local community to regenerate inner-city areas.

- *Funding by competitive bidding.* The City Challenge program was launched in 1991, allowing urban regeneration funding to be allocated through a process of competitive bidding based on clear objectives, output measures, and value for money. The new policy gave the local authorities a key role by letting them draw up plans for the regeneration of areas that they felt were pivotal for the region's resurgence.

A successful urban regeneration needs not only improvement of the physical environment, but also empowerment of the people via public involvement and job training. The implementation of urban regeneration would unavoidably cause redistribution of benefits among different interest groups; therefore, it is important that the vision of urban regeneration be built through a process of public involvement. Meanwhile, since job opportunities newly introduced into the regeneration area often need different work skills and management know-how, training and education are required to help local laborers prepare themselves.

Among various types of redevelopment-based urban regeneration, the most complicated one is the redevelopment of contaminated urban land left by manufacturing plants. According to Schoenbaum (2002), the U.S. Environmental Protection Agency has defined brownfields as "abandoned, idled, or under-used industrial and commercial facilities where expansion or redevelopment is complicated by real or perceived environmental contamination." To encourage redevelopment of brownfields, many states in the United States had passed so-called brownfields legislation, which limits the financial liability of innocent redevelopers of contaminated property (Schoenbaum 2002). Given the complex technological and legal aspects of brownfields redevelopment, a team of experts across different disciplines is needed to help with the cleanup, recycling, and reuse of such contaminated urban sites. The cost, time, and technology needed are often beyond the capability of private firms, and thus special teams and extra government assistance are usually needed (Walker and Owen 2001).

## THE CONSERVATION-BASED APPROACH

In contrast to the redevelopment-based regeneration approach, the conservation-based approach emphasizes the reuse of existing buildings and environmental settings to conserve cultural, historic, and natural elements. This approach can be further divided into two types, culture conservation–based and nature conservation–based approaches. While the culture conservation–based approach makes use of existing old buildings and environmental settings, the nature conservation–based approach emphasizes conservation of the natural environment for sustainable development.

### Culture Conservation

Old buildings are often imbued with traditional culture and historic memory and, with the rapid development of the culture and tourism industries, can be important cultural capital for local development. Historic places and landscapes tell the story of collective memories and help people shape their perceptions of the past. Preservation of a historic heritage can play an important role in cultural industry (Hagen 2006). Furthermore, with advanced technology and adaptive rehabilitation, historic buildings can be reused in an innovative, modern way for many purposes. Such structures can be a symbolic asset in attracting production units, such as design houses and offices, or a place for tourists to visit and shop. In other words, an urban regeneration project rooted in the historic or symbolic character of the buildings can create "scarcity" or "locational" synergy for the redeveloped area.

**Figure 5.1:** Relationship Between Tourism and the Natural Environment

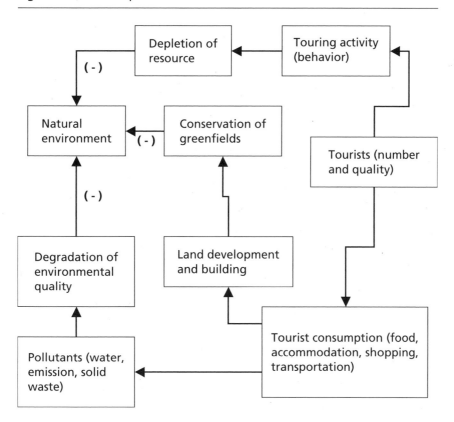

## Nature Conservation

If a city attracts tourists because of its beautiful natural environment, unless that environment is strictly protected and the tourists are well managed, neither will be sustainable. To explain the importance and necessity of the nature conservation–based approach for urban regeneration in such an area, a framework of the relationship between quality of the natural environment and tourism has been established.

Figure 5.1 shows that tourists affect environmental quality directly and indirectly, in three ways:

1. Through tour experiences and activities, the number and behavior (quality) of tourists directly affect the environment negatively.
2. Tourists need local commercial services such as dining, lodging, trans-

portation, and shopping. To meet those demands, new hotels, restaurants, and shops are built, creating additional pressures on greenfield land.

3. Tourists also produce pollutants (wasted water, vehicle emissions, solid waste, etc.) and thus directly affect environmental quality if pollutants are not well processed and disposed of.

To maintain the beauty and well-being of the environment and ensure the sustainability of such a tourist city, the urban regeneration approach has to be based on conservation of the natural environment.

The conservation-based approach is much more complicated and difficult to carry out than the redevelopment-based approach; in addition to the skills and tools needed for redevelopment, knowledge and management skills related to culture and nature conservation are needed. The nature conservation–based approach is especially difficult because the size of the tourism market has to be limited to protect the conserved nature resource according to its carrying capacity. In other words, that approach will limit potential market income, on one hand, and require higher costs for the conservation of natural resources, on the other hand. Because of such difficulties, more cautions in environmental planning and management and government assistance are particularly needed for nature conservation–based regeneration projects.

## NATURE CONSERVATION–BASED STRATEGY FOR GREEN ISLAND

Green Island is a small volcanic island located off the southeastern coast of Taiwan (see figure 5.2). It covers only 16.2 square kilometers and had a population of about 3,200 people in 2005. The island is famous for housing many political prisoners between the 1950s and the 1970s; the current vice president of Taiwan, Hsiu-lien Lu, was jailed there in the 1970s. The jail has been preserved as a historic building for tourists. The various ecological resources of Green Island are well preserved due to its unique historical development. About 200 years ago, Han (Chinese) people began arriving. The basic economy of the island has traditionally been fishing and raising deer, but recently it has changed to tourism. On such a small island, there is no opportunity for the development of manufacturing, and as the agriculture industry becomes less competitive, the tourism industry seems to offer the only opportunity for local economic development on Green Island.

The tourism industry on Green Island has developed rapidly and has become the most important part of the local economy. The number of

**Figure 5.2:** Map of Green Island

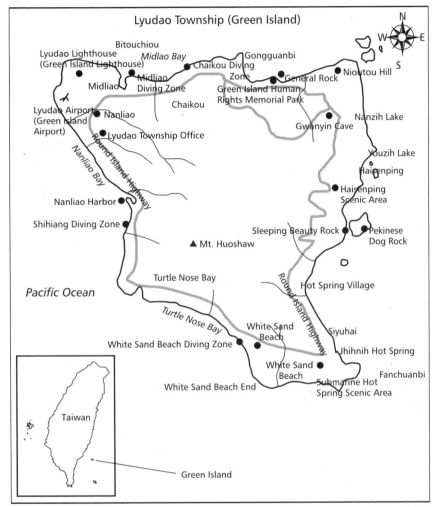

*Source*: Modified from Tourism Bureau, Ministry of Transportation & Communications, Republic of China (Taiwan).

tourists increased sharply in the last decade, from about 60,000 people per year in 1991 to about 400,000 people in 2004. In 2005, there were about 380,000 tourists, a slight decrease from the previous year. Summer is the peak season on Green Island. The number of tourists in July has averaged about 70,000 over the last five years, roughly 22 times the size of the local population. Tourism development has provided new employment and incomes and additional tax receipts to local communities, enhancing the community infrastructure. However, mass tourism also puts enormous pressure on both the coastal ecology and the local society.

Ocean and coastal tourism is one of the fastest-growing areas of contemporary tourism, but mass tourism endangers the sustainability of coastal environments. Tourism activities have already widely affected the ecological systems of Green Island. Large numbers of tourists come to the island without adequate information or effective management of their recreation activities. Up to 2,500 tourists per day visit Green Island in the summer season, and 90 percent of them go to the beach for swimming, surfing, diving, and even fishing. In the evening most tourists gather in the only main street on the island. Tourists' recreational activities have damaged the marine resources in the coastal areas; their consumption activities (lodging, dining, drinking, shopping, etc.) have produced tremendous pollutants and land development pressure on the greenfields. There is no sewer treatment system, for example, so wastewater flows directly to the sea.

A recent survey of coastal species (Chen, Lin, and Wang 2004) confirmed that the populations of crabs and other species on Green Island are declining at an unprecedented rate. The marine landscape is not as attractive as before. In other words, the environmental impact of tourism has exceeded the carrying capacity of the natural environment; the quality of the tourism experience is thus degraded along with the beauty of the natural environment. Under the pressure of mass tourism, neither the tourism industry nor the natural environment can be sustained. The decrease of tourists by about 20,000 in 2005 may be considered a warning signal to the tourism industry on Green Island.

To save Green Island from the decline caused by mass tourism, conservation of natural resources, especially the coral reef ecosystems and the coastal zone, is critically needed. Only through regeneration by means of the conservation-based approach can the tourism industry be directed toward sustainable development. To distinguish it from traditional mass tourism, the terms *sustainable tourism* and *ecotourism* are used to describe nature conservation–based tourism.

In 1991, the Ecotourism Society defined *ecotourism* as "responsible travel to natural areas that conserves the environment and improves the well-being of local people" (Honey 1999, 6). *Sustainable tourism* can be defined as tourism that makes a notable contribution to or at least does not conflict with maintaining the principles of tourism development indefinitely without compromising the ability of future generations to satisfy their own needs and desires (Tosun 2001).

The underlying concept of sustainable tourism is tourism with ecological and social responsibility. Its aim is to meet the needs of tourists and host regions while protecting and enhancing the environmental, social, and economic values of those regions for the future. Sustainable tourism is envisaged as leading to the management of all resources in such a way that it can fulfill economic, social, and aesthetic needs while maintaining cultural integrity, essential ecological processes, biological diversity, and life support systems.

Ecotourism is an important alternative to mass tourism due to its small-scale construction and the minimization of environmental impacts that follow from it. This suggests that tourism can be regulated and controlled at a sustainable level. Sustainable tourism produces economic advantages in addition to maintaining environmental diversity and quality, thus combining conservation with economic development (Wearing and Neil 1999).

To sustain the tourism industry on Green Island, a nature conservation–based regeneration strategy to support ecotourism is critically needed. The actions are proposed as follows:

1. Establish a consensus on the vision of ecotourism on Green Island through public education and participation. This will encounter difficulties because of different stakeholder interests. Active governance will be needed to facilitate the political process.
2. Identify the cultural and natural resources that need to be preserved and conserved. The coral reef ecosystems and coast areas around Green Island should be the top priority.
3. Prepare a land use plan that clearly indicates conservation areas and development areas. Growth management schemes should be implemented to protect natural and cultural resources in the conservation areas and to control buildings in the development areas.
4. Identify the carrying capacity of each zone and the whole island so that the appropriate total number of visitors can be planned for and targeted for related development.
5. Educate tourists about how to conduct themselves during their stay on Green Island, especially during recreation activities in protected marine areas, to minimize their negative impacts on the natural environment.
6. Educate and train residents in the concepts and skills needed for the management and development of ecotourism.
7. Redevelop the area of the main street, improving the infrastructure and landscapes to provide a better-quality sustainable environment for tourists.
8. Take advantage of the high percentage of public land on Green Island. The sale of public land in conservation areas should be stopped, and public land in the street area should be used as an incentive to encourage redevelopment in that area.

## CONCLUSIONS

Sustainable urban development has gained more and more attention from land policy makers and environmental planners. Articles in *Land Lines* about urban regeneration projects by Randy Gragg (2006) and nature conservation issues by James Levitt (2006) have indicated the increasing importance of urban regeneration in the development of sustainable environments.

Some cities decline due to deterioration of the physical environment, while others lose economic competitiveness because of the depletion of natural resources or changes of external environments. Given the nature of urban development dynamics, cities need different approaches of urban regeneration at different stages of their development. In other words, urban regeneration is a continuous process, and it needs to be shaped in a dynamic way.

So far, most urban regeneration projects have been conducted through the so-called redevelopment-based approach. Through the provision of various incentives, redevelopments with reconstruction of housing and commercial properties are promoted to attract inward investment and immigration. Recently, the importance of the conservation-based approach has begun to be recognized in many areas, particularly in tourism-based cities. Through the culture conservation–based approach, historic buildings and districts of local cultures are being conserved and reused in new economic activities.

In this chapter, a nature conservation–based regeneration approach is proposed for the sustainable development of Green Island, where natural marine resources and landscapes are the key attractions of the local tourism industry.

Green Island may be too small to qualify as a city, although its main street serves as the commercial center. However, it is significant enough to reflect the critical need for urban regeneration to deal with economic restructuring in the age of changing global environments, and it is also simple enough to demonstrate the relationship of nature conservation and economic development in the context of sustainability. The nature conservation–based approach proposed for Green Island could be applied to other cities with similar situations in Taiwan and other places in the world.

As mentioned previously, redevelopment in an inner-city area is much less attractive to developers than new development in a suburban area, unless financial incentives are provided. Compared to the redevelopment-based approach, the conservation-based approach is more difficult because it affords lower market profits. Development of a more sustainable environment requires both effective governance and more knowledge to deal with urban regeneration. In the real world, cities with different problems and conditions need a balanced approach with different combinations of conservation and redevelopment. How to appropriately formulate an integrated urban regeneration approach for different cities is a critical challenge for policy makers and planners as we prepare for the future.

The case of Green Island has demonstrated that among the required efforts to promote conservation-based urban regeneration, an important task is to educate residents to understand and support the necessity of conservation in certain areas, and to train local people in the skills needed for the new labor market. Local people often fear that giving up the short-term revenues may not ensure long-term benefits. In addition, environmental education is critically needed to help politicians, policy makers, scholars, and professional planners be more capable in the promotion of urban regeneration.

## REFERENCES

Cater, A. 2000. Strategy and partnership in urban regeneration. In *Urban regeneration: A handbook*. P. Roberts and H. Sykes, eds., 37–58. London: Sage Publications.

Chen, C-P., S-T. Lin, and F-L. Wang. 2004. Coconut crabs as a target for promoting the establishment of marine protected areas on Green Island, Taiwan. In *Islands of the World VIII International Conference*, Taiwan, November 1–7.

Couch, C., and A. Dennemann. 2000. Urban regeneration and sustainable development in Britain. *Cities* 17(2):137–147.

Gragg, R. 2006. London's large-scale regeneration projects offer community benefits. *Land Lines* (October):2–7.

Hagen, J. 2006. *Preservation, tourism and nationalism*. Aldershot, U.K.: Ashgate.

Hall, P. 1991. The restructuring of urban economies integrating urban and sectoral policies. In *Urban regeneration in a changing economy*. J. Fox-Przeworski, J. Goddard, and M. Jong, eds. Oxford: Clarendon Press.

Honey, M. 1999. *Ecotourism and sustainable development*. Washington, DC: Island Press.

Levitt, J. N. 2006. Conservation incentives in America's heartland. *Land Lines* (October):8–11.

Noon, D., J. Smith-Canham, and M. Eagland. 2000. Economic regeneration and funding. In *Urban regeneration: A handbook*. P. Roberts and H. Sykes, eds., 61–85. London: Sage Publications.

Register, R. 2002. *Ecocities*. Berkeley, CA: Berkeley Hills Books.

Roberts, P. 2000. The evolution, definition and purpose of urban regeneration. In *Urban regeneration: A handbook*. P. Roberts and H. Sykes, eds., 9–36. London: Sage Publications.

Schoenbaum, M. 2002. Environmental contamination, brownfield policy, and economic redevelopment in an industrial area of Baltimore, Maryland. *Land Economics* 78(February):60–71.

Shutt, J. 2000. Lessons from America in the 1990s. In *Urban regeneration: A handbook*. P. Roberts and H. Sykes, eds., 257–280. London: Sage Publications.

Tosun, C. 2001. Challenges of sustainable tourism development in the development world: The case of Turkey. *Tourism Management* 22:289–303.

Urban Task Force. 2002. *Towards an urban renaissance*. London: HMSO.

Walker, L., and R. Owen. 2001. Regeneration: Vision, courage, and patience. In *Manufactured sites: Re-thinking the post-industrial landscape*. N. Kirkwood, ed., 82–101. London: Spon Press.

Wearing, S., and J. Neil. 1999. *Ecotourism: Impacts, potentials and possibilities*. Oxford: Butterworth-Heinemann.

World Commission on Environment and Development. 1987. *Our common future*. Oxford: Oxford University Press.

# 6

# The Role of Local Government in Contemporary Economic Development

## Michael I. Luger

The purpose of this chapter is to review the role subnational governments play in contemporary economic development, with particular reference to the United States.[1] In the United States, municipal (local) governments play a central role in land use policy (often following model state legislation) and the provision of common infrastructure. County, multicounty, and other regional governments are central actors in the United States in other areas of economic development as well. The intergovernmental distribution of responsibilities differs from country to country elsewhere in the world, but with few exceptions, there are important roles for subnational governments in land use and other aspects of economic development policy.[2] A common theme internationally is that there is increasing competition within and between countries for economic activity, especially for higher-skilled and better-paying jobs. That is entrenched in the structure of most governments, where responsibility for various important functions is devolved to state (prefecture, Länder, canton, etc.), regional, and municipal levels. The advisability of such competition is open to debate, but it is a feature of most governments that will continue to at least 2015.

---

[1]An earlier version of this chapter was presented at REDE's International Conference on the Role of Government in Regional Economic Government in Baiona (Galicia), Spain, 19–20 September, 2005. (REDE is the Centre for Research in Energy, Economics and the Environment.)

[2]The best author on international comparisons of intergovernmental relations, particularly between the United States, Korea, and Japan, is Deil S. Wright, professor emeritus, University of North Carolina, Chapel Hill.

The public sector has been engaged in economic development since the founding of the United States (and from the early days of other countries, as well). Today, the local economic development apparatus is so entrenched around the world that it is hard to imagine regions without government involvement. To the extent that there is discussion in the literature about government and local (regional) economic development, it tends to revolve around the appropriate unit of government, the extent and timing of involvement, and the type of interventions to use.

In the United States, the United Kingdom, and elsewhere, local governments are the principal providers of infrastructure services, notably water, wastewater, sewer, local roads, public transit, and, in some cases, power.[3] Local governments also are the primary source of land use regulations. Throughout U.S. history, all of these services and powers have been used, either explicitly or implicitly, as tools of business development. From the latter decades of the twentieth century to today, local governments have used their tools as a means to recruit and retain businesses, raising some interesting constitutional challenges.

## KEY DEFINITIONS

The chapter's title includes three terms that tend to be used loosely in the literature and in practice: "local government," "the role of government," and "economic development."

In the narrowest, political administrative sense, *local government* refers to the smallest incorporated municipal unit, such as a city, town, township, or village. Dillon's Rule states that those units of government are "creatures of the state" bestowed by the legislature with certain functional and fiscal responsibilities and rights.[4] Counties are also local governmental units with separate political apparatuses, in most cases.[5] But unlike cities, towns, townships, and villages, counties have functional authority stipulated in state constitutions, including health and welfare, the courts, and policing by a sheriff.

---

[3]Provision includes responsibility for the service when it is delivered by a private sector contractor.

[4]For Dillon's Rule, see Frug, Ford, and Barron (2001). Some states allow "home rule," which loosens the connection between local and state governments. Dillon's Rule is based on English common law, as exemplified in this 1726 quote from Thomas Madox, British historiographer: "Who so desireth to discourse in a proper manner concerning incorporated towns and communities must take in a great variety of matter and should be allowed a great deal of time and preparation. . . . The subject is extensive and difficult" (Rhyne 1980, 1).

[5]There are several successful models of consolidated city-county governments—Miami-Dade in Florida and Nashville-Davidson in Tennessee, for example—but they are exceptions to the rule.

Economists are less concerned about the political administration definition of local government than about the economic definition. "Local economies" and "local labor market areas" to an economist refer to the functional economic region, defined by the commuting shed. The U.S. Census Bureau operationalizes that concept as a metropolitan area.[6]

I use both the political and economic definitions in the discussion that follows. When I talk about service provision, I refer to the cities, towns, townships, villages, and counties that provide those local services. When I talk about local economic outcomes, I refer to the economic region, since those outcomes do not stop at municipal borders.

The textbook definition for the *local government's role* includes the following activities and range of subactivities:

- Planning—objective setting, *ex ante* assessment (usually cost-benefit analysis), and rule making
- Financing—development of capital for long-term projects from both taxes and fees, paying as you go and through bonds, and the provision of inducements, incentives, and subsidies
- Delivering—using public-sector employees to deliver services, including, for example, teachers, firemen, policemen, sanitation workers, and public works personnel
- Regulating—establishment and enforcement of property rights, taxation, and any other rules governing behavior
- Managing—coordination, contracting out, and *ex post* evaluation, inter alia

There is little debate about whether government *should* play those roles. Regions differ, however, in the mix of those roles by local governments. Indeed, the absence of government is itself an act of governance, as would pertain to privatization and deregulation.

By "local (or regional) economic development" I mean efforts to enhance employment, income, wealth, and opportunity within a defined geographic area. Regional economic development subsumes industrial, workforce, infrastructure, and other types of development efforts. Figure 6.1 presents a schematic of economic development.

We can see in figure 6.1 that economic development can be interpreted as both a noun and a verb. As a noun it is an outcome, equated to a better quality of life for citizens. Ultimately, that means a more vibrant social and cultural milieu, financial security, physical health and well-being, and a sustainable environment. The weights attached to each of those ultimate outcomes typically

---

[6]The Census Bureau defines several types of statistical regions, including metropolitan statistical areas, consolidated statistical areas, and micropolitan areas, for example.

**Figure 6.1:** Regional Economic Development

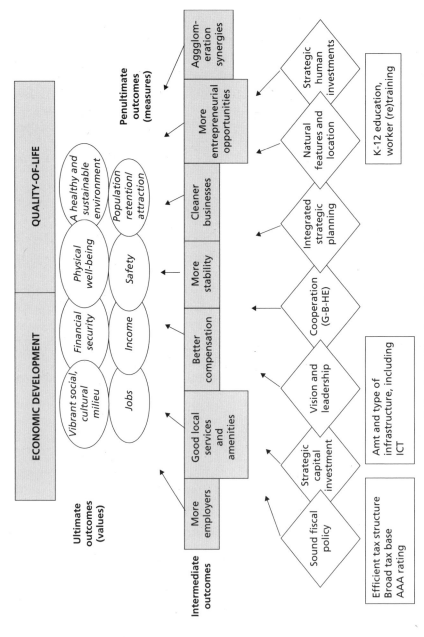

differ as a matter of political ideology: Green parties stress environmental out-comes; conservative regimes focus more on financial security for incumbents.

The figure shows that those outcomes are commonly understood in terms of jobs and income created, safety, and retention and attraction of population (brain-draw and brain-drain). Indeed, those are the very "penultimate out-come" measures used in commercial software that is employed by consultants and researchers to measure the economic impact of new business locations.

Much of the literature and many professional reports focus on what are really intermediate outcomes, at least in terms of economic development (it may be legitimate to consider them as ends in themselves in more limited studies). They are shown as the shaded boxes in the center of figure 6.1: more employers, better compensation, more stability, more entrepreneurial oppor-tunities, and agglomeration and synergies. Those intermediate outcomes are also the grist for political debates, in which credit for success and blame for failure are assigned.

The role of government (and other inputs) in this schematic is shown at the bottom of the figure. Among the important policy, institutional, and behavioral inputs are provision of a sound fiscal environment and strategic investments in capital and labor (Tabellini 2005). This shows economic development as a verb—the things we do to develop economically.[7]

This schematic applies to other countries besides the United States, though (as previously noted) the weights attached to the outcomes (top of the figure) vary, as do the types of interventions employed (bottom of the figure). Germany has been a leader in technical education; Finland has been a leader in the provision of information and communication technology (ICT) infrastructure; Taiwan and South Korea, for example, have made enormous investments in physical infrastructure. Fuller discussion of national differ-ences in policy approach is beyond the scope of this chapter.

## THE CHANGING INTERGOVERNMENTAL ROLE

The public sector's role in local (regional) development predated the Ameri-can Revolution, when the colonies invested in port and waterway improve-ment and began to build roads (Schultz 2004). By the early nineteenth century, the new nation was building canals and then railroads. That role was at the center of both constitutional and other legislative acts in the early years of the United States. The Interstate Commerce Clause of the Constitution

---

[7]See Luger (1987) for an explanation of the practice of scholarly evaluation in this area.

and federal funding for postal roads recognized the importance of facilitating the flow of goods, people, and information to all parts of the developing nation, including the frontier.[8] That continued after the Civil War into what is now called the era of bridge building (ibid.). Federal involvement expanded into the twentieth century with further development of roads (including the construction of interstate highways starting in the 1950s), water systems, electrification projects, and the development of airports and seaports. Today, government has added investments in information and advanced communications technology to its list of responsibilities (Luger and Stewart 2003; Luger 2001, 2005). All these activities may not have been explicitly for regional development, but they are recognized to have had profound regional effects.

More explicit attention to regional development by the federal government was intended to alleviate pockets of poverty. Many New Deal programs were directed where unemployment was highest or where infrastructure needs were greatest—for example, the Works Projects Administration (WPA), the Tennessee Valley Authority (TVA), the Appalachian Regional Commission (ARC), and the Rural Electrification Administration (REA) were targeted to laggard regions. Some of those regional development efforts continue today, with the TVA and ARC as prime examples of federal programs that have survived for decades. The longevity of those programs is proof not of their success in promoting economic development within their regions, but rather of the staying power of the political institutions. Both the TVA and ARC cover multiple states within their regions; the ARC includes 13 state governors within its commission and converts that participation into the political support necessary for continued funding (Bradshaw 1992). ARC has expanded into new areas, including the metropolitan area of Pittsburgh, as congressmen and senators look to expand the benefits of the commission across their districts. The TVA, at its heart a rural electrification program, has also been shown to have limited economic impact on its region despite decades of regional investments (Chandler 1984).

Large federal projects like the construction of the Hoover and Grand Coulee dams in Nevada and Washington (and many other large hydro projects), flood control on the Mississippi and other rivers, and more have had profound effects on regional development. The federal government also has used the location of large federal facilities, including military bases and

---

[8]The Interstate Commerce Clause grants the U.S. Congress the power to regulate international and interstate trade. This clause was used in the nineteenth and twentieth centuries to expand federal regulatory power at the expense of the states. The clause became the basis for federal environmental, safety, and labor standards, among others.

national laboratories, to enhance regional development (see Markusen et al. 1991). Today, there are ongoing regional development programs sponsored by the U.S. Department of Agriculture in rural areas, the U.S. Economic Development Administration, and to lesser degrees other federal agencies. Of course, there is also a history of programs targeted to subregions or neighborhoods, including, for example, Model Cities, Community Development Block Grants, and other programs with income or unemployment criteria in their allocation formula.

The federal government's activities just summarized have a mix of what the literature calls intended and unintended or derivative regional consequences. Many authors have pointed out that there are really no geographically neutral federal policies. Luger (1984), among others, has shown that the federal tax code has distinct spatial biases. There was a period during the presidency of Jimmy Carter when the federal government sought to use the federal tax system explicitly to help laggard regions. But that attempted targeting of the tax system was short lived.

Also in the 1970s there was discussion in the United States about national industrial policy. Robert Reich, Ira Magaziner, and other progressive writers at the time advocated for an open debate about what industries should be supported by policy (Reich and Magaziner 1982). In short, that would make the selection of winners and losers among America's businesses more explicit. But that also had a relatively short half-life.

Today the literature is relatively quiet on these macro questions about the federal government's responsibility for and effect on economic development. Central government in the United States continues to fund (although at increasingly lower levels) the ARC, along with the Economic Development Administration (EDA) and other federal agencies that help distressed regions more than others. And questions of regional economic impact are part of discussions about military base closings and realignments, for example. Some new federal programs require a regional (or distressed community) economic impact assessment—for example, New Market Tax Credits are now available to taxpayers who invest in designated Community Development Entities that can demonstrate the use of the funds for job creation and income enhancement.[9]

Rather than directing multistate or regional development efforts, the federal government has become a source of funding and other support for state and local efforts. One clear advantage of devolution in the economic development system is the creation of national competition and innovation across states and regions, which can quickly develop best practices for regional

---

[9]http://cdfifund.gov/.

development. Unencumbered by the federal government, state and regional leaders are free to pursue innovative policies and programs to address economic shortfalls, as suggested by David Osborne in *Laboratories of Democracy* (1988). However, without a coordinated public-private dissemination effort, these best practices fail to spread across areas (McDowell 1995) concentrating program benefits and potentially widening regional disparities. Those regions without the infrastructure, expertise, and technology to replace declining industries may also experience destructive competition, which can lead to a race to the bottom for financial incentives, limited cross-state cooperation, and a duplication of development efforts within a single geographic area (Cooke, Gomez Uranga, and Etxebarria 1997). Whether the outcome of this devolution is net positive or negative, there are significant consequences for regional economic developers who must work within this new system.

It is now common for states to have an economic development program whose purpose is to grow industry, mostly by tax incentives and recruiting. The strategic development of those programs in many cases is overseen by an economic development board at the gubernatorial or legislative level. In many states, multicounty economic development organizations also provide services. In addition, there are over 2,500 cities, towns, and counties across the United States with full-time economic development professionals, often reporting to an economic development commission. Those state, regional, and local economic developers; Chambers of Commerce and issue groups with names like "the Committee of 100"; economic development "allies," including law firms, banks, and utilities; elected officials; nongovernmental organizations (NGOs); foundations; consultants; the education sector; state legislative "standing committees"; and several federal agencies all constitute a broad and deep professional community of interest around economic development. Those stakeholders have no shortage of statewide and national meetings to attend, sponsored by such organizations as the International Economic Development Council (IEDC), the State Science and Technology Institute (SSTI), the EDA, and state economic development associations. And several professional publications are outlets for information about economic development at the state, regional, and local levels, including *Applied Research in Economic Development* (published by the Council for Community and Economic Research, or ACCRA), *Economic Development Journal* (IEDC), *Economic Development Now* (IEDC), and *Economic Development America* (IEDC and the National Association of Regional Councils, NARC), to name a few. There is also a community of scholarship around economic development, in many universities and colleges, and a corresponding set of organizations and journals to create legitimacy (see Luger and Stewart 2003).

Tax incentives are perhaps the most common state-level policy used to recruit businesses from other states, assist existing businesses, and induce new start-ups (Luger and Bae 2005). For example, while 24 states offered tax incentives for job creation in 1984, 43 states offered incentives in 1998. R&D tax incentives were offered to businesses by 9 states in 1977 and 39 states in 1998 (Chi 1989; Chi and Hofmann 2000).[10]

There is considerable debate in the literature and among policy makers about the effectiveness of these state tax incentive programs and whether they are justified as public policy.[11] A review of legislative intent indicates that state tax incentive programs usually are enacted and implemented for political rather than cost-benefit or cost-effectiveness reasons. Brunori (2001) argues that most business tax incentives are the product of interstate competition to attract businesses from other states, or what he calls an "arms-race mentality." State policy makers appear to be obliged to offer tax incentives to businesses when other states are implementing tax incentive programs. They fear that they will lose businesses already located in their states to other states with tax incentive programs.[12] On the other hand, Greenstone and Moretti (2004) estimated that jurisdictions that won the competition for "million-dollar plants" gained welfare relative to the runners-up, in terms of wage and property tax premia and, consequently, more spending on services, in their and neighboring jurisdictions.

Given the growth of tax incentive programs at the state level over the past 25 years, the stakes involved with their use also have grown. The tax expenditure nationally from state business tax incentives is substantial. For example, in California, the estimated loss of revenue from business tax incentives was approxi-

---

[10]The term *business tax incentives* is used in different ways in the literature. Some scholars include any subsidy to a company, including below-market rate loans, free real estate, job training assistance, and below-cost infrastructure (see, for example, Coenen 1998; Coenen and Hellerstein 1996, 1997). Glaeser (2001) suggests two rival definitions: (1) as tax rates chosen on a firm-by-firm basis, and as such, they are highly discretionary; (2) as reductions in the total tax rate. That latter definition is associated with Garcia-Mila and McGuire (2002). The definition I have used in my tax incentive research is more precise. Start with a defined, or statutory tax code for individuals or businesses. That code specifies what is supposed to be taxed and by how much. Tax incentives reduce that statutory liability by allowing lower tax rates to be used, or by providing exemptions (abatements), exclusions from the base, tax credits, and tax deductions (reductions in the relevant taxable base). Those rate reductions, exemptions, exclusions, and deductions can be across the board, for specific types of businesses, or for specific behavior (types of investments including in R&D and in types of equipment, hiring and/or training workers, locating in a particular place, etc.). Those incentives drive a wedge between nominal and real tax burdens.

[11]For pros and cons on state tax incentives, see Lynch (1996), Fisher and Peters (1996), and Chi and Hofmann (2000).

[12]This can be verified with any state Department of Commerce secretary. Quotes are available from authors.

mately $15 billion in 2001–2002.[13] New York forwent approximately $2 billion in 2002.[14] And North Carolina spent some $74 million on business tax incentive programs in 1997–1999.[15] In addition, Thomas (2000, 159) estimated that state and local corporate subsidies in the United States reached approximately $48.8 billion in 1995–1996. This large tax expenditure justifies a careful look at whether business tax incentive programs are justified as public policy. Indeed, several states have sunset provisions or required reviews written into the legislature (e.g., North Carolina, Oregon, and Texas). The need for careful reviews has been amplified in the past fiscal year by serious budget crises in many states,[16] often accompanied by renewed cries from legislators to curtail incentive programs (an action also referred to as closing tax loopholes).[17]

Today it is also common for local governments to sweeten recruitment deals with offers of property tax abatements (except in states that proscribe that), straight-out cash subsidies and employment-based grants, below-market-price land deals, subsidized industrial buildings, and concessionary utility rates. The reduction of property tax liabilities for qualifying businesses is of particular relevance for this volume. Two of those programs, personal property exemptions and accelerated depreciation, can be used by almost any commercial or industrial operation to reduce its property tax liability on machinery and equipment. Foreign trade zone programs also confer property

---

[13]This amount does not cover all tax credit expenses. It covers only four types of tax credits: Manufacturers' Investment Credit, Research and Development Tax Credit, Carryover of Net Operating Losses, and Enterprise Zone Hiring and Sales Tax Credits. See California Department of Finance, *Tax Expenditure Report 2001–02.*

[14]This amount covers only five types of tax credits in New York: New Capital Investment Tax Credits, Research and Development Credit, Emerging Industries Jobs Act, Credit for Hiring Persons With Disabilities, and Alternative Fuel Vehicle Credit. See New York Division of Budget and Department of Taxation & Finance, *Annual Report on New York State Tax Expenditures 2002–2003.*

[15]In addition, Massachusetts spent about $220 million in 1997–1998 for Investment Tax Credit, Research and Development Tax Credit, and Economic Opportunity Area Credit. Iowa spent about $61 million for New Jobs Credit, Research and Development Credit, and Investment Credit in 2000. See Luger (2001); Massachusetts Fiscal Affairs Division, *The Governor's Budget Recommendation Fiscal Year 1999*; and Iowa Department of Revenue and Finance, *Iowa Tax Expenditures 2000.*

[16]For example, North Carolina and California faced budget shortfalls in 2002–2003 of upward of $2 billion and $23 billion, respectively; 2004–2005 saw some improvement, but still tight budget times.

[17]The North Carolina House decided to close $60 million in corporate tax loopholes in 2002–2003 and additional tax loopholes in 2003–2004. The Missouri House planned to close or cut corporate tax breaks and loopholes to cover expenses for elementary and secondary schools in 2003–2004. Bill Ratliff, Texas lieutenant governor, proposed to close some corporate tax loopholes to address school financing problems in 2002–2003. See the *Charlotte Observer* (July 12, 2001); the *News & Observer* (February 13, 2002); the *St. Louis Post-Dispatch* (April 8, 2002); and the *Houston Chronicle* (October 20, 2001).

**Figure 6.2:** The Economic Development Process

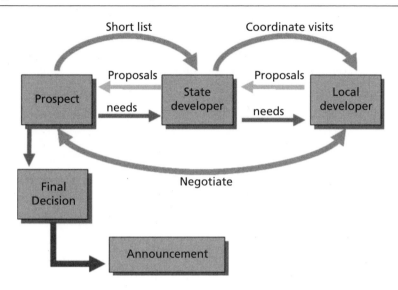

tax benefits to companies that do business internationally. In addition, state enterprise zones offer property tax incentives.

Variants of those incentives are used in Europe, as well, often in a targeted fashion—that is, to induce development in the city center, in distressed places, in historic structures, in brownfield sites, for "green technologies," etc.[18] Those are likely to become even more common in locations around the world to which U.S.-owned companies are seeking to move.

Within this wide range of state- and local-level efforts, the typical goal and most common metric of success is the number of new business announcements. Figure 6.2 shows the typical process to achieve that end. State and local developers not only are involved in prospect handling, but increasingly provide financial incentives to lure the prospect. Some of the incentives that are offered are based on federal (mostly EDA) grant and loan programs; others use state and local taxpayers' money. The figure shows the interconnection among actors. A prospect tells a state agency that it is potentially interested in a site somewhere in the region and provides general criteria. The state then sends requests for

---

[18]See http://www.pinsentmasons.com/media/1847864368.htm. A quick scan of the Internet reveals Web sites on those types of incentives in Spain, Ireland, and several other countries.

proposals to many local authorities who choose how to respond, including what local incentives to bring to the table. The prospect visits the most attractive locations and negotiates a final package with the state and the local entity.

Economic development scholars and some enlightened practitioners long have argued that too much attention is focused on business recruitment, as opposed to business retention and entrepreneurship (see Luger and Stewart 2003). The commitment to this more balanced approach varies among jurisdictions. In any case, those who hold that alternative view require another (overlapping) set of stakeholders, including Small Business Development Centers, community colleges, manufacturing (industrial) extension partnership programs, entrepreneurship support networks, loan and equity funds, and more. Many of those resources are provided or subsidized by government.

The review so far has focused on the United States. But as noted in several places above, similar trends can be found in Europe. One of the European Commission's major activities over much of its existence has been to reallocate "structural adjustment funds" to regions of countries deemed to be relatively distressed. And within countries, regional authorities were created to help with industrial development. The Northwest Development Agency, for example, provides incentives for businesses locating or expanding in the northwest of England.

Over the past 50 years we have moved farther away from the laissez-faire notion of businesses seeking location based on their assessment of resource and transportation costs, and business performance driven solely by the company's inherent efficiency. And over the past several decades local governments have moved from providing services to providing incentives, along with their regional and state government counterparts. That role for local and state government has been contested in the courts; its foundation in law has been shaken but is still intact.

For example, in *Maready v. City of Winston-Salem*, William F. Maready, a trial lawyer, successfully argued in state superior court that his city and the surrounding county violated the state's constitution by giving taxpayer money to private companies for such incentives as helping to rent an office building and providing subsidized parking. The judge, ruling in August 1995, also found that the statute authorizing local government expenditures for economic development was impermissibly vague. Local governments throughout North Carolina began to question their own use of incentives. State officials worried that if the ruling were upheld on appeal, other statutes governing state-level expenditures for economic development might be cast into doubt. In that case, the ruling was reversed in the state supreme court. The Democratic majority accepted the argument that incentives "are directly aimed at furthering the general economic welfare," while one dissenting judge castigated the state for justifying its use of incentives on the rationale that "all the states are doing it."

That provided a reprieve for state and local governments to continue offering incentives, and between 1996 and 2004, the repertoire was expanded, using several new incentive programs to lure corporate giants Merck and Dell (among other companies) to North Carolina. The opposition to incentives intensified in response, led by former state supreme court justice Robert Orr, who formed the North Carolina Institute for Constitutional Law to oppose business incentives.[19] An odd coalition of progressive and libertarian groups has joined Orr in opposing the state's use of incentives, including the Corporation for Enterprise Development on the left and the John Locke Foundation on the right.[20]

To date, the political center that supports the use of incentives has prevailed in North Carolina (as elsewhere), but pressure for reform is mounting. In 2004, the *Daimler Chrysler v. Cuno* decision in the U.S. Court of Appeals created a specter for economic developers throughout the United States. The court upheld the plaintiff's claim that a Toledo, Ohio, investment tax credit violated the Interstate Commerce Clause of the constitution. It remains to be seen how broadly that decision will apply.

The impact of the *Cuno* case was muted somewhat by *Kelo v. City of New London*, decided by the U.S. Supreme Court in June 2005. In *Kelo*, the court affirmed the use of eminent domain when the result would be jobs for the community: "The City's proposed disposition of petitioner's property qualifies as 'public use' within the meaning of the Takings Clause" (pp. 6–20). In a highly publicized dissent, Justice Sandra Day O'Connor said, "Under the banner of economic development, all private property is now vulnerable to being taken and transferred to another private owner, so long as it might be upgraded."

The bottom line should be very clear: The government's role in local (regional) economic development is broad and deep. In general, it is not disputed. It is firmly entrenched with many stakeholders who derive financial benefit from the system.

## INCREASING DISPARITIES IN ECONOMIC DEVELOPMENT

Since the mid-1980s the United States has experienced widening economic disparities among socioeconomic groups and regions (Luger 1993). Arguably, that is the result of macro policies that have reduced tax burdens and regulations more for upper- than for lower-income Americans. But it also is a consequence

---

[19]Web address: www.ncicl.org.
[20]Web addresses: www.cfed.org and www.johnlocke.org.

of the knowledge (or "new") economy, in which workers are increasingly foot-loose and gravitate to places with concentrations of amenities. Florida (2003) refers to those workers as the creative class and those places as creative communities. What we see is that the "have regions" get richer and the "have not" regions get poorer.

These growing disparities show up in all sorts of outcome and input indicators. On the outcome side, consider table 6.1. The largest 50 metropolitan statistical areas (MSAs) have been divided into three tiers, based on population size: very large (generally above 4 million), medium large (roughly 2 to 4 million), and large (above 1 million). The groupings are inexact because of the differences in population rankings (and MSA definitions) between the two years examined — 1999 and 2005. The key insight is that the higher the population tier, the more the MSA's population has been able to increase its per capita personal income. In short, the rich get richer.

A unique data set — RaDiUS, assembled by the RAND Corporation — is used to illustrate increasing concentration on the input side. RaDiUS shows the volume and types of federal R&D grants made, by recipient, sorted by type of research, location, and other attributes. If the future of regions in the "new economy" depends on their ability to innovate, and innovation is somehow related to R&D, then growing concentrations of R&D dollars are both a coincident and leading indicator of imbalanced growth.

Table 6.2 presents the top 50 MSAs in the United States (as of 2004) in three population tiers: very large (above 4 million), medium large (2 to 4 million), and large (the remaining 50 below 2 million). The MSAs have been divided this way so that we can see if there has been an increasing concentration of R&D dollars in the largest cities that have the greatest critical mass of knowledge resources. The answer is clearly yes. In 1994, average funding per capita for tiers 1, 2, and 3 was $3.80, $4.20, and $5.90, respectively. The percent deviation from lowest to highest ratio was 55.2. Just 10 years later, the per capita figures were $12, $6.70, and $9.10. The top-tier cities not only sprang into the lead, but by a large margin. The percent deviation lowest to highest was 79.1. The same pattern occurs for funding per S&T (science and technology) worker and per full-time professor. The same story emerges using concentration indices. In short, critical mass is attracting more critical mass.

As interesting, and more pertinent for the purposes of this chapter, are the differences among MSAs within the tiers. Not surprisingly, those MSAs with concentrations of universities, research labs, hospitals, and high-tech consulting companies do much better than the others.

**TABLE 6.1**  Changes in Per Capita Personal Income by Size Tier of Metropolitan Statistical Areas

| Area name | 2005 | | | Area name | 1999 | | | Percent change, 1999-2005 |
|---|---|---|---|---|---|---|---|---|
| | Personal income | Per capita personal income* | Population | | Personal income | Per capita personal income* | Population | |
| New York-Northern New Jersey-Long Island, NY-NJ-PA | 854,317 | 45,570 | 18,747,356 | New York-Northern New Jersey-Long Island, NY-NJ | 653,173 | 37,019 | 17,644,286 | |
| Los Angeles-Long Beach-Santa Ana, CA | 477,101 | 36,917 | 12,923,612 | Los Angeles-Long Beach-Santa Ana, CA | 357,595 | 29,184 | 12,253,326 | |
| Chicago-Naperville-Joliet, IL-IN-WI | 362,994 | 38,439 | 9,443,378 | Chicago, IL | 275,684 | 33,569 | 8,212,458 | |
| Philadelphia-Camden-Wilmington, PA-NJ-DE-MD | 235,657 | 40,468 | 5,823,292 | Boston-Worcester-Lawrence-Lowell-Brockton, MA-NH | 211,837 | 35,178 | 6,021,860 | |
| Dallas-Fort Worth-Arlington, TX | 215,756 | 37,075 | 5,819,447 | Dallas-Fort Worth-Arlington, TX | 159,254 | 13,854 | 5,119,852 | |
| Miami-Fort Lauderdale-Miami Beach, FL | 196,789 | 36,293 | 5,422,230 | Philadelphia, PA-NJ | 162,176 | 31,896 | 5,084,525 | |
| Houston-Sugar Land-Baytown, TX | 206,198 | 39,052 | 5,280,088 | Washington, DC-MD-VA-WV | 182,722 | 37,693 | 4,847,637 | |
| Washington-Arlington-Alexandria, DC-VA-MD-WV | 258,281 | 49,530 | 5,214,638 | Detroit, MI | 140,791 | 31,716 | 4,439,116 | |

(continued)

**TABLE 6.1**  (continued)

| | 2005 | | | 1999 | | | | Percent change, 1999-2005 |
|---|---|---|---|---|---|---|---|---|
| Area name | Personal income | Per capita personal income* | Population | Area name | Personal income | Per capita personal income* | Population | |
| Atlanta-Sandy Springs-Marietta, GA | 172,164 | 35,009 | 4,917,707 | Houston, TX | 131,601 | 31,995 | 4,113,174 | |
| Detroit-Warren-Livonia, MI | 169,183 | 37,694 | 4,488,327 | San Francisco-Oakland, CA | 170,460 | 41,681 | 4,089,625 | |
| Boston-Cambridge-Quincy, MA-NH | 212,464 | 48,158 | 4,411,811 | Atlanta, GA | 126,446 | 31,534 | 4,009,831 | |
| San Francisco-Oakland-Fremont, CA | 215,791 | 51,964 | 4,152,702 | Miami-Ft. Lauderdale, FL | 100,297 | 26,289 | 3,815,102 | |
| | 3,576,695 | 41,280 | 86,644,588 | | 2,672,036 | 33,547 | 79,650,792 | 23.1 |
| Riverside-San Bernardino-Ontario, CA | 103,944 | 26,584 | 3,910,021 | Riverside-San Bernardino, CA | 70,928 | 22,238 | 3,189,495 | |
| Phoenix-Mesa-Scottsdale, AZ | 125,755 | 32,536 | 3,865,103 | Phoenix-Mesa, AZ | 83,347 | 26,223 | 3,178,393 | |
| Seattle-Tacoma-Bellevue, WA | 133,452 | 41,661 | 3,203,284 | Minneapolis-St. Paul, MN-WI | 101,664 | 34,671 | 2,932,249 | |
| Minneapolis-St. Paul-Bloomington, MN-WI | 132,258 | 42,083 | 3,142,789 | San Diego, CA | 84,585 | 30,322 | 2,789,559 | |
| San Diego-Carlsbad-San Marcos, CA | 116,986 | 39,880 | 2,933,450 | St. Louis, MO-IL | 77,424 | 29,838 | 2,594,812 | |

(continued)

| | | | | | | | | |
|---|---|---|---|---|---|---|---|---|
| St. Louis, MO-IL | 100,511 | 36,174 | 2,778,543 | Baltimore, MD | 78,303 | 30,824 | 2,540,326 | |
| Baltimore-Towson, MD | 108,475 | 40,846 | 2,655,707 | Seattle-Bellevue-Everett, WA | 93,047 | 38,811 | 2,397,439 | |
| Tampa-St. Petersburg-Clearwater, FL | 87,393 | 33,008 | 2,647,631 | Tampa-St. Petersburg-Clearwater, FL | 64,205 | 27,101 | 2,369,101 | |
| Pittsburgh, PA | 86,396 | 36,208 | 2,386,103 | Pittsburgh, PA | 68,830 | 29,092 | 2,365,943 | |
| Denver-Aurora, CO | 100,473 | 42,574 | 2,359,961 | Cleveland-Lorain-Elyria, OH | 67,035 | 29,757 | 2,252,747 | |
| Cleveland-Elyria-Mentor, OH | 75,573 | 35,542 | 2,126,301 | Denver, CO | 71,496 | 34,515 | 2,071,447 | |
| Portland-Vancouver-Beaverton, OR-WA | 73,806 | 35,215 | 2,095,868 | Portland-Vancouver, OR-WA | 56,125 | 29,594 | 1,896,499 | |
| Cincinnati-Middletown, OH-KY-IN | 73,745 | 35,618 | 2,070,442 | Cincinnati, OH-KY-IN | 48,424 | 29,561 | 1,638,104 | |
| Sacramento-Arden-Arcade-Roseville, CA | 71,082 | 34,805 | 2,042,293 | Sacramento, CA | 45,588 | 28,457 | 1,601,996 | |
| | 1,389,849 | 36,367 | 38,217,496 | | 1,011,001 | 29,895 | 33,818,110 | **21.6** |
| Virginia Beach-Norfolk-Newport News, VA-NC | 54,883 | 33,316 | 1,647,347 | Kansas City, MO-KS | 52,969 | 30,063 | 1,761,933 | |
| San Jose-Sunnyvale-Santa Clara, CA | 88,404 | 50,373 | 1,754,988 | San Jose, CA | 76,443 | 45,733 | 1,671,506 | |
| San Antonio, TX | 56,901 | 30,109 | 1,889,834 | Orlando, FL | 41,313 | 25,692 | 1,608,010 | |

**TABLE 6.1** *(continued)*

| | 2005 | | | 1999 | | | | Percent change, 1999-2005 |
|---|---|---|---|---|---|---|---|---|
| Area name | Personal income | Per capita personal income* | Population | Area name | Personal income | Per capita personal income* | Population | |
| Salt Lake City, UT | 34,426 | 33,279 | 1,034,466 | Indianapolis, IN | 46,760 | 29,427 | 1,589,017 | |
| Raleigh-Durham-Cary, NC | 48,972 | 34,833 | 1,405,897 | San Antonio, TX | 39,188 | 24,920 | 1,572,552 | |
| Orlando-Kissimmee, FL | 60,148 | 31,112 | 1,933,273 | Norfolk-Virginia Beach-Newport News, VA-NC | 38,799 | 24,905 | 1,557,880 | |
| New Orleans-Metairie-Kenner, LA | 27,340 | 20,722 | 1,319,371 | Columbus, OH | 44,563 | 29,228 | 1,524,668 | |
| Nashville-Davidson-Murfreesboro, TN | 51,845 | 36,445 | 1,422,555 | Las Vegas, NV-AZ | 40,406 | 26,882 | 1,503,088 | |
| Milwaukee-Waukesha-West Allis, WI | 57,279 | 37,862 | 1,512,836 | Milwaukee-Waukesha, WI | 46,584 | 31,134 | 1,496,242 | |
| Memphis, TN-MS-AR | 42,720 | 33,880 | 1,260,921 | Charlotte-Gastonia-Rock Hill, NC-SC | 43,384 | 29,481 | 1,471,592 | |
| Louisville-Jefferson County, KY-IN | 41,208 | 34,100 | 1,208,446 | New Orleans, LA | 33,672 | 25,159 | 1,338,368 | |
| Las Vegas-Paradise, NV | 59,682 | 34,890 | 1,710,576 | Salt Lake City-Ogden, UT | 32,685 | 24,748 | 1,320,713 | |
| Kansas City, MO-KS | 69,843 | 35,859 | 1,947,712 | Nashville, TN | 36,409 | 29,973 | 1,214,727 | |

| | | | | | | | | |
|---|---|---|---|---|---|---|---|---|
| Jacksonville, FL | 42,110 | 33,732 | 1,248,370 | Austin-San Marcos, TX | 36,852 | 30,560 | 1,205,890 | |
| Indianapolis-Carmel, IN | 59,440 | 36,231 | 1,640,584 | Buffalo-Niagara Falls, NY | 30,386 | 25,902 | 1,173,114 | |
| Hartford-West Hartford-East Hartford, CT | 50,745 | 42,706 | 1,188,241 | Raleigh-Durham-Chapel Hill, NC | 35,568 | 30,613 | 1,161,859 | |
| Columbus, OH | 60,188 | 35,226 | 1,708,624 | Hartford, CT (NECMA) | 39,199 | 34,345 | 1,141,331 | |
| Charlotte-Gastonia-Concord, NC-SC | 54,996 | 36,151 | 1,521,286 | Memphis, TN-AR-MS | 32,011 | 28,431 | 1,125,919 | |
| Buffalo-Niagara Falls, NY | 36,741 | 32,012 | 1,147,726 | Rochester, NY | 30,339 | 27,675 | 1,096,260 | |
| Austin-Round Rock, TX | 49,394 | 34,005 | 1,452,551 | Jacksonville, FL | 29,903 | 27,475 | 1,088,371 | |
| Rochester, NY | 34,930 | 33,618 | 1,039,027 | Oklahoma City, OK | 25,953 | 24,117 | 1,076,129 | |
| Oklahoma City, OK | 36,590 | 31,630 | 1,156,813 | Louisville, KY-IN | 29,253 | 28,677 | 1,020,086 | |
| Providence-New Bedford-Fall River, RI-MA | 57,588 | 35,493 | 1,622,517 | Richmond-Petersburg, VA | 29,131 | 29,513 | 987,057 | |
| Richmond, VA | 43,697 | 37,169 | 1,175,630 | Providence-Warwick-Pawtucket, RI (NECMA) | 26,040 | 27,251 | 955,561 | |
| | 1,220,070 | 34,909 | 34,949,589 | | 917,810 | 28,988 | 31,661,873 | **20.4** |

Notes: * = weighted averages; NECMA = New England Country Metropolitan Area.
*Source:* U.S. Department of Commerce, Bureau of the Census, MSA data.

| TABLE 6.2 | R&D Disparities Among Metropolitan Areas | | | | | | |
|---|---|---|---|---|---|---|---|
| Tier | City | Population | | Funding per capita | | Per S&T worker | | Per full-time professor at top 50 research university |
| | | 1994 | 2004 | 1994 | 2004 | 1999* | 2004 | 2004 |
| 1 | New York | 19,788,963 | 18,709,802 | 2.4 | 5.8 | 283.9 | 607.9 | 22,895 |
| | Los Angeles | 15,302,000 | 12,925,330 | 0.0 | 0.5 | 0.6 | 31.7 | 1,282 |
| | Chicago | 8,527,000 | 9,391,515 | 6.0 | 8.6 | 248.7 | 396.5 | 18,834 |
| | Philadelphia | 5,957,000 | 5,800,614 | 4.7 | 6.0 | 232.1 | 269.0 | 13,402 |
| | Dallas | 4,362,000 | 5,700,256 | 1.1 | 1.8 | 33.5 | 76.9 | 7,324 |
| | Miami | 3,408,000 | 5,361,723 | 0.9 | 1.3 | 89.6 | 184.8 | 7,749 |
| | Houston | 4,099,000 | 5,180,443 | 4.9 | 5.1 | 137.9 | 204.6 | 15,236 |
| | Washington, DC | 7,059,000 | 5,139,549 | 2.0 | 60.9 | 57.3 | 965.0 | 449,332 |
| | Atlanta | 3,331,000 | 4,708,297 | 0.0 | 0.0 | 0.0 | 0.0 | N/A |
| | Detroit | 5,255,000 | 4,493,165 | 0.8 | 1.8 | 22.4 | 54.1 | N/A |
| | Boston | 5,730,000 | 4,424,649 | 15.7 | 34.1 | 552.4 | 907.3 | 23,722 |
| | San Francisco | 6,513,000 | 4,153,870 | 7.1 | 17.6 | 500.0 | 910.5 | 22,982 |
| | **AVERAGE** | **7,444,330** | **7,165,768** | **3.8** | **12.0** | **179.9** | **384.0** | **58,276** |
| 2 | Phoenix | 2,473,000 | 3,715,360 | 0.0 | 0.1 | 1.2 | 5.7 | N/A |
| | Seattle | 3,225,000 | 3,166,828 | 11.3 | 19.9 | 263.8 | 482.8 | 22,037 |
| | Minneapolis | 2,688,000 | 3,116,206 | 19.4 | 16.5 | 433.4 | 440.0 | 30,736 |
| | San Diego | 2,632,000 | 2,931,714 | 12.6 | 27.6 | 471.2 | 920.4 | 83,853 |
| | St Louis | 2,536,000 | 2,764,054 | 0.1 | 1.2 | 2.7 | 48.9 | 3,461 |
| | Tampa | 2,157,000 | 2,587,967 | 1.1 | 2.9 | 44.7 | 145.6 | N/A |
| | Pittsburgh | 2,402,000 | 2,401,575 | 9.9 | 26.6 | 490.5 | 1173.2 | 27,148 |
| | Denver | 2,190,000 | 2,330,146 | 1.5 | 1.4 | 39.8 | 40.5 | 3,972 |
| | San Juan | 2,450,292 | 2,270,808 | 0.8 | 3.2 | 101.8 | 347.1 | N/A |
| | Cleveland | 2,899,000 | 2,137,073 | 1.9 | 3.9 | 95.3 | 181.4 | 13,286 |
| | Portland | 1,982,000 | 2,064,336 | 0.5 | 0.3 | 18.7 | 10.9 | 766 |
| | Cincinnati | 1,894,000 | 2,058,221 | 1.3 | 3.2 | 57.3 | 145.6 | 5,729 |
| | Sacramento | 1,588,000 | 2,016,702 | 0.9 | 0.1 | 40.4 | 3.9 | N/A |
| | Kansas City | 1,647,000 | 1,925,319 | 0.2 | 0.0 | 7.4 | 0.0 | N/A |
| | Orlando | 1,361,000 | 1,861,707 | 1.3 | 2.6 | 52.6 | 108.5 | N/A |

**TABLE 6.2** *(continued)*

| Tier | City | Population | | Funding per capita | | Per S&T worker | | Per full-time professor at top 50 research university |
|---|---|---|---|---|---|---|---|---|
| | | 1994 | 2004 | 1994 | 2004 | 1999* | 2004 | 2004 |
| | San Antonio | 1,437,000 | 1,854,050 | 0.9 | 1.6 | 50.2 | 97.9 | N/A |
| | Columbus | 1,423,000 | 1,693,906 | 10.5 | 18.4 | 316.3 | 665.1 | 11,170 |
| | Las Vegas | 1,076,000 | 1,650,671 | 2.0 | 1.3 | 123.4 | 94.3 | N/A |
| | Virginia Beach-Norfolk | 1,529,000 | 1,644,250 | 1.9 | 5.0 | 86.3 | 186.4 | N/A |
| | Providence | 912,000 | 1,628,808 | 12.5 | 8.0 | 762.3 | 639.3 | 21,140 |
| | Indianapolis | 1,462,000 | 1,621,613 | 0.0 | 0.0 | 0.0 | 0.0 | N/A |
| | Milwaukee | 1,637,000 | 1,515,738 | 1.8 | 3.4 | 70.5 | 119.5 | N/A |
| | **AVERAGE** | **1,981,831** | **2,225,321** | **4.2** | **6.7** | **160.5** | **266.2** | **20,300** |
| 3 | Charlotte | 1,260,000 | 1,474,734 | 0.9 | 2.0 | 31.1 | 74.7 | N/A |
| | Raleigh-Durham-Chapel Hill | 965,000 | 1,415,260 | 34.1 | 47.0 | 528.5 | 924.8 | 17,114 |
| | Austin | 964,000 | 1,412,271 | 20.2 | 24.4 | 338.0 | 265.4 | 13,955 |
| | Nashville | 1,070,000 | 1,395,879 | 3.0 | 6.9 | 157.7 | 366.2 | 12,353 |
| | New Orleans | 1,309,000 | 1,319,589 | 1.5 | 6.5 | 89.9 | 397.4 | N/A |
| | Memphis | 1,056,000 | 1,250,293 | 1.2 | 2.0 | 71.6 | 125.6 | N/A |
| | Jacksonville | 972,000 | 1,225,381 | 0.1 | 0.2 | 4.7 | 10.5 | N/A |
| | Louisville | 981,000 | 1,200,847 | 0.4 | 1.6 | 21.0 | 95.6 | N/A |
| | Hartford | 1,117,000 | 1,184,564 | 2.4 | 1.2 | 63.9 | 32.5 | N/A |
| | Buffalo | 1,189,000 | 1,154,378 | 7.6 | 14.1 | 440.0 | 728.3 | 14,203 |
| | Richmond | 917,000 | 1,154,317 | 0.9 | 2.3 | 33.7 | 78.2 | N/A |
| | Oklahoma City | 1,007,000 | 1,144,327 | 0.1 | 0.6 | 6.0 | 27.7 | N/A |
| | Rochester | 1,090,000 | 1,041,499 | 10.2 | 10.9 | 370.2 | 372.0 | 22.422 |
| | Salt Lake City | 1,178,000 | 1,018,826 | 11.5 | 20.6 | 408.3 | 521.5 | 18,664 |
| | Grand Rapids | 985,000 | 767,539 | 0.1 | 0.3 | N/A | 9.0 | N/A |
| | Greensboro-Winston Salem | 1,107,000 | 667,542 | 0.9 | 4.8 | 32.9 | 141.5 | N/A |
| | **AVERAGE** | **1,072,938** | **1,176,703** | **5.9** | **9.1** | **173.2** | **260.7** | **16,452** |

*1994 data were not available.
*Source:* Compiled from the RaDiUS data set. Courtesy of RAND Corporation.

The point of this exercise is twofold. First, it suggests that the traditional things state and local governments have been doing to develop their economies—notably, providing infrastructure and location incentives—are necessary but not sufficient to compete in the twenty-first century. Those places with concentrations of knowledge resources are moving ahead; those without are falling behind. Second, knowledge resources can be created as a matter of policy; indeed, that type of government intervention can be justified, as is shown in the next section. These conclusions apply not only in the United States, but also in Europe and increasingly in Asia.

## RATIONALES FOR GOVERNMENT INTERVENTION

Implicit in the foregoing discussion were rationales for government involvement in local (regional) economic development. The justifications are a combination of market failure, equity, and efficiency—all related to the inability of the unfettered market to deliver the outcomes shown at the top of figure 6.1. In practice, the case for government action includes the following (which are not necessarily mutually exclusive), which go beyond simple textbook rationales (they can be contested, and often are by libertarian groups):

- *Capital barriers can preclude a critical level of infrastructure.* This is true in most places, but certainly in poor regions. The physical infrastructure needed to support growth and development is lumpy. There are economies of scale in its provision, and because it is long-lived, equity considerations require its costs to be spread over time. The number of future users and their median incomes may dwindle, requiring a subsidy. Or the initial cost to provide a level of service adequate for health and safety may be beyond the means of the users.
- *The market may not value economic "transformation" adequately.* Economists who have studied the rapid development of the Asian dragons and tigers note the massive investments made by central government, building entire science cities, universities, and other research facilities; investing in transportation and communications infrastructure, including high-speed rail and large airports; and luring expatriates back from the west (see World Bank 1993). That has enabled economies like Taiwan, Singapore, and Korea to leapfrog ahead, moving up the economic development trajectory in figure 6.2 quite rapidly. There is no market mechanism for that type of progress.
- *Economic development is a merit good and is associated with cross-border flows.* Some of the inputs used to achieve economic development (the

noun) can be mobile. Trained workers and educated students can move to jurisdictions different from where they were trained and educated, and students from elsewhere can attend local colleges. This type of externality warrants government action.

- *As trade barriers are lifted, unfettered global competition may overwhelm indigenous industries.* In the short term, the government can play a central role in supporting industries that are newly opened to competition while retraining workers who are forced out of the sector. Over the long term, the government's role shifts to become more promotional, identifying local sectors with global competitive advantage and bolstering their growth, and more managerial, monitoring trade partners and foreign corporations to ensure a fair playing field for the local private sector.

- *Economic development is a "public purpose," so that government involvement to achieve social benefit is justified.* The U.S. Constitution identifies the promotion of health, safety, and welfare as the raison d'être of government. That has been used to justify public provision of environmental infrastructure, occupational safety and health regulation, and food and drug oversight, for example. General welfare also has been claimed as a basis for "takings" under eminent domain, where the good of the many are weighed against the sanctity of individual property rights. The legal challenges to the government's role in economic development mentioned earlier revolve around whether economic development is to be regarded as essential for the public good. So far it has been.

- *Strategic investment can be efficient, by returning more than itself in benefits.* There is such a focus on "multipliers" in economic development because, in principle, a value greater than one passes the benefit-cost test of efficiency.

## CONCLUSIONS AND IMPLICATIONS FOR POLICY

This chapter summarizes the sense of the literature about the role of government in local (regional) economic development, focusing mostly on the United States and using examples from North Carolina. But the lessons are more broadly applicable. The main take-aways are the following: (1) economic development is so entrenched as an activity of government that there is little debate about its legitimacy; (2) all levels of government have been involved in economic development, but the balance of responsibility and types of intervention have changed over the course of history; (3) in the knowledge economy of the twenty-first century, traditional types of intervention (providing water, sewers, and roads, or even conventional tax incentives, for example) may not be enough for lagging regions to compete—attention needs to be focused on the development of knowledge infrastructure that allows regions to attract R&D dollars and become more innovative; and (4) several "stylized" rationales for government intervention can be applied to the activities observed.

The third of these observations has considerable import for policy making. Unlike the presence of a deep-water seaport, proximity to natural resources, or accessibility to markets, for example, largely "natural advantages" that accounted for the growth of America's largest cities through the twentieth century, the presence of universities, research centers, and cultural amenities can be enhanced anywhere. The Research Triangle Region of North Carolina, the Huntsville-Birmingham corridor, and the Daejon region in Korea, to name just three of many examples, were economic backwaters at one time but have become successful high-tech regions through strategic action. Those actions can be justified by several of the arguments listed above, including their ability to be "transformational," and to generate net welfare benefits.

## REFERENCES

Bradshaw, M. J. 1992. *The Appalachian Regional Commission: Twenty-five years of government policy.* Lexington: University Press of Kentucky.

Brunori, D. 2001. *State tax policy: A political perspective.* Washington, DC: Urban Institute Press.

Chandler, W. U. 1984. *The myth of TVA: Conservation and development in the Tennessee Valley, 1933–1983.* Cambridge, MA: Ballinger.

Chi, K. S. 1989. *The states and business incentives: An inventory of tax and financial incentive programs.* Lexington, KY: Council of State Governments, Division of Policy Analysis Services.

Chi, K. S., and D. J. Hofmann. 2000. *State business incentives: Trends and options for the future.* Lexington, KY: Council of State Governments.

Coenen, D. T. 1998. Business subsidies and the dormant Commerce Clause. *Yale Law Journal* 107(4):965–1053.

Coenen, D. T., and W. Hellerstein. 1996. Commerce Clause restraints on state business development incentives. *Cornell Law Review* 81(May):789–878.

———. 1997. Suspect linkage: The interplay of state taxing and spending measures in the application of constitutional antidiscrimination rules. *Michigan Law Review* 95(7):2167–2233.

Cooke, P., M. Gomez Uranga, and G. Etxebarria. 1997. Regional innovation systems: Institutional and organisational dimensions. *Research Policy* 26(4–5):475–491.

*Daimler Chrysler Corporation, et al., petitioners, v. Charlotte Cuno, et al., and William H. Wilkens, Tax Commissioner for the State of Ohio, et al., petitioner, v. Charlotte Cuno, et al.,* 547 US ___ (2006), Nos. 04-1704 and 14-1724.

Fisher, P., and A. Peters. 1996. Taxes, incentives and competition for investment. *The Region* (Federal Reserve Bank of Minneapolis) 10(2):52–57.

Florida, R. 2003. *The rise of the creative class: And how it's transforming work, leisure, community and everyday life*. New York: Basic Books.

Frug, G. E., R. Ford, and D. Barron. 2001. *Local government law*, 3rd ed., 139–158. Eagan, MN: West.

Garcia-Mila, T., and T. McGuire. 2002. Tax incentives and the city. In *Brookings-Wharton Papers on Urban Affairs*. J. R. Pack and W. G. Gale, eds., 95–114. Washington, DC: Brookings Institution Press.

Glaeser, E. L. 2001. The economics of location-based tax incentives. Discussion Paper No. 1932. Cambridge, MA: Harvard Institute of Economic Research.

Greenstone, M., and E. Moretti. 2004. Bidding for industrial plants: Does winning a "million dollar plant" increase welfare? Working Paper No. 04-39. Cambridge, MA: MIT Department of Economics.

*Kelo et al. v. City of New London et al.*, 545 U.S. 469 (2005).

Luger, M. I. 1984. Tax incentives as industrial and urban policy. In *Sunbelt-frostbelt: Urban development and regional restructuring*. W. Tabb and L. Sawers, eds., 201–234. New York: Oxford University Press.

———. 1987. State subsidies for industrial development: Program mix and policy effectiveness. In *Perspectives on local public finance and public policy*. J. M. Quigley, ed., 29–61. Greenwich, CT: JAI Press.

———. 1993. Technology development programs, intergovernmental relations and balanced regional growth. In *Comparisons of urban economic development in the U.S. and western Europe*. A. A. Summers and L. Sen, eds., 493–529. Washington, DC: Urban Institute Press.

———. 2001. Assessment of the William S. Lee Tax Act for the North Carolina Department of Commerce (July).

———. 2005. Information and communications technology and the places left behind. Working paper. Chapel Hill: University of North Carolina, Center for Competitive Economies.

Luger, M. I., and S. Bae. 2005. The economic effects of business tax incentives: The case of North Carolina. *Economic Development Quarterly* 11(19):327–345.

Luger, M. I., and L. Stewart. 2003. *Improving North Carolina's economic development delivery system*. Published for the North Carolina General Assembly (March).

Lynch, R. G. 1996. The effectiveness of state and local tax cuts and incentives: A review of the literature. *State Tax Notes* (September).

*Maready v. City of Winston-Salem*, 342 NC 708, 467 S.E. 2d 615, 620 (1996).

Markusen, A., P. Hall, S. Campbell, and S. Deitrick. 1991. *The rise of the gunbelt*. New York: Oxford University Press.

McDowell, G. R. 1995. Some communities are successful, others are not: Toward an institutional framework for understanding the reasons why. In *Rural development strategies*. D. W. Sears and J. N. Reid, eds, 269–281. Chicago: Nelson-Hall.

Osborne, D. 1988. *Laboratories of democracy*. Boston: Harvard Business School Press.

Reich, R. B., and I. C. Magaziner. 1982. *Minding America's business: The decline and rise of the American economy.* New York: Harcourt Brace Jovanovich.

Rhyne, C. S. 1980. *The law of local government operations.* Washington, DC: Law of Local Government Operations Project.

Schultz, D. F. 2004. Big projects in America. Research report from the Infrastructure Technology Institute, Northwestern University, Evanston, IL.

Tabellini, G. 2005. The role of the state in economic development. *Kyklos* 58(2): 283–303.

Thomas, K. P. 2000. *Competing for capital: Europe and North America in a global era.* Washington, DC: Georgetown University Press.

World Bank. 1993. *The East Asian miracle: Economic growth and public policy.* New York: Oxford University Press.

# Institutional Reform

# 7

# Property Valuation in the Twenty-First Century

## Peter F. Colwell and Joseph W. Trefzger

V*aluation* is the term generally used for the process of estimating some measure of the economic worth of an asset, particularly real estate. While the practice of valuation always has drawn on technology— especially the technology of finance and, more recently, econometrics—it is based, more fundamentally, on ideas regarding what notions of economic worth are being estimated. Technology has been evolving, of course, but the ideas are evolving as well. To a great degree, it is possible to predict the direction of future stages in the evolution of real estate valuation ideas based on recent academic work, because the world of real estate valuation practice— appraisal and assessment—traditionally has lagged behind the academic literature by a few generations. The valuation technology used by practitioners in the twenty-first century also is likely to be largely dependent on the valuation technology that has been developed by academics over the last several decades of the twentieth century. Predicting the nature of future developments in valuation ideas and technology is useful not only for helping practitioners anticipate the skills they will need to master, but also for helping a wider audience to better understand the great public issues related to real estate valuation.

The authors thank Carolyn Dehring, Max Kummerow, Tzu-Chin Lin, and Henry Munneke for their comments. All errors, omissions, and unfortunate inclusions are the responsibility of the authors.

## VALUATION TECHNOLOGY

The technology applied in real estate valuation practice often is subsumed under the three approaches to valuation traditionally identified by appraisers: the market comparison, income, and cost approaches. The twentieth century was characterized by some movement at the practitioner level from traditional adjustment grids to regression analysis within the market comparison approach. The income approach actually experienced a narrowed array of choices during the twentieth century. The cost approach, on the other hand, changed little; it remains rather primitive even today, and not much of consequence seems to be afoot that would bring about immediate changes.

### The Market Comparison Approach

Most of the academic effort in creating new valuation technology has focused on the market comparison approach.

*Adjustment Grids.* As in so many areas of human endeavor, the growth in computing power in the second half of the twentieth century was both the enabling force and the driving force behind the movement from the appraisal industry's longtime standard market comparison technique, the adjustment grid, to other methods. Of course, increased computing power also allowed the grids to be adjusted in a more automated fashion, but primitive equipment has never been the main problem with the technique. One central conceptual problem associated with adjustment grids is reconciliation: producing a single, defensible point estimate from individual estimates related to a small number of comparable sales (Colwell, Cannaday, and Wu 1984).

Another conceptual problem is the estimation of adjustment factors (Colwell, Cannaday, and Wu 1983). While it can be argued that the most supportable adjustment factors are the coefficients produced in a regression analysis, that view does not address the problem for a practitioner whose tool kit is limited to matched pairs. It is fortunate that matched pairs can be elevated to contemporary statistical standards through the use of nonparametric tests of hypotheses and yet can be made simple enough for application by most practitioners through the availability of preset spreadsheet templates.[1]

Remaining problems with adjustment grids—such as *collinearity* (the tendency of seemingly separate value determinants to be related, as when larger homes in a particular market generally have been built with better-quality

---

[1] Work on this problem is at an early stage. Contact Peter Colwell (pcolwell@uiuc.edu) or Bruce Vanderporten (bvander@luc.edu) for details.

materials and workmanship) and *excluded variables* (the inadvertent failure to recognize important value-determining features within a regression model, as when an analyst is unaware that houses built by a particular contractor consistently sell for higher prices in the affected locality)—are those that vex econometricians in other applications as well.

Adjustment grids do have one primary advantage over much of the academic valuation work of the twentieth century. With their focus on a few comparable sales in close proximity to the subject property, they are useful in producing reasonable predictions of value. However, they effectively obscure the reasons for value differentials across neighborhoods. Of course, if there are sufficient comparables within neighborhoods to allow for the use of adjustment grids, analysts who wish only to estimate specific properties' values find it unnecessary to estimate or understand the sources of value differences across neighborhoods.

*Hedonic Regression.* Regression analysis (hedonics) represents the first major property valuation technology transferred from academics to practitioners (Colwell and Dilmore 1999). Academics began using regression analysis, in fact, in the 1920s. An auto industry analyst gave the technology the name *hedonics* in the 1930s, to convey the idea that value relates to features that provide the user of an item with pleasure or utility, borrowing from a psychological term involving pleasant states of mind. Although hedonics has not become widely adopted yet within the appraisal profession, its use has moved beyond such great pioneering practitioners as Gene Dilmore. Regression has found a place among many more private appraisers of the next generation, and also among some important public-sector jurisdictions where assessment officials use regressions in mass appraisals for ad valorem tax assessments. The cost of regression analysis programs is extremely low (e.g., it is a feature within Microsoft Excel), so it is available to virtually any valuation practitioner who would care to use it.

By the end of the twentieth century, academics had moved well beyond straightforward regression analysis, as the size of available data sets grew along with computing power. The increasing availability of relatively large sets of sales data has been instrumental, along with increased computing power, in facilitating appraisers' movement toward the use of hedonics. However, a problem with basing a regression analysis on a large data set is that a single pricing model is unlikely to have relevance over a geographical area sufficiently wide to provide a substantial quantity of observations. The analysis might produce positive *spatial autocorrelation*, meaning that similar values would be attributed to properties simply because they are located "near" each other. Alternative computational solutions to this problem reflect, to some extent, deeply held points of view on the merits of improved technical response to error terms versus improved theoretical understanding: Is the solution one of better handling the part of value that remains unexplained by the regression, or one of developing spatial models that provide richer explanations of variations in value?

One solution is to take spatial modeling much more seriously. The econometrician/appraiser of the future may look to more sophisticated variables that represent the abstract characteristics of important spatial phenomena. Neighborhoods might be better represented by the population characteristics of the residents (Colwell and Munneke 2006), or there might be price (i.e., boundary) effects at the edges of neighborhoods. There could be local pimples and pocks on the value surface that reflect minor shopping, work, or industrial centers (i.e., *positive* spatial autocorrelation, as noted above, in which high values are associated with other high values) (Colwell and Munneke 1997); or the price surface could exhibit scallops—alternating high and low values—within certain types of blocks where corner lots might be more or less valuable than interior lots (i.e., *negative* spatial autocorrelation, in which lower values are found close to high values). These features can be modeled without disruptions to the entire value surface.

Similarly, the impact of odd linear features, such as a railroad crossing the cityscape, can be modeled. Other examples include limited-access highways and important surface features such as streets, lakefronts, and rivers. Those features can be handled like one-dimensional versions of the two-dimensional pimples and pocks described in the previous paragraph.

The value *gradient*, the function that describes how changes in land value relate to movement away from the central business district (CBD) center or other important location, can be modeled flexibly so that the parameter estimate depends on direction, and not merely on distance. Including both distance and direction accommodates the star-shaped city so frequently theorized by early economists, illustrated in textbooks, and observed in many modern urban areas but infrequently found in the models of modern empirical researchers (Colwell and Munneke forthcoming). Those sorts of enhancements to empirical models are not difficult to make, so once they have been demonstrated—by academics or by practitioners—it is reasonable to expect that they will find their way into a broad range of valuation tools over time.

A radically different kind of solution is to use some type of mechanistic approach to estimating property values. Mechanistic approaches include spatial autocorrelation schemes, kernel methods, and splines, such as piecewise parabolic multiple regression analysis. If those approaches were to lead researchers away from carefully modeling the true spatial relationships, their adherents could be considered members of cults of ignorance. Nevertheless, there is legitimacy in the views that those approaches represent. First, there is beauty in a cult of ignorance if a simple prediction of individual property selling prices, and not a fuller explanation of underlying relationships, is the only goal. Second, new phenomena (i.e., blips in the value function appearing in space where they were not anticipated) may be observed in the results of those methods.

Those who favor spatial autocorrelation schemes attempt to adjust for the positive spatial autocorrelation often found in property sales data. Making the needed adjustments requires that the analyst weight observations based on some proximity measure, like geographical distance. The technique is referred to by its proponents, immodestly, as spatial econometrics. It addresses the error of assuming that the value function is constant across space; its kinship to the traditional adjustment grid is obvious where comparables are weighted to produce a point estimate of value for the subject property (Dubin, Pace, and Thibodeau 1999). Unfortunately, its application requires some ready measure of comparability, such as simple distance, without regard to the comparable's direction from the subject property.

Using distance alone is wrongheaded, but the problem certainly will be corrected in the near future—the next decade or so. The correction will make use, no doubt, of the notion that many value anomalies in the urban setting are linear: best modeled not as hills or craters in the value surface, but as ridges or valleys. That is, similar pricing effects are often found along roads, rivers, or lakes, with profound differences from values of otherwise similar properties a block or two away. So looking only at distance from an important reference point does a poor job of explaining value differences. Distance in a particular direction, such as along the same road or even on the same side of the road as the subject property, may do much better. Addressing the central deficiency of this solution to the problem (treating value models as constant across space) may prove to be relatively simple. A rich solution may be one that incorporates both improved modeling and adjustments for spatial autocorrelation.

Still another solution is to use a kernel, semi-parametric technique referred to as LOWESS, an acronym for LOcally Weighted regrESSion (McMillen 1996). This sort of application is much like the previous solution, in that it allows for a variable pricing model. But it does so based on the crude assumption that distance from a subject property (actually, distance from a point in space) is what determines comparability; a function such as the tricube is used in weighting the sales surrounding the subject. Imagine a circular window of data that is centered geographically on each prediction or subject property. A separate regression is run for each such window. For a

Gaussian kernel (i.e., weighting based on the normal density function), all the data are used for each regression. The LOWESS technology produces a value estimate for each point on which a regression is run. More than likely, those points are on a spatial grid. LOWESS does not produce a value surface. The reader who sees that the estimated points have been connected to construct a surface should realize that there is no econometric justification for that surface to exist. It is always possible to run more and more regressions in order to make the spatial grid finer and finer, and in the limit, there is a smooth surface.[2] However, questions arise regarding the informational content obtained from, say, more regressions than data points.

Finally, there is a semi-parametric solution that allows for the entire data set to be utilized in one regression, but that solution fails to address the possibility that the parametric coefficients on the nonspatial variables might vary across space (of course, restraint in the area of coverage can reduce that problem). This solution, called piecewise parabolic regression, is essentially a simple spline (Colwell 1998; Colwell and Munneke 2003). It utilizes a notion called barycentric coordinates to locate the data points within the squares of a spatial grid. That technique legitimately produces a value surface that is continuous: kinked at the grid lines but smooth (i.e., differentiable) within the grid lines (i.e., the iso-value curves are hyperbolic, whereas vertical sections are parabolic).

*Repeat Sales Analysis.* Academics and practitioners mean rather different things when referring to the analysis of repeat sales. To practitioners, repeat sales analysis involves taking differences or ratios for the purpose of estimating appreciation in value relative to an initial date or condition. According to traditional textbook presentations, for example, a house selling in December 2007 for 10 percent more than the seller paid in December 2005 provides evidence that local market values have been rising by about 5 percent per year; a higher resale price subsequent to major renovations provides evidence of the market value of the improvements made. To academics, repeat sales analysis is a regression technique in which the ratio of prices is the dependent variable (in contrast to hedonic analysis, in which the price, or perhaps the logarithm of price, is the dependent variable). The initial academic use of repeat sales analysis was to develop price indexes through time; however, the technique can be hybridized with hedonics to reveal changes in spatial

---

[2]The technique described is called a smoother, because there generally is little effort to model space within each data window. The result is that extreme values are eliminated, an undesirable outcome. The technique is not a smoother in the sense of producing a smooth value surface, except in the limit.

relationships, such as the introduction of new positive or negative externality sources (Case et al. 2006). The point of repeat sales technology is that inferences can be drawn when sales data omit important property attributes, if there are sufficient numbers of repeat sales and if the repeat sales properly represent the population of interest.

*Geographic Information Systems.* There are valuation applications that are not part of the econometric tradition. Geographical information systems (GIS) may contain some of those applications. Of course, those systems are perfectly fine spatial databases, but they may be pushed beyond their true capabilities. They may have features that draw maps of value (e.g., iso-value maps or 3D-value maps) based on data points in space. Since those features are black boxes, it must be assumed that the systems' ability to produce surfaces from point data is based on some type of averaging routine, but not on econometrics. If that assumption is correct, professional users of GIS should be wary of the systems' seemingly amazing features. Instead, it is best to use GIS for its database features, and to stick with standard econometrics for the analysis.

Any map of value needs to be based on a program that holds a lot of property features constant, if it is to be useful in any practical sense. For example, property improvements might be held constant for some purposes. Holding improvements constant leads toward the ability to map land value. However, unless the analyst realizes that land value is a nonlinear function of parcel size and thus holds size constant as well, the result is useless. On the other hand, if the GIS is provided with econometrically estimated land values for a constant-sized parcel, the system can produce credible maps, with appropriate caveats for the interpolation of values between actual points at which there are estimated values. It is even better to estimate a value surface econometrically and represent that surface graphically[3] than to estimate discrete points and then provide some mysterious interpolation between the points to allow for graphical representations.

*Contingent Valuation.* Contingent valuation (CV) has been gaining adherents, particularly among those who would estimate the value of environmental features. CV analysis is based on survey research: asking respondents hypothetical questions, such as "What would you require as a discount if you were to purchase property that is impacted by (insert some horrible condition

---

[3]Microsoft Excel actually is relatively good at producing this graphical representation, although there are peculiarities, notably the program's implicit assumption that the value surface is composed of triangular planes.

here)?" This technique not only is subject to all the common criticisms of surveys, but in addition is subject to a fundamental criticism from neoclassical economics: that the survey addresses only the demand side of the market. It does not reflect the market's supply side; that is, it does not reveal the frequency with which the horrible condition is found within the region surveyed (Colwell and Trefzger 2005). For example, if 70 of 100 potential buyers would insist on paying prices lower than they would pay for otherwise similar property unaffected by the adverse condition, but only 20 of the 60 available local properties suffered from the condition, the expectation should be that the affected properties would be purchased by 20 of the 30 buyers not requiring discounts. Their outbidding of those who were troubled by the condition would lead to sale prices not substantially discounted from those expected for unaffected parcels.

Thus, the analyst cannot determine the horrible condition's pricing effect by the survey alone; no manipulation of the survey results can lead, by itself, to any conclusion regarding expected prices in market transactions. No averages or more sophisticated statistics, no charts—nothing will produce a legitimate estimate of the impact on expected prices unless information about supply is simultaneously incorporated with the results of the survey. Because this simple principle should not be difficult to communicate, there is reason to hope that the future will hold more sensible uses of contingent valuation than have been seen in the past.

## The Income Approach

Early in the twentieth century, appraisers used a wide range of income approach applications (Colwell and Cannaday 1981a, 1981b, 1981c), but by the century's end those applications had narrowed to gross income multipliers, net income multipliers (direct capitalization), and detailed pro forma discounted cash flow analysis (manual, and later electronic, spreadsheets with income, expense, net present value, and internal rate of return calculations). Multiplier applications, in which value is estimated as a function of a single year's income (gross income for gross income multiplier [GIM] analysis, net income for direct capitalization), continue to be important to valuation practitioners. However, academics never really have bonded to the use of multipliers, and, as a result, practitioners have not moved beyond determining multipliers by computing averages. It should have been recognized that the relationship between a property's value and its ability to generate a given gross or net income is instead one that can, and should, be estimated with conventional econometric techniques (Colwell and Sirmans 1980). That oversight is another problem that is likely to be remedied in the near future.

The reduced cost of computing power has tremendously influenced the nature of the income approach. The numerous income approach applications that were used by appraisers during much of the previous century emerged primarily to keep computing costs in check. They were based on various simplifying assumptions to make the valuation equation more compact, thereby reducing the need for computation. One such assumption holds that buildings or other capital improvements will produce constant annual income streams during their useful lives, and when an improvement's useful life comes to an implicitly assumed abrupt end, the income immediately goes to zero (because with no remaining life for the improvements, the property is worth the land value only). This "one-hoss-shay" assumption (so named from an Oliver Wendell Holmes poem about a buggy that provides 100 years of reliable service and then immediately falls apart), which is familiar to economists who are capital theorists, was commonly included in simplified applications of the income approach. Fortunately, the need for that sort of simplifying assumption was eliminated by the advent of electronic spreadsheets. It is no longer especially helpful to find some clever, or not-so-clever, means of making a single equation easier to compute. The computer's brute computational force easily can produce a present value or rate of return estimate for any projected stream of future cash flows.

The interesting question regarding computational aspects of the income approach is whether all the evolution that is going to be seen has been seen. The answer is that it *probably* has not. There is an intended play on words here; future developments in pro forma analysis may be probabilistic. A natural extension of the use of spreadsheets is to want to see them become animated, to employ them in exploring the implications of alternate futures. Monte Carlo simulation allows for the analysis of different states of the world by incorporating one or more stochastic processes. For example, if a random walk were incorporated into the projected stream of income or expenses (or some other parameter, like the vacancy rate), each period for which the model is run would show the magnitude increasing or decreasing by some amount, with, say, a 50 percent chance of each. Averaging the results of a very large number of runs provides a more reliable estimate of value than could any traditional pro forma analysis based on a single set of assumed parameter magnitudes.

The analyst could enhance a Monte Carlo analysis with a Wiener process, in which some important variable would change through time by moving, each period, according to a particular probability distribution. Brownian motion is a more elaborate process, in which the analyst allows a drift term to be added to the Wiener process. Of course, a question that must be addressed is how the analyst chooses the distributions. The answer may be through surveying experts in the market. An especially compelling survey question would involve the greatest, the most common, and the smallest year-to-year change in a relevant variable that the expert has observed during his or her years of experience. Those three magnitudes can become the parameters of a triangular probability distribution, one that resonates with many practitioners. Through an averaging of repeated simulations of the future, the Monte Carlo analysis can produce estimates of the expected value and standard deviation of a property's likely selling price and internal rate of return, along with estimates of such conditions as the probability of default on a mortgage loan. Since there are commercial add-ins for Excel that offer Monte Carlo capability (e.g., @RISK and Crystal Ball), incorporating simulation analysis into appraisals has become a fairly simple matter.

While this type of attention to quantitative techniques could put the income approach on a more secure computational footing, some observers would contend that what the approach needs instead is simplification through a theoretical reexamination (Colwell and Cannaday 1986). For example, constraints imposed by market participants and regulators may limit value in ways not recognized by those who would view more computation, in an era of declining computing costs, as a perfect substitute for thinking.

## The Cost Approach

Cost approach applications are built on three important components: building cost, land value, and depreciation. Weaknesses exist in our current abilities to handle each of the three. Practitioners continue to deal with depreciation often through some form of rule of thumb; and when using the cost approach, they frequently give short shrift to land valuation. Academics generally have steered clear of the cost approach almost entirely, as if it were an unwelcome carryover from classical economics in the neoclassical age.

Because all three cost approach components have been insufficiently studied, they are subjects that are ripe for innovation. But innovation may not come.

*Building Cost.* Appraisers often compute estimated building costs by referring to, or at least double-checking with, commercially available cost manuals. Despite their widespread use, however, those manuals have not been critically reviewed by independent researchers intent on explaining the assumptions—which might be highly questionable—incorporated in the figures presented. For example, what happens to the cost estimate as square footage is increased and quality is held constant, or as square footage is increased and quality is increased, or as a constant square footage is spread over one story rather than two? How reliable are the local market area adjustment factors? Because appraisers often find talking with contractors more enlightening than using cost manuals, an important question that academics might address is whether the analysis of local builders' invoice data is a more theoretically supportable way to estimate construction costs than the seemingly more scientific use of cost manuals (Colwell and Marshall 2002).

*Land Value.* Valuation practitioners tend to estimate land value using rules of thumb, such as price per square foot or per acre. Today academics know, however, what the savviest practitioners knew a century ago: that the assumptions underlying such rules are often completely wrong (Colwell and Sirmans 1993; Colwell and Scheu 1994). Value is not likely to be proportional to land area; for example, a residential lot with 50 feet of frontage and 600 feet of depth is not likely to sell for the same price as a nearby lot with 150 feet of frontage and 200 feet of depth. This lack of proportionality may be one of the most stable relationships observed in connection with land values, yet today many appraisers fail to recognize it—or at least to incorporate it in their work.

A number of findings from academic research deserve to be incorporated into appraisal practitioners' tool kits for valuing land. First among these findings is the importance of value gradients; Colwell and Munneke (1997) provide a review of the related literature.[4] Although academic research has focused on gradients that are region wide, some focus on subregional gradients is also worthy (Colwell, Dehring, and Lash 2000; Colwell, Gujral, and Coley 1985; Colwell, Munneke, and Trefzger 1998). The importance of relative lot size within a neighborhood, an idea that relates to the public good aspect of private lots, is another significant development (Colwell and Asabere 1985). Finally, variation in nonlinear pricing of land across an identified market may indicate whether assembly (creating one large parcel from smaller existing parcels) or subdivision (creating many smaller parcels from one large existing parcel) is land developers' more typical activity (Colwell and Munneke 1999).

*Depreciation.* More fully explaining depreciation is an important key to developing coherence in the cost approach. Unfortunately, not much theoretical work has been done toward helping academics and practitioners understand depreciation (Colwell, Kinnard, and Beron 2003; Colwell and Ramsland 2003). For example, it is not unusual for a depreciation model to

---

[4]In a subsequent work the authors show how to allow gradients to vary by direction; see Colwell and Munneke (forthcoming).

treat an asset as losing value continuously over a presumed useful life, whereas the reality may be that the emergence of conditions that cause value losses, and the undertaking of cures to address those conditions, are lumpy in terms of their timing and severity. Finding a valid way to quantify that lumpiness would have a great impact on the estimation of depreciation schedules. If an analyst knew the prices at which a sample of properties recently had sold, and possessed reliable estimates of land values and the current cost of constructing improvements of the type in question, computing actual depreciation for the sold properties would be simple. The next step would be developing a regression model to explain the variation in depreciation based on relevant property attributes known to the investigator. Of course, as always in the use of regression analysis, there would be concerns over modeling and data problems, but the results would be much more defensible than standard, straight-line age/life applications are. Depreciation is ultimately an empirical question, a market phenomenon that should be estimated based on some form of market comparison.

## Reconciliation of Approaches to Value

Practitioners traditionally have devoted considerable time and thought to reconciling their findings from the three valuation approaches into a single value estimate. There is a high probability that future appraisers, on the other hand, will feel less driven to reconcile the various approaches to value. The reason is that appraisers are not likely to rely on multiple valuation approaches in the future. After all, if the approaches are used correctly, each tends to be applicable to a particular context, and in some cases there is little crossover.

The market comparison approach has the widest applicability; it is useful in valuing residential, commercial, industrial, and agricultural property and in applications involving both the type of property that typically would be occupied by its owner and the type that is rented to tenants. It is used most commonly when data on property attributes are available. An appraiser who lacks sufficient knowledge of property attributes can make effective use of repeat sales analysis, as long as there have been a sufficient number of repeat sales of a relevant type. Hybrid methods can infuse property attributes, especially changes in location such as the appearance of an externality, into repeat sales analysis when information on property attributes is scarce but not totally unavailable.

The income approach is applicable only to property of a type that is purchased primarily for its ability to generate income. Otherwise, it can lead to biased results. For example, it will produce too low a value estimate systematically when used in estimating the value of a single-family residential property in a neighborhood where houses seldom are rented because landlords in that area have lost the bidding wars to owner-occupants who value housing there more. The beauty of the income approach is that its use does not require much data on physical property attributes, as long as the appraiser has identified a relationship between value and a measure of income for the applicable type of property in the applicable market area.

However, making effective use of the income approach is increasingly dependent on more complete and accurate income and expense information. Long gone are the days when appraisers could get away with the same assumption of vacancy rate or expense ratio across their many income property appraisals. The application of gross income multipliers will require, in the future, econometric estimation since, for example, GIMs vary systematically with age (a newer rental property might be expected to generate its income stream for longer than a property with older improvements, such that the newer income property's GIM would be higher). At the same time, GIMs tend to decline systematically as gross income increases, presumably reflecting higher expense ratios incurred in maintaining larger properties. It is meaningful to relate value to a gross income measure, of course, only if it can be assumed that all similarly classified properties have the same expense ratios; the GIM, therefore, is a fairly blunt instrument. Yet appraisers using the slightly more surgical net income multiplier (direct capitalization) technique also will have to meet tougher standards, as more complete data and better data management tools force them to limit their use of a given capitalization rate to properties that meet increasingly stringent tests of comparability.

The cost approach is useful primarily for setting an upper bound on the value of property with newly constructed improvements. It is a competitor of the market comparison approach when data include property attributes, such that depreciation can be meaningfully estimated. (Why some tout the cost approach as the preferred method for valuing specialized or infrequently sold property types—situations in which estimating depreciation is especially difficult—remains a mystery.) However, it is not likely that the cost approach will fare well in the competition, since it is based on more indirect comparisons than the market comparison approach is.

## VALUATION IDEAS

The ideas that underlie the need for estimating real estate value are profound. Takings, taxation, and transitions are the big three; they are reasons for valuation that provoke great public controversy. The outrage felt by most citizens when land is taken for public "purposes" rather than direct public uses may spill over into such related areas as how just compensation is conceived of and estimated, as well as whether more restrictive zoning regulations require compensation. Property taxation is a topic that will continue to generate controversy. Caps on permitted annual increases in assessed values create impediments to the transfer of real estate ownership that gum up the national labor market. Assessment advantages provided to farmland interfere with our rural to urban land use transitions, while overzoning in favor of certain land uses (e.g., residential zones and exclusive industrial zones) distorts relative land values and the balance of land uses.

## Takings

The taking of property rights, which governmental units complete under their eminent domain power to condemn privately owned real estate, rocketed into the public consciousness recently with the famous case of *Kelo v. City of New London*. In that case a Connecticut municipal authority condemned homes in a nonblighted area as part of a plan to promote private economic development in the city. The U.S. Supreme Court's support of the takings in its *Kelo* ruling provides the natural conclusion to the decades-earlier *Poletown Neighborhood Council v. City of Detroit* case, in which the Michigan supreme court in 1981 affirmed Detroit's right to condemn long-time residents' modest houses, business properties, and churches for resale to General Motors for the stated "public purpose" of creating jobs (actually, moving jobs) and strengthening the local property tax base. The *Poletown* ruling rested on a questionable idea, since the city paid substantially more to buy Poletown neighborhood properties than it charged GM for them, and the state supreme court ultimately (and unanimously) reversed the *Poletown* decision in 2004's *County of Wayne v. Hathcock* case. But in the wake of the U.S. Supreme Court's *Kelo* decision, local governments now might appear to be largely unconstrained in their ability to take private property for the express purpose of selling it to another private owner to develop.

Appearances, however, can be deceiving. An important point raised by the high court in *Kelo* is that local jurisdictions have broad takings powers *unless* applicable state or local laws restrict them.[5] Reacting to their own

---

[5]After offering general allusions to the power of state legislatures and judges, the Court majority concludes its *Kelo* opinion with a paragraph that includes the passage "nothing in our opinion precludes any State from placing further restrictions on its exercise of the takings power. Indeed, many States already impose 'public use' requirements that are stricter than the federal baseline."

newfound powers, and to outrage expressed by large numbers of citizens, some officials at U.S. state and local levels have undertaken aggressive measures. Supreme courts in some states (notably Michigan and Ohio) have found the taking of private land for a mere public "purpose" to be unconstitutional. In addition, legislatures in a number of states (including Illinois) have begun passing statutes that close down municipalities' option to take property for economic reasons alone, while ordinances proposed in some communities would prohibit the acquisition of property under eminent domain unless supermajorities of local councils voted in support. Direct voter initiatives on November 2006 ballots in several states (including Arizona, Florida, Georgia, and Michigan) also limited governmental takings powers.[6] The public's outrage might be expected to spill over into such related areas as how "just" compensation is conceived of and estimated.

*The Price of Everything, and the Value of Nothing.* To modify a quote by Oscar Wilde, standard appraisal tools disclose the price of everything and the value of nothing. The point of this modification is that there are value concepts that have been beyond the realm of the appraiser—although limitations imposed on appraisers may have been too constraining in some contexts. One constraint that has the potential for creating trouble is the definition of *just* compensation for eminent domain takings: market value. That definition is something akin to the expected price (some appraisers think in terms of the most probable price) under a particular set of conditions (Colwell 1979). There must be something wrong with that limitation, because almost everyone who has had their property taken has been angry with the compensation. What is wrong is that market value does not fully compensate for what most owners lose in a taking.

Compensation is too low because there is an accompanying *consumer surplus* that currently is not compensable but is a real component of value. Total value for an owner, sometimes called *investment value* in appraisal, is the sum of the expected selling price and the surplus. The total market value plus consumer surplus for all the property in a particular local market is the area under the demand curve for that market. Urban economists who focus on the long run, the open city, imagine that the surplus ultimately is bid away. But that view is erroneous. Consumer surplus for real estate is durable;

---

[6]The passage of Michigan's Proposal 06–4 codifies the state supreme court's *Hathcock* ruling that takings for economic reasons are unconstitutional; see Michigan Initiatives and Referenda (2006). Results of the many November 2006 eminent domain ballot initiatives were covered extensively in the press; see, for example, "Kelo's Revenge: Voters Restrict Eminent Domain" (2006).

it cannot be bid away by identical bidders from other cities. The reason is that the long-lasting surplus, which tends to relate closely to tenure in a given location, is costly to create yet cannot be sold. The basis for the surplus consists largely of advantages such as information and social contracts that emerge through longevity; examples would be trusted relationships with neighbors and local service businesses. It also can be affected by the property's suitability to an owner's unique circumstances, such as special improvements that an owner favors but a typical buyer would not, or proximity to the home of an elderly parent; it also might reflect an owner's sentimental attachment to a property (Trefzger 1995).

Those types of advantages cannot meaningfully be transferred to a buyer when the property is conveyed, so consumer surplus generally does not affect the estimation of compensation owed for takings in U.S. jurisdictions; the surplus above market value typically does not enter the analysis. The idea that it could, though, is not as far-fetched as it once might have seemed. England's "home loss payment" system, which statutorily awards an additional 10 percent of market value when owner-occupants lose their homes to "compulsory purchase" (eminent domain), reflects an attempt to compensate for lost surplus,[7] while France provides for an even more substantive 20 percent premium over market value (Almond and Plummer 1997). Even more compelling is a successful November 2006 Michigan ballot proposition that created a payment standard of *at least* 125 percent of market value for forcible takings in that state.[8]

The Mill Acts in colonial America, often cited as a key point in the history of U.S. takings law, reveal an intention to address, if perhaps indirectly, issues relating to the owner's surplus. Operators of mill ponds, which were the public utilities of the day, were required to pay 150 percent of the market value of the loss when they flooded the land of others. The direct purpose of that sort of compensation requirement was to ensure that there would be a limit on such takings, and to increase the likelihood that property moved from lower- to higher-valued uses. (In addition to the intended improvement in allocative efficiency, that sort of requirement might be used to achieve distributional

---

[7]The Land Compensation Act of 1973 establishes the 10 percent premium as a statutory right. There are, however, ceiling and floor levels adjusted annually for inflation (dispossessed owners could receive premiums of no more than £40,000 and no less than £4,000 in 2006), and even rental tenants displaced by compulsory takings—since they, and not the landlords, are losing their homes—could receive fixed £4,000 payments. See Statutory Instrument 2006.

[8]With the passage of Proposal 06–4, the Michigan state constitution now prevents governmental units from forcing the sale of private property for economic development or tax enhancement purposes, requires those units to meet a high standard of proof if property is said to be taken to eliminate blight, and further requires them to pay dispossessed private owners at least 125 percent of market value. See Michigan Initiatives and Referenda (2006).

justice.) Questions arise in the *Poletown* and *Kelo* cases regarding the possibility that the property did, in fact, move from higher- to lower-valued uses. If the designated buyer would be willing to pay no more than market value, while any existing consumer surplus would cause the current owner to attribute a higher-than-market value to the property, a forced sale under eminent domain would displace a higher-valued use with a lower-valued use.

Because the price someone would willingly pay relates directly to the productive value that could be derived from the purchased item, a condemnation sale priced to include only market value could easily pass ownership to a party that would use it less productively, for individual or commercial benefit, than the displaced owner. Movement from higher- to lower-valued uses therefore is inefficient. An eminent domain system that legally permits public bodies to ignore a private owner's idiosyncratic value determinants thereby leads to an inefficient level of compensation,[9] which in turn could bring about a less-than-optimal investment in physical capital on land, as well as too little investment in social contracts and information.

Imagine an eminent domain compensation schedule that is intended to deal with the kind of consumer surplus described.[10] Suppose that someone who has purchased property within a year of when it is taken is paid 100 percent of the estimated market value (plus a slight premium to compensate for transaction costs such as searching and moving), whereas someone who has held property 10 years or more gets 150 percent of market value (plus the relocation premium). Some kind of schedule of intermediate compensation could fall to owners with more than 1 year but less than 10 years of tenure. Clearly, some dispossessed owners would be overcompensated, because after a tenure of many years changes in their circumstances would have devalued their special information, social contracts, or access to specialized improvements or proximate properties in the given location, such that they might have already considered selling voluntarily despite the expectation of receiving only the "bricks and mortar" value. (Indeed, it typically is when changed circumstances devalue the surplus that an owner puts up a "for sale" sign, advertising a willingness to sell at a market price that excludes the nontransferable surplus.)

Some owners also would be overcompensated or undercompensated by that type of plan based on the size of the premium; the 50 percent figure used for illustrative purposes here is, of course, arbitrary. A more rigorously

---

[9]The literature on the efficiency of compensation abstracts from the existence of a surplus. For a review of that literature, see Trefzger and Colwell (1996).

[10]A system for compensating with a premium above market value, in cases involving a range of public and private incursions on private property rights, is discussed in Colwell (1990).

estimated magnitude might be attributed to particular household or business characteristics through survey research, involving questions such as the percentage premium over market value the respondent would require for willingly selling on the survey date. (It would not be surprising, for example, to see very high premiums required by business owners who had made capital investments to serve specific needs of nearby land users more effectively, or by owners forced to sell land held by their families for many generations.) The analyst would use econometrics to relate the expected premium to the household or business characteristics found.

A system of premiums based on owner attributes would be likely to capture the effects of longevity, and perhaps of special improvements. Of course, because surveys can be fraught with their own problems, an inexpensively administered compensation plan based on an arbitrary premium over market value, such as England's or Michigan's, might be the most practical means of realizing significant improvements over current compensation practice. While this type of plan could not fully prevent the transfer of land to a party that valued it less than the current holder (whose consumer surplus might be far more than the 50 percent or other administered premium over the market value), it would enhance efficiency by ensuring that any transfer would be to a user who at least valued the acquired property substantially more than the marginal (market-value paying) transactor.

***Partial Rights.*** More and more, partial property rights are being conveyed through voluntary or involuntary arrangements. Examples include such real estate interests as conservation easements and pipeline easements. A group concerned with maintaining open space might purchase a conservation easement on a parcel, through which the owner subsequently is prevented from developing the land. It should be intuitively clear that the value of the right to prevent development depends on the likelihood that the land would have been developed in the absence of the easement. In economic terminology, it would be said that a conservation easement's value is based on the value of the owner's implicit option to undertake development: The higher the development option value, the higher the easement value. The value of the development option obviously varies directly with the land's suitability for development (by features such as location and topography).

The value of the right to wait—to monitor changes in the economy and the progression of development in the nearby area—can result in a parcel's highest and best use actually being to remain vacant. Therein lies a dilemma for land markets and communities. For a conservation easement to be highly valuable, it would have to remain operative for a long period of time, perhaps saddling future generations with higher construction, infrastructure, and commuting costs as they must develop around protected locations. Conversely, such an easement lasting for a short number of years might be essentially worthless to the grantee, because even if the easement did not exist, some time would have passed before development occurred.

A coherent use of the eminent domain power is for obtaining pipeline, and other public utility, easements. The reason is that the holdout problem is accentuated when a network of pipes or wires must connect to be valuable. Ordinarily, a pipeline easement is worth considerably less than the fee value of the land burdened by the easement (it should cost less to obtain the right to bury some pipe on a strip of land than to buy the strip outright). Theoretically, the right to run the pipeline *could* be worth more (require a higher payment in an arm's-length transaction) than the fee value if that right substantially disrupted the use of the remainder (i.e., the part of the parcel not affected by the easement). But that circumstance is hard to imagine on a practical level, especially if the pipeline company is responsible for any damages resulting from pipeline accidents. Indeed, a buried pipeline would more likely enhance the remainder's value through the resulting open space. If a holdout could demand an excessive price for granting the pipeline company an easement on a parcel that had become strategically critical solely because of the pipeline company's earlier actions, the result would be to prevent property rights from moving to a truly higher-valued use. The primary reason for eminent domain is to address this type of holdout situation, in which public officials fear that the community will see too little in public capital improvements if each investment a public utility makes merely raises the expected cost of obtaining additional needed land.

## Taxation

Property taxation is a subject that will continue to generate controversy. Issues such as caps on assessments will have to be addressed. Most jurisdictions in the United States have graded taxation systems, under which land is taxed at lower rates than buildings, resulting primarily from attempts to favor farmland—a sort of anti-Georgist sentiment that should be corrected, unless the intention is to continue impeding both investment in capital improvements and the application of land to its highest-valued use.

*Assessment Caps.* A number of states, including Michigan, have instituted assessment caps in California's Proposition 13 mold. Caps of that nature limit the annual increases in assessed property values to some small specified percentage or to the rate of growth in the Consumer Price Index, whichever is lower. That limit remains in place until there is a sale. Of course, if everyone in the state has the same legislated advantage, there is no absolute benefit for the taxed population; tax rates simply adjust to generate the revenue that voters approve of through their elected representatives.

What rate caps actually do is to confer a *relative* advantage on residential properties with the most widely sought physical or locational features. Those houses' values would appreciate the most rapidly, and their owners would face skyrocketing value assessments, in an unfettered market accompanied by a nondiscriminatory tax regime. Therefore, the caps create unfairness through allowing for disparate treatment. Even more troubling is that inefficiency engendered by the caps, and by that questionable relative advantage, imposes a tremendous burden on the economy. The burden is that consumer surplus is increased for greater tenure far beyond what normal conditions (such as informational advantages) would dictate: Those who have considerable longevity at particular locations are likely to value their properties more than any new buyers conceivably would, solely because of a legislated tax benefit. The result is that property fails to move to higher-valued uses, or at least into the hands of parties who would value it more highly than the current owners if not for an artificial constraint on the market. The economy is less able to direct labor resources (typically younger households) to where they might be needed; relocation costs are kept prohibitively high because housing capital remains in the control of favored parties (often older households) who otherwise would find it socially and economically advantageous to live elsewhere.

The reluctance to sell exhibited by those who own the fixed number of advantaged properties indirectly affects the demand side of the market, as those owners reserve their homes for themselves rather than to transact with others who might derive high utility from the physical or locational features but would not be entitled to the tax advantages. That "reservation demand" on the part of the current owners constitutes part of the total demand relationship for the type of property with the most desired features (Wicksteed 1933).[11] The result is a slowing in the rate of transactions, and the sales that do occur are characterized by higher prices than would be observed in a market driven by more typical economic motivations. (It should not be surprising that the movement of property to higher-valued uses is impeded when buyers not only must pay excessively high prices, but also, as new owners, must then pay inordinately high ad valorem taxes.) The reduction in transactions surely is apparent to real estate brokers, title insurers, and other industries that benefit from property sales.

---

[11]Early-twentieth-century economist P. H. Wicksteed introduced the idea of reservation demand, observing that if an item's quantity is essentially fixed, "what is usually called the supply curve is in reality the demand curve of those who possess the commodity."

*Agricultural Land.* Contemporary property taxation regimes do not treat all land uses equivalently; farmland, for example, often is afforded favorable treatment. In Illinois, farmland is assessed under a formula that appears to be something like value-in-use. It is not precisely value-in-use, because the statutory capitalization rate and theoretical income are conceptually incompatible. The capitalization rate is based on a nominal discount rate, whereas the projected income concept is a real, rather than a nominal, magnitude. Thus, assessed value is a function of the rate of inflation. Farm assessments therefore fluctuate; they fall with higher inflation and rise as inflation declines. What is not incorporated into the assessments that determine property taxes on farmland is the value of the development option, which generally is quite high for unimproved land located near sites that are already intensively developed. As a result, farmland in close proximity to cities is undertaxed and therefore is held out of development longer than it otherwise would be. The outcome obviously is similar to that brought on by assessment caps on homes: Real estate fails to move to uses that would be higher valued in an unfettered market.

Yet whereas assessment cap proponents seem most concerned with the potential "sticker shock" of rising tax bills, rather than with changes in ownership or use, proponents of a property tax system biased in favor of farmland sometimes are motivated by a desire to see farm property remain in agricultural use. The irony is that a favorable tax on farming use merely reduces the intrinsic value of the development option, leading the owner to speculate by withholding, but only for the time being, the land from the development market. Opponents of tax preferences for agricultural use would point out that, regardless of how worthwhile the speculative motive is, policies that subsidize speculation are not efficient (but neither should speculation be singled out for targeted penalties, such as special taxes on capital gains). The point is that there are conflicts surrounding agricultural land assessment that may have to be dealt with differently in the future than they are in the present.

## Transitions

Transitions in land use will depend on the sophistication of property value estimation, primarily estimation techniques relating to land (and land versus capital improvement) values. Reductions in land value caused by regulations such as zoning will focus the attention of both developers and public-sector decision makers on modifying those regulations.

*Zoning.* In a situation involving two contiguous land uses that have evolved in the absence of any zoning restrictions—think of a residential area and a commercial area, with a boundary separating the two—the equilibrium allocation of land to the different uses would not be the economically efficient allocation. The equilibrium condition is for land within the interior of the residential area to sell for more than an equal-sized and topographically similar parcel in the nearby commercial area. The reason is that buyers would offer less for residential land bounding on the commercial area than for buffered land in the interior of the residential area; residential boundary land is negatively affected by noise, light, and congestion from adjoining commercial activity.

In that equilibrium situation, land in the commercial area but bounding on the residential area should sell for the same price as land on the residential side of the boundary. If it did not, buyers in that unrestricted environment could engage in a form of arbitrage by buying lower-cost commercial land and putting it to residential use without facing further exposure to negative influences than the boundary residential land already endures. And because nearby residential activity creates no additional problems for commercial users (rendering residential the "higher" use), commercial land along the boundary would be expected to sell for the same price per unit as land in the interior of the commercial area.

An efficient outcome, on the other hand, would be for prices in the *interiors* of the two land use areas to be the same; if efficient conditions prevail, two equal-sized parcels that are physically and locationally similar should not sell for different prices merely because of their expected uses. (Lower prices would be expected along the boundary, where the boundary residential land faces the negative impact of adjoining commercial use.) Therefore, if a zoning regime were to determine the amount of land that could be put to each use, and if the zoning were to be allocatively efficient, the outcome would be equal land values in the interiors of the land use areas (Colwell and Trefzger 1994). For this reason there is tension between free-market equilibrium and efficient zoning; it should be a common occurrence for developers to attempt to get zoning changed (moving toward the equilibrium outcome) even if zoning officials do an efficient job of allocating land to various uses.

If, however, a zoning plan is accompanied by different interior land prices in the two zones, the regime is characterized by an efficiency problem. If the commercial zone has a higher price per unit of land—indeed, what is observed in the presence of the most common zoning error—the zoning authority has overzoned for the residential use by constraining commercial use too much. For the commercial zone to demonstrate the lower price per unit of land, there would have to be an exclusive zoning plan under which too much land has been designated solely for commercial use. That result would be impossible in the presence of cumulative zoning, which allows higher uses in the zoning hierarchy to operate in lower-use zones and thus prevents the forced expansion of the lower use, a situation that would be analogous to pushing on a string (finding too few designated residential parcels, residential developers would become active bidders for vacant commercially zoned land).

One important aspect of the appraiser's job is to value land. Through appraisers' professional efforts, the correctness or error in zoning policy is made clear. Thus, planners should look to appraisal as a check on the efficiency of their activities.

*What Is Land Value?* The challenging question of capital improvements plays a critical role in the ideas surrounding real estate valuation. The zoning conundrum, for example, relates to the efficient application of capital improvements *on* land (most prominently, buildings). At the same time, what generally is thought of as pure land value in the United States often is largely the value of capital improvements *to* the land. The reason is that land developers in the United States are responsible for producing the on-site infrastructure that serves their developments. Thus, the price a developer receives for "land" includes compensation for providing such improvements *to* the land as streets, sidewalks, and utility distribution facilities (e.g., sewers, water and gas pipes, and electric cables). In a new development project, the value of that capital tends to be worth approximately half of what often is mistakenly thought of as the value of land.

It is important to identify the value of land, as opposed to a combined value of land and any capital attached to the land, because the implicit tax rates on land and capital cannot be understood unless the value of each component is known. Public officials cannot administer a conscious graded tax system, or a total site-value tax system, without the means of estimating the value of land and the value of capital improvements. Alternatively, if the goal of an ad valorem taxation system is to tax land and capital equally, it is necessary to estimate accurately the value of land so that any inequality that exists in the tax rate applied to land and the rate applied to physical capital can be identified.

Because of the inherent difficulty of separating the land component of real estate sales data from capital, determining land value may continue to perplex both valuation practitioners and academic theorists. Longstanding logical conjecture on what creates value in land parcels of different size or configuration is, to some extent, unsupported by systematic studies; at the very least the received doctrine seems to tell an incomplete story (Ecker and Isakson 2005; Colwell and Munneke 1997, 1999). Previous conjecture has suggested, for example, that a parcel's value first increases at an increasing rate as size increases from a very small level, a phenomenon called assemblage or plottage. The underlying logic is that someone with a parcel too small to put to an economically beneficial use would pay a premium price for added acreage up to the minimally effective size; while such a relationship may indeed exist, it has not been validated repeatedly by empirical evidence.[12] Beyond that critical size, denoted by an inflection point in the value function, previous conjecture posited value increasing at a decreasing rate (as implied by depth rules), a phenomenon that has been called plattage.[13] The underlying logic is that the price of buildable land must include a premium for the infrastructure. Here the described relationship is unlikely to be correct with respect to very large parcels having essentially no infrastructure. There is no great amount of evidence that average price per acre is less for very large parcels than for those that are merely large.[14]

A new conjecture that may be worth exploring is that, at least for parcels exceeding a fairly large number of acres (i.e., beyond sizes for which plattage exists), value once again increases at an increasing rate, approaching a proportional relationship asymptotically from above as size grows. That conjecture may suggest that analysts should develop new functional forms to model land markets. It might be possible to estimate that asymptotic value, albeit with large forecast errors, even though data on very large tracts (e.g., a section or larger) are not available in statistically useful quantities.

***Concurrency.*** Some states are requiring "concurrency" for new developments. This strange language means that developers must either produce the public off-site infrastructure needed to serve a new development (e.g., schools, fire houses, police equipment, sewer treatment facilities), or finance the public sector's provision of infrastructure by depositing sufficient money into a government fund prior to proceeding with their development activity. Concurrency, therefore, is an extreme version of an impact fee. It is sold to voters as simply a user charge (a payment required to offset the public sector's cost of providing the service), but it actually represents a huge new lump-sum tax on capital investment.

Because this severe tax interferes with the efficient allocation of capital, it is important to find ways to reduce concurrency requirements. First, it may

---

[12]The most credible discovery of plottage is provided in Ecker and Isakson (2005). Highly suggestive confirmation of the plottage conjecture is offered in Colwell and Munneke (1999).

[13]Much stronger confirmation exists with regard to the plattage than to the plottage conjecture; see Colwell and Munneke (1997).

[14]An exception is found in Chicoine (1981).

be necessary to educate people that a stream of taxes through time can be financially equivalent to a lump-sum tax. The mathematics to show this equivalence is straightforward; it is a simple present value of an annuity function. The financial device for spreading a lump-sum tax over time is a bond: Municipal governments can issue bonds to raise the money to provide infrastructure for new developments. The lenders who buy the bonds willingly accept lower payments than on bonds of equal risk issued by corporations, because the interest they receive on municipal bonds is not taxed as income at the federal level; the federal government thereby provides an interest subsidy to local taxpayers in jurisdictions that borrow money to provide infrastructure or other public services. Yet because revenue bonds' lenders are repaid solely from revenues generated by the funded projects—not from general tax receipts, for which local residents bear direct responsibility—municipal revenue bonds would be an attractive financing device even in the absence of the interest subsidy.

Second, many new developments are net tax contributors even in the absence of concurrency requirements. Luxury housing and many other types of projects could be expected to generate yearly property taxes that more than pay for their annual use of public services, including infrastructure. Thus, the cumulative effect of the concurrency mandate on developers (whether passed along to buyers or extracted from the selling price of undeveloped property), plus the ordinary annual property tax that purchasers of newly built houses pay, is a cost to the ultimate owner that greatly exceeds—perhaps more than doubles—what a full annual user charge would be.

A common misconception is that if all citizens are taxed when the infrastructure required by new development is paid for by a bond issue, preexisting taxpayers are subsidizing the new taxpayers. Existing residents, as some would see it, already have their schools, parks, and fire stations in place, so newcomers should have to ante up to provide such support facilities for themselves. That view is wrong on two fronts. First, existing residents do not come to the bargaining table with infrastructure services eternally in place. They bring the remaining lives of wasting physical assets that will have to be maintained, and ultimately replaced, with tax money (possibly fronted by bond issues) collected from the entire community. Thus the newcomers' tax payments will, at the very least, play the same role in replacing existing infrastructure that longstanding residents' payments play in providing infrastructure to new neighborhoods.

Yet property owners in the new development could well do more than merely trade tax dollars with those having longer tenure. If a new development is a net tax contributor, the taxes it generates will more than cover the payments on bonds issued to pay for its infrastructure, as well as operation and maintenance, and the new development will end up subsidizing the pre-existing properties, even without a concurrency requirement. The likelihood that a new development would be a net tax contributor is high, if only because brand-new improvements would tend to have higher market, and therefore assessed, values than otherwise similar older, existing improvements. Requiring concurrency for net tax contributors is less the application of a user charge than a form of extortion. A societal problem results, in that concurrency represents a profound disincentive to produce productive developments and thus acts as a brake on economic activity—once again, the result of what effectively is a tax on capital improvements.

Newcomers certainly should pay their fair share of the cost of local government services, and a reasonable argument could be offered that it is appropriate to pay for those services with ongoing user charges. Of course, as noted, a stream of ongoing fees can be replaced with a financially equivalent lump-sum payment. If part of public services' expected cost is handled through a required lump-sum impact fee, that lump sum should be computed as the negative of the present value of the expected net tax contribution. Therefore, while the levying of impact fees can be justified when a new development is expected to be a net user of local tax dollars, there should be a greater use of *negative* impact fees, in the form of lump-sum payments *from* jurisdictions *to* developers, since there are so many cases in which projects are expected to be net tax contributors. An important task for assessors particularly, but also for appraisers asked to value proposed or existing projects, is to identify which developments are expected to be net tax contributors, and which are not, so that communities will not impede the efficient allocation of capital. Local officials should encourage activities that can provide long-term fiscal benefits, rather than subsidizing high-visibility projects, such as civic centers, that actually may be net tax consumers.

## CONCLUSIONS

Although it may seem that the technology and ideas surrounding real estate valuation are headed in extremely complex directions, the changes will be less overwhelming if their nature can be anticipated. It is useful to keep in mind that the movement to multiple regression analysis began only about half a century ago, as access to computers became widely available; the use of that now-common technique had been thought to be quite complicated, even exotic. Computer hardware will continue to evolve, but more important for valuation practitioners, the software that supports hedonic applications will evolve in the very near future in a way that allows what still seems exotic and complex, in many ways, to become common and accessible.

Yet at the same time that analysts come to benefit from desktop tools that are easier to use, they will have to deal with the problem of diverging market comparison applications. While it is possible that a winning technique, or a winning combination, will emerge, it is more likely that different tastes and different objectives will drive continued divergence. With regard to taste differences, some will try to build hedonic models that include all possible variables, whereas others will try to capture blips in the value surface with autoregressive schemes, kernel methods, or splines. Creative combinations of the two different viewpoints may prove to be especially productive. On the other hand, it seems unlikely that combinations of autoregressive schemes, kernel methods, and splines would be productive, because those techniques are similar in their objectives.

Applications of the income approach have moved away from the multiplicity of reduced form equations toward complex pro forma spreadsheets and toward empirical direct capitalization and multipliers. That pattern can be expected to continue, but it also is likely that spreadsheet applications will incorporate Monte Carlo analysis in the future.

The cost approach continues to exist in a very primitive state. While there are obvious enhancements that could be made, it is doubtful that any of those will be explored and implemented in the world of valuation practice. The reason is that more carefully crafted and substantiated depreciation estimation techniques require the same type of data that are found in hedonics, yet the application is less direct. There is also much that could be done in terms of reviewing, as well as moving beyond, the cost manuals; the question is whether anyone will be motivated to do the necessary work.

Land value estimation is an activity especially in need of ongoing study and experimentation. The good news here, however, is that the motivation for creating better techniques is substantial, because land valuation plays a profound role in guiding development, regulation, and taxation.

Indeed, the ideas that support real estate valuation, and that drive the demand for estimating property values, will continue to evolve. It can be anticipated that sophisticated valuation methodology will be thrust into the public arena in the future to a greater extent than is seen today. The fields of real estate taxation and land use regulation are two of the public policy arenas in which valuation theory and practice might be expected to become much more important. Their importance relates not only to compelling economic questions of efficient allocations and fair outcomes, but also to political realities. Great controversies are likely to emerge with regard to valuation's role in taxing and regulating land and its improvements, because entrenched interests will be affected.[15]

## REFERENCES

Almond, N., and F. Plummer. 1997. An investigation into the use of compulsory acquisitions by agreement. *Property Management* 15(1):38–48.

Case, B., P. F. Colwell, C. Leishman, and C. Watkins. 2006. The impact of environmental contamination on condo prices: A hybrid repeat-sale/hedonic approach. *Real Estate Economics* 34(1):77–107.

Chicoine, D. L. 1981. Farmland values at the urban fringe: An analysis of sale prices. *Land Economics* 57(3):353–362.

Colwell, P. F. 1979. A statistically oriented definition of market value. *Appraisal Journal* 48(1):53–58.

——. 1990. Privatization of assessment, zoning, and eminent domain. *ORER Letter* 4(2):1–7.

——. 1998. A primer on piecewise parabolic multiple regression analysis via estimations of Chicago CBD land prices. *Journal of Real Estate Finance and Economics* 17(1):87–97 (special issue on spatial econometrics).

Colwell, P. F., and P. K. Asabere. 1985. A relative lot area hypothesis: An empirical note. *Urban Studies* 22(4):355–357.

Colwell, P. F., and R. E. Cannaday. 1981a. A unified field theory of the income approach to appraisal: Part I. *Real Estate Appraiser and Analyst* 47(1):5–9.

——. 1981b. A unified field theory of the income approach to appraisal: Part II. *Real Estate Appraiser and Analyst* 47(2):29–43.

——. 1981c. A unified field theory of the income approach to appraisal: Part III. *Real Estate Appraiser and Analyst* 47(3):25–37.

---

[15]Entrenched interests that affect appraisal have grown as secondary market investors have displaced originating institutions as the major holders of mortgage notes. In earlier times, for example, developers and home sellers sometimes had cause to pressure or mislead lenders' appraisers into justifying unrealistically high sale prices. The recent subprime residential lending crisis, however, highlights the more widespread agency problems that arise when fee-earning loan originators, and buyers with zero or negative amounts at risk, care more about completing transactions than about supporting careful underwriting. Lenders' reluctance to foreclose in a period of tightened lending standards and generally declining home prices has led to greater frequency of such practices as improperly including personal property or sums to be rebated in the transaction prices reported in public records not only by sellers, but also by lenders and the borrowers who are buying or refinancing property. Because even the most theoretically defensible appraisal techniques produce meaningless results if the underlying data are unreliable, the growth of entrenched parties' potential to affect the appraisal process should be a matter of ongoing concern to academic theorists, appraisal practitioners, regulatory bodies, and legislators.

———. 1986. Real estate valuation models: Lender and equity investor criteria. *AREUEA Journal* 14(2):317–337.

Colwell, P. F., R. E. Cannaday, and C. Wu. 1983. The analytical foundations of adjustment grid methods. *AREUEA Journal* 11(1):11–29.

———. 1984. Weighting schemes for adjustment grid methods of appraisal. *Appraisal Review Journal* 7(1):24–31.

Colwell, P. F., C. A. Dehring, and N. A. Lash. 2000. The effect of group homes on neighborhood property values. *Land Economics* 76(4):615–636.

Colwell, P. F., and G. Dilmore. 1999. Who was first? An examination of an early hedonic study. *Land Economics* 75(4):620–626.

Colwell, P. F., S. S. Gujral, and C. Coley. 1985. The impact of a shopping center on the value of surrounding properties. *Real Estate Issues* 10(1):35–39.

Colwell, P. F., W. N. Kinnard, and G. Beron. 2003. The cost approach and functional obsolescence. In *Essays in honor of William N. Kinnard, Jr.* C. F. Sirmans and E. M. Worzala, eds., 65–80. Boston: Kluwer Academic Publishers.

Colwell, P. F., and D. W. Marshall. 2002. The unit-comparison cost approach in residential appraisal. In *Real estate valuation theory.* K. Wang and M. L. Wolverton, eds., 357–372. Boston: Kluwer Academic Publishers.

Colwell, P. F., and H. J. Munneke. 1997. The structure of urban land prices. *Journal of Urban Economics* 41(3):321–336.

———. 1999. Land prices and land assembly in the CBD. *Journal of Real Estate Finance and Economics* 18(2):163–180.

———. 2003. Estimating a price surface for vacant land in an urban area. *Land Economics* 79(1):15–28.

———. 2006. Bargaining strength and property class in the office market. *Journal of Real Estate Finance and Economics* 33(3):197–213.

———. Forthcoming. Directional land value gradients. *Journal of Real Estate Finance and Economics.*

Colwell, P. F., H. J. Munneke, and J. W. Trefzger. 1998. Chicago's office market: Price indices, location, and time. *Real Estate Economics* 26(1):83–106.

Colwell, P. F., and M. Ramsland. 2003. Coping with technological change: The case of retail. *Journal of Real Estate Finance and Economics* 26(1):47–63.

Colwell, P. F., and T. F. Scheu. 1994. A history of site valuation rules: Functions and empirical evidence. *Journal of Real Estate Research* 9(3):353–368.

Colwell, P. F., and C. F. Sirmans. 1980. The value of multi-family housing. *Review of Regional Studies* 10(3):60–67.

———. 1993. A comment on zoning, returns to scale, and the value of underdeveloped land. *Review of Economics and Statistics* 75(4):783–786.

Colwell, P. F., and J. W. Trefzger. 1994. Allocation, externalities, and building value. *Journal of Real Estate Finance and Economics* 8(1):53–69.

———. 2005. Supply-side effects and contingent valuation analysis. *Journal of Real Estate Practice and Education* 8(1):45–60.

*County of Wayne v. Hathcock,* 471 Mich. 445 (2004).

Dubin, R., R. K. Pace, and T. Thibodeau. 1999. Spatial autoregression techniques for real estate data. *Journal of Real Estate Literature* 7(1):79–95.

Ecker, M. D., and H. R. Isakson. 2005. A unified convex-concave model of urban land values. *Regional Science and Urban Economics* 35(3):265–277.

*Kelo et al. v. City of New London et al.*, 545 U.S. 469 (2005).

Kelo's revenge: Voters restrict eminent domain. 2006. CNN Money.com. http://money .cnn.com/2006/11/08/real_estate/kelos_revenge/index.htm?postversion=2006110811.

McMillen, D. P. 1996. One hundred fifty years of land value in Chicago: A nonparametric approach. *Journal of Urban Economics* 40(1):100–124.

Michigan Initiatives and Referenda. 2006. National Conference of State Legislatures. http://www.ncsl.org/ncsldb/elect98/irsrch.cfm?recid=2753.

*Poletown Neighborhood Council v. City of Detroit*, 410 Mich. 616 (1981).

Statutory Instrument. 2006. No. 1658: The Home Loss Payments (Prescribed Amounts) (England) Regulations 2006. http://www.opsi.gov.uk/si/si2006/20061658.htm.

Trefzger, J. W. 1995. Efficient compensation for regulatory takings: Some thoughts following the *Lucas* ruling. *Real Estate Law Journal* 23(3):191–204.

Trefzger, J. W., and P. F. Colwell. 1996. Investor efficiency in the face of takings. *Journal of Real Estate Finance and Economics* 12(1):23–35.

Wicksteed, P. H. 1933. *The common sense of political economy and selected papers and reviews on economic theory*, vol. 2. London: Routledge & Kegan Paul.

# 8

# Global Challenges for Land Administration and Sustainable Development

## Ian Williamson

Land surveyors, lawyers, and land administrators are experts in designing, building, and managing our land administration systems (LAS). They are experienced in creating, describing, and defining land parcels and associated rights. Historically, society required those skills to support an efficient and effective land market in which rights in land are traded to promote economic development. By the mid-nineteenth century, trading involved buying, selling, mortgaging, and leasing of rights in land. By the mid-twentieth century, land administration and cadastral officials, and associated legal and surveying professionals, assumed that they understood land markets and that they had developed appropriate professional skills to serve the needs of those markets.

Surveyors who worked from "whole to part" designed the tools to support land markets—the LAS, cadastres, and supporting technical and administrative skills. Unfortunately, those tools were involved in supporting the land trading activities. Designing a land market, of itself, is another question. From the point of view of land administrators, there is little documentation in

This chapter draws on the collegiate creative efforts of staff, students, and professionals in the Centre for Spatial Data Infrastructures and Land Administration, Department of Geomatics, University of Melbourne, Australia, in joint publications with the Centre's colleagues, and with Dr. Abbas Rajabifard and Ms. Jude Wallace. The research is supported by grants from the International Science Linkages program established under the Australian Government's Innovation statement *Backing Australia's Ability*, by the Australian Research Council, and by state Departments of Sustainability and Environment (Victoria), Land Information (Western Australia), and Lands (New South Wales). Any errors are entirely the author's responsibility.

the literature on how to design and build a land market or even on the development and growth of land markets (however, see Wallace and Williamson 2006a).

Historically, existing land administration (LA) skills are appropriate for simple land markets that focus on traditional land development and simple land trading. However, land markets have evolved dramatically in the last 50 years and are now very complex, with the major wealth creation mechanisms focused on the trading of complex commodities. While the potential expansion of our LAS to support the trading of complex commodities offers many opportunities for land administrators, one particular commodity—land information—has the potential to significantly change the way societies operate, and how governments and the private sector do business.

The growth of markets in complex commodities is a logical evolution of our people-to-land relationships, and our evolving cadastral and LAS. The changing people-to-land relationships, the need to pursue sustainable development, and the increasing need to administer complex commodities within an ICT-enabled virtual world offer new opportunities for our LAS. Many challenges need to be overcome, however, before those opportunities can be exploited.

Research aimed at understanding and meeting those challenges has been undertaken within the Centre for Spatial Data Infrastructures and Land Administration, Department of Geomatics, University of Melbourne (http://www.geom.unimelb.edu.au/research/SDI_research/). The overarching focus of the Centre's research projects is spatially enabling government in support of sustainable development. The Centre has identified a potential for land information that goes far beyond the land administration endeavor. That potential is called spatially enabling government. One key to achieving it involves using land information in entirely new ways, gathering the momentum of technological changes and using that momentum to invigorate land administration functions.

This new vision for managing land information to spatially enable governments is called iLand. The components of the iLand vision include the following:

- A collaborative whole-government approach to managing spatial information using spatial data infrastructure (SDI) principles
- Better understanding of the role that LAS plays in integrated land management (e.g., land markets, land use planning, land taxation)
- Seamless integration of built and environmental spatial data in order to deliver sustainable development objectives

- Improved interoperability between our land information silos through e-land administration
- More flexible technology and models to support cadastres, especially to introduce a third dimension of height and a fourth dimension of time
- A national geo-coded street address file linked to the cadastre
- Better management of the complex issues in our expanding multiunit developments and vertical villages
- Better management of the ever-increasing restrictions and responsibilities relating to land
- Incorporation of a marine dimension into both our cadastres and our (land) administration systems

The fundamental idea is to rebuild LAS to support the emerging needs of government, business, and society; to deliver more integrated and effective information; and to use that information throughout government and nongovernment processes by organizing technical systems in the virtual environment around "place" or "location."

To understand the descriptions of a possible invigorated LAS future, it is useful to trace how land administration has met the challenges of economic development and social change in the past.

## LAND ADMINISTRATION SYSTEMS

An understanding of the components of LAS and their evolution can help predict how they will develop.

### The Importance of the Cadastre

Digital information about land is central to the policy framework of modern land administration and sustainability accounting (Williamson, Enemark, and Wallace 2006b). The cadastre, or the large-scale land parcel map related to parcel indices, is the vital information layer of an integrated land management system and, in the future, will underpin the information systems of modern governments.

While some developed countries do without a formal cadastre, most generate digital parcel maps (or a digital cadastral database, or DCDB) that reflect land allocation patterns and uses and subdivision patterns, and even addresses and photographs. A country's DCDB is its core information layer. It is destined for a much broader role as a fundamental part of government

infrastructure equivalent to a major highway or railway, though it was originally created on behalf of taxpayers merely for better internal administration
of taxation and, more recently, titling of land. Without such digital facilities,
modern governments have no means of understanding the built environment
of cities, managing land competently, using computer capacity to assist in
policy making regarding land management, or retrieving significant value
out of land.

The greatest potential of the DCDB lies with the information industry at
large, as the principal means of translating geographic coordinates and spatial descriptors of land parcels into meaningful descriptions of places that
everybody can understand. Land parcels describe the way people physically
use and think about their land. The familiar configuration of parcel-based descriptions in the DCDB allows a people-friendly identification of the precise
locations of the impact of private ownership and, more vitally, of government,
business, and community policies, regulations, and actions. In cadastres supported by professional surveyors, the descriptions have the added advantage
of being legally authoritative.

While having a cadastre is not mandatory for LAS, all modern economies
recognize its importance and incorporate either a cadastre or its key components into their LAS. For example, Australian LAS did not evolve from a traditional cadastral focus, as did their European counterparts, but their cadastres
are equal to, and sometimes improve upon, the classic European approach.

The cadastral concept shown in figure 8.1 (International Federation of
Surveyors 1995) is simple and clearly shows the textual and spatial components, which are the focus of land surveyors and land registry and cadastral
officials. The cadastre provides a spatial integrity and unique identification
for land parcels within LAS. However, while the cadastral concept is simple,
implementation is difficult and complex, especially when linked to a national geo-coded street address database. After 10 years, the model shown remains a useful depiction of a cadastre. However, it needs to be extended to
incorporate the evolving and complex rights, restrictions, and responsibilities
operating in a modern society concerned with delivering sustainable development. It also does not show the important roles for the cadastre in supporting integrated land management, or in providing critically important land
information to enable the creation of a virtual environment, at a more practical level e-government, and eventually a spatially enabled government. However, other initiatives of the International Federation of Surveyors (FIG),
such as CADASTRE 2014 (International Federation of Surveyors 1998) and
the Bathurst Declaration on Land Administration for Sustainable Development (International Federation of Surveyors 1999), do highlight the changing roles of the cadastre.

**Figure 8.1:** The Cadastral Concept

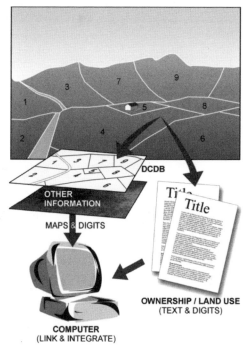

*Source*: International Federation of Surveyors (1995).

## The Evolution of Land Administration Systems

The evolution of LAS is influenced by the changing people-to-land relationship over the centuries. Even though figure 8.2 depicts a Western example of this evolving relationship, a similar evolution can be plotted for most societies. This diagram highlights the evolution of feudal tenures to individual ownership, the growth of land markets driven by the Industrial Revolution, the impact of a greater consciousness about managing land by formal land use planning, and, in recent times, the environmental and social dimensions of land (Ting et al. 1999). Historically, an economic paradigm drove land markets; however, that paradigm has now been significantly tempered by environmental (e.g., Agenda 21) and, more recently, social paradigms (e.g., Native Title). Simply, the people-to-land relationships in any society are not stable but are continually evolving.

In turn, Western nations developed land administration or cadastral responses to evolutionary changes in people-to-land relationships over the last 300 years, shown in figure 8.3. The original focus on land taxation expanded

**Figure 8.2:** Evolution of People-to-Land Relationships

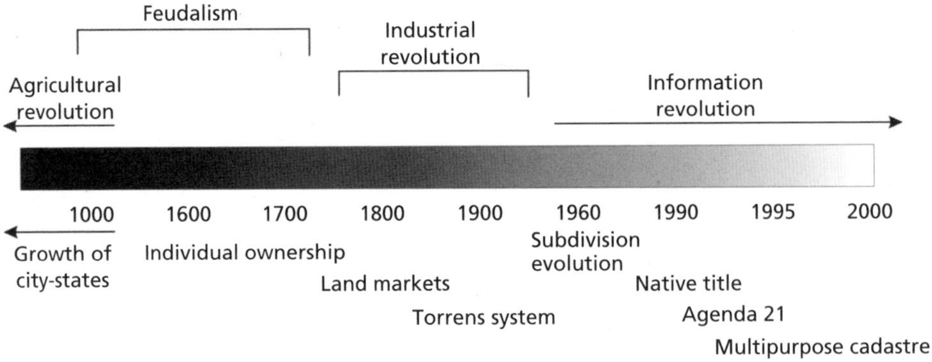

Source: Ting et al. (1999).

to support land markets, then land use planning, and, over the last decade or so, to provide a multipurpose role supporting sustainable development objectives (Ting and Williamson 1999).

Even within this evolution, LAS must continue to service the nineteenth-century economic paradigm by defining simple land commodities and supporting simple trading patterns (buying, selling, leasing, and mortgaging), particularly by providing a remarkably secure parcel titling system, an easy and relatively cheap land transfer system, and reliable parcel definition through attainable surveying standards (World Bank 2004, 2005).

Arguably, Australia was a world leader in adapting its LAS to support land parcel marketing. Its major innovations of the Torrens system of land registration and of strata titles are copied in many other countries. However, because of the pace of change, the capacity of LAS to meet market needs diminished. The land market of, say, 1940, would be unrecognizable today. After World War II, new trading opportunities and new products were invented. Vertical villages, time-shares, mortgage-backed certificates used in the secondary mortgage market, insurance-based products (including deposit bonds), land information, property and unit trusts, and many more commodities now offer investment and participation opportunities to millions, either directly or through investment or superannuation schemes, trusts, and property investment vehicles. Meanwhile, the controls and restrictions over land became multipurpose and aimed at ensuring safety standards, durable building structures, adequate service provision, business standards, social and land use planning, and sustainable development. The replication of land-

**Figure 8.3:** The Land Administration Response

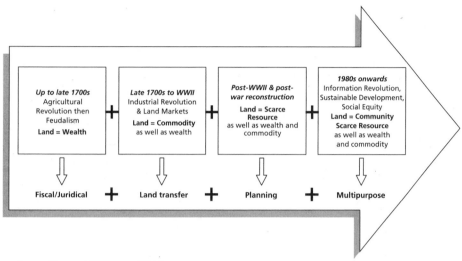

*Source:* Ting and Williamson (1999).

related systems in resource and water contexts is demanding new flexibility in our approaches to land administration (Wallace and Williamson 2006a).

Also in Australia, the combination of new management styles; computerization of activities; creation of databases containing a wealth of land information; and improved interoperability of valuation, planning, address, spatial, and registration information allowed much more flexibility. However, Australian LAS remain creatures of their historical state and territory formation. They do not service national-level trading and are especially inept in servicing the trading of new commodities that Australians continue to invent as they "unbundle" land. Moreover, modern societies, which are responding to the needs of sustainable development, are now required to administer a complex system of overlapping rights, restrictions, and responsibilities relating to land—existing land administration and cadastral systems do not service that need. A diagrammatic representation of the development of land administration (and cadastral) systems from a policy focus is shown in figure 8.4.

## The Formalization of Tenures

The situation is just as complex at the other end of the economic spectrum when land use of traditionally organized societies needs to be reflected in

**Figure 8.4:** Development of Land Administration

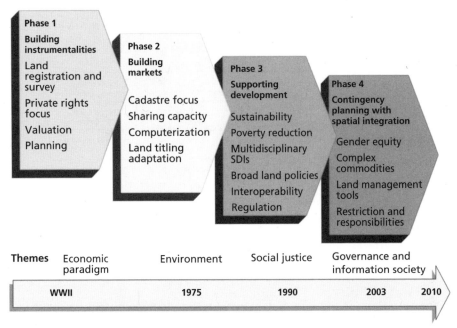

*Source*: Wallace and Williamson (2005).

LAS. Modern societies are also now realizing that many rights, restrictions, and responsibilities (RRR) relating to land exist without formalization by governments for various policy or political reasons. This does not mean those rights, restrictions, and responsibilities do not exist; it means that they have not been formalized in recognizable land administration or equivalent frameworks. A good example is the recognition of indigenous aboriginal rights in land in Australia in the 1980s. Prior to the Mabo and Wik High Court decisions and the resulting legislation in Australia, indigenous rights did not formally exist. Their existence was informal but strongly evidenced by song lines, cultural norms, and other indigenous systems, a situation still familiar in the developing world where indigenous titles await more formal construction.

The process of formalizing tenure and rights, restrictions, and responsibilities in land is depicted in figure 8.5 (Dalrymple, Wallace, and Williamson 2004). An understanding of both formal and informal rights is important as we move to develop land administration and cadastral systems that are

**Figure 8.5:** Formalization of Tenures

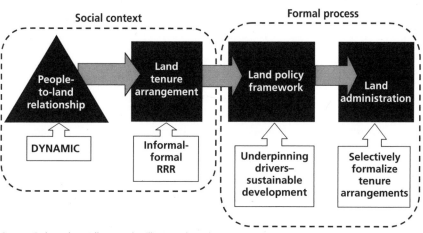

*Source*: Dalrymple, Wallace, and Williamson (2004).

sensitive to the underpinning drivers associated with sustainable development (economic, environmental, social, and governance dimensions). Change management processes and adaptation of formal systems always lag behind reality: All mature systems will simultaneously sustain both informal and highly formalized rights while they adjust to absorb emerging interests. Frequently, some rights will be deliberately held in informal systems: One of the largest and most significant commercial management tools in Australia, the trust, remains beyond the land administration infrastructure and relies on formalities generated by client-based practices of lawyers and accountants, held in their filing drawers.

Other rights involve minimal formalization for different reasons. Residential leases, too common and too short term to warrant much administrative action, are traditionally organized outside LAS. Those rent-based distribution systems nevertheless remain potentially within the purview of modern LAS, policy makers, and administrators, as illustrated by Australia's development of a geo-referenced national address file (GNAF). Indeed the development of spatial, as distinct from survey, information provides the timeliest reminder that information about land is potentially one of the most remarkable commodities in the modern land market. Certainly, it is of core interest to land administrators. Its power is exemplified by Google Maps, which will display the up-to-date cadastral parcel layer for any Australian street address typed into its search window.

## Implementing and Understanding Regulations and Restrictions

Many rights, restrictions, and responsibilities in land are not formalized, and many are established by statute or regulation but not recorded in land registries or any other form of register. Land uses over time must be managed to mitigate long-term deleterious impacts and support sustainable development. Over time, for example, attempts to manage the Australian problems of erosion, salinity, and acidity by regulating tree clearance, water access, soil removal, chemical use, building standards, and more led to a great increase in the number of laws, regulations, and standards that apply to land-based activities. The lack of coherent management of the restrictions and the information they generate is now apparent. The increasing complexity of social and environmental restrictions over land is straining our systems and in some cases failing. The state of Victoria now implements over 600 pieces of legislation that relate to land, and the national Australian government implements a similar number. Most of those are administered outside our LAS. Similar experiences occur worldwide. Calls for including restrictions on land in traditionally organized LAS are therefore common and international. The idea of including all restrictions in the land register was a first-grab solution that is now recognized as impractical, however. Society needs more transparent and consistent approaches to dealing with such restrictions and the information they generate. While modern registries are adapting to manage those restrictions compatible with their traditional functions, spatially enabling governments and businesses offers different solutions in the context of iLand (Bennett, Wallace, and Williamson 2005, 2008).

## The Changing Nature of Ownership

The rapid growth of restrictions on land in modern societies is paralleled by a change in the nature of land ownership. Nations are building genuine partnerships between communities and landowners, so that environmental and business controls are more mutual endeavors. Rather than approach controls as restrictions, the nature of ownership is redesigned to define the opportunities of owners within a framework of responsible land uses for delivery of environmental and other gains. This stewardship concept is familiar to Europeans long used to the historical, social, and environmental importance of land. For Europeans, the social responsibilities of landowners have a much longer heritage, with the exemplar provision in the German constitution insisting on the landowner's social role. The nature of land use in The Netherlands, given that much of the land mass is below sea level, presupposes high levels of community cooperation and integrates landownership responsibilities into the broader common good. The long history of rural villages in Denmark and public support for the Danes who live in rural areas also encourage collaboration (Williamson, Enemark, and Wallace 2006a).

The Australian mining industry provides typical examples of the collaborative engagement of local people, aboriginal owners, and the broader public. The Australian National Water Initiative and the National Land and Water Resources Audit reinforce the realization that the activities of one landowner affect others. The development of market-based instruments (MBIs) such as EcoTenders and BushTenders, which attempt to use trading mechanisms, auctions, and price signals to positively influence the behavior of people managing natural resources and environmental assets, is an Australian attempt to build environmental consequences into land management. Australia's initiatives in the "unbundling" of land to create separate, tradable commodities, including water titles, are now built into existing LAS as far as possible. The processes, however, are far from integrated. As yet a comprehensive analysis of the impact of unbundling land interests on property theory and comprehensive land management is not available.

Whatever the mechanism, modern landownership has taken on social and environmental consequences at odds with the idea of an absolute property owner. Australian and European approaches to land management are inherently different. While Europe is generally approaching land management as a comprehensive and holistic challenge requiring strong government information and administration systems, Australia is creating layers of separate commodities out of land and adapting existing LAS as much as possible to accommodate this trading, without an overarching national administrative approach. In these varying national contexts, the one commonality, the need for land information to drive land management in support of sustainable development, will remain the universal land administration driver of the future (Williamson, Enemark, and Wallace 2006a).

## LAND MARKETS

As stated, modern land markets have evolved from systems for simple land trading to trading complex commodities (figure 8.6). New trading opportunities and new products were, and continue to be, invented. The controls and restrictions over land became multipurpose with an increasing focus on achieving sustainable development objectives.

As with simple commodities such as land parcels, all commodities require quantification and precise definition (de Soto 2000). While LAS have not yet incorporated the administration of complex commodities to a

**Figure 8.6:** Evolution of Land Markets

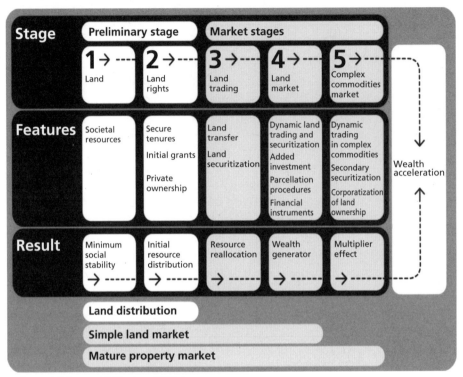

*Source*: Wallace and Williamson (2006a).

significant degree, these modern complex land markets offer many opportunities for land administrators and associated professionals if they are prepared to think laterally and capitalize on their traditional measurement, legal, technical, and land management skills.

This complexity is compounded by the unbundling of rights in land (e.g., water, carbon, salinity, biota), thereby adding to the range of complex commodities available for trading. For example, the replication of land-related systems in resource and water contexts is demanding new flexibilities in our approaches to land administration (Wallace and Williamson 2006a). These emerging demands will stimulate different approaches to using cadastral information.

Our understanding of the evolution of land markets is limited, but it must be developed if land administrators are going to maximize the potential of trading in complex commodities by developing appropriate LAS (Wallace and Williamson 2006a). Figure 8.6 shows the various stages in the evolution

**Figure 8.7:** Complex Commodities Markets

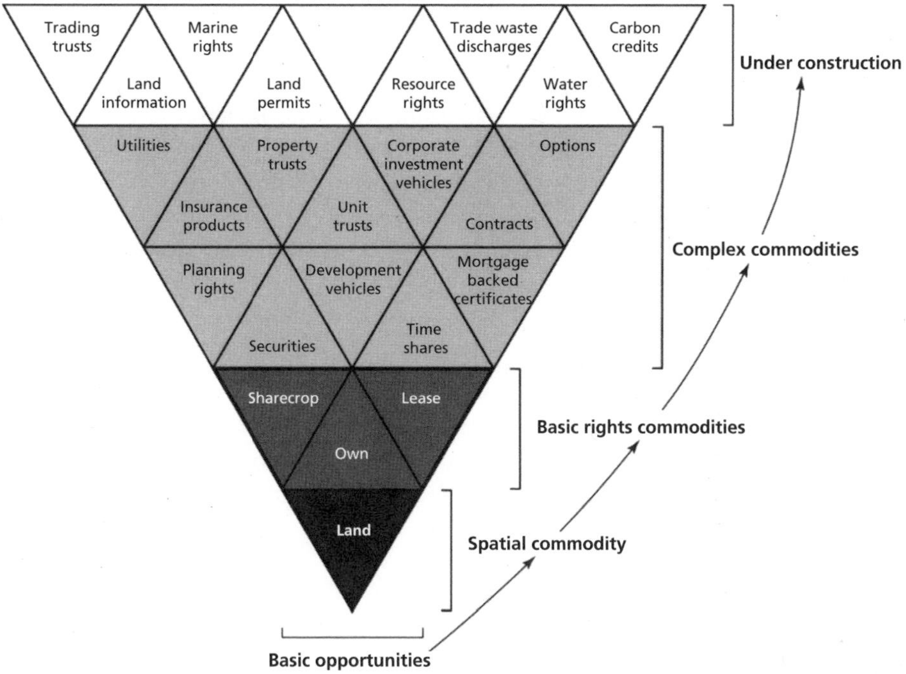

*Source*: Wallace and Williamson (2006a).

of land markets from simple land trading to markets in complex commodities. The growth of a complex commodities market that also shows examples of complex commodities is presented diagrammatically in figure 8.7.

## THE IMPORTANCE OF SPATIAL DATA INFRASTRUCTURES

All LAS require some form of spatial data infrastructure to provide the spatial integrity for rights, restrictions, and responsibilities relating to land, and the resulting land information. The concept of an SDI continues to evolve, however. In simple terms, it is an enabling platform linking data producers, providers, and value adders to data users. SDIs are crucial tools to facilitate use of spatial data and spatial information systems. They allow data sharing and enable users to save resources, time, and effort when acquiring new data sets. Many nations and jurisdictions are investing in development of such platforms and infrastructures to enable their stakeholders to adopt compatible approaches to creation of distributed virtual systems. Two drivers are evident:

(1) the need to organize information to better support decision making; and (2) elimination of expensive duplication. The success of these systems depends on collaboration between all parties and on system design to support efficient access, retrieval, and delivery of spatial information.

The steps to develop an SDI model vary, depending on a country's background and needs. However, it is important that countries develop and follow a road map for SDI implementation. The road map should include development of an SDI vision, required improvements in national capacity, integration of different spatial data sets, establishment of partnerships, and financial support for an SDI. A vision within the SDI initiative is essential for sectors involved within an SDI project and for the general public. The SDI vision helps people to understand the government's objectives and work toward them. Unfortunately, many land administrators underestimate the importance of SDIs in building efficient and effective LAS. They focus on the immediate administrative needs and tasks to provide security of tenure and the support for simple land trading, a narrow focus that restricts the ability of LAS organizations to contribute to the whole of government and wider society through spatial enablement.

## SDI as an Enabling Platform

Effective use of spatial information requires the optimization of SDIs to support system design and applications and subsequent business uses. Initially, SDIs were implemented as a mechanism to facilitate access and sharing of spatial data hosted in distributed geographical information systems (GIS). Users now require precise spatial information in real time about real-world objects, however, along with the ability to develop and implement cross-jurisdictional and interagency solutions to meet priorities, such as emergency management; natural resource management; water rights trading; and animal, pest, and disease controls.

To achieve this, the concept of an SDI is moving to a new business model in which the SDI promotes partnerships of spatial information organizations (public-private), allowing access to a wider scope of data and services of greater size and complexity than they could individually provide. SDI as an enabling platform can be viewed as an infrastructure linking people to data (Rajabifard, Binns, and Williamson 2006) through linking data users and providers on the basis of the common goal of data sharing (figure 8.8). However, there is a need to move beyond a simple understanding of SDI and to create a common rail gauge to support initiatives aimed at solving cross-jurisdictional and national issues. This SDI will be the main gateway through

**Figure 8.8:** SDI Connecting People to Data

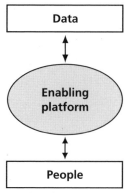

*Source:* Rajabifard, Binns, and Williamson (2006).

which to discover, access, and communicate spatially enabled data and information about the jurisdiction.

According to Masser, Rajabifard, and Williamson (2007), the development of SDIs over the last 15 years and the vision of spatially enabled government have many parallels, but there are also important differences. The challenge is to develop an effective SDI that will support the vast majority of society members, who are not spatially aware, in a transparent manner. All types of participating organizations (including governments, industries, and academic institutions) could thus gain access to a wider share of the information market. This could be done by organizations providing access to their own spatial data and services, becoming contributors in return, and hence gaining access to the next generation of different and more complex services. The vision is to facilitate integration of existing government spatial data initiatives for access and delivery of data and information. Such an environment would be more than just a simple representation of the features in a virtual world. It would also include the administration and institutional aspects of those features, enabling both technical and institutional aspects to be incorporated into decision making. Following this direction, in Australia, for example, researchers have defined an enabling platform called Virtual Australia (Rajabifard, Binns, and Williamson 2006), which aims to enable government and other users from all industries and information sectors to access both spatial information (generally held by governments) and applications that use spatial information (developed by the private sector and governments).

## SDI and Sustainable Development

While SDIs play an essential role in supporting LAS, they also have a wider role in supporting sustainable development objectives. Achievement of sustainable development is not possible without a comprehensive understanding of the changing natural environment. The impact of human activities on the natural environment can be monitored by integrating virtual representations of the built and natural environments. Despite the significance of data integration, however, many jurisdictions fragment institutional arrangements and data custodianship in the built and natural information areas. For example, the land administration, cadastral, or land titles office (which has a key role in providing built-environment, people-relevant data) is often separated from state or national mapping organizations responsible for managing the natural environment data. Fragmentation among data custodians produces diverse approaches to data acquisition, models, maintenance, and sharing. Many countries attempt to address the inconsistencies through development of national SDIs. However, a framework and associated tools to facilitate integration of multisourced data are also needed (Mohammadi et al. 2006). An SDI can provide the institutional, administrative, and technical basis to ensure the national consistency of content to meet user needs in the context of sustainable development.

## THE POTENTIAL OF LAND ADMINISTRATION SYSTEMS

This brief review of the evolution of cadastres, LAS, SDIs, and land markets shows that the tradition of cadastral parcels representing the built environmental landscape is being replaced by a complex arrangement of overlapping tenures reflecting a wide range of rights, restrictions, and responsibilities, and that a new range of complex commodities building on this trend is emerging. To a large extent these developments are driven by the desire of societies to better meet sustainable development objectives. There is no reason to believe that these trends will not continue as all societies better appreciate the need to manage the environment for future generations and to deliver stable tenure and equity in land distribution.

While the growth of complex commodities offers huge potential for cadastral systems to play a greater role in delivering sustainable development objectives, and in supporting the trading of these complex commodities in particular, one complex commodity, land information, is capable of transforming the way government and the private sector do business. The potential offered by land information in a virtual world in spatially enabling government is

**Figure 8.9:** Technical Evolution of Land Administration

Source: Williamson (2006).

so large it is difficult to contemplate. We are starting to glimpse this potential in initiatives such as Google Earth and Microsoft's Virtual Earth, as previously mentioned, but that is barely a start. Predictions of the importance of spatial information have been recognized in many influential forums, including the prestigious journal *Nature* and in Australian prime minister John Winston Howard's December 2002 statement on frontier technologies for building and transforming Australia's industries. Both these examples place the growth and importance of the geosciences alongside nanotechnology and biotechnology as transformational technologies in the decade ahead.

The significance of land administration and its cadastral core are indicated in figure 8.9 (Williamson 2006), which shows the transformation of land administration and cadastral systems over the last three decades. The figure shows five stages in the evolution of our cadastral systems from a technology perspective. The first stage recognizes that historically cadastral systems were manually operated and all maps and indexes were in hard copy. At that stage, the cadastre focused on security of tenure and simple land trading. The 1980s saw the computerization of records with the creation of digital cadastral databases and computerized indexes. While that did not change the role of the land registry or cadastre, it was a catalyst felt worldwide, initiating institutional change to start bringing the traditionally separate functions of surveying and mapping, cadastre and land registration together.

With the growth of the Internet, the 1990s saw governments start to put information about their land administration systems online, as they became more service oriented. As a result, Internet access to cadastral maps and data was possible. This facilitated digital lodgment of cadastral data and opened up the era of electronic conveyancing or electronic land transfer (*e-conveyancing*). However, the focus on security of tenure and simple land trading within separate institutional data silos continued. At the same time, the era saw the establishment of the SDI concept (Williamson, Rajabifard, and Feeney 2003; Rajabifard, Binns, and Williamson 2005). The SDI concept, together with Web enablement, stimulated the integration of different data sets (particularly the natural and built environment data sets) with these integrated data sets, now considered critical infrastructure for any nation-state.

Now a significant refinement of Web-enabled LAS aims to achieve inter-operability between disparate data sets, facilitated by the partnership business model. This marks the start of an era in which basic land, property, and cadastral information can form an integrating technology between many different sectors of government, such as planning, taxation, land development, and local government. An example is the new Shared Land Information Platform (SLIP) being developed by the state government of Western Australia (Searle and Britton 2005). A key catalyst for interoperability is the development of high-integrity geo-coded national street address files, notably the Australian GNAF (Paull and Marwick 2005). Similarly, "mesh blocks," small aggregations of land parcels, are revolutionizing the way census and demographic data are collected, managed, and used (Toole and Blanchfield 2005). These refinements potentially extend to better management of the complex arrangement of rights, restrictions, and responsibilities relating to land that are essential to achieving sustainable development objectives (Bennett, Wallace, and Williamson 2005). They also stimulate reengineering of cadastral data models to facilitate interoperability between the cadastre, land use planning, and land taxation, for example (Kalantari et al. 2005).

## THE POTENTIAL OF LAND INFORMATION: ILAND

The next chapter of the story requires practitioners, big business, and government to see the potential from linking "location" or the "where" to most activities, policies, and strategies, just over the horizon. This is the emerging era of spatial enablement of government and wider society. Companies like Google are actively negotiating to gain access to the world's large-scale built and natural environment databases. In Australia, Google has negotiated access to the national cadastral and property maps, as well as to GNAF. At the same time, new technologies—such as the Spatial Smart Tag, which is a joint initiative in Australia between government, the private sector, and Microsoft—are being built on top of those enabling infrastructures (McKenzie 2005). We are starting to realize that cadastral and land-related information will dramatically spatially enable both government and the private sector, and society in general. In the near future, spatially enabled systems will underpin health delivery, all forms of taxation, counterterrorism, environmental management, most business processes, elections, and emergency responses, for example.

All these initiatives come together to support a new vision for managing land information—iLand (Wallace and Williamson, 2005; Williamson 2006). The focus on realizing the potential of land and cadastral information will transform iLand into an enabling technology or infrastructure capable of deliv-

**Figure 8.10:** The iLand Vision

**Information**
Government's basic activities are organized and linked to a location. Businesses, people, transactions, and processes are linked to the land and buildings where they take place.

**Interactive**
Government and citizens have open access to land information and use it for personal and governmental decision making.

**Integration**
Activities, standards, laws, processes, and information of government, private sector, and citizens are integrated.

*iLand*

**Internet and Tools**
Spatial technologies: GIS, web mapping services, GPS are used to record, integrate and provide access to spatial information and services.

**Institutions**
Land and spatial information is used ubiquitously across government departments and the private sector.

*Source*: Williamson and Wallace (2006).

ering value to government that far outweighs its value as a support for simple land trading and security of tenure. Cadastres will not stop at the water's edge; they will include a marine dimension where there is a continuum between land and marine environments. Without that basic infrastructure, management of the exceptionally sensitive coastal zone is very difficult, if not impossible (Strain, Rajabifard, and Williamson 2006; Wallace and Williamson 2006c).

In the future, cadastral data will be seen as information, and iLand will become the paradigm for the next decade. iLand is a vision of integrated, spatially enabled land information available on the Internet. iLand enables the "where" in government policies and information. The vision, as shown diagrammatically in figure 8.10, is based on the engineering paradigm in which hard questions receive "design, construct, implement and manage" solutions. The LAS and cadastre are even more significant in iLand. Modern land administration demands an infrastructure such as iLand if land information is to be capable of supporting those "relative" information attributes about people, interests, prices, and transactions so vital for land registries and taxation.

## THE ROLE OF LAND ADMINISTRATION IN SPATIALLY ENABLING GOVERNMENT

Most governments already have considerable infrastructure and administrative systems for better management of land and resources. Basic information-creating processes are cadastral surveying that identifies land; its supporting digital cadastral database, which provides the spatial integrity and unique land parcel identification; registering land that supports simple land trading (buying, selling, mortgaging, and leasing land); running land information systems (LIS) for land development, valuation, and land use planning; and geographic information systems, which provide mapping and resource information. For modern governments at all stages of development, one question is how best to integrate those processes, especially to offer them in an Internet-enabled e-government environment.

Twenty years ago, each of the above processes and the associated collection of information was distinct and separate. Two changes in the world at large challenged that silo approach. First, thanks to improvements in technology, the infrastructure available to support modern land and resource management now spans three distinct environments: the natural, the built, and the virtual. Second, the pressures on managers created by increased populations, environmental degradation, water scarcity, and climate change require governments to have more accurate and comprehensive information than ever before.

How governments treat their land information will define their transformation or reengineering of internal and external government processes as a result of spatial enablement. The e-land administration concept as part of e-government initiatives is now moving to a wider use of spatially enabled land information, expressed in the concept of iLand—integrated, interactive spatial information available on the Internet. The conversion of existing government processes to spatially enabled systems will increase usability of, access to, and visualization of information.

Governments can be regarded as spatially enabled when they treat location and spatial information as common goods made available to citizens and businesses to encourage creativity and product development, and use "place," or location, as a means of organizing their information, and even their activities. The vision of a spatially enabled government involves establishing an enabling infrastructure to facilitate that use of place or location to organize information about activities of people and businesses, and about government actions, decisions, and policies. Central to spatial enablement as a process is spatial enablement of information in LAS. Given the potential of new technologies, once the infrastructure is built, use of place or location will facilitate the evaluation and analysis of both spatial and nonspatial relationships among people, business transactions, and government (Williamson and Wallace 2006).

An infrastructure capable of supporting spatial enablement of governments and societies includes technical, institutional, legal, social, and knowledge transfer issues. All of these need to be identified. In Australia and other countries at similar levels of development, given current technologies, the path to spatial enablement could involve the steps identified in table 8.1.

For other countries with different institutions, laws, and information technologies, the appropriate steps will be different. Whatever the steps in a

**TABLE 8.1** Ten Tools to Spatially Enable Australian Governments for Sustainable Development

| No. | Tool | Description |
|---|---|---|
| 1 | *Use of spatial information* | Major departments and agencies use maps and visualizations to present information and permit interactive interrogation. Australia already has significant expertise. |
| 2 | *Spatial information availability policy* | Spatial information is available as a common good on a free or low-cost basis, encouraging innovation throughout government, the private sector, and the community. |
| 3 | *Cadastre as the fundamental layer of information* | The cadastre is the primary source of technical, accurate, large-scale, digital information about how land is used. It must be converted into an *authoritative register* of spatial land information (Wallace and Williamson 2006b). |
| 4 | *Easily understood mechanism for using spatial enablement throughout agencies* | Spatially enabled land information from the cadastre, land and resource registries, land planning and valuation flows through to tax offices, emergency services, health services, census offices, service utilities, and so on by consistent geo-coding or other means—for example, Australia's geo-coded national address file and The Netherlands' Kadaster compliance with XML-compatible data for a multinational system, in The International Spatial Infrastructure project (INSPIRE) of EU. |
| 5 | *A national and widely implemented land information policy: iLand* | Whole of government land information policy aims to ensure that basic land information, especially the cadastre, is both spatially enabled and authoritative. |
| 6 | *Interoperability of spatial information— Australian SDI* | A national SDI provides the Web-enabling platform; solutions to interoperability of information about natural and built environments; and coordination of terrestrial, coastal, and marine information. |
| 7 | *Interoperability of all government information and services* | All government information becomes interoperable, initially via geo-coding and related IT systems (not just geo-coded land information as in 2006), in sufficiently flexible arrays to take advantage of technical and institutional innovations. |
| 8 | *Service delivery through e-government* | Government services, not merely information, are provided through spatially enabled, Web-enabled, or portable instrument–enabled, and interactive, systems. |

*(continued)*

| No. | Tool | Description |
|-----|------|-------------|
| 9 | *Use of "place" to organize information, services, and activities* | Government organizes information and activities around unique geo-codes and other spatial information relating to places and locations, in addition to, or in place of, unique business file numbers, identification numbers, dates, and so on, that now populate standard relational databases and object recognition systems in object-oriented architectures, merging into service-oriented architectures. This involves reorganization of government activities—at local, state, and national levels—and introduction of new legal, technical, and organizational frameworks. New business models are invented. |
| 10 | *Monitoring and evaluation* | Continuous reappraisal of processes against policies is carried out. |

*Source:* Compiled by the researchers in the Centre for Spatial Data Infrastructures and Land Administration, Department of Geomatics, University of Melbourne, 2006.

nation's path, the need to improve availability of information to inform policy decisions remains universal.

## THE ROLE OF LAND ADMINISTRATION IN SUPPORTING SUSTAINABLE DEVELOPMENT

These developments and drivers will introduce complexity into the design of LAS as they adapt to assist delivery of a broader range of public policy and economic goals, the most important of which is sustainable development. Reengineering LAS to support sustainable development objectives is a major change in direction for traditional LAS and is a significant challenge (Enemark, Williamson, and Wallace 2005).

The global trends to move LAS down this path, and the national and historical methods used to incorporate sustainable development objectives into national LAS, were examined in an Expert Group Meeting (EGM) in Melbourne in December 2005 with leading stakeholders and land policy experts from Australia and Europe (Williamson, Enemark, and Wallace 2006b). Distinctions between approaches used in modern European democracies and in Australia were identified. The European approach showed more integration between the standard LAS activities and measures of sustainability. Australian policy was more fractured, partly due to federation and the

**Figure 8.11:** Land Management Vision

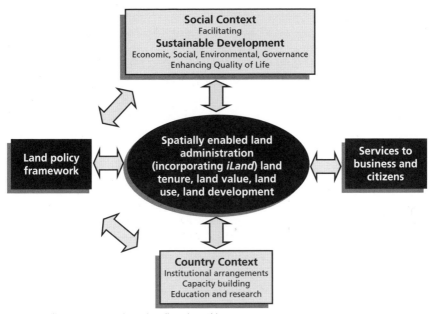

*Source*: Williamson, Enemark, and Wallace (2006b).

constitutional distribution of powers. In contrast, Australian LAS pioneering lay in incorporating market-based instruments (MBIs) and complex commodities into LAS, and revitalization of land information through inventive Web-based initiatives.

The EGM developed a vision for future LAS sufficiently flexible to adapt to this changing world of new technology, novel market demands, and sustainable development, as shown in figure 8.11. This vision incorporates and builds upon the vision of iLand and can be considered an infrastructure or enabling platform to support spatial enablement of government (Wallace, Williamson, and Enemark 2006; Williamson, Enemark, and Wallace 2006a, 2006b).

## CONCLUSION

People-to-land relationships are dynamic. The land administration and cadastral responses to managing those relationships are also dynamic and continually evolving. For developed countries, a central objective of LAS is to serve efficient and effective land markets. Because of sustainable development and technology drivers, modern land markets now trade in complex commodities; however, existing LAS, and the companion skills of land surveyors, lawyers, and administrators, remain focused on the more traditional processes supporting simple land trading. The growth in complex commodities offers many opportunities for land administrators who are prepared to think laterally and more strategically.

The importance of land information has grown over the last few decades. It is now more important and useful to government than merely providing traditional support for security of tenure and simple land trading. LAS, and their core cadastral components, are evolving into an essential infrastructure embracing SDIs, iLand, and new technologies to spatially enable governments, and to identify the "where" for all government decisions, policies, and implementation strategies. Eventually, although probably sooner rather than later, spatial enablement of governments and societies will provide links between land administration and sustainable development so that sustainability accounting measures are fed into monitoring and evaluation systems.

This brief account of the future challenges land administration officials to design and build modern land administration and cadastral systems capable of supporting the creation, administration, and trading of complex commodities, and of providing reliable land information to spatially enable governments and societies in general. Unfortunately, unless LAS are refocused on delivering transparent and vital land information and enabling platforms, modern economies will have difficulty meeting sustainable development objectives and achieving their economic potential.

## REFERENCES

Note: Most referenced articles that have been authored or coauthored by I. P. Williamson are available at http://www.geom.unimelb.edu.au/people/ipw.html.

Bennett, R., J. Wallace, and I. P. Williamson. 2005. Integrated land administration in Australia. *Proceedings of the Spatial Sciences Institute Biennial Conference*, Melbourne, Australia, September 12–16. CD-ROM.
———. 2008. Towards sustainable land management: A tool for describing and holistically understanding property interests. *Journal of Land Use Policy* 25(1):126–138.
Dalrymple, K., J. Wallace, and I. P. Williamson. 2004. Innovations in rural land policy and tenure in Southeast Asia. Paper presented at the Third FIG Regional Conference, Jakarta, Indonesia, October 4–7. http://www.fig.net/pub/jakarta/papers/ts _10/ts_10_1_dalrymple_etal.pdf.
de Soto, H. 2000. *The mystery of capital: Why capitalism triumphs in the west and fails everywhere else*. London: Bantam Press.

Enemark, S., I. P. Williamson, and J. Wallace. 2005. Building modern land administration systems in developed economies. *Journal of Spatial Science* 2(50):51–68.

International Federation of Surveyors. 1995. *The FIG statement on the cadastre*. FIG Publication No. 11. Copenhagen: International Federation of Surveyors. http://www.fig.net/commission7/reports/cadastre/statement_on_cadastre.html.

———. 1998. *Cadastre 2014*. Copenhagen: International Federation of Surveyors. http://www.fig.net/commission7/reports/cad2014/.

———. 1999. *The Bathurst declaration on land administration for sustainable development*. Copenhagen: International Federation of Surveyors. http://www.fig.net/pub/figpub/pub21/figpub21.htm.

Kalantari, M., A. Rajabifard, J. Wallace, and I. P. Williamson. 2005. Towards e-land administration: Australian on-line land information services. *Proceedings of the Spatial Sciences Institute Biennial Conference*, Melbourne, Australia, September 12–16. CD-ROM.

Masser, I., A. Rajabifard, and I. P. Williamson. 2007. Spatially enabling governments through SDI implementation. *International Journal of Geographical Information Science* 21(July):1–16.

McKenzie, D. 2005. Victorian spatial smart tag: How to bring spatial information to government's nontechnical users. *Proceedings of the Spatial Sciences Institute Biennial Conference*, Melbourne, Australia, September 12–16. CD-ROM.

Mohammadi, H., A. Rajabifard, A. Binns, and I. P. Williamson. 2006. Bridging SDI design gaps to facilitate multi-source data integration. *Coordinates* 2(5):26–29.

Paull, D., and B. Marwick. 2005. Maintaining Australia's geocoded national address file (GNAF). *Proceedings of the Spatial Sciences Institute Biennial Conference*, Melbourne, Australia, September 12–16. CD-ROM.

Rajabifard, A., A. Binns, and I. P. Williamson. 2005. Development of a virtual Australia utilising an SDI enabled platform. *Global Spatial Data Infrastructure 8 and FIG Working Week Conference*, Cairo, Egypt, April 14–18.

———. 2006. Virtual Australia: An enabling platform to improve opportunities in the spatial information industry. *Journal of Spatial Science* 51(1) (special edition).

Searle, G., and D. M. Britton. 2005. Government working together through a shared land information platform (SLIP). *Proceedings of the Spatial Sciences Institute Biennial Conference*, Melbourne, Australia, September 12–16. CD-ROM.

Strain, L., A. Rajabifard, and I. P. Williamson. 2006. Marine administration and spatial data infrastructures. *International Journal of Marine Policy* 30:431–441.

Ting, L., and I. P. Williamson. 1999. Cadastral trends: A synthesis. *Australian Surveyor* 4(1):46–54.

Ting, L., I. P. Williamson, D. Grant, and J. Parker. 1999. Understanding the evolution of land administration systems in some common law countries. *Survey Review* 35(272):83–102.

Toole, M., and F. Blanchfield. 2005. Mesh blocks: From theory to practice. *Proceedings of the Spatial Sciences Institute Biennial Conference*, Melbourne, Australia, September 12–16. CD-ROM.

Wallace, J., and I. P. Williamson. 2005. A vision for spatially informed land administration in Australia. *Proceedings of the Spatial Sciences Institute Biennial Conference*, Melbourne, Australia, September 12–16. CD-ROM.

———. 2006a. Building land markets. *Journal of Land Use Policy* 23(2):123–135.

———. 2006b. Building sustainability accounting in land administration systems in Australia. In *Sustainability and land administration systems*. I. P. Williamson, S. Enemark, and J. Wallace, eds., 31–46. Melbourne, Australia: Centre for Spatial Data Infrastructures and Land Administration, Department of Geomatics.

———. 2006c. Registration of marine interests in Asia-Pacific region. *International Journal of Marine Policy* 30(3):207–219.

Wallace, J., I. P. Williamson, and S. Enemark. 2006. Building a national vision for spatially enabled land administration in Australia. In *Sustainability and land administration systems*. I. P. Williamson, S. Enemark, and J. Wallace, eds., 237–250. Melbourne, Australia: Centre for Spatial Data Infrastructures and Land Administration, Department of Geomatics.

Williamson, I. P. 2006. A land administration vision. In *Sustainability and land administration systems*. I. P. Williamson, S. Enemark, and J. Wallace, eds., 3–16. Melbourne, Australia: Centre for Spatial Data Infrastructures and Land Administration, Department of Geomatics.

Williamson, I. P., S. Enemark, and J. Wallace. 2006a. Incorporating sustainable development objectives into land administration. *Proceedings of the XXIII FIG Congress: Shaping the Change*, TS 22, Munich, Germany, October 8–13.

———, eds. 2006b. Executive summary. In *Sustainability and land administration systems*. Melbourne, Australia: Centre for Spatial Data Infrastructures and Land Administration, Department of Geomatics.

Williamson, I. P., A. Rajabifard, and M-E. F. Feeney, eds. 2003. *Developing spatial data infrastructures: From concept to reality*. London: Taylor and Francis.

Williamson, I. P., and J. Wallace. 2006. Spatially enabling governments: A new direction for land administration systems. *Proceedings of the XXIII FIG Congress: Shaping the Change*, TS 22, Munich, Germany, October 8–13.

Williamson, I. P., J. Wallace, and A. Rajabifard. 2006. Spatially enabling governments: A new vision for spatial information. Paper presented at the Seventeenth UNRCC-AP Conference and Twelfth Meeting of the PCGIAP, Bangkok, Thailand, September 18–22.

World Bank. 2004. Doing business in 2004: Understanding regulation. Washington, DC: World Bank. http://www.doingbusiness.org/Documents/DB2004-full-report.pdf

———. 2005. Doing business in 2005: Removing obstacles to growth. Washington, DC: World Bank. http://www.doingbusiness.org/documents/DoingBusiness2005.pdf.

# 9

# The Multilateral Development Bank as Legal Midwife: Delivering Property Rights Reform

John W. Bruce

A number of chapters in this volume—particularly chapters 10 and 11, by Bromley and Bebbington, respectively—raise questions about the relevance and adequacy for developing countries of received notions about property rights in land, at least the versions conveyed by development institutions such as the multilateral development banks (MDBs). Bebbington, noting that such outside players now influence local perceptions of meanings of land, suggests that it is important that we explore *how* these outside influences operate. Many multilateral and bilateral donors are actively involved in the promotion of land tenure reform,[1] but this chapter describes the mechanics and substance of the promotion of property rights reform by the World Bank, drawing on my seven years in its Legal Department. The World Bank is the development agency whose research has most influenced thinking on property rights reform in the developing world.[2] To what extent can we observe the future of property rights in developing countries in the bank's efforts?

---

[1] Among the multilaterals, the Inter-American Development Bank and the Asian Development Bank are both important actors in the land tenure reform field. The U.S. Agency for International Development (USAID), the U.K. Department for International Development (DFID), Australia's AusAID, and the Deutsche Gesellschaft für Technische Zusammenarbeit (German Technical Cooperation, or GTZ) are among the more active bilaterals.

[2] The World Bank established its preeminence in this area through the writings of Gershon Feder of the bank's Development Research Group. See Feder's landmark Thailand study (1988) and, more generally, Feder and Nishio (1999).

## PROPERTY RIGHTS REFORM AS A GROWTH AREA

The bilateral and multilateral donor organizations that manage development assistance are more focused on property rights reform today than at any time in the last half century. Concerns for land reform from cold war days have given way to an emphasis on the need for secure, marketable property rights in land. The insights that provide the economic basis for land tenure reform are not new but come out of early work in agricultural economics, notably the eighteenth-century debate on the impacts of tenancy on productivity. In chapter 10 of this volume Bromley reviews those developments through the work of several economic thinkers. In the less nuanced world of development "common knowledge," however, the idea that stands out is that strong property rights can enhance farmer incentives and, in the words of Adam Smith, "turn sand to gold."

Today, equally dramatic propositions about the role of property rights in development are being put forward. Due largely to the work of Hernando de Soto, and in particular his book *The Mystery of Capital*, property rights are urged as fundamental to the process of capital building. The extensive lands held without benefit of formal property rights are characterized as constituting a vast fund of "dead capital," which can be brought to life through the conferring of formal, transferable, and mortgageable property rights. Because the poor hold much of the world's land under informal and customary tenures, it is suggested that they would be major beneficiaries of this change (de Soto 2000).

This is obviously a gross oversimplification. Property rights are only one of the cogs that need to be in place in order for the complex gears of a market economy to engage and move the development process forward. Failure to recognize this and a tendency to see property rights reform as the removal of a "bottleneck" led donors in the 1960s to serious overpromising on the impacts of rural property rights reform and titling. The results were disappointing and gave rise to disillusionment with the strategy (Bruce and Migot-Adholla 1994). Moreover, the poor, given marketable property rights, may lose their land through ill-considered and desperate sales rather than using it to access formal credit (Bledsoe 2006; Quan 2000; de Janvry et al. 2001). When one adds the fact that in many developing countries land is not just an object of investment, but is also the principal resource for social security, is often entangled in a web of kinship relations, and is embedded in local cultures and governance system, the complexity of the task of property rights reform becomes clearer.

What constitutes "reform" of land rights will not mean the same thing at all places and times, and certainly does not mean the same thing to everyone. As Bebbington makes clear, one's idea of what makes sense as land policy and property rights depends on how one can benefit from the land, and different actors bring different values and claims to policy discussions. As he suggests, "It is not simply the case that the meaning of land has changed over time . . . it is also that these different meanings co-exist, and can come into conflict with each other." Land is thus political. Vested and powerful interests are involved, and property rights reform is a task to be tackled carefully. Often it can be achieved only incrementally. Poorly conceived or overambitious property rights reforms sow normative confusion and seriously decrease security of tenure. This is a lesson learned from early land privatization reforms of the 1960s in Kenya and elsewhere (Shipton 1988; Migot-Adholla, Place, and Oluoch-Kosua 1993). But it has been largely disregarded in the enthusiasm for formalization of property rights in land.

What are the main focuses of reforms of property rights today? In countries transitioning out of state ownership and management of land, donor agencies have sought to use technical assistance in law and technology to deliver new property rights systems almost overnight. In eastern and central Europe those efforts have met with considerable success, and, given impetus by the desire of those nations to join the European Union, those reforms will continue to move steadily forward. In former Soviet Central Asia, the process has proved much more difficult and halting, and authoritarian governments have manipulated the privatization process to concentrate land in the hands of the former farm management class and political cronies (Bloch 2002). In China, land has been decollectivized and farmers given greater freedom to produce and market their produce; reforms to further strengthen tenure security are under consideration.[3]

In Latin America, South and Southeast Asia, and especially Africa, the process of property rights reform has been complex, and accurate generalization is more difficult. Many of those countries, especially in Africa, have substantial areas where land rights are governed by custom, plus colonial statutes are still in force and judge-made law by colonial courts is still applicable. Later deposits of legal detritus from attempts at either (or both) land nationalization

---

[3]The major returns to agrarian reform in China appear to have come from the return to family farming and the relief of farmers from production quotas, rather than tenure reforms. Only as the productivity increases due to those initial reforms have tapered off has government granted increments of tenure security; such security is only partial, and the potential of full tenure security has still not been tapped. A great deal is at stake in current discussions of a new property rights law in the People's Congress. I am working on these issues in connection with technical assistance to a World Bank–funded study of tenure issues carried out by the Development Research Center, a research institute of the State Council.

and privatization may further litter the normative landscape. One finds layer upon layer of land legislation like geologic strata, piled upon each other without much attention to repeals or reconciliation, in desperate need of restructuring for accessibility and intelligibility (McAuslan 2000). A housecleaning is clearly needed.

The really challenging issue, however, is that of the future of customary land tenure. In Africa, as Bromley suggests, early efforts at tenure reform and titling met with disappointing results, resulting in a barrage of critical studies. Those efforts underestimated the cultural embeddedness of customary systems: A customary tenure system is not a case of informality, but constitutes an alternative formality with its own values and vested interests. Some critics have urged that such programs were premature (Bruce and Migot-Adholla 1994), others that they misconceived the process of evolution of property rights (Platteau 2000). Bruce and Migot-Adholla (1994) argued for much more selective use of tenure reform and titling, focusing on lands in urban and peri-urban areas, and for development of supplemental strategies that encourage customary land tenure to evolve in response to changing conditions, instead of government seeking to transform it overnight in a forced march toward individual ownership. Still others have argued, as does Bromley, that these titling efforts represent a failed attempt to transplant values about land developed in European cultural and agronomic contexts into African contexts where they simply do not fit, and that fundamentally new approaches are needed.

In spite of some disappointing experiences with these programs, land law and property rights reform remains a staple of development assistance. How exactly does a multilateral development bank such as the World Bank assist client governments in the process of land law reform? National law is made by national institutions, and so the role of an MDB in law reform can only be encouragement and support; however much influence the bank may have, it does not have the final say. Drawing on the recent experience of the World Bank, the flagship of the MDBs, this chapter describes how World Bank task managers decide what reforms to encourage and how those reforms are pursued within the context of the bank's lending programs, then evaluates the relative effectiveness of the different approaches reflected in current practice.

## THE WORLD BANK AND THE CONTENT
## OF PROPERTY RIGHTS REFORM

Neither the World Bank nor any of the other multilateral development banks has a land policy.[4] Do they simply follow the classic prescriptions of neo-classical economics? In fact, World Bank research has produced serious qual-ifications of the property rights prescriptions generally associated with neoclassical economics, and those qualifications have been embraced by the bank in policy papers. The 1988 econometric study of impacts of land titling in Thailand by Gershon Feder made a compelling case for the credit and in-vestment benefits of titling and registering land (Feder 1988). But Bin-swanger, Deininger, and Feder's "Power, Distortion, Revolt and Reform in Agricultural Land Relations" (1995) is an astute analysis of the issues of land tenure and land reform from a political economy perspective. Bruce and Migot-Adholla's *Searching for Security of Land Tenure in Africa* (1994) re-ported survey results from studies jointly funded by USAID and the World Bank in several African countries that raised doubts about whether registra-tion of private ownership would significantly increase investment, and at the same time drew attention to the ability of customary tenure to evolve to meet new needs. A comprehensive statement of the World Bank's approach to land tenure, the 2003 policy research paper *Land Policies for Growth and Poverty Reduction* (Deininger 2003) largely accepts those critiques and embraces a variety of tenure forms including leasehold and the customary tenure system as workable in market economic contexts. Much of the recent work of the World Bank on negotiated land reform (government funding provided to groups of the poor to purchase land in the market) reflects an understanding that land markets will not, left to themselves, deliver land to poor but efficient producers (Deininger 1999).[5] Most recently, a volume on land law reform published by the World Bank's Legal Vice-Presidency urges refocusing land law reform efforts to prioritize gender equity, poverty reduction, and natural resource conservation (Bruce 2006).

The relatively innovative perspectives developed from World Bank research are not always reflected in its lending, however. It is not the bank's researchers or

---

[4]It should be noted that the World Bank does have two operational policies that have land law content, but they are narrowly focused. Denominated safeguard policies because they seek to avoid or mitigate negative effects of World Bank–funded projects, these are Operational Policy 4.12, Involuntary Resettlement (April 2004) and Operational Policy 4.1 Indigenous Peoples (May 2005). The former deals with the protection of land users displaced by World Bank–funded activities, the latter with the protection of indigenous land rights.

[5]"Negotiated land reform" seems an appropriate term for the approach, as opposed to the mis-leading "community-based land reform" used in some later bank documents.

the policy wonks in the central (or "anchor") units who work with client countries to develop and deliver bankable projects for board consideration. That work is done by the bank's task managers, based in the regional vice-presidencies. Task managers of land projects exhibit very different levels of experience and expertise in the land area. Some are deeply committed to work on land issues, have substantial experience, and have developed a sophisticated and pragmatic understanding of the economic and political issues at stake.[6] But there are other bank staff managing land projects with little or no specialist knowledge; that is considered acceptable on the questionable reasoning that a good manager can access the expertise needed through the hiring of consultants.

How is new knowledge generated by research and related best practices communicated to this task manager cadre? The most important conduit is the Land Policy and Administration Thematic Group. Thematic groups are voluntary associations of staff with common interests, sponsored and funded at a modest level by anchor units, in this case the Rural Development Department.[7] These thematic groups mix "anchor" staff (staff from central units in the bank whose job is to provide expertise and advice to colleagues and clients) with staff from the regional lending units, in particular the task manager cadre. Research results and field experience are exchanged largely through brown-bag lunches, seminars, and presentations during the bank's annual Rural Week.

New knowledge and understandings from research do reach bank lending staff, but they do so slowly and imperfectly, and when faced with decisions, bank task managers sometimes fall back on economic first principles. They tend to assume, for instance, that land markets are benign, will distribute land fairly, and will produce more efficient and productive land use. The roughly 20 ongoing World Bank land administration projects, whose land titling and registration support the development of land markets, dwarf the four ongoing projects supporting negotiated land reform.[8]

---

[6]Specialization beyond a certain point is not an advantage for advancement in the World Bank, and those who do specialize may do so at some cost to any aspirations they have for advancement into management.

[7]I served as the "anchor" (management representative for the Rural Development Department) for this group, in the capacity as land tenure expert for that department. With a core group of perhaps 15 active members and officers elected by the membership, it is one of the most effective thematic groups (TGs) in the bank. Its Web site can be accessed under the Rural Development heading in the World Bank site at http://www.worldbank.org. Its members are heavily but not exclusively from regional lending operations rather than the central advisory, or "anchor" units. The bank has a matrix management system, and most of the TG members are part of the "Rural Family" under that system. The TG serves a knowledge-sharing function but also serves as an advocacy group within the bank, committed to keeping land matters high on the agenda of the institution.

[8]The countries in which the bank supports negotiated land reform include Brazil, Malawi, South Africa, and Bolivia. A 2005 list of countries in which the bank is supporting land administration

The bank's task managers seek to implement their understandings of the need for property rights system reforms in two distinct lending contexts. One is the policy lending context, in which bank lending is specifically framed to promote policy change and legal reforms. The other is investment lending, in projects that invest in land administration or other concrete activities such as the construction of infrastructure or agricultural development. While the latter projects do not have law reform as a primary objective, law reform may be seen as needed for project success, and so a "policy and regulatory framework" component will be included in the project to support reform efforts.

The World Bank cannot compel legal change by sovereign states, but it does create incentives for governments to change laws: Funding for a project or part of a project may be conditioned on certain legal reforms. It generally does so in partnership with the ministry or other government agency with which it is working, often the recipient of its funds, and in support of local champions of such reforms. It focuses on changes in law rather than only policy, because policy is ephemeral and binds only the government of the day, whereas legal changes remain the law even after governments change.

## LAW REFORM IN THE POLICY LENDING CONTEXT

An ever-larger part of bank lending, more than a fourth of new commitments in the 2005 fiscal year, falls outside traditional investment projects and in the realm of policy lending.[9] The relevant lending instruments were previously Structural Adjustment Loans but today are largely Poverty Reduction Support Credits (PRSCs) (World Bank 2003b). For a PRSC, the policy or legal reforms needed are typically described in a Letter of Development Policy exchanged between the bank and the government as a prelude to the loan.[10] These typically deal with numerous reforms stretching across sectors. The Letter of Development Policy is written by a client government official to the

---

reform lists projects in Armenia, Bulgaria, Cambodia, El Salvador, Guatemala, Ghana, Indonesia, Ivory Coast, Kyrgyz Republic, Laos, Moldova, Nicaragua, Philippines, Romania, Russia, Slovenia, Sri Lanka, Ukraine, and West Bank and Gaza.

[9] FY 2005 new commitments consisted of US$16,215.44 million for investment projects and US$6,604.68 for development policy projects. See http://web/worldbank.org/ external/projects.

[10] Footnote 14 to paragraph 14 of Operational Policy (OP) 7.0 goes on to explain, "Development policy loans require often [sic] entail significant changes in existing laws, regulations, and administrative practices. The legislative steps to be undertaken are normally described in the Letter of Development Policy (see para. 16), but may also be part of the specific actions incorporated in the Loan Agreement as conditions of Board presentation or conditions of disbursement of particular loan tranches, rather than as covenants."

World Bank as part of the lead-up to the PRSC. Progress in achieving reforms is later reviewed in the PRSC Program Document and the subsequent aide-mémoires from bank supervision missions. As countries usually have a succession of PRSCs, this process repeats itself: a statement of intention in a policy letter followed by assessments of progress under the PRSC, followed by a further policy letter, followed by another PRSC, and so on.

For example, the bank is currently working with the government of Vietnam on land policy and legal development, which are dealt with under the Vietnam Second Poverty Reduction Support Credit, 2003 (P075398). The Letter of Development Policy (LDP) for the credit provides, in paragraph 54, that the program will support issuance of land tenure certificates, noting that land use rights that can be traded and mortgaged provide several benefits, especially for the poor. The Development Credit Agreement (DCA) for the project, in schedule 2, notes progress made to date: issuance of land use right certificates (1) to about 35 percent of users of urban residential land; and (2) in forest areas, to about 60 percent of households and individual land users who have received or rented forest land directly from the state. The letter goes on to state, in paragraph 80, that under future PRSCs

> the National Assembly is expected to adopt a new, substantially revised Land Law, which will provide greater land-tenure security and equal access to land by all sectors, that is correspondent with the customs and habits of the communities that are using the land legally. Registration and other civil transactions relating to land use rights will be simplified. Especially, land use rights and project bidding methods will be applied widely for the cases when credit organizations fail to collect their debts. Issuance of Land Tenure Certificates will be continued under PRSCs.[11]

Policy lending is a powerful tool for law reform because PRSCs provide largely untied and thus very attractive funding. But they have some drawbacks as vehicles for law reforms as well. First, in contrast to land investment projects, project preparation for PRSCs sometimes does not effectively mobilize expertise on land law and policy from within and outside the bank at the time the conditionality is designed. This is because the project is not focused on land, but is being used to leverage numerous and diverse policy changes. The bank staff involved represent a variety of sectoral interests and often lack the land-specific expertise of bank staff working on investment projects that deal directly with land. These nonspecialists are more likely to

---

[11]Letter of Development Policy from the governor of the Bank of Vietnam to the president of the World Bank (30 May 2003). This and many similar documents are available in the Project section of the Bank's Web site at http://www.worldbank.org.

fall back on economic "first principles" rather than the more nuanced prescriptions indicated by recent research and experience. Second, a policy loan often does not provide for effective technical assistance to the client government in meeting its policy and law reform obligations in relation to the loan. Third, the PRSC context does not allow focused application of loan funds to support particular activities; the assistance consists of broad support for government across a wide range of deserving purposes. Follow-through in terms of support for implementation of legal reforms is often not present.

## LAW REFORM IN THE INVESTMENT POLICY CONTEXT

During preparation of any investment project, the Task Team entrusted with developing the project asks if the legal conditions needed to achieve project objectives exist. How rights are defined and distributed can affect both how intended beneficiaries will respond to the opportunities offered by the project and how the benefits of the project will be distributed. The team may recommend a condition in the credit agreement requiring legal change, for instance, a condition involving law reform that must be met before funds are disbursed. In many cases, the legal problem affects some subset of activities under the project, so the condition on disbursement may apply only to the relevant component of the project. Recognizing the need for government to respect the legislative branch's prerogatives—here the rationale is quite different than in policy lending—the bank is careful regarding the legal form of obligation taken government commitments to enact laws. They are inserted in the loan agreement using conditions rather than covenants, whose violation has more serious consequences than failure to meet a condition. Often, the condition will take the form of a commitment by the executive branch of government to prepare and submit legislation to the legislative branch by a particular date, rather than a commitment to enact the legislation.[12]

It is rare that projects that are not "land" projects call for legal change, and conventional wisdom among task managers of World Bank land projects is that it will usually be futile to tackle land policy and law reform without the

---

[12]The World Bank's OP 7.00 *Lending Operations: Choice of Borrower and Contractual Arrangements* (February 2001) provides in paragraph 14 the following: "The Bank does not stipulate covenants that require the member to enact legislation, and tries to work within existing law to the extent possible. If enactment of particular legislation is necessary to achieve the project's objectives, the appropriate steps to be taken for such enactment should be clearly defined; and such enactment is made a condition of negotiation, Board presentation, effectiveness, or disbursement, rather than a covenant."

strong focus on those issues provided by a land project. They simply require focused attention and substantial resources if changes are to be achieved.

Most land law reform support then takes place in the context of investment projects that are focused primarily on land issues. These tend to fall into three major categories: (1) land administration projects; (2) land reform projects; and (3) natural resource management projects. Land law reform in each of these project contexts is reviewed in turn.

## Land Administration Projects

Land administration projects account for the majority of "land lending" by the World Bank. The objective of these projects is to provide security of tenure and enable the development of land markets, and they do that by supporting the provision and documentation of land rights. While such a project usually has several components, a look at the budgets makes clear that these are essentially land titling and registration projects. Such projects are common in countries of Eastern Europe and the former Soviet Union, and there are also a substantial number in East Asia and Latin America; there are fewer in Africa and other regions. On both efficiency and equity grounds, the bank has supported primarily systematic titling and title registration, based on a field operation for demarcation and survey of boundaries and adjudication of rights. At best, that process moves from parcel to parcel in a locale officially declared an "adjudication area," gathering the needed information and informally mediating disputes. The approach is especially useful in major transitions, as when (1) customary or informal rights are to be formalized; (2) state or collective land is being broken up into smaller holdings and privatized; or (3) it is simply desired to bring all land in an area onto a single efficient rights database. Because the process is painstaking and participatory, fraud is minimized and the results are reliable, so registration of a title can be given conclusive or other strong legal effect. The certainty created allows anyone contemplating a transaction to rely confidently on the register to show who is the legal owner of the land (Simpson 1976; Dale and McLaughlin 1999; Deininger 2003). A review of these projects shows a variety of legal reform issues arising, pursued under subcomponents for "policy and legal reform" or "the regulatory framework."

First, there are sometimes issues with the content of the rights to be registered. While the bank has become far more flexible over the years in this regard, and is comfortable funding titling of customary rights, use rights, and leasehold rights, it must still ask whether the tenure available is robust enough to provide landholders with the incentives needed to invest and is secure under national law. There is, after all, little point in documenting rights that may be arbitrarily withdrawn or casually overridden by government or powerful private interests. This issue surfaces only occasionally in land administration projects, because it is so fundamental that it should be addressed before such a project will even be considered. It is especially important in countries in transition out of state ownership of all land, such as those in Eastern and Central Europe and Central Asia. Some of the Eastern European countries, such as Poland, Yugoslavia, and Hungary, retained a limited amount of land under private ownership (household food plots, for instance) even under communism, and so property rights reforms come relatively easily. In countries of the former Soviet Union the process has been more difficult. In former Soviet Central Asia, some countries, such as the Kyrgyz Republic, have made the transition to private property relatively quickly, but in others, such as Azerbaijan, Kazakhstan, Tajikistan, and Uzbekistan, the reform process has been halting and has delayed World Bank–funded support for land administration.[13]

The World Bank does sometimes commit to land administration projects, however, in countries where improvements in the content of property rights are a concern. For example, the loan agreement concluded for the Ghana Land Administration Project, 2003 (P071157), reflects a concern with security of tenure through a disbursement condition that requires clarification satisfactory to the bank of a constitutional issue concerning the continued validity of customary land rights. This assurance, in the form of memoranda from the ministry and the attorney general, were provided and the condition met. In another example, the Nicaragua Agricultural Technology and Land Management Project, 2002 (P056018), supported a national Committee for the Study of Agrarian Legislation in the hope of drafting a new law to consolidate and guarantee property rights.

Second, and by far the most common, land administration projects support reform of the legal framework for three basic tasks in the process of land titling and registration itself: rights adjudication, survey, and titling. Bank task managers experienced in these projects are knowledgeable about the legal issues and models involved. The key statutes for titling and registration are typically a land registration act, a land adjudication act, and a land survey act. One sometimes finds these dealt with in broad terms in a single land law, with specifics left to regulations.

---

[13]An anticipated land administration project in Kazakhstan was cancelled in part because an earlier project failed in its attempt to obtain a revision of the 1994 Land Code, which left landholders vulnerable to revocation of their land rights by officials and was not adequate for a market-oriented land economy.

In Cambodia, for example, the Land Law of 2001 contains the basic legal framework for title registration, adjudication, and survey, but few details. The multidonor Cambodia Land Management and Administration Project (LMAP) supported by the World Bank has focused its legal reform assistance on elaboration of the subsidiary legislation related to adjudication and titling. Technical assistance has been provided by an Asian Development Bank team working within the Ministry of Lands, and the ministry has produced and enacted a broad range of subsidiary laws and regulations under which an ambitious program of systematic titling and registration is going forward.[14]

Specific legal issues that arise with some frequency in land administration projects and for which legal reforms have been sought include the needs to (1) create one-stop shops to better service clients; (2) strengthen provisions on the legal conclusiveness of titling; (3) provide more adequately for systematic adjudication of land rights; (4) provide public access to the land register; (5) give field adjudication officers the authority to make decisions based on incomplete documentary evidence and to rely upon oral evidence; and (6) provide more rigorous standards for correction of mistakes in the register (Bruce 2006). While some of these may seem "technical matters," there is often opposition from attorneys and notaries to simplifying reforms of land registration law, because they see their incomes as threatened by simpler, cheaper approaches.

Third, there are sometimes institutional reform issues to be addressed that require legal change. The World Bank often urges consolidation of several institutions with roles in the land registration and titling process into a single agency to reduce the alarming transaction costs that can be involved in registration. Commonly, for instance, survey and title adjudication functions are in a lands agency, while the title register is managed by the Ministry of Justice. Bank experts insist that land administration projects in one-agency countries (Armenia, Moldova, and Kyrgyz Republic) are performing well, but not those in two-agency countries (Bulgaria, Croatia, and Romania). The World Bank's project on land registration in Macedonia only moved forward

---

[14]Land Law, promulgated as Royal Decree NS/RKM/0801/14, 30 August 2001, deals with land registration in articles 226–246. The regulations promulgated under LMAP to date include Sub-Decree No. 46 ANK/BK of 31 May 2002, "Procedures of Establishment Cadastral Index Map and Land Register"; Sub-Decree No. 47 ANK/BK of 31 May 2002, "Organization and Functioning of the Cadastral Commission"; Sub-Decree No. 48 ANK/BK of 31 May 2002, "Sporadic Land Registration"; Prakas (regulation) of the Ministry of Land Management, Urban Planning and Construction No. 112 DNS/BrK of 21 August 2002, "Guidelines and Procedures of the Cadastral Commission"; and Ministry of Land Management, Urban Planning and Construction, No. 001DNS/SD of 19 August 2002, "Instructive Circular Relating to the Implementation of the Procedure of Establishing the Cadastral Index Map and the Land Register (Systematic Registration)."

to signature once the title registration function was moved from the Ministry of Justice to the state agency for geodetic works. This can be a contentious issue with Western European donors, who are familiar with and quite comfortable with the two-agency model. And the bank is not always successful in achieving the sought-after reform. Under the Philippines Land Administration and Management Project, 2000 (P066069), a proposal to consolidate the land titling function in the Ministry of Natural Resources, which already did land titling and already operated a title registry, was successfully resisted by the Ministry of Justice, which operated a parallel judicial titling system. In Ghana, in connection with the bank's Ghana Land Administration Project, 2004 (P071157), the cabinet has committed itself to reorganizing an older deeds registration and a modern title registry under the commissioner of lands, to promote an effective transition to the modern system and end the competition that had existed between the two units.

Fourth, there are now World Bank projects that seek to register customary rights. In some cases, national statutes do not make provision for this. In Indonesia, the Project Appraisal Document (PAD) for the Indonesia Land Administration Project, 1994 (P003984), spells out a phased approach to customary land rights: (1) excluding areas under customary communal tenure from areas chosen for systematic adjudication; (2) bypassing those areas when found in an adjudication area; (3) examining the feasibility, desirability, and methodology of registering *hak ulayat* [communal property] in three selected areas through *adat* [customary] land right studies; and (4) engaging government in needed reforms. Toward the end of the project, as a result of these discussions, the government enacted a regulation providing for registration of communal land rights.[15]

In Malawi, the Malawi Community-Based Rural Land Development Project, 2004 (P075247), is supporting development of a new land law that will provide for full recognition and certification of customary rights. The Cambodia Land Management and Administration Project, 2002 (P070875), is working in a context in which the legal authority for registering customary rights exists, but the modalities for adjudication and titling need to be worked out.[16] The project is working with local NGOs to develop satisfactory approaches to get this land on the register. The Ghana Land Administration Project, Ghana Land Administration Project, 2003 (P071157), is working

---

[15]Regulation of Minister of State for Agrarian Affairs/Head of BPN, No. 5 of 1999, "Guide to Settlement of Issues Related to Adat Law, Communities' Ulayat Rights," in article 4. This is a less than comprehensive legal solution to the issue, however, and the extent of implementation is unclear.

[16]The Land Act 2001 provides for the ownership of land by indigenous peoples and for the titling of that land in articles 23–28.

with a land registration act that provides specifically for registration of customary land rights and is developing a pilot for registration of the allodial land rights of traditional communities.

Another potential front in land law reform in land administration projects is gender equity. The World Bank's OP 4.20, *Gender and Development* (World Bank 2003a), while it calls for nondiscrimination, does not specifically mention property rights, nor does it provide explicit guidance on how to pursue nondiscrimination in project contexts. Task managers sometimes face legal systems that discriminate against women in land rights, and it can reasonably be asked whether land administration projects should proceed in such a context. That question is not generally asked, however, and the bank's land administration projects have rarely faced up to the need for legal reforms in that area. One exception is the Philippines Land Administration and Management Project, 2000 (P066069), which played a major role in obtaining the 2002 repeal of a 1936 administrative order; the repeal removed explicit gender bias in provisions on the acceptance and processing of applications for homestead patents and other applications for public lands.[17]

More commonly, the gender equity issue in land administration projects arises as an issue of how to keep the project's titling from actually disadvantaging women landholders. This issue has generally been neglected because task managers have assumed that a national law is adequate if it does not de jure discriminate against women with regard to land access and rights. Recently, the bank has studied the gendered impact of land titling and registration projects (World Bank 2005),[18] and it is better understood (if not universally accepted) by task managers that even where women have valid legal claims on land, they can be lost in the registration process if adjudication staff do not take affirmative action to ensure they are registered. This can often be handled at the level of regulations, instructions, and training for staff; World Bank land administration projects in Laos and Vietnam are good practice examples in this area.[19]

---

[17]Para. 8 of the Land Administrative Order 7–1 (30 April 1936), "Rules and Regulations Governing the Filing and Disposition of Applications of Alienable Lands of the Public Domain or for Real Properties in the Commonwealth of the Philippines," was repealed by Department of Natural Resources Administration Order No. 13, Series of 2002.

[18]This is an unusually thorough and frank look at the handling of gender issues in four World Bank land projects, in Kazakhstan, Laos, Bolivia, and Ghana,

[19]The Lao PDR Land Titling Project, 1996 (P004208), incorporated gender sensitivity training for field adjudication staff and conducted public education campaigns that covered, inter alia, women's land rights issues; the Lao Women's Union plays a key sensitization role in implementation of the project (Li 2004). In Vietnam, the 2001 Decree No. 70, "Implementation of the Marriage and Family Law," required that all registrations of land use rights must be in the names of both spouses. The World Bank supported a pilot program that focused on such activities as ensuring that forms used in adjudication were appropriate for joint titling and that

Finally, land administration projects frequently break new legal ground in the provision of alternative mechanisms for resolution of land disputes. The World Bank has sponsored regulations for systematic adjudication that provide for mediation in the field by project staff, subject to appeal to administrative authorities or the courts. This topic deserves a chapter or paper of its own. For example, the Cambodia Land Management and Administration Project, 2002 (P070875), supports a system of cadastral commissions at the district, provincial, and national levels to hear appeals of field adjudications. The project has funded the drafting of regulations to govern the proceedings of the commissions, as well as training and equipping them. In addition, the project is funding NGO legal assistance to poor and disadvantaged parties appearing before the commissions.[20]

## Negotiated Land Reform Projects

Today a new generation of World Bank land reform projects is implementing "negotiated" or "community-based" land reform, in which bank funds are provided to groups of beneficiaries to purchase land. Early experience suggests that this reform model is a relatively efficient way to move land to the poor because it reduces political tensions, bureaucratic inefficiencies and corruption, and court disputes.

The World Bank's pilot work with this concept was hampered by a bank rule against disbursement against land, but in 2003 the managing director exempted community-based land reform projects from that prohibition and set up a Community Land Purchase Committee within the bank to vet projects and monitor success. In August 2004, the "expenditure eligibility" reform, designed to loosen a variety of restrictions on the activities the bank can fund, did away completely with the prohibition.[21] The Land Purchase Committee continues to review projects seeking approval for land purchases and to craft guidance for bank staff on use of land purchases in a much broader range of contexts.

The community-based land reform approach uses the market mechanism, and that affects the legal issues that arise, which are quite different from

requirements of documentation (for example, tax receipts, usually in the husband's name) did not stand in the way of women asserting their rights. The project substantially increased the number of parcels registered to women, especially the number of parcels registered jointly to husbands and wives. The case makes the point that simply reframing forms can have a major impact (Kumar 2002).

[20] Sub-Decree No. 47 ANK/BK of 31 May 2002, "Organization and Functioning of the Cadastral Commission."

[21] The prohibition was included in para. 2(b) of OP 12.00, "Disbursement" (February 1997), now repealed. Land was listed among items against which bank funds could not be disbursed.

those arising in compulsory land acquisition programs. Under the criteria applied by the Land Purchase Committee, a project will be approved to purchase land only when the purchase is for a productive purpose, when the land market is sufficiently developed to provide an efficient means of transferring land, and when mechanisms are in place to ensure safe handling of funds. The committee asks the task manager to inquire closely into (1) the forms of tenure available; (2) whether the sellers can provide good title to the land to be purchased; (3) the efficiency of the land market (including regulatory restrictions, credit market imperfections, and the distortions that both introduce into the land market itself); and (4) the forms of organization available for beneficiary groups, which must provide the juridical personality required to hold land.

The flagship project is the Brazil Land-Based Poverty Alleviation Project, 2001 (P050772). This project extends to several Brazilian states a program piloted in 1996–1997 in the state of Ceara.[22] The PADs and the DCAs for both the pilot and the new project raised none of the legal issues mentioned. This was not surprising since the large holdings to be purchased under this program belong to a formalized land sector, one in which full private ownership is well established, land is registered, and the legal framework for land transactions is well developed. Unlike land reform programs involving compulsory acquisitions, there is not a series of legal hurdles to be surmounted under this model — just the normal requirements for valid land transactions.

The first project operating under the exception allowing the purchase of land with World Bank funds for community-based land reform is the Andhra Pradesh Rural Poverty Reduction Project, 2003 (IDA-37320/P071272). Land purchases are budgeted at $4 million, with land purchase being one possible use of funds under the project's Community Investment Fund. Investment funds will also be provided to beneficiary groups. The project commissioned studies of the operation of land markets and the land administration machinery prior to appraisal and concluded that, with precautions, those could safely be used. The project benefited from two detailed legal reviews of the arrangements, one by a legal consultant hired by the project design team and the other as part of the external review process used by the Land Purchase Committee. Again, it was concluded that the project could proceed within the existing legal framework.

The next project, the Malawi Community-Based Rural Land Development Project, 2004 (P075247), has been approved and implementation has

---

[22]Ceara Rural Poverty Alleviation Project, loan number 3918-BR. These projects could proceed prior to the removal of the prohibition of bank expenditures on land because the states themselves funded the land purchases, the bank loans funding resettlement and other costs involved.

begun. The project will provide funds for land purchases by poor members of local communities from freehold and long-term leasehold estates in southern Malawi. In this case, the funding was provided to the government in the form of an Individual Development Account (IDA) grant. Legal issues did arise during appraisal, concerning the type of land registration, purchases of leaseholds, an option for the purchasers to fold the land purchased back into the customary land tenure system if they chose to do so, and the appropriate form of association for land purchase groups. Again, laws did not need to be changed to achieve the aims of the project.[23]

These early community-based land reform projects represent an important departure for the World Bank and raise important legal issues for consideration during the design process, but they have not so far required reforms of land law. They do require a legal framework that allows secure transactions in land rights, of course, but it appears that projects in this early stage are moving forward only where those conditions already exist. This may change with time if the model continues to prove its worth.

## Natural Resource Management Projects

The World Bank has far fewer natural resource management projects than land administration projects. Many are focused on protection activities and regrettably pay scarce attention to property rights issues, but there are exceptions. The exceptions have focused not on individual property rights but on the rights of communities in natural resources (Bruce and Mearns 2002; Bruce 2003).

One of the most systematic and substantial reforms of land policy and law supported by the Bank in Africa began in the context of a forestry project, the Tanzania Forest Resources Management Project, 1992 (P002785). Building on a landmark public consultation and report by the Presidential Commission of Inquiry into Land Matters (Government of Tanzania 1991), the policy development process under the project produced a new land policy in 1995 and, with DFID technical assistance, resulted in the enactment of an important new law in 1999, the final year of the project.[24] The new law, inter alia, affirms the right of villages to use bylaws to manage their natural resources; bylaws are facilitating the replication of a number of the household and community forestry initiatives developed under the project (Wiley 1997).

---

[23]The relevant laws in Malawi are the Land Act, 1965, and the Registered Land Act, 1967, both of which were used for land titling and registration under the bank's Lilongwe Land Development Project, 1980 (P001598).
[24]Tanzania Land Act, 1999, and Village Land Act, 1999.

Another World Bank–supported natural resource management project that advocated property rights reform was the Colombia Natural Resource Management Program, 1993 (P006868). According to the PAD, local communities in Colombia's Choco Region on the Pacific were unable to manage their natural resources as the project envisaged because the entire region was classified as a forest reserve: "Clarification of the land ownership situation is essential for the design of resource management and conservation policies, in order to assess the convergence of interests of the parties affected and involved, [and] the distribution of economic benefits and costs." A legal regime for titling indigenous reservations had existed for some time, and land was titled both to individuals and to Amerindian communities. The project worked on regulations and contractual arrangements for implementation of these legal reforms in the Choco Region, and for the coordination of claims from the different ethnic communities. It eventually issued 83 titles covering 404 communities containing nearly 40,000 families and covering nearly 2 million acres, but a growing insurgency in the region precluded a follow-on project (Ng'weno 2000).[25]

Where World Bank natural resource management projects have confronted access issues concerning state-owned forest resources, the bank has encouraged governments to work with contractual solutions. These involve agreement between the forestry department and a community or resource user group on a forest management plan (Lynch and Talbott 1995). For example, the Lao PDR Forestry Management and Conservation Project, 1994 (P004169), funded the launching of a pilot program for participatory management of production forests in 60 villages in two provinces. The Forestry Law of 1996 (article 7) allowed for the organization of village forestry associations, agreement between governments and associations on 10-year management plans, and 50-year management contracts between the state and associations for association use of state forest land, with sharing of revenues (Williams 2000).

Usually such agreements do not confer property rights, and they often fall short of providing secure tenure (Bruce 1999). The World Bank–supported Vietnam Forest Sector Development Project, 2004 (P066051), does better, aiming to provide long-term leases to local communities. Forest plantations (fast-growing trees, mixed plantations, and fruit trees) are to be established on state land (all land in Vietnam being state land) with 40- to 50-year Land Use Certificates, using a participatory approach involving village consultations, land allocation, and certification of land use rights.

---

[25]This study documents the land work under this project and gives considerable attention to the legal framework.

In the arid pastures context, a context occasionally addressed in World Bank projects in client countries in Africa and Asia, the bank has faced similar issues of state land ownership and reluctance on the part of governments to accord secure use rights to user communities. In Mongolia, through a Japan Social Development Fund (JSDF) grant and a Sustainable Livelihoods Project, 2002 (P067770), the bank encouraged the government to pursue a system of community-access commons, which were allowed under the 1994 Land Law. In an unfortunate regression, a 2003 Land Law in effect returned pastureland to the status of an open-access resource.

World Bank projects on natural resource management and forestry have not generally sought property rights and titles for resource users, though communities may be as badly in need of those for their forests and pastures as individuals are for their residences and farms. Nor have the needs for tenure and title been addressed in World Bank–funded land administration projects, which have avoided titling on forestland, given the frequent lack of a legal framework for property rights there, rather than confronting that lack as a legal reform issue. There is, in fact, a serious and unfortunate disconnect between the bank's work on land law reform and reform of the law relating to common property. Bank land administration projects in Cambodia and Laos lack the legal basis for registering local land resources[26]—the village soccer field, the village temple, the village commons—to local communities, and so those resources are registered in the name of the state. The Bank has failed to seek legal reforms needed to remedy these situations, and lost an important opportunity to clarify the legal status of local communities.

## BLIND SPOTS AND PROMISING APPROACHES

This chapter has reviewed the processes by which the World Bank pursues land law reform in various project contexts and has provided a good many concrete examples. It hopefully is enlightening as to the processes and substance of World Bank–promoted reforms. The bank, which lends to governments, tends to support land administration, a key government function. It supports primarily to titling and registration of individual property rights, secondarily land reform and natural resource management, and only very rarely for a broad range of other legitimate land activities by the state: land use planning, state land management, and sustainable land management.

---

[26]The Laos Land Titling Project, 1997 (P004208), and the Cambodia Land Management and Administration Project, 2002 (P070875).

The emphasis on land titling reflects the bank's conviction of the transformative power of property rights. Laws create property rights, but it is land titling and registration that make them effective. They identify the land, identify the right holder, and document the link between the two in ways that promote security of tenure and marketability of land. The World Bank has been practicing this for decades, and its land experts are nonplussed by the new enthusiasm for formalizing property rights and the fanfare that has accompanied it. Like the Native Americans whose continent was discovered by Europeans, they wonder how their territory could have just been "discovered" when they have always lived there. They know, moreover, and from hard experience, that property rights reforms are never simple or easy. Still, they are themselves believers in strong property rights, and new generations of PADs repeat the lessons of the Thailand Land Titling Project. Unfortunately, often they do not probe seriously the extent to which the country at hand is like or unlike Thailand, and the financial analysis of returns to the investment is constructed on the basis of assumptions that may or may not be applicable.

There are some surprising blind spots that recur in World Bank land administration projects, and two are particularly serious. First, the emphasis in bank thinking and projects remains on individual rights; bank projects now work with long-term use rights and leases and even customary rights, but they still tend to focus, with a few exceptions, on individual rights. Some natural resource management projects have embraced common property solutions, vesting land rights in communities rather than individuals, but the mainstream land administration projects have paid remarkably little attention to such rights, even where they have been reflected in local practice (if not national law). The bank has not, as it should have done, identified this as a key area for policy dialogue and legal reform.

A second blind spot is reflected in the lack of incorporation of land use planning in its land administration projects. There is skepticism among many bank land administration staff as to the enforceability of such restrictions in many developing countries—not unreasonable given the experience. They are also leery of land use planning because, especially in recently socialist polities, officials sometimes seek to use it to revert to command agriculture—for example, assessing soil quality and dictating crops to be planted in given areas.[27] In addition, bringing land use planning within a land administration project often requires involving another ministry—

---

[27] The problem is real, and I have recently grappled with this tendency during consultancies in Mozambique and Rwanda. In neither country does government have genuine confidence in farmers to manage their own holdings. The assumptions inculcated by command economies often live on long after the ideologies that underpinned them have been abandoned.

administration of property rights and land use planning are rarely in the same ministry or agency—and that greatly adds to project complexity. Bank task managers, quite rightly, value simplicity in project design.

But failure to include land use planning creates an imbalance. Property rights in western economies can be framed in a relatively absolute fashion because the legitimate claims of the state to social control of land are achieved through legal controls characterized as regulatory and situated outside land law, in planning law. Property rights and regulatory restrictions exist in a creative tension, providing the balance that makes them both work. This understanding is largely absent from discussions dealing with land in the World Bank, and from its land projects. I do not want to gainsay the difficulty of working both these sides of the fence in a given project, which often involves working with two or more different government institutions, and yet it is important that the bank try to find ways to do that.

These two issues concern the substance of property rights reform, but what about process? The World Bank has considerable experience in this area, and most task managers of land projects understand that land law reform is not just a matter of enacting good laws but of translating them into reality on the ground. This cannot be dealt with at any length in this chapter, but some remarks are appropriate, given the importance of the topic and the fact that some bank land projects have in fact worked quite effectively to achieve land law reform.

This has happened primarily in the bank's land investment projects. Those projects may lack the weight of policy lending to leverage reform, but they have other advantages that may be more important in the end. First, land projects more often involve bank specialist staff members who understand land policy and law reform well. In a policy lending project, a great diversity of staff is needed, and a land specialist may or may not be included on the team. Specialists are important because they understand that it is not useful to simply postulate "the good property rights system" and demand that it be enacted. Different countries begin reform processes from quite different places, and how far governments can go at a point in time will differ from case to case. It is a political matter, and bank task managers with specialist knowledge recognize that, implicitly if not explicitly.

Second, these land investment projects work with bureaucracies that often are important opponents of reform, having vested interests in the corruption that is all too common in systems with weak, heavily "administered" property rights. In fact, growing land administration systems offer substantial revenue and an opportunity to move to self-supporting land administration institutions with salary levels that make it more realistic to eliminate corrupt practices. Land administration projects that incorporate such changes, rather than those that focus too exclusively on the need for high-level political "champions," will produce more sustainable impetus for change. With such a vision in hand, champions for reforms sometimes emerge within the land administration institutions themselves.

Third, these investment projects can provide effective support for an extended process of land law reform, for public and stakeholder consultation, for legal education, and for legal aid to those struggling with problems under the new systems.

Fourth, where property rights reforms are involved, investment projects provide immediate opportunities for piloting and then more broadly implementing reforms. In a remarkable number of cases, policy studies and debates sponsored by the World Bank under policy lending have resulted in enactment of major new land legislation—in Uganda, Tanzania, and Mozambique, in particular—only to have the bank drop the ball when it came to support for implementation.

Finally, the role of conditionality in property rights reform needs to be reassessed. Conditionality is not objectionable in principle, as the bank clearly has the right to attach conditions to its loans. Conditions should have some logical connection to the purposes of the loan, of course, and that is usually the case. The important question is whether conditionality is an effective way to achieve broad property rights reform. It may do the job well enough in technical matters, but it does not work as well where a broad reform of property rights is needed. If the objective is to change reality on the ground, a law with strong country ownership is needed, and in my experience that requires a process involving broad public participation in development of the law.

In recent years I have dealt with two laws that have exhibited such strong ownership, the 1997 Land Law in Mozambique and the 1998 Land Law in Cambodia. Both involved up-front studies and considerable public discussion, leading to the development of a substantial consensus. In the case of the law in Cambodia, the parliamentary debates were broadcast on national television, providing extraordinary exposure of the issues to the public eye. Implementation has not been easy due to limited capacity, but the political will has been there, and attempts to weaken the laws have been resisted vigorously by a wide range of government and civil society actors.

Such commitment is produced by extended reasoning together, not by conditionality, though conditionality can help launch such a reasoning process. There is a questioning of conditionality going on within the World Bank today, and rightly so (Abdildina and Jaramillo-Vallejo 2005). Conditionality should be used only with considerable caution, because it too often produces compliance without ownership and laws that are dead on arrival. If overused, it may also render World Bank loans, available at concessionary rates, less attractive than commercial bank lending at slightly higher rates, unencumbered by such conditionality.

In conclusion, how should we see these efforts by the World Bank and other donors to support property rights reforms? Is donor-supported land law reform likely to be a feature of land tenure in 2015? In all likelihood it will be, and the real question is how to make it better. As a participant in some of these efforts, I believe they are potentially valuable, the potential achieved in some cases and squandered in others. A great deal depends on proper diagnosis of local needs, and that calls for both research and better spatial targeting reforms, even within a given country. Bromley contrasts European and African circumstances, but it is not possible to lay out prescriptions using such a broad brush. Even within the landscape of a single country, levels of development and land potential differ dramatically, and needs for property rights will vary as well. One set of rules may be needed for urban and peri-urban areas, where pressure on land is considerable and active markets of all kinds exist, and another for deep rural areas. A mechanism at the interface between these contexts is also needed, to allow land to shift between these systems. The Thailand model, stressing "whole country" titling and registration, will usually not be appropriate.

The need is not for the World Bank or other donor agencies to withdraw from support of property rights reform and land administration. They have staff with a great deal of experience and insight to offer developing countries. But there is a need for those donors to (1) target their efforts more selectively, on areas where they are really needed; (2) recognize and register not only individual but community land rights; (3) develop a broader menu of reforms, one that includes but does not rely so heavily on land registration, and (4) develop more effective strategies and project approaches to support the evolution of customary land tenure systems. Hopefully that will be the shape of things by 2015.

## REFERENCES

Abdildina, Z., and J. Jaramillo-Vallejo. 2005. Streamlining conditionality in World Bank– and International Monetary Fund–supported programs. In *Conditionality revisited: Concepts, experiences, and lessons.* S. Koeberle, H. Bedoya, P. Silarszky, and G. Verheyen, eds. Washington, DC: World Bank.

Binswanger, H., K. Deininger, and G. Feder. 1995. Power, distortion, revolt, and reform in agricultural land relations. In *Handbook of development economics*, vol. 3. J. Behrman and T. N. Srinivasan, eds., 2659–2772. New York: Elsevier Science.

Bledsoe, D. 2006. Can land titling and registration reduce poverty? In *Land law reform: Achieving development policy objectives.* J. W. Bruce, ed., 143–174. Washington, DC: World Bank.

Bloch, P. 2002. Land reform in Uzbekistan and other Central Asian countries. Working Paper No. 49. Madison: University of Wisconsin Land Tenure Center.

Bruce, J. W. 1999. *Legal bases for the management of forest resources as common property.* Rome: United Nations Food and Agriculture Organization.

———. 2003. Property rights issues in common property regimes for forestry. *World Bank Legal Review: Law and Justice for Development* 1:257.

———, ed. 2006. *Land law reform: Achieving development policy objectives.* Washington, DC: World Bank.

Bruce, J. W., and R. Mearns. 2002. Natural resource management and land policy in developing countries: Lessons learned and new challenges for the World Bank. IIED Issue Paper No. 115. London: International Institute for Environment and Development.

Bruce, J. W., and S. Migot-Adholla, eds. 1994. *Searching for security of land tenure in Africa.* Dubuque, IA: Kendall/Hunt.

Dale, P. F., and J. D. McLaughlin. 1999. *Land administration.* Oxford: Oxford University Press.

de Janvry, A., G. Gordillo, J. Plateau, and E. Sadoulet, eds. 2001. *Access to land, rural poverty and public action.* Oxford: Oxford University Press.

de Soto, H. 2000. *The mystery of capital: Why capitalism triumphs in the west and fails everywhere else.* New York: Basic Books.

Deininger, K. 1999. Making negotiated land reform work: Initial experience from Brazil, Colombia, and South Africa. World Bank Policy Research Working Paper No. 2040. Washington, DC: World Bank.

———. 2003. *Land policies for growth and poverty reduction.* World Bank Policy Research Report. Washington, DC: World Bank and Oxford University Press.

Feder, G. 1988. *Land policies and farm productivity in Thailand.* Baltimore: Johns Hopkins University Press.

Feder, G., and A. Nishio. 1999. The benefits of land registration and titling: Economic and social perspectives. *Land Use Policy* 15(1):143–169.

Government of Tanzania. 1991. *Report of the Presidential Commission on Land Policy Reform* (Shivji Commission). Dar es Salaam: Government Printer.

Kumar, K. 2002. *Land use rights and gender equality in Vietnam.* Washington, DC: World Bank.

Li, Z. 2004. The Lao People's Democratic Republic: Preserving women's rights in land titling (in Module 9, Investments in land administration, policy and markets). In *Agricultural investment sourcebook.* Washington, DC: World Bank.

Lynch, O. J., and K. Talbott. 1995. *Balancing acts: Community-based forestry management and national law in East Asia and the Pacific.* Washington, DC: World Resources Institute.

McAuslan, P. 2000. Only the name of the country changes: The diaspora of "European" land law in Commonwealth Africa. In *Evolving land rights; policy and tenure in Africa.* C. Toulmin and J. Quan, eds., 75–96. London: International Institute for Environment and Development and Natural Resources Institute.

Migot-Adholla, S., F. Place, and W. Oluoch-Kosua. 1993. Security of tenure and land productivity in Kenya. In *Searching for land tenure security in Africa*. J. W. Bruce and S. Migot-Adholla, eds., 119–140. Dubuque, IA: Kendall/Hunt.

Ng'weno, B. 2000. *On titling collective property, participation, and natural resource management: Implementing indigenous and Afro-Colombian demands*. Washington, DC: World Bank.

Platteau, J. 2000. Does Africa need land reform? In *Evolving land rights, policy and tenure in Africa*. C. Toulmin and J. Quan, eds., 51–73. London: International Institute for Environment and Development and Natural Resources Institute.

Quan, J. 2000. Land tenure, economic growth and poverty in sub-Saharan Africa. In *Evolving land rights, policy and tenure in Africa*. C. Toulmin and J. Quan, eds., 31–49. London: International Institute for Environment and Development and Natural Resources Institute.

Shipton, P. 1988. The Kenyan land tenure reform: Misunderstandings in the public creation of private property. In *Land and society in contemporary Africa*. R. E. Downs and S. P. Reyna, eds., 91–135. Durham: University of New Hampshire Press.

Simpson, S. R. 1976. *Land law and registration*. Cambridge: Cambridge University Press.

Wiley, L. 1997. *Finding the right legal and institutional framework for community-based natural forest management: The Tanzania case*. CIFOR Special Publication. Jakarta, Indonesia: CIFOR.

Williams, P. 2000. Evaluation of three pilot models for participation forest management: Village involvement in production forestry in Lao PDR. Draft evaluation summary. Washington, DC: World Bank.

World Bank. 2003a. *Gender and development*. Operational Manual 4.20. Washington, DC: World Bank.

———. 2003b. *World Bank lending instruments: Resources for development*. Washington, DC: World Bank.

———. 2005. *Gender issues and best practices in land administration projects: A synthesis report*. Washington, DC: World Bank.

# Changing Visions
of Land

# 10

## Land and Economic Development: New Institutional Arrangements

**Daniel W. Bromley**

For those who study world poverty, the year 2015 has a special ominous ring to it. That is the year by which the so-called developing countries are to achieve the Millennium Development Goals. Unfortunately, most of the poorest 20 to 25 countries, almost all of which are in sub-Saharan Africa, will not even come close. Indeed, it is doubtful that most of them warrant the term "developing," since that suggests an ongoing process of improvement across a spectrum of pertinent indicators. I suggest that *immiserization* is a more fitting descriptor. I will return to the special challenge of sub-Saharan Africa in a moment. For now, it is necessary to set the stage by surveying a somewhat wider set of ideas about the role of land in economic development. And that requires that we address the *idea of land* in economic affairs.

### THE EVOLUTION OF THE IDEA OF LAND

The prominence of land in economic theory and economic affairs is long and profound. Some of the greatest thinkers in our discipline have been concerned with the role of land in the creation of economic wealth. David Ricardo comes immediately to mind. Thomas Malthus, Karl Marx, Henry George, and Karl Polanyi also figure prominently. These five individuals capture the essential aspects of land as an economic asset: Ricardo on differen-

I am grateful to Gregory Ingram for comments on an earlier draft of this chapter.

tial land quality; Malthus on the overall scarcity of land and its products; Marx on the economic and political advantages to emerge from the control over land; Henry George on the appropriable fiscal dividend associated with that differential advantage; and, of course, Polanyi for reminding us of the "fictitious" nature of land as a commodity. Moving beyond the material realm, Aldo Leopold gave us the idea of a "land ethic," while John Muir and Henry David Thoreau reminded us that our existence—both material and spiritual—is tied up in land, broadly defined.

As we trace the lessons of those profound thinkers, we are reminded of the evolutionary nature of the conception of land, and how changed conceptions reflect the *evolving purposes of land*. The appropriate place to start is with the philosopher Charles Sanders Peirce, the intellectual fount of philosophical pragmatism. Peirce's "pragmatic maxim" states the following: "Consider what effects, that might conceivably have practical bearings, we conceive the object of our conception to have. Then, our conception of these effects is the whole of our conception of the object" (Peirce 1934, 1).

Since the "object of our conception" here is land, the pragmatic maxim reminds us that the *meaning to us* of that object is captured, and exhausted, by the effects that land holds for us (Bromley 2006). With that foundation, we can see that over the course of human history land has held varying—and often quite distinct—meanings to humans. And we are reminded that political tensions arise when those meanings are found to be suddenly unwelcome or are found to be in conflict. Let us start with land in its material sense. Here there are two subcategories: land as a direct materialist asset, and land as a necessary yet ancillary materialist asset.[1]

## Land as Direct Materialist Asset

The earliest purpose of land was, of course, to provide food and necessary materials for human survival. Paradoxically, we may think of land in that time as essential for survival but of little interest to humans. In a sense, it was merely space over which humans moved in the quest for survival. As populations increased, and as human aggregations became larger and more concentrated, land came to be seen in terms of the idea of belonging and possession. Agriculture, the essential materialist idea of land, became an urban activity—of necessity. Transportation was difficult, and so it was essential to live close to (indeed, among) places where sustenance was assured. As domesticated animals became an increasing part of the agricultural enterprise,

---

[1] See Hubacek and van den Bergh (2006) for a nice account of the changing concept of land in economic theory.

and as transport improved, agriculture (food provision) once again became a "rural" activity—it was pushed out of urban areas. Of course, general security conditions continued to influence the distance at which agriculture could be carried on with respect to settled communities. A close look at rural landscapes in various parts of Europe reveals much about how secure agricultural producers must have felt at various times. Sometimes we see scattered farmsteads, and at other times we see clustered villages and scattered fields to which people traveled each day.

It is in that general setting that the writings of Ricardo and Malthus figure in economic history. Differential land quality, an aspect that had heretofore been associated with broad sweeps of landscape and the spatial distribution of plants and animals thereon, began to take on immediate pertinence. Malthus worried that there would not be enough "good" land to keep up with population growth. Ricardo focused attention on the unequal availability of "good" and "bad" land. The Ricardian rent arising from this differential motivated the work of Marx, George, and Polanyi.

We see that there were three attributes of land that dominated early economic thought. The first was a static Ricardian idea of the inherent quality of land. The second aspect, popularized by Arthur Young in England, was the ability of certain parcels of land to become, in essence, a different asset. Young made Ricardian land quality an endogenous variable. Natural capital could be augmented—rotations and green manure crops changed the historic "iron law" of natural fertility. The third attribute, as agriculture developed, became the location of parcels of land with respect to markets for inputs and outputs. And as transportation improved, we see that even that dimension of capital could be "augmented." Specifically, improved transportation (reduced costs of transportation) served to transform the locational attributes of a parcel—in essence "moving" a parcel closer to market so that its value was increased. This brings us to the idea of land as an ancillary asset.

## Land as Ancillary Asset

With the transition from agrarian to industrial economies, land takes on a new and quite different role. Now the "inherent" qualities of land—the differential gift of nature—decline in economic importance and are replaced by a differential advantage associated with spatial proximity to other economic activities. The properties (attributes) of land as a direct materialist asset diminish, and location begins to dominate the discourse about land. We can think of this in terms of Ricardo being reinterpreted in a spatial sense. While Malthus drops from sight, Polanyi, Marx, and George continue to be relevant.

The transition from land as a direct materialist asset to land as an ancillary asset is coincident with increased aggregations of people into urbanized settings. As with agriculture in earlier history, early manufacturing was basically an urban endeavor. And, as with agriculture, when the scale of manufacturing—and the associated externalities—became bothersome to urban neighbors, large-scale manufacturing moved out of urban areas. Indeed, urban zoning arose to address precisely that issue. The increased urbanization, and the associated tight clustering of people into unpleasant settings and circumstances, can be seen as the impetus behind a newfound appreciation of the natural environment beyond the bounds of unpleasant cities. To compress human history in the language of Leo (not Karl) Marx, we went from the "garden" to the "machine in the garden," and we now long to return to the garden (Marx 1964). It is here that Leopold, Muir, and Thoreau enter the picture.

## Land as a Consumption Asset

The third general idea about land and its purpose seeks to recapture a vision of the garden we lost as humans became seriously agricultural, and then seriously urbanized and industrial. The three writers mentioned immediately above sought to remind us of the deeper meaning of land—and of a landscape—that had become, in the extreme, simply a materialist asset. We see that the idea and meaning of land progressed from strictly a factor of production in agriculture or industry to a consumption item—as an amenity and as a provider of environmental and ecological services (Bromley 2000a).

To return to Peirce's pragmatic maxim, the meaning of land is nothing but the effects that land has on us—and the implications that land holds for us. The essentialist will insist that there is something fundamental about land—and will proceed to romanticize land in rather odd ways. Those of us who deny essentialism will simply insist that land is what we make of it. Charles Darwin showed us that "finchness" is a variable, and pragmatism teaches us to see land as a variable. In economic terms, the idea and meaning of land are endogenous variables. One central influence on that endogeneity is simply the nature of the dominant economic activity—is it agricultural, is it industrial, or is it postindustrial?

## The Evolving Focus of Land Economics Research

Though the time horizon is truncated from the long sweep of history just described, we do have one recent gauge of the changes in the meaning (and importance) of land as an economic and social artifact. A recent paper catalogued the 2,139 articles published in the journal *Land Economics* from its founding in 1925 up through the year 1999 (Roulac et al. 2005). Before getting to that summary, the authors of the paper discuss the first article to appear in that inaugural issue (January 1925). The author was Richard T. Ely, the founding editor of *Land Economics* (the original name of which was the *Journal of Land and Public Utility Economics*) and a cofounder of the American Economic Association. Roulac et al. write:

> In this one seminal article, Ely set the stage for eight decades of research in the field of land and public utility economics. . . . Ely identified the following topics areas for promising research:
> - optimal allocation of land uses
> - optimal utilization of agricultural lands
> - optimal urban land development
> - housing policy
> - traffic congestion
> - comprehensive city planning
> - land tenure (tenancy versus ownership)
> - land tenure (public versus private ownership)
> - financial returns to real estate investment
> - relationship between construction costs and the production of income
> - the use of land as a basis for credit
> - the impact of taxation on the economic activity and use of land
> - the economics of public utilities (Roulac et al. 2005, 458)

With the benefit of hindsight, it would seem that Ely got it mostly right. As for the evolving content of the journal, consider table 10.1. One is struck by the early dominance of concern for land as a "public utility"—Roulac and his coauthors were considering land as a special type of commodity, perhaps with some monopoly aspects to it. Along with that attribute, much early research concerned the agricultural, wildlife, and timber aspects of land. The third dominant concern early in the twentieth century was that of tenure. By the 1990s, only agriculture, timber, and wildlife remained dominant—now as part of the broader environmental concerns that dominate public discourse. Table 10.2, also from Roulac et al. (2005), depicts the extent to which *Land Economics*—and presumably the field of land economics research—became much more diversified over time.

**TABLE 10.1** Top 20 Topics of Papers Published in *Land Economics* in the Twentieth Century

| Rank | | Number of articles published in each decade | | | | | | | | Total | Percent of total articles |
|---|---|---|---|---|---|---|---|---|---|---|---|
| | | 1920s | 1930s | 1940s | 1950s | 1960s | 1970s | 1980s | 1990s | | |
| 1 | Real estate as a public utility | 72 | 171 | 79 | 59 | 41 | 31 | 36 | 9 | 498 | 23.3 |
| 2 | Agriculture/wildlife/timber | 13 | 2 | 27 | 25 | 25 | 24 | 45 | 28 | 189 | 8.8 |
| 3 | Lease/own (tenure decisions) | 17 | 20 | 38 | 51 | 29 | 13 | 7 | 1 | 176 | 8.2 |
| 4 | Urban/regional planning and economic development | 4 | 11 | 24 | 19 | 40 | 6 | | 5 | 109 | 5.1 |
| 5 | Land use control | 2 | 15 | 15 | 6 | 9 | 15 | 15 | 14 | 91 | 4.3 |
| 6 | Property taxation | 3 | 15 | 12 | 4 | 5 | 12 | 26 | 7 | 84 | 3.9 |
| 7 | Demographic analysis | 4 | 3 | 6 | 9 | 11 | 17 | 11 | 23 | 84 | 3.9 |
| 8 | Value creation | 4 | 3 | 4 | 3 | 10 | 14 | 29 | 10 | 77 | 3.6 |
| 9 | Decision process: appraisal | 7 | 1 | 2 | | | 1 | 9 | 45 | 65 | 3.0 |
| 10 | Spatial location theory | | 2 | 2 | 4 | 12 | 13 | 14 | 6 | 53 | 2.5 |
| 11 | Transportation linkage and theory | | 11 | 2 | 6 | 5 | 11 | 14 | 1 | 50 | 2.3 |

| | | | | | | | | | | | |
|---|---|---|---|---|---|---|---|---|---|---|---|
| 12 | Water and irrigation | 2 | 1 | 5 | 10 | 7 | 8 | 10 | 6 | 49 | 2.3 |
| 13 | Urban development patterns | 3 | 3 | 8 | 4 | 13 | 8 | 8 | 2 | 49 | 2.3 |
| 14 | Housing policy: public housing projects | 3 | 7 | 12 | | 10 | 13 | 3 | | 48 | 2.2 |
| 15 | Market structure: housing market | 2 | 9 | 6 | 11 | 5 | 5 | | | 38 | 1.8 |
| 16 | Environmental impact on value | | | | | | | 2 | 29 | 31 | 1.4 |
| 17 | Impact of law/regulation on environment | | | | | | 5 | 9 | 16 | 30 | 1.4 |
| 18 | Property rights | | 3 | 1 | 2 | 2 | 7 | 11 | 3 | 29 | 1.4 |
| 19 | Economic base | | | | 15 | 6 | 3 | 2 | 2 | 28 | 1.3 |
| 20 | Emergence of land economics as a discipline | 8 | 1 | 15 | 3 | 4 | 2 | | | 33 | 1.5 |
| | Total number of articles on all topics | 171 | 341 | 300 | 258 | 305 | 285 | 306 | 344 | 2,310 | |

*Source:* Roulac et al. (2005).

**TABLE 10.2** Evolving Composition of Leading Articles Published in *Land Economics*

| Decade | Relative composition of leading topics | | | |
|---|---|---|---|---|
| | Top 10 topics (percent) | Top 5 topics (percent) | Top 3 topics (percent) | Top topic (percent) |
| 1920s | 78.9 | 68.4 | 59.6 | 42.1 |
| 1930s | 80.9 | 68.0 | 60.4 | 50.1 |
| 1940s | 69.6 | 53.6 | 42.2 | 23.2 |
| 1950s | 80.5 | 64.5 | 51.5 | 22.5 |
| 1960s | 66.3 | 48.5 | 36.0 | 13.4 |
| 1970s | 54.5 | 32.8 | 23.7 | 10.5 |
| 1980s | 62.6 | 44.9 | 32.7 | 13.4 |
| 1990s | 54.4 | 36.1 | 25.6 | 11.3 |

*Source:* Roulac et al. (2005).

## THE ROLE OF LAND IN ECONOMIC DEVELOPMENT

Following World War II, as many colonies were gaining their independence, interest in land reform became a dominant theme in economic development. Landlordism and plantation agriculture (pineapples, bananas, tea, coffee, sugar) were seen as serious impediments to economic progress—and as perpetuating unjustified inequities. While the Reagan administration (1981–1989) essentially ended U.S. interest and involvement in land reform, international agencies have continued to work on the problem—particularly in a few countries in Latin America, Southeast Asia, and, more recently, South Africa. But two new issues soon arose to occupy those who cared about land and the development process.

The first issue concerned converting so-called informal tenure into formal tenure through registering and titling agricultural land (and urban housing). It was alleged that with "secure" tenure farmers would invest to bring about increased productivity, an agricultural surplus would soon materialize, and poor countries would be launched on a new sustainable development trajectory. Here was land in its materialist role giving rise to higher incomes and economic development, as we had known it in western Europe.

The second issue concerned not producing new income and wealth from land, but using land as an instrument to lock in the nascent economic reforms in the aftermath of the dissolution of the Soviet Union. In that setting, land was to form the new secure institutional foundations of a market economy out of the ashes of Stalinist collectivization. Land would not necessarily bring about development in the poor nations of the world, but it would be a central component in the triumph of markets over "godless communism."

Ironically, both of these optimistic visions for land were overdone. In sub-Saharan Africa, formalization of tenure seems to have virtually no effect on agricultural productivity. And in the former Soviet Union, the role of land and associated agrarian relations as an impediment to economic success during Soviet times was seriously overrated. As we will see, the failure of both of these economic "truths" to stand up under close examination holds important implications for economic institutions, but in quite unexpected ways.

## Formalization of Tenure

The interest in the development community to promote land registration schemes leading to the issuance of formal titles received much of its early support from a study of squatters on government forestland in Thailand. In that study, Feder and Onchan (1987, 311–312) sought to "confirm empirically that ownership security induces higher farm investment and land improvements and to estimate the magnitude of the effects." Unfortunately, the empirical model was mis-specified, and they did not measure the effects of tenure security on investment behavior by farmers. In the study area, even farmers without any title (squatters on government land) were extremely unlikely to face eviction, and so it could not be claimed that the absence of a title produced insecure tenure. What Feder and Onchan did estimate was the effect of formal title on the probability of obtaining credit from the formal credit system. Despite how this research has been portrayed in the literature, here is a study of how the formal credit sector discriminates between two classes of farmers—some of whom have title, and some of whom do not. If we are interested in the role of formal tenure in promoting enhanced agricultural productivity, the research question worth asking is the following: Given equal access to credit on the part of farmers with and without "tenure security" (proper title), can we detect a difference in their investment behavior with respect to agricultural productivity? If we can detect a difference in their behavior *unconstrained by the vagaries of the agricultural credit market*, formalization of tenure (via the issuance of proper titles) will have a positive effect on the investment behavior of farmers. If we cannot detect a difference in investment behavior when credit is *not* rationed on the basis of titles, formalization (titles) is irrelevant for agricultural progress.

The general perception in the development literature of the Feder-Onchan study has been that it confirmed the importance of titles for agricultural investments and thus productivity. Given the persistence of poverty in sub-Saharan Africa, and the fact that the development community often seems unable to understand communal tenures, it was not long before the assertion about formalizing tenure gained credibility as a strategy for inducing development in sub-Saharan Africa. Hernando de Soto played a prominent role here (de Soto 2000).

Interestingly, the abundant empirical work in Africa fails to support this emphasis on formalizing tenure. In Kenya and Ghana, researchers state, "We found no relationship between land rights and plot yields in Kenya and Ghana. . . . We also found that the mode of acquisition had no effect on plot yields" (Migot-Adholla et al. 1993, 282). In Ghana Timothy Besley observed that "the analysis of this paper warns against viewing [formalizing land rights] as a panacea for problems of low growth and investment before the process determining the evolution of rights is properly understood" (1995, 936). In Burkina Faso, differences in land productivity are said to depend on factors "other than property rights, mainly the natural fertility and climate conditions" (Ouedraogo et al. 1996, 232). In Rwanda, Migot-Adholla et al. found that " 'short-term use rights' parcels were more productive than parcels in all other land rights categories. . . . Farmers who rent land may generally be in dire need of land resources and apply greater amounts of labour in order to provide subsistence for their families" (1993, 281). In a detailed study in Ghana, Kenya, and Rwanda, researchers found, "Rights which farmers hold over individual parcels of land vary widely, and are in many cases surprisingly privatized. Yet with few exceptions, land rights are not found to be a significant factor in determining investments in land improvements, use of inputs, access to credit, or the productivity of land. These results cast doubt on the need for ambitious land registration and titling programs at this time" (Place and Hazell 1993, 10). And David Atwood found that "if potential purchasers tend to see land as an investment with a high potential for appreciation or as a hedge against inflation, rather than as a factor of production, reducing their transaction costs and risks may lead to poorer land use and reduced production as land is held idle or used in a non-intensive way after its transfer" (1990, 663–664).

Klaus Deininger of the World Bank has written, "Increasing security of tenure does not necessarily require issuing formal individual titles and in many circumstances more simple measures to enhance tenure security can make a big difference at much lower cost than formal titles . . . formal title is not always necessary or sufficient for high levels of tenure security" (2003, 39). A similar point is offered by Deininger and Feder: "Formal documentation (i.e. titling) is not crucial where customary tenure systems provide sufficient security to facilitate the level of investment and land transactions that are relevant for the prevailing economic environment" (2001, 314).

Similar points have been made by Carter and Olinto (2003). De Janvry et al. have noted, "Intensification of land use can occur without formal property rights. . . . In many situations, titling may increase transaction costs in the circulation of land, create new sources of conflicts if formal land rights are assigned without due recognition of customary arrangements . . . and not add anything to efficiency in resource use" (2001, 13).

Daniel Fitzpatrick (2005) has written in a similar vein regarding the case for formalization. In addition, Lund (2000) reminds us of yet another confounding influence: Most African property regimes are notable in their multiplicity of interests and tenures on the same parcel of land. That is, various members of the family (and the village) will often have socially recognized claims on different attributes (and products) of the same parcel—one individual may cultivate and harvest the crops on that parcel, another individual may gather fuelwood on that parcel, and yet another may obtain dry-season forage or fodder from that parcel. Which use—which claimant—is to be made more secure by the issuance of "formal" titles? Who is the "primary" right holder, and who is the "secondary" right holder? On this same general theme, Platteau points out:

> In a social context dominated by huge differences in educational levels and by differential access to the state administration, there is a great risk that the adjudication/registration process will be manipulated by the elite to its advantage. . . . The fact of the matter is that, insofar as it encourages the assertion of greedy interests with powerful backing and is likely, wittingly or not, to reward cunning, titling opens *new* possibilities of conflict and insecurity that can have disastrous consequences for vulnerable sections of the population *at a time when their livelihood crucially depends on their access to land.* (1996, 43–45)

The irony here is that the *World Development Report 2006* declares with obvious certainty, "Despite *potentially large benefits from titling,* there are challenges in urban and rural contexts" (World Bank 2006, 165; emphasis added). Can it be that those who are responsible for producing the *World Development Report* are innocent of the empirical research on titling? Or do we see here a set of "truths" about titling that resists contrary empirical evidence? Indeed, with respect to sub-Saharan Africa, Espen Sjaastad and I have argued the following:

> The common assertion that tenure security is necessary to promote investment may—in many cases—be reversed. That is, investment is necessary to obtain security. Investments in trees, irrigation furrows, buildings or other fixed structures may provide a litigant in a land dispute with an unassailable case. Thus, although insecurity of tenure is a disincentive to

invest, it is—paradoxically—often also an incentive because investment in itself increases security. . . . If one accepts that certain types of investment in land are a legitimate way of claiming more secure rights to land, and that investments may be recovered even when land is lost, the assertion that insecurity of land rights in indigenous tenure systems is a serious impediment to investment seems less convincing. (Sjaastad and Bromley 1997, 553)

## Privatization

Given the general impression of widespread failures in Soviet agriculture, it was thought to be self-evident that once the Soviet Union collapsed, privatization would produce immediate and profound results. I have written on this matter elsewhere and will only summarize those arguments here (Bromley 2000b, 2005).

First, it is important to recognize that Soviet "land tenure" (ownership) carries only a portion of the blame for the dissolute performance of Soviet agriculture. Wheat yields were usually within 75 to 80 percent of what good Canadian farmers in similar agroecological zones managed to obtain. Second, there were bizarre arrangements for allocating agricultural inputs. I have in mind here "tractor stations" and a range of other institutional arrangements that precluded timely application of necessary fertilizers and pesticides. Third, the specific institutional arrangements inside Soviet farms virtually assured serious incentive problems. Much of the food for household consumption came from the farm itself, giving rise to perverse incentives to pilfer and reallocate inputs, to shirk so that labor could be devoted to one's own production, and to manipulate production schedules to enhance appropriable commodities. Fourth, much agricultural produce was lost because of flaws in the agricultural marketing system. Finally, it is important to recall that Stalin destroyed many rural towns and villages and relocated villagers on state and collective farms. That meant that farms came to represent—and to function as—virtual towns and villages. The disbursement of widows' and veterans' benefits, schooling, transportation, postal services, and communications (telephone and telegraph) are just a few of the services for which Soviet farms were often the sole provider. In other words, Soviet farms represented a curious mix of industrial-scale farming and required civic functions. Those two purposes often competed for scarce labor, financial resources, and managerial talent.

With input and output markets seriously distorted by the central planning apparatus, and with the internal management of farms responsible for a wide range of nonagricultural imperatives, there can be little surprise that Soviet agriculture was in disarray. Interestingly, efforts to "unpack" the large multipurpose structures and create viable small-scale "family farms" often stalled.

While there was much interest in breaking up Soviet farms because they were too large, Poland, which managed to avoid Soviet-style collectivization, abounds in family farms that are alleged to be too small. It seems that the ideology of privatization still precludes clarity in thinking about agricultural land in the former Soviet Union.

While on the subject of land in agriculture, it seems appropriate to offer a few brief observations concerning the agricultural transformation in the People's Republic of China (PRC). Since the experimental reforms in 1978 endorsed by Anhui's provincial governor Wan Li, China's agriculture has been in constant institutional flux (Bromley 2005; Bromley and Yao 2006; Xue-Lascoux and Bromley 1996). Many economists find it difficult to understand how China's agriculture can be successful in the absence of private ownership of land. My response to that puzzlement is to suggest that those economists should pay more attention to the theory of contracts.

There is, in economics, a general sense that private ownership of land is necessary for economic efficiency and high productivity. Such belief springs from a failure to understand one of the two fundamental theorems of welfare economics. Specifically, the second theorem tells us that economic efficiency can result from *any* possible structure of endowments (land and capital) and associated institutional arrangements—as long as competitive bargaining across all pertinent margins is possible (Bromley 2006). This means that it does not matter who owns agricultural land (the state, an individual farmer) as along as it is possible for rather complete contracts to be written in a bargaining arrangement between the owner (acting as a competitive landlord) and a class of renters. With complete contracting possibilities, incentives can be aligned in such a way that both economic efficiency (a concept at the margin) and productivity (a concept concerning averages) can be ensured. If we start with this theoretical apparatus, emphasis could shift from puzzlement about ownership and instead focus on how to make sure that competitive contracts are possible. While such contracting possibilities may still be somewhat attenuated in China, evidence suggests that reforms are certainly pushing in that direction.

## INSTITUTIONS, LAND, AND THE DEVELOPMENT PROCESS

In most of the developed world, land no longer plays the role of an essential materialist input. In such settings, primary production from land is a small share of GNP, and that land is evolving into an asset of greater significance for producing amenities and ecosystem services. In these circumstances, the institutional issues concern how to insure the long-run economic viability of an agricultural sector whose primary raison d'être is to manage landscapes and to provide ecological benefits (Bromley 2000a).

In the middle-income countries, primary production is rather more prominent, yet even there the institutional issues pertaining to land often concern its conversion from primary production into an ancillary asset for urban and industrial uses. The institutional tensions tend to concern the means of implementing the transition from agriculture and forestry to other uses. We see a politically dangerous aspect of this conversion process along the east coast of the PRC, where industrialization and urbanization are pushing into productive agricultural areas. In such settings, private ownership of agricultural land—and associated legal procedures to ensure compensation of those being displaced—would mitigate the economic losses from conversion and would tend to quell the political outrage. We might predict that the frequent and highly visible confrontations between farmers and local authorities will soon lead to the establishment of clear compensation procedures, even in the absence of private ownership of agricultural land. At the moment, the process is impeded by the sweeping economic and political autonomy granted to provincial authorities, and the seeming reluctance of the political leadership of the PRC to interfere with the robust economic growth brought on by that extraordinary provincial autonomy.

That brings us, once again, to the debilitating and persistent immiserization of many countries in sub-Saharan Africa. As I survey the economic landscape of that part of the world, I am now prepared to conclude that the "development" prescriptions that seem to have worked in Southeast Asia, in much of Latin America, and with some tentative success in parts of South Asia, will not work in sub-Saharan Africa. Others seem to share my concerns (Easterly 2001; Stiglitz 2002; Pritchett 1997). In the face of this realization, we see several responses. One response has been to relieve the extraordinary debt overhang of many countries and then get back to work with much the same medicine that has heretofore failed to produce promising results. A related response in the absence of debt relief is to persist in what has been tried before, except to push in more money—and do more hand holding. Perhaps the most alarming response is to bring in a rock star or two so that they can adopt a village in Malawi, Zambia, or Niger. Related to that bizarre idea is the felt need to distribute free mosquito nets or other items thought to be catalysts to "get the economy moving." Only to express surprise when said nets end up being used in fishing activities.

My conclusion from these desperate measures is that the standard development model that has guided the international community for the past 40–50 years is a spent force. Those of us who have been involved in the development enterprise over the past several decades have watched in amusement (and frequent dismay) as a succession of magic solutions has been offered. The failure of those prescriptions to do the necessary work, especially in sub-Saharan Africa, has then led to a new generation of studies proposing "reasons" for their failure—for example, politicians and government officials are corrupt, we are dealing here with "failed states," colonial boundaries are badly drawn, countries are land-locked, and ethnic tensions undermine good outcomes. There are as many rationalizations as there are excuses to be made. In the case of sub-Saharan Africa, the development community seems to have concluded that *all* of the above reasons are present in most countries and so how can we possibly expect development progress?

However, to the best of my knowledge, no one has been willing to entertain the hypothesis that the received development *model* is itself inappropriate to sub-Saharan Africa. Instead, we have consistently blamed the patient for a failure to respond favorably to our dubious medicine. If our diagnosis is flawed, however, the medicine cannot possibly be of help. This interesting possibility is pertinent to our deliberations here because at the center of my hypothesis is a proposition that the idea and the meaning of land in sub-Saharan Africa differs profoundly from the idea and meaning of land in those settings and circumstances out of which the standard development model emerged (Bromley 1995).

The standard development "model" was not handed down to us by divine revelation. Rather, it is simply the creation of the human mind as successive generations of individuals have struggled with the age-old question of how to bring about economic progress. The development model was created—it was not discovered lying around someplace (Bromley 2006). Its creation story is one of a slow accretion of empirical "regularities" (not laws) as different nations engaged in a continual process of diagnosis, experimentation, learning, and adaptive response. That diagnostic imperative is what pragmatists call abduction (Bromley 2006). But almost without exception, this creation story has concerned nations in the temperate zone, where agriculture differs profoundly from agriculture in the tropics (Rutenberg 1980). Even those accounts that *seem* pertinent to circumstances in the tropics apply the standard model from temperate settings (Boserup 1965).

However, the idea and the meaning of land are endogenously prefigured by the agroecological circumstances specific to the society that exists in those settings and circumstances. It cannot possibly be a surprise that pastoral peoples embedded in a highly varied and extensive agroecological environment would work out an idea and a meaning for land that differs profoundly from that endemic to more temperate settings. And if land plays a different economic role, it must, of necessity, play different social and cultural roles.

Consider two agroecological histories—one from Europe and one from sub-Saharan Africa. The European history is one of relentless intensification.

Under that model, the point is to impose ever-increasing quantities of labor and capital on individually owned parcels of land. Land was necessarily commoditized (fictitiously so in the Polanyi sense), and it ultimately became the focus of family, economy, and polity. Feudalism arose as an economic system predicated on the control of high-quality land (*pace* Ricardo) and the constant investment in land in order to support military and political ends. Over time, as the idea and reality of nation-states evolved, and as the power of a centralized state materialized, feudalism gave way to a system in which former vassals became freeholders—and the consistent imperative to one who owns land is to keep investing so as to make that particular asset produce competitive revenue streams. Once taxation of land became common, the costs of holding (hoarding) land were such that an owner had little choice but to keep investing, or sell it to others who would keep investing.

In temperate zones, with deep and agreeable soils, with rather predictable and standard rainfall, and with an infrastructure that evolves in conjunction with those agroecological circumstances, intensification is mutually reinforcing. Investments in agricultural land are enhanced by correlated investments in the associated service industries—processing, marketing—and the value of agricultural land is thereby ratcheted up even more. Coevolution comes to mind (Norgaard 1981).

In contrast to this intensification model, the indigenous agrarian model in much of Africa is one of extensification. In the language of economic anthropology, the intensification model is a narrow-spectrum provisioning strategy, while extensification is a broad-spectrum provisioning strategy. The point in such agroecological systems is not to invest in individual parcels of land, rendering them more productive than before, but to focus one's livelihood strategies across highly variable microclimates and to invest in personal relations across that heterogeneous space. The economy is not predicated on an abundance of labor and capital applied to individual parcels for the quite plausible reason that the economic returns from such a strategy are insufficient to support that strategy. We must understand the economy as an extension of the family—whose relations developed for both political and material purposes. Land is not commoditized because there is no economic reason for it to be. What benefits flow from the control of small (or large) parcels of land? Belonging to an ordered community is not predicated on the ability to mobilize grain, sturdy horses, and well-fed men to the campaign as we knew it during high feudalism. Rather, belonging is predicated on the willingness (indeed, the obligation) to join together in group political and military endeavors when called upon. In this economy, labor power is more important than ensured (state-protected) control over specific pieces of Cartesian space.

The reigning model of development advocates greater intensification of land on the dubious presumption that land in sub-Saharan Africa is the same thing as land in France or England. However, there is no such thing as land—there is only land tenure. And land tenure is simply the culturally particularized ideas of land. From this it follows that agriculture as an engine of agrarian development in sub-Saharan Africa remains problematic precisely because the development prescriptions for agriculture are predicated on the wrong model. Not having been socialized into the model of intensification and fictitious commoditization of land, many in sub-Saharan Africa are often content to see land as something to which they belong, rather than as something that belongs to them. Try fitting that into microeconomic theory and the derived models of "development economics."

## IMPLICATIONS

My task here has been to address new institutional arrangements for land in the twenty-first century, with particular reference to economic development. I believe that several implications flow from this exercise.

First, the idea of land is subject to constant evolution, and it therefore follows that the institutional arrangements pertinent to land are in continual flux. Land is not some static essence but is merely the artificial creation of culturally disparate social entities intent on securing a better future. And land cannot be understood as something apart from the web of institutional arrangements situating it in a multifaceted relationship that entails the object of interest (a parcel of land) and two or more parties (individuals or groups of individuals) with differing ideas and aspirations with respect to that parcel (Bromley 1991, 2004). Land, as with an economy, is always in the process of becoming (Bromley 2006).

The second implication to flow from this assessment is that the idea of ownership, so central in both a political and an economic sense, is overplayed and conceptually incoherent. Ownership is overplayed because it is thought to represent some timeless assurances essential to political liberty and economic efficiency. But, of course, ownership is necessarily in a state of evolution because the object "owned"—land, in this case—is constantly evolving. So the static concept of ownership is incoherent. With everything in motion, what is there representing stability that is worth celebrating? Only romantics can find something durable in such a world.

Land as space and place—and as part of the revered natural world—will continue to take on greater social and economic significance. As it does that, the related institutional arrangements that will secure multiple interests in specific parcels will take on additional political importance. We have not yet scratched the surface on crafting new institutional arrangements pertinent to land in this broader sense.

My final observation is that the entire development enterprise must be subjected to a radical reformulation. The insistence that introducing (imposing) "formal" tenures in the poorest countries in the world will be a plausible strategy to induce agricultural investment and economic development cannot be supported by the empirical evidence. More important, the entire conceptualization of land and investment leading to economic advancement is the worn-out residue of a flawed model of the development challenge. Land will continue to matter for livelihoods in sub-Saharan Africa, but the place-centric concept of intensification and resulting investment fails to accord with the broad-spectrum survival strategy so central to highly variable agroecological settings. Of course, there will be those who advocate irrigation investments— or green revolution crop varieties—and who then will assume that those actions will somehow give rise to a narrow-spectrum economic strategy in these highly variable settings and circumstances. I suggest such optimists investigate the residues of massive irrigation infrastructures visited on the Indians, the Pakistanis, and the Sudanese during the years of high British colonialism.

As with other things, the current degraded state of those capital structures will be blamed on corruption, or political incompetence, or the tyranny of engineers, or some other mysterious force. Lost in fixing blame will be the distinct possibility that those irrigation investments were undertaken by foreigners for the clear purpose of producing cotton or some other export crop that could be sent back to the colonial master for manufacture and possible reimportation into the colonies. Can there be any mystery in why these investments have not been maintained?

New institutional arrangements for the twenty-first century, if they are to bring about economic development, will need to start from a clean slate (a tabula rasa). The models we seem to draw on are flawed by their cultural idiosyncracy—and by their ideology (Sjaastad and Bromley 2000). As such, they offer too little to the profound challenge of lifting millions of the world's poorest out of their miserable existence.

## REFERENCES

Atwood, D. A. 1990. Land registration in Africa: The impact on agricultural production. *World Development* 18(5):659–671.

Besley, T. 1995. Property rights and investment incentives: Theory and evidence from Ghana. *Journal of Political Economy* 103(5):903–937.

Boserup, E. 1965. *The conditions of agricultural growth.* London: Allen & Unwin.

Bromley, D. W. 1991. *Environment and economy: Property rights and public policy.* Oxford: Blackwell.

———. 1995. Development reconsidered: The African challenge. *Food Policy* 20(5):425–438.

———. 2000a. Can agriculture become an environmental asset? *World Economics* 1(3):127–139.

———. 2000b. A most difficult passage: The economic transition in Central and Eastern Europe and the former Soviet Union. *Emergo: Journal of Transforming Economies and Societies* 7(3):3–23.

———. 2004. Property rights: Locke, Kant, Peirce, and the logic of volitional pragmatism. In *Property rights in the 21st century.* H. M. Jacobs, ed. Cheltenham, U.K.: Edward Elgar.

———. 2005. Property rights and land in ex-socialist states. In *Developmental dilemmas: Land reform and institutional change in China.* P. Ho, ed. London: Routledge.

———. 2006. *Sufficient reason: Volitional pragmatism and the meaning of economic institutions.* Princeton, NJ: Princeton University Press.

Bromley, D. W., and Y. Yao. 2006. Understanding China's economic transformation: Are there lessons here for the developing world? *World Economics* 7(2):73–95.

Carter, M., and P. Olinto. 2003. Getting institutions right for whom: Credit constraints and the impact of property rights on the quantity and composition of investment. *American Journal of Agricultural Economics* 85(1):173–186.

de Janvry, A., J-P. Platteau, G. Gordillo, and E. Sadoulet. 2001. Access to land and land policy reforms. In *Access to land, rural poverty, and public action.* A. de Janvry, G. Gordillo, J-P. Platteau, and E. Sadoulet, eds., 1–26. New York: Oxford University Press.

de Soto, H. 2000. *The mystery of capital: Why capitalism triumphs in the west and fails everywhere else.* New York: Basic Books.

Deininger, K. 2003. *Land policies for growth and poverty reduction.* Washington, DC: World Bank.

Deininger, K., and G. Feder. 2001. Land institutions and land markets. In *Handbook of agricultural economics.* B. Gardner and G. Rausser, eds., 288–331. Amsterdam: Elsevier.

Easterly, W. 2001. *The elusive quest for growth.* Cambridge, MA: MIT Press.

Feder, G., and T. Onchan. 1987. Land ownership security and farm investment in Thailand. *American Journal of Agricultural Economics* 69(2):311–320.

Fitzpatrick, D. 2005. "Best practice" options for the legal recognition of customary tenure. *Development and Change* 36(3):449–475.

Hubacek, K., and J. C. J. M. van den Bergh. 2006. Changing concepts of "land" in economic theory: From single to multi-disciplinary approaches. *Ecological Economics* 56:5–27.

Lund, C. 2000. African land tenure: Questioning basic assumptions. Drylands Issue Paper E100. London: IIED.

Marx, L. 1964. *The machine in the garden*. Oxford: Oxford University Press.

Migot-Adholla, S., P. B. Hazell, B. Blarel, and F. Place. 1993. Indigenous land rights systems in sub-Saharan Africa: A constraint on productivity? In *The economics of rural organization*. K. Hoff, A. Braverman, and J. Stiglitz, eds., 269–291. Oxford: Oxford University Press. Also in: *The World Bank Economic Review* 5(1):155–175 (published in 1991).

Norgaard, R. B. 1981. Sociosystem and ecosystem coevolution in the Amazon. *Journal of Environmental Economics and Management* 8:238–254.

Ouedraogo, R. S., J-P. Sawadogo, V. Stamm, and T. Thombiano. 1996. Tenure, agricultural practices and land productivity in Burkina Faso: Some recent results. *Land Use Policy* 13(3):229–232.

Peirce, C. S. 1934. *Collected papers*, vol. 5. Cambridge, MA: Harvard University Press.

Place, F., and P. Hazell. 1993. Productivity effects of indigenous land tenure systems in sub-Saharan Africa. *American Journal of Agricultural Economics* 75(1):10–19.

Platteau, J-P. 1996. The evolutionary theory of land rights as applied to sub-Saharan Africa: A critical assessment. *Development and Change* 27(1):29–86.

Pritchett, L. 1997. Divergence, big time. *Journal of Economic Perspectives* 11(3): 3–17.

Roulac, S. E., M. O. Dotzour, P. Cheng, and J. R. Webb. 2005. Evolving research priorities: The contents of *Land Economics*. *Land Economics* 81(4):457–476.

Rutenberg, H. 1980. *Farming systems in the tropics*. Oxford: Clarendon House.

Sjaastad, E., and D. W. Bromley. 1997. Indigenous land rights in sub-Saharan Africa: Appropriation, security and investment demand. *World Development* 25(4): 549–562.

———. 2000. The prejudices of property rights: On individualism, specificity, and security in property regimes. *Development Policy Review* 18(4):365–389.

Stiglitz, J. E. 2002. *Globalization and its discontents*. New York: Norton.

World Bank. 2006. *World Development Report 2006: Equity and development*. Washington, DC: World Bank.

Xue-Lascoux, Z., and D. W. Bromley. 1996. Necessity and purpose in Chinese agriculture: 1949–95. *Oxford Development Studies* 24(3):261–280.

# 11

# Social Dimensions of Rural Resource Sustainability

## Anthony Bebbington

I wrote this chapter while living in Peru. During the course of thinking about it and preparing for it I watched a closely fought national election, which divided the country. One vote was concentrated largely in metropolitan Lima and the Peruvian coast, where the bulk of Peru's large cities and its export agriculture are found. The other vote was concentrated in Peru's two other mega-ecological regions: the Andean highlands, an area of intermediate cities, small-scale (peasant and indigenous) farming, and a rapidly growing (but still enclave-like) mining economy; and the jungle to the east, a lowland area of tropical agriculture, hydrocarbon and timber extraction, colonization from the highlands and indigenous populations whose territories suffer increasing pressures of invasion, and de facto expropriation. In the second round of the elections (in May 2006), the highland and jungle vote was for a candidate who called for radical change, spoke against the system, and called for far greater controls on, and taxation of, a highly profitable, largely

I am grateful to the International Center for Land Policy Studies and Training and the Lincoln Institute of Land Policy for the invitation to prepare this chapter. I am also grateful to the Centro Peruano de Estudios Sociales (CEPES, the Peruvian Centre for Sòcial Studies) for providing such an enjoyable home while I prepared the chapter. Thanks to Denise Humphreys Bebbington, Jim Riddell, Gary Cornia, and conference participants for comments. The chapter draws on different bodies of work conducted over the years, but in particular on research funded by the International Development Research Centre (Canada) through its program Social Movements, Environmental Governance and Territorial Rural Development, a program coordinated by the Latin American Centre for Rural Development (RIMISP). Research for the chapter was partly supported by an Economic and Social Research Council Professorial Fellowship, Award Number RES-051-27-0191.

foreign owned, mining sector. The coastal and, above all, Lima vote, on the other hand, supported a candidate calling for more continuity, for the promotion of agricultural exports (from both coast and highlands), and for more (but also more responsible) mining investment.

What does a national election in Peru have to do with my theme, the social dimensions of rural resource sustainability? I suggest two ways in which it is relevant and helps frame the discussion here. First, natural resources occupied a prominent place in these electoral arguments, in the form of debates on the roles that mining and hydrocarbons ought to play in national development. Arguments were passionate about how much taxes and royalties mining should pay, about the extent to which foreign direct investment (FDI) in mining ought to be subject to government regulation and control (if not nationalized), and about the imperative of making mining a force for progressive forms of rural development (as opposed to a vehicle for the extraction of value inhering in natural resources). In many regards this was a debate about how far the extraction of a particular form of natural capital should be allowed to damage other forms of natural capital (land and water) and how far (and through which mechanisms) it should be transformed into different forms of rural capital (e.g., human, financial, physical). It was a debate about the relative substitutability of different forms of capital, and about how the substitution should be defined and managed, and by whom.

This leads to the second point. The highland vote was an angry vote, reflecting a deeply felt sense that highland, rural, and provincial populations have had little say in framing debates on, policies for, or concepts of development in Peru. It was a vote against a metropolitan, white, coastal, and elite domination of these debates and a demand for increased involvement of the highlands in determining what natural resources should be used for and where the wealth that they generate should be reinvested.

These elections therefore drew attention to several building blocks for this chapter. First, the roles that rural resources ought to play in society can be a deeply contentious issue. Second, it matters greatly whose sets of ideas come to dominate national debates and policies on how these resources should be used. Third, some groups in society dominate and define these debates and ideas far more than do others. Fourth, in these debates—even if the term *sustainability* is not used explicitly—different groups have quite different ideas of what constitutes a sustainable management of rural resources. For some groups the large-scale extraction of subsoil resources can be considered sustainable resource use, as long as some of the income derived is paid as tax revenue and then invested back into the formation of other resources; for others, if such extraction implies permanent change to and loss of landscape, water, and financial resources (through capital flows from Peru to the global North), there is no imaginable way that such extraction could be thought of as sustainable resource management.

With these contemporary observations in mind (and we will return to them later), let me change tempo and lay out how this chapter will proceed. The purpose of the following section is to explore, criticize, and expand on frameworks for thinking about sustainability and rural resources. The section first lays out two related frameworks for thinking about rural resource sustainability, one operating at an aggregate (regional and national) level, the other at the level of the household. The discussion here explores the contributions that "capital"-based approaches to sustainable development and livelihoods might make to an understanding of the social factors that underlie rural resource sustainability. In particular, it suggests that these frameworks leave pending a series of questions that should also be central in any reflection of the social dimensions of sustainability. Inter alia, they fail to consider how it is that certain *things* come to be seen as *resources*, or *capital assets*, in some contexts and not in others; how actors (at distinct scales) determine the goals to which different asset portfolios should be put; how actors (again at different scales) come to decide the terms of exchange between different assets—how they decide that the loss of a given amount of asset X can be justified by a gain in another amount of asset Y; and how resources come to be unevenly distributed.

Building on these reflections, the text then adds two core geographical concepts into this discussion of assets, asset mixes, and asset portfolios. These are the concepts of space and of scale. The discussion first suggests that these concepts are also central to how "rural" sustainability might be thought of. Indeed, they lead us to question any attempts to think only of rural sustainability without also considering urban-rural interactions within wider territories, or the relationships between a given territory and actors and processes operating at other scales of analysis. The introduction of concepts of scale and scale relations also opens up a reflection on the wider economic and sociopolitical networks running across localities both close to and at great distances from the resource in question that influence the control, management, and relative sustainability of particular resources and particular livelihoods.

These discussions raise the specter of a series of social processes and social relationships that appear to merit more attention in any reflection on the social dimensions of rural resource sustainability. The section therefore closes with a discussion of one particular type of actor—social movements—that in many cases brings these more contentious social dimensions into the open. In particular, this discussion explores both how livelihoods and capital asset frameworks can help observers understand why such movements emerge, as well as the ways in which the nature and actions of these social movements speak back to and help elaborate livelihood frameworks. The discussion also suggests that such movements raise questions not only about different ways of conceiving of resource sustainability, but also about ways of understanding the relationships between land and territory.

In the following section, these ideas are explored empirically for the case of areas affected by rapid increases in external investment in natural resource extraction. The examples—drawing on our recent and ongoing research[1]— explore the social dimensions that surround conflicts over resource use that are triggered by such forms of development. At their core they make clear the way in which any notion of sustainable rural resource management is itself a social construct, that different actors have different understandings of the role of land in such strategies for sustainability (cf. chapter 10 in this volume), and that the processes through which certain notions of sustainability and land become dominant are themselves social, characterized as much by conflict as by collaboration and dialogue. While the examples come from Latin America, once they are considered in the context of the broader spatial and scale relationships of the places discussed, they quickly become cases that are at once Latin American, global, and multiregional.[2] Building on these case-based discussions, the conclusions bring the discussion back to a larger reflection on what we might mean by (or at the very least include within any reflection on) the "social dimensions of rural resource sustainability."

## SUSTAINABILITY AND SOCIAL MOVEMENTS

### Capitals and Sustainability

During the 1990s, one of the more interesting and influential turns in the ways development studies discussed resources was to experiment with the use of a language of different forms of "capital." One of the early statements in this vein was that of Ismail Serageldin and Andrew Steer (1994)—at that time, respectively, the World Bank's vice president for environmentally sustainable development and the director of the Bank's Environment Department. The statement grew, in part, out of an effort on Serageldin's part to suggest alternative ways of assessing the "wealth of nations" (Serageldin

---

[1]Conducted with Jeffrey Bury, Denise Humphreys Bebbington, Jeannet Lingan, Juan Pablo Muñoz, and Martin Scurrah.

[2]Indeed, both cases have an important East Asian component—in one instance as a source of investment and in both as a source of demand.

1996), an effort first influenced by Herman Daly's work on natural capital (e.g., Daly and Townsend 1993), and subsequently by Putnam's promotion of the concept of social capital. Daly had helped introduce notions of natural capital into the vice-presidency—with a view to pushing the Bank to think more critically about the value of the environment and about the costs of environmental damage caused by its operations. Meanwhile, Putnam (1993) had just argued—on the basis of work in Italy—that an undervalued resource in development was the social capital that exists as norms and networks of reciprocity in society. This social capital, he suggested, was directly implicated in the production of economic capital (and more generally of good government). Regardless of later debates (Tendler 1997) that questioned Putnam's arguments about causality, the idea found fertile ground in the World Bank, and in particular in the vice-presidency that had already experimented with the concept of natural capital and was itself the home for the Bank's social development work (Bebbington et al. 2004).

Serageldin took these ideas and suggested that a more complete assessment of the wealth of nations should include—indeed, account separately for—national stocks not only of financial and fixed capital, but also of human, natural, and social capital. The argument was that gross national product, gross domestic product (GDP), and income per capita measures alone were inadequate measures of wealth. Wealth had to be assessed across a range of asset or (in their language) capital domains. It was but a short step, of course, to relate this discussion to a reflection on sustainability. In their 1994 publication, Serageldin and Steer argued that sustainability could best be thought of in terms of the mixes and trade-offs among produced capital, natural capital, human capital, and social capital. They suggested that levels of sustainability could be conceptualized in terms of the rules governing the substitution among these different stocks of capital. A "weak" concept of sustainability, they argued, would consider development as sustainable as long as the overall capital stock increased, regardless of the substitutions occurring among different types of capital. This would therefore qualify as sustainable a form of development that drew down natural capital on a massive scale, as long as this formed enough human, produced, financial, and social capital to offset this cost. At the other extreme, an "absurdly strong" notion of sustainability would not allow drawdown in any of these forms of capital—to be able to speak of sustainable *development*, the overall stock would have to grow without loss in any single form of capital.

In between the two extremes, Serageldin and Steer located two more pragmatic notions of sustainable resource use: *sensible* sustainability (in which total capital stock remains intact, and development processes avoid depletion of any particular capital stock beyond critical levels, which, since these critical levels are unknown, should be defined conservatively and monitored carefully); and *strong* sustainability (which would imply maintaining each component of capital intact, meaning that if natural capital is destroyed in one place, it should be replaced by cultivated natural capital in other places, as, for instance, in carbon sequestration and trading arrangements) (Serageldin and Steer 1994, 31–32).

Of course, such ideas are both value laden (the adjectives that the authors used made clear their own preferences) and more heuristic than analytical—the latter because any effort to generate a common metric against which each of these capital assets could be valued would inevitably become subject to analytical scrutiny and political contention (a point to which we return later). Nonetheless, the framework remains useful and intriguing (and in this sense it is a good heuristic) because it helps make explicit some of the general senses in which societies (and sociopolitically distinct subgroups within societies) form views on acceptable types of trade-off among, and acceptable critical or threshold levels of, each of these different capitals. What remains pending is how these decisions are made in society, but before we move to that point we first address a particularly fruitful elaboration of this schema.

While Serageldin and Steer (1994) appeared to be talking about regional and national levels when they were considering the relative substitutability of different types of capital, other authors and organizations have taken the basic elements of this same schema and applied them at the level of households—with a view to elaborating frameworks for understanding livelihood dynamics and decisions. This interest in livelihoods, of course, has a history that predates these analytical experiments in the 1990s. In the 1970–1980s, research informed by dependency and world systems theory often drew links between processes of underdevelopment and the dependent nature of poor people's livelihoods. This work emphasized the extent to which the broader development model constrained and undermined people's livelihoods and the resources at their disposal.[3]

More recent approaches, while not eschewing the ways broad processes of capitalist development limit livelihood options, have taken a somewhat different approach. They have argued that a careful analysis of how people compose livelihood strategies can suggest ways that openings in the overall development model might be reworked and exploited by poor people and the

---

[3]The concept of functional dualism (de Janvry 1981), for instance, embodied the notion of structural relations among modernizing and popular sectors of the economy in which the modern economy *needed* the popular economy as a source of cheap labor, foodstuffs, goods, and services. Similar ideas characterized work on urban survival strategies and took on particular force in critiques of self-help housing and of de Soto's interpretation of the informal economy (Bromley 1994; Bromley and Gerry 1979; de Soto 1989).

organizations that work alongside them (Chambers 1987; Chambers and Conway 1992). These approaches combine a concern for poor people's agency, an interest in the resource bases of their livelihoods, and an acknowledgment of the ways institutions and structures affect livelihood options.

Some of these approaches focus particularly on the ways people gain access to and control over a diversity of resources, combining them in different ways in order to pursue their aspirations.[4] Such frameworks focus on "what the poor have, rather than what they do not have" (Moser 1998, 1) and understand livelihood strategies as the ways people gain access to those assets, combine them, and transform them into livelihood outcomes. In particular, the following types of assets tend to be emphasized (Bebbington 1999):

- Human capital—the assets that one has as a consequence of one's body (knowledge, health, skills, time, etc.)
- Social capital—the assets that one has as a consequence of one's relationships with others and one's membership in organizations, and which also facilitate access to other resources
- Produced capital—both physical assets (infrastructure, technology, livestock, seeds, etc.) and financial assets (money, working capital, and assets easily converted into money)
- Natural capital—the quality and quantity of the natural resources to which one has access
- Cultural capital—the symbolic resources that one has as a result of the social structures within which one is embedded

In addition to having a broad view of the assets upon which people draw, some of these frameworks also have a wide view of what people pursue in their livelihoods—in other words, what they produce when they transform these assets. These frameworks thus work with a multidimensional view of poverty (Moser 1998) and aspiration (Appadurai 2004). The framework portrayed in figure 11.1 conveys the notion that through their practices and strategies of resource management, people seek to generate not only material

---

[4]See, for instance, Bebbington (1997, 1999), Carney (1998), Moser (1998), Scoones (1998), and Zoomers (1999). There is a certain bias toward rural applications of these asset-based approaches to livelihoods. This is perhaps not surprising. Not only does the bias reflect the intellectual roots of such approaches (in farming systems research, etc.), but it may also reflect the work that such approaches are made to do—in particular, they have been used to draw attention to the increasing importance of nonfarm dimensions of rural life and economy, and to the (relatively) diminishing significance of natural resources in rural livelihoods (Escobál 2001; Reardon, Berdegué, and Escobar 2001; Zoomers 1999). Indirectly, they have also been caught up in those discussions of agricultural extension and technology transfer that have implied—or directly argued—that for poorer rural households, public resources would be better spent on education (directly or via vouchers) than on agricultural extension (López 1995).

**Figure 11.1:** A Livelihoods Framework

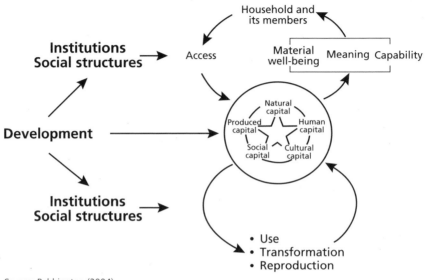

Source: Bebbington (2004).

income (or income in kind), but also meaning and sociopolitical capabilities. There is thus an inherent relationship between livelihood and culture, and between livelihood and political capacity: Livelihoods are in and of themselves meaningful, and a change or loss of livelihood possibilities necessarily implies cultural change. Likewise, a reworking of assets necessarily means a change in a person's ability to participate politically and in the concerns he or she will pursue in that political participation.

As they combine their assets in pursuit of their objectives, it is supposed that people tend to pursue those livelihood strategies that (1) are the most consistent with the portfolio of assets they control at that point in time; (2) reflect both long-term aspirations and immediate needs; and (3) seem the most viable given the opportunities and constraints of the circumstances within which they live. In such conceptions of livelihoods, it is important to introduce a time dimension in the sense that people's livelihood practices in the present may differ from their strategies for the future. Thus, where people invest the majority of their time and effort now may not reflect their aspirations for the future. Indeed, livelihood strategies may work at two levels simultaneously, with people accessing and using the resources they need to meet immediate family needs, while also trying to build up those assets that, when accumulated over time, will allow them or their children to pursue a different sort of livelihood.

An example is rural families who not only pursue agriculture to meet their immediate needs, but also invest in assets that allow their children to gain education so that they can shift out of agriculture (and even out of the countryside). In the language of Serageldin and Steer (1994), this is a process of substitution among different forms of household capital over time.

In emphasizing the importance of *access* to resources, such frameworks also emphasize the ways in which broader social structures and market, state, and civil society institutions affect this access and people's abilities to transform, reproduce, and accumulate resources (see figure 11.1). The influence of the state on livelihoods can be profound and is exercised in many ways, through laws that influence who has access to resources; public policies and programs that provide resources and influence market conditions; state-sanctioned violence that renders assets insecure and depresses local economies; levels of repression or democratization that influence the relative inclination of more powerful social groups to steal the assets of the poor; and so on. The influences of racism, patriarchy, and dominant notions of authority are equally significant. The politics of economic policy making—that privileges particular macroeconomic strategies, sectors of the economy, and regions over others—also has a critical influence on what people can do with their assets and on their long-term livelihood aspirations. While a policy framework that does little to offset the stagnation of peasant agriculture might elicit forms of collective rural radicalism as a response, at an individual level it is at least as likely to translate into family strategies that aim to lay the bases for children to leave—to leave agriculture, to leave the countryside, and to leave economically depressed regions.

Notwithstanding their potential utility, the Serageldin and Steer framework and the livelihoods framework share several points on which they are relatively silent, yet which are central to any appreciation of the social dimensions of the sustainability that each professes an interest in.

First, while each framework emphasizes that sustainability is a function of various asset types (not only land and natural resources) and that different strategies for sustainability involve distinct mixes and trade-offs among these assets, the processes through which decisions about trade-offs are made remain unexamined. At an individual or household level, these processes will depend greatly on how different assets are valued, both by the individual and by the political economic environment within which that individual is putting a livelihood strategy together. At a collective level (region, country, etc.), the process involves interaction among distinct actors, each with their respective valuation of these assets and linked by social relationships that confer far more power to some of these actors than to others. Thus, the trade-offs made may reflect imposition of particular valuations as much as they reflect choice.

Second, while each framework presumes the existence of different types of capital, they fail to explore how certain things, or attributes, come to be viewed as resources (or forms of capital) in the first place. For instance, what are the processes through which the subsoil ceases to be something that merely "is there" under the ground, and begins to be viewed as a source of mineral or hydrocarbon resources—that is, as capital assets with a particular value? What are the processes through which certain cultural practices or forms of social organization come to be valued or, indeed, cease to be valued? Or again, how is it that a certain body of knowledge begins to be viewed as a resource or an asset, rather than simply part of culture, tradition, or even backwardness?

Each of these processes changes any subsequent decisions about acceptable or necessary trade-offs among capital assets, and so becomes formative of subsequent resource management practices. And, for the purposes of this chapter, each of these processes is inherently social and in many senses discursive. The value of a given extension of headwater land, vegetated with cloud forest, located in community territory, and with subsoil deposits of copper, depends greatly, for instance, on how far prior debate, media activity, and curriculum development in that society have come to frame the relative weights of the society's commitments to biodiversity, endangered species, landscapes, minerals, and indigenous culture. Put another way, that same piece of land can have quite distinct functions and meanings, depending on what it is valued for and who is looking at it.

Similar observations apply to the third gap in these frameworks. While each presumes a larger goal to which actions are oriented, they do not address the processes through which this goal is defined. Thus, for instance, in livelihood frameworks, how do individuals determine the meanings they want their lives to fulfill, and the relative balance among these meanings, personal empowerment, and material security? In Serageldin and Steer's framework, how is the collective "development" project whose relative sustainability is to be enhanced defined, and by whom? This definition is key—for it will influence what are deemed to be acceptable trade-offs among different resources, the "level" of sustainability that a society's collective efforts will opt for, and the "critical levels" below which a society will not allow particular assets to be drawn down.

Fourth, and finally for our purposes here, these frameworks pay scant attention to the social distribution of these different capitals. Although some livelihoods frameworks do make explicit the sense in which particular structures and institutions govern access to assets, as well as their security and productivity, the socially differentiated distribution of these assets—and thus of the livelihood options of different individuals—is hardly prominent in livelihood analysis. One effect of this is to understate the ways different livelihoods (and thus the management of different asset bases controlled by different actors) are structurally related to each other. Ownership regimes—and rules governing what needs to be done to demonstrate and secure control, access, and ownership—will, for instance, determine which actors can and cannot draw on particular resources in their livelihoods. They can also go a long way in determining which livelihoods will revolve around asset management as a laborer, which around asset management as an employer, which around asset management as a purchaser, and which around asset management as a trader.

Much of this can seem at once obvious and fuzzy. Yet I want to suggest—for the purposes of a chapter on the social dimensions of rural resource sustainability—that it is critically important. These social processes define the resources that any given actor and collectivity have at their disposal to manage and sustain; the goals toward which they will orient these strategies of management and sustainability; and the social relationships through which some actors in society will have far more power to determine all this than do others. As the vote in Peru suggests, these are relevant, contentious, and burning issues for those in society who feel they have fewer resources to manage, who disagree with currently hegemonic ideas about to what (and whose) ends resources should be managed, and who believe that they have had little say in defining either these goals or these distributions. As we shall suggest in a following section, certain social processes—in particular those involving the emergence of social movements—have helped bring greater visibility to these social dimensions of sustainability.

## Space and Scale in Rural Resource Sustainability

*Rural* is both a social and a spatial concept. Socially, it invokes a notion of low population densities, economic activities in which natural resources play a role (through agriculture, tourism, heritage management, and so on), and a range of cultural attributes and practices. Spatially, it invokes a notion of places that are located beyond concentrated human settlements of a given size,[5] and that are characterized by significant natural or cultivated land cover (as opposed to built forms).

*Rural* is also a concept that can often be packaged with a certain conception of scale. *Local* would seem to be the scale most instinctively associated with rural—an association that is so often manifest in the somewhat strange notion of "local people." Rural development projects, participatory natural resource management initiatives, and rural research projects repeatedly talk

---

[5]Whose census definition varies among countries.

about consulting with local people, as if people in other parts of the world are not local. This use of *local* is itself often imbued with social meanings, seeming to imply people who have more grounded knowledge, more right to have a say in how resources in particular places should be used, who are more noble, more legitimate, more authentic.

Yet the spatial and scalar associations often linked with the word *rural* are highly questionable. Indeed, livelihoods research has done a lot in recent years to demonstrate the extent to which many "rural" livelihoods are no longer primarily agrarian, but involve a range of nonfarm activities, many of which have clear urban components—because of migration, because of strategies to gain access to schooling or other services, or because of families making a steady transfer over time of their investments from rural to urban space (Reardon, Berdegué, and Escobar 2001). In a similar vein, an increasingly strong current of thought in rural development debates argues, in essence, that it is no longer helpful to think of *rural* development. Instead, the focus should be on understanding the processes through which development occurs in wider territories that encompass both rural and urban spaces (Schejtman and Berdegué 2003). This orientation is already a pillar of the Inter-American Development Bank's rural development strategy and policy and is prominent in agencies such as the International Fund for Agricultural Development.

These approaches emphasize the extent to which rural economies are linked by a range of commodity chains to urban, national, and more distant economies. They also insist, increasingly, that for a process of territorial development to occur, the economic linkages between rural spaces and dynamic markets need to be deepened, and that institutions need to be built to facilitate that deepening and enable poorer rural residents to participate in the economic transformations that market deepening would engender.

Thus, whether the focus is on rural livelihoods or the economic development options of rural territories, the tendency is to deemphasize the very idea of rural and to think instead of linkages, networks, and chains in which economic processes cut across space, link actors in different locations, and draw resources into these economic dynamics. The relevant space for thinking about rural resource use thus ceases to be rural and becomes regional and multilayered, and the scale for thinking about "rural" ceases to be local and becomes multiscalar—or perhaps multilocal.

Several implications seem to flow from this for our interest in rural resource sustainability. One is that it may simply be unhelpful to think of "rural resources." Rather, resources are embedded in networks that run across a range of locations and involve a range of actors. Indeed, to return to a point in the previous section, these networks go a long way in determining the processes through which a "thing" in rural areas becomes a "resource." Indeed, in many instances it may be the case that something is never a rural resource—rather, it transitions from being a "rural thing" to a "regional/national multilocal resource." This is most clearly the case for minerals and hydrocarbons, but it is also true for certain timbers, plants, and landscapes.

Second, the calculations that influence the ways in which these resources are managed are certainly not bounded by a rural space. Markets, prices, and policies in distinct locations each have a great influence, of course—not only on how a given resource sold on those markets is managed, but also on how other resources are managed, mixed, and traded off as a function of the management of this marketable resource. But it is not only distant markets that affect these resource management practices in a given rural space. The use and control of rural water is (and will increasingly be) affected by urban and industrial demands for water—demands still transmitted and made effective by bureaucracies and laws as much as markets. Likewise, valuations made elsewhere of biodiversity, cultural diversity, landscapes, and other "things" creates linkages that then impinge directly on the use of rural things, bringing them into wider networks that turn these things into resources. Some of these networks might operate through markets (as in the case of tourism), others through hierarchies and bureaucracies (as in the case of international conservation organizations).

Third, and directly related, the "relevant" actors in rural resource management become anything but rural. In cases that we will discuss in the empirical section, a small sample of the actors relevant in influencing rural resource use would include traders and investment firms operating on the Toronto, New York, London, and Philadelphia stock markets; environmental activists of a range of political hues operating in the Bay Area and Washington, D.C.; members of Congress in Peru and Ecuador; human rights and development activists in London, Boston, Quito, Lima, and Colorado; companies legally based in London, Denver, and Vancouver; the World Bank group—as well, of course, as a range of national ministries.

Again this may seem obvious, but whatever the case, the important point is that the relevant spaces and scales at which rural resource sustainability is determined go far beyond the rural, and are multiple—with, by the same token, multiple actors involved. While this can bring opportunity, it also brings a far broader range of valuations to bear on given resources (in addition to the valuations made by those people who live more closely to them) and as a result increases the likelihood of conflicts over how rural resources should be managed, by whom, and to what ends.

Such networks and the ways they affect the use of rural resources have only recently become an object of serious research. Furthermore, what research has been done has been far more focused on activist networks and networks linked to the multilateral development agencies (formative works here are Keck and Sikkink 1998; Fox and Brown 1998). Far less progress has been made in understanding the parts of these networks that operate through businesses, stock markets, venture capital markets, and the like. Even less has been done to understand the ways distinct types of network coexist and interact with each other—and again, what has been done has focused more on interactions between activist or social movement networks and the development banks than on their interactions with international market actors.

One important and interesting exception in this regard is the work of anthropologist Anna Tsing (2004). Tsing explores the ways timber and minerals in Indonesia become resources within international economic circuits, and the networks, ideas, and images that are mobilized in these processes. At the same time, she traces the relationships between environmental activists working at different locations along the same networks—activists in provincial localities in Indonesia, in Jakarta, and in the Americas. Again, reflecting the relative difficulty of research access, the activist networks are more deeply analyzed than those linking market actors, but still her ability to get inside each allows her to trace how the workings of these different networks interact with each other and ultimately influence the ways resources across distinct locations of the Indonesian archipelago are managed, extracted, protected, fought over, traded off, and sustained.

Tsing uses the term *friction* to refer to these interactions and does so in a double sense. The first sense is that activist networks present a certain friction to market processes, slowing or modifying their fluidity of operation. The second sense is to refer to friction within environmental activist networks—tensions among actors working at the same spatial scale, as well as, and especially, among actors operating at different scales (or different points along the network). These frictions can emerge for a number of reasons, including tensions over who exercises more influence in setting agendas for local action and for international campaigns; who determines the use of resources; the simultaneous existence of relationships of solidarity and of audit; the coexistence within networks of conservationist agendas and environmental justice agendas; and so on. Whatever the specific explanation in any given case, however, the existence of these tensions reflects the more general fact that along these chains of solidarity and activism there exists a series of actors—located at quite different physical and social distances from particular natural resources—who have an influence (and aim to expand that influence) on the ways in which land and natural resources are used, and the ways in which this use is debated. Rural resource sustainability becomes again—in activist networks as much as economic ones—subject to actors operating at a range of scales and across wide spaces, some very far from the resource and land in question.

## Social Movements and Sustainability: Making the Social Dimensions Visible

In discussing international activist networks and the ways they interact with economic networks and together affect what happens to rural resources, Tsing (2004) draws attention to the place of social activism and mobilization as part of the social dimensions of rural resource sustainability. What these movements do (in part) is argue the case for a particular notion of sustainability—in general, a relatively strong notion, to use Serageldin and Steer's (1994) terms. As such, they also constitute one of the actors struggling to define the concepts of sustainability that will ultimately inform policy and political decisions about resource use. These international (multiscalar) actors, however, often interface with more localized forms of social mobilization that also aim to influence the ways capitals are substituted one for another, as well as the social distribution of the costs and benefits associated with these processes of capital substitution. In many cases, these more localized mobilizations might usefully be understood in terms of the asset-based livelihoods frameworks discussed earlier, though, as we will see, their actions also reveal, and in some way compensate for, the gaps in those frameworks.

As noted earlier, livelihoods are a function of assets and structures, and a source of subsistence, income, identity, and meaning (Bebbington 1999; Moser 1998; Scoones 1998). Some social movements seek, above all, to expand or maintain people's asset bases. These movements may engage in direct resource management activities; in activities that provide new, or complement existing, resources; and in activities that involve the transformation of resources (marketing, processing, etc.). I have discussed these organizations elsewhere (Bebbington 1996, 1997). In this section I focus on those social movements that instead emerge to contest patterns of resource control and access and, in some sense, to resist economic processes that lead to asset dispossession (cf. Harvey 2003; Hickey and Bracking 2005, 853). The emergence of such movements might be understood as an attempt to defend livelihood, assets, and territory (Escobar 1995) by challenging the structures, discourses, and institutions that drive and permit their exploitation and dispossession (or, in other terms, as an effort to sustain one particular way of controlling and managing resources rather than another).[6]

Over the last decade in Latin America, movements with these characteristics have increased in importance in response to the increased investment

---

[6]For the specific case of the Peruvian Andes, Gavin Smith (1989) has explored in dense ethnographic and historical detail the many ways resistance and livelihood are linked. For a more general discussion of this link, see Bebbington (2004).

in rural resource extraction driven by growing demand for minerals (especially from East and South Asia), price increases for minerals and hydrocarbons, and technological changes that have turned many once uninteresting deposits into technically exploitable and commercially viable propositions. As a result of these different changes, the economic and technological frontier for extractive industry has been pushed deep into already occupied areas. This brings new threats to the material and cultural resource bases of livelihood, eliciting new types of movement—ones that contest issues of dispossession.

The complaints of movements in the face of these forms of dispossession can be understood in terms of the frameworks explored earlier. That is, they emerge to contest the terms of exchange when one form of capital is substituted for another, and to contest the levels below which certain resources (water, land, wildlife, etc.) are drawn down as a result of extractive industrial activity. For their part, companies and governments reply either that movements have no need to worry (that drawdown has not passed critical levels) or that drawdown of natural capital is more than compensated for through gains in financial capital (in the form of business investment) and in human and physical capital (as a result of investments by company social responsibility programs or by government programs funded by taxes generated by extractive industries). Standoffs between companies and movements thus reflect struggles over who should define acceptable levels of trade-offs, and in this sense they politicize one of the social dimensions on which Serageldin and Steer are silent. At the same time, movements contest the social distribution of the resource gains and losses created by extraction—again making clear a social dimension not made explicit in these frameworks.

While movements might share a broad concern about dispossession, there can still be considerable diversity among and within movements as to the *specific* types of dispossession they are contesting. Likewise, different actors within movements may offer distinct critiques of the issues they are addressing, and different proposals for alternative policies (cf. Perreault 2006). These alternatives can range from complete rejection of resource extraction and the concepts of resource governance and sustainability that they bring with them, to demands for greater participation in decisions regarding resource management and more equitable distribution of the benefits derived from resource exploitation. Some groups within movements might be open to deal with resource extraction companies; others, not at all (and vice versa). Some may prefer strategies of negotiation; others, of confrontation and direct action.

We might hypothesize that the positions and strategies that dominate within movements will have distinct implications for the types of negotiation and articulation that ultimately occur between movements and resource extraction industries, and thus for the types of rural resource management that ensue from these articulations. At one extreme, one can imagine the existence of movements with unified and forceful positions reflecting their sense that they are being dispossessed both of a way of life and of exchange value, and who are therefore unwilling to negotiate. At another extreme, one can imagine the existence of movements whose concern is to negotiate compensation for dispossession or guarantees against dispossession of asset *quality*, and who would withdraw contestation once the extractive industry had put in place plans for environmental remediation and social compensation.

It is important not to romanticize about such movements, because they fail as often as they succeed. This propensity for failure reflects an inherent fragility in movements, one that has to be understood in terms of their internal dynamics and the contexts in which they operate. Movements are constituted by distinct currents, groupings of actors, local leaderships, and organizations. As a result, holding a movement together around a shared agenda for sustainability is an immensely difficult feat and always a fragile achievement, not least because internal sources of weakness can be compounded by external factors. In particular, while many livelihoods might be threatened by extractive industry development, others will stand to gain as the capital investment and substitution effects of the industry also create new livelihood opportunities. This can easily lead to situations in which the social mobilization that emerges to contest extractive industry development exists alongside quite distinct forms of mobilization that seek to defend and support the industry (and may well receive direct support and encouragement from the industry itself).

The effect that this mix of social actors ultimately has on resource management depends greatly on their relative power and the relative importance of the extractive industry within both the national and regional economies. Where the industry is that much more important, one would expect state and other social forces to be more determined to question, delegitimize, and repress movements and more generally expose their internal fragilities. Likewise, the greater the resources at the disposal of other economic actors, the more able they will be to deepen the inherent fractures in movements. At a more general level of abstraction, in this triad of relationships between movement, business, and state, it may well be that the outcome of conflicts over what sort of resource sustainability and livelihood mixes are to be pursued hinges around how far state agencies ultimately identify with one set of claims over another.

## EXTRACTIVE INDUSTRIES, ACTOR NETWORKS, AND CONFLICTS OVER SUSTAINABILITY

In this section I wish to explore a particular case that throws light on some of the issues raised in previous sections, and that helps ground some of these more abstract reflections on what might be taken to constitute social dimensions of sustainability. The case is of a particular form of extractive industries development—large-scale mining—with a geographical focus on Peru. Peru has a long history of mineral extraction. However, since the mid 1990s, reflecting a series of changes in mining and tax codes—changes linked to the more general implementation of a neoliberal model of economic management in Peru—the mining industry has expanded rapidly (Bridge 2004). By the year 2000 three departments of the country had between 30 percent and 50 percent of their terrain under mining claims, and a further seven had between 20 percent and 30 percent (Bury 2005).

Accompanying this growth in investment in extractive industries has been an equally remarkable surge in social mobilization and conflict. Thus, in 2005 a report to the Peruvian Defensoría del Pueblo (Ombudsman's Office) recorded 33 separate conflicts related to mining (Ormachea Choque 2005). In many respects these conflicts can be understood as confrontations between different models of sustainability. In a very simple sense, mining companies and ministries of energy and mines manage a concept of resource sustainability that allows for substantial substitution among forms of capital, as well as significant changes in the asset mixes on which rural livelihoods are built (changes that would essentially force many families into new types of livelihood). They also—somewhat against the suggestions of Serageldin and Stéer—manage optimistic notions of how far particular capitals can be drawn down before passing critical levels. Those contesting this mineral development—both local movements and wider activist networks—work with stronger concepts of sustainability, allow less substitution among capital, and are far more conservative and risk averse in the types of capital drawdown they deem acceptable.

These conflicts over models of sustainability have involved a wide range of actors operating at different scales. In much the same way as Tsing (2004) describes, we encounter on one hand networks that bring together miners, investors, stock markets, and ministries of mining and finance. Actors in these networks by and large seek to promote mining and the models of sustainability that this implies. They also argue that decisions on whether mining should proceed should be made at a national (rather than local) level, on the grounds that mining is a national priority. Of course, substitution and drawdown of capital is easier to accept at this level because those making de-

cisions do not experience the effects of the substitutions in their own livelihoods.

On the other hand are a range of activist and social movement organizations operating at various scales and questioning the current forms assumed
by mineral extraction projects. Actors in these networks may push for anything from more responsible mining to no mining at all—depending on their
respective understandings of sustainability. These networks bring together international actors—Oxfam, Friends of the Earth International, U.S. Bay Area
environmental groups, human and indigenous rights groups, and others—as
well as local and national nongovernmental organizations (NGOs) and social organizations. National-level indigenous organizations are also prominent in these networks, and tend to argue that land and subsoil ought to be
understood as territory rather than resources. As such, they have increasingly
argued that these spaces ought to be managed so as to sustain indigenous territory rather than with a view to extracting natural capital and building up
other forms of capital. They also tend to argue that decisions on the forms of
sustainability to be pursued should be made either at international levels
(where the emphasis is on protecting global commons) or local levels (where
people are directly affected by the capital substitution and drawdown fostered
by mining).

Variants of these networks have interacted and clashed on a number of extractive industry development projects in Peru over the last decade. In some
cases the clashes have led to some slight modification of the resource management and capital formation effects of mining—examples here would include more careful environmental management practices or expanded social
responsibility programs investing in both human capital formation and local
business development. In other instances, the clashes have had far more significant effects on rural resource management. In August 2006 in Peru—
following the election discussed at the beginning of the chapter, and a rising
tide of social conflict—a group of mining companies, encouraged by the new
government, agreed to contribute an additional US$782 million over five
years to government social programs[7]—a significant change in the terms of
substitution among forms of capital at a national level.

Experiences such as these suggest several important points about the ways
these different actor networks, stretching across distinct locations and scales,

---

[7]"Additional," that is, to the taxes and royalties they were already paying. That said, most of the
largest companies already had very favorable arrangements in which their taxes were low and
they paid no royalties. Indeed, this situation (which in effect reduced the extent to which natural capital was being turned into anything other than financial capital controlled as company
profit) had much to do with the discontent that underlay some of the electoral discussion on
mining and much of the social protest against the sector.

influence resource management. First, they help turn things into resources and also help give distinct values to these resources; second, they each influence the ways discussions of resource management are framed—indeed, there exists something of a tussle among them to determine the terms of debate as to what constitutes sustainability and how resources ought best be managed in Peru; and third, even if certain networks and actors consistently tend to have more power than others, there is always an element of contingency in how these power relationships will work out and in the resource management effects that flow from this.

The following comparative study of two regions in the north of Peru, each affected by mining, explores in somewhat more detail how these networks operate, and some of the factors that seem to determine the ultimate resource management effects of their interactions. The first case comes from the department of Cajamarca. The mine studied—which we refer to as MYSA—is jointly owned by Newmont Mining Corporation (a United States–based multinational with head offices in Denver, Colorado) with a 51.35 percent share in the ownership; the Peruvian Compañía de Minas Buenaventura, with 43.65 percent; and the International Finance Corporation (IFC), with 5 percent. MYSA is a particularly significant mine, not only because it is the largest gold mine in Latin America,[8] but also because it was the first large-scale foreign direct investment in Peru following the 1980s, a decade of loss to hyperinflation and civil war. While exploration was under way during the 1980s, the first significant investment was made only in 1992, and the first gold presented to the public in 1993.

The second case—or, more exactly, pair of cases—come from the department of Piura, which sits between Cajamarca and the Pacific Coast of Peru. The first experience comes from the town of Tambogrande, and the second from the provinces of Huancabamba and Ayabaca. In each instance, the case is of an (as yet) non-mine. That is to say, these are cases in which mineral exploration has not yet been able to progress into mineral extraction, in part because the exploration activities have catalyzed processes of social mobilization that emerged to resist the conversion of land to mining.

The comparison between these cases helps us to reflect on the conditions under which social movements have more and less effect on natural resource extraction industries and the types of land use and landscape they produce. Indeed, the comparison is one of extremes—between one case in which a social movement has been little more than a spectator to the creation of Latin America's largest gold mine, and another a case (Tambogrande) in which

---

[8]Even though, initially, the company insisted that the mine would be small.

mobilization has had the effect that—for the time being—an agrarian landscape is still an agrarian landscape, and land is still used primarily for agriculture and human settlement. What might this comparison have to tell us about the social dimensions of rural resource sustainability?

## Cajamarca: Rural Resource Transformation and Weak Sustainability

The acquisition of land is central to the success of an open-cast mine for the obvious reason that such operations require that the mine own surface as well as subsurface rights. Land has long been a point of political contention in the Andes, however, and, indeed, MYSA's land acquisition program triggered the first rumblings of discontent with the mine. Interestingly, the rumblings were less due to asset loss per se than to the conditions under which land was being acquired. Complaints began to emerge about prices paid, undue pressure exercised on families to sell their land, and people selling land that did not belong to them. The first stop for these complainants was the parish church in the area most affected by the early activities of the mine. The priest conveyed the complaints to the diocesan human rights office as well as other human rights organizations in Peru—organizations that presented the complaints to MYSA as well as Newmont in Denver.

While the local church played the initial role in linking communities with proto-social movement organizations, this soon came to an end when the priest was sent to Rome. At this point, however, another actor began to assume this articulating role. This actor was the nascent federation of *rondas campesinas*, peasant vigilante groups whose primary purpose had been to guard against cattle rustling and later to ensure community security more generally during the times of rural violence in Peru (Starn 1999). A number of people active within the federation (FEROCAFENOP) were affected by the expansion and land purchasing activities of the mine, and the federation became a vehicle for contesting these adverse impacts. It began to organize protests in Cajamarca and further developed its links to international environmental groups (in particular in the Bay Area of the United States), which also helped it engage in advocacy in the United States. In the process, its complaints became more visible nationally and internationally; federation activists of this period remember it as one when international support and involvement were far greater than support from urban Cajamarca, where these rural grievances passed as largely invisible and irrelevant.

Significantly, though, notwithstanding the grievances that peasants and the federation had with the mine, the protest during this period was not so much oriented toward getting rid of MYSA as toward demanding a different relationship between mine and communities: a relationship characterized by fair compensation, more civil treatment, and greater participation in the benefits the mine was generating. In other words, the protesters were looking for a relationship in which the natural capital of the mine (i.e., gold) and of the community (i.e., land) would be converted into greater amounts of other forms of capital over which community members would have control and on the basis of which they could build improved livelihoods.

Meanwhile, concerns about the mine were beginning to grow in the city of Cajamarca—not so much because of any sympathy with the plight of rural communities but rather because of the accumulating evidence that the mine was beginning to have adverse effects on the rural sources of urban water. A mercury spill in 2000 further consolidated these concerns while also gaining greater international attention because of a highly successful video (supported financially and distributed by several international activist organizations) that documented the spill. Urban environmentalist groups found themselves somewhat strengthened by these events.

Around the same time as these publicly visible rural resource management failures of the mine, MYSA finally succeeded in channeling some of its social responsibility program financing to FEROCAFENOP,[9] the federation that had long been the main organized face of rural contention against the actions of the mine. This immediately undermined the legitimacy and power of the federation, and as a direct consequence, the anchor of the social movement shifted from organizations based in rural community groups to ones based in urban and professional groups. In the process, movement discourses also began to change. While the rural movement of the 1990s had been openly confrontational, it had been neither an environmentalist movement nor an anti-mining movement. Instead, it had been a movement that was more concerned with obtaining fair treatment and adequate compensation for the forms of dispossession that had occurred in rural communities, and a fuller inclusion of rural people in the mine's activities. In this sense it might be argued that it sought a far clearer and more synergistic articulation of the mining economy and rural livelihoods and a "sensible" (Serageldin and Steer 1994) sustainability—rather than the dispossession and weak sustainability model of mining that dominated in the 1990s. With the shift to an urban-led movement, movement discourses on sustainability changed, with some

---

[9]We remain unable to explain how this occurred. It is a case so full of mutual recriminations that it is difficult to know what actually happened. What is clear is (1) that the mine had already invested (through its hiring practices) in finding ways into social movement organizations; and (2) that at least some of the leaders of the federation were always more of a mind to ensure adequate community compensation for the mine than to ensure closure of the mine. These two postures certainly helped make this financial flow possible.

groups calling for a "strong sustainability" environmentalism demanding far greater protection of natural capital, while others merely called for greater national and state participation in the control of the mine and its profits. In this far weaker view of sustainability, the mine would continue drawing down natural capital, but increased state control of the mine would mean that the income from this drawdown would be invested in society-wide human and social capital formation rather than company-controlled financial capital formation (i.e., profit).

Environmental concerns remained at the forefront of debate in Cajamarca during the early 2000s, as arguments emerged about whether mercury had seeped into the urban water supply and whether the overall quantity of the water supply was being threatened. At the center of this latter discussion was an argument about MYSA's desire to expand operations into an area known as Cerro Quilish. Initial peasant protests against this expansion in the late 1990s had ultimately led to a municipal ordinance that declared Quilish a protected area on the grounds that it was the source of the cities' water supply—a definition of a critical level below which a particular part of the region's natural capital should not be drawn down. The ordinance was contested by MYSA, however, and after drawn out legal proceedings, a constitutional tribunal concluded that the mine's rights to explore in Quilish preceded the powers of the municipality to declare it a protected area. In July 2004, on the basis of this judgment and an environmental impact assessment, the central government gave MYSA the right to recommence exploration on Quilish. Immediately, protests erupted and quickly escalated to the point that the city of Cajamarca and the mine were effectively paralyzed until the central government once more shifted its stance. Confronted with a situation in which its "social license to operate" seemed increasingly in the balance, MYSA withdrew its request for permission to explore in Quilish.[10]

As the process of social mobilization has unfolded in Cajamarca, it has incorporated a growing number of actors. These actors, while united by a general sense that MYSA has dispossessed them of something, differ in the specific nature of their concerns. These include worries over threats to rural water, concerns for the supply of urban water, desires to see the mine subject to national ownership, annoyance at the relative loss of middle- and upper-middle-class status and authority, and annoyance at the seeming impenetrability of the mine and its unwillingness to listen. The positions ranged from anti-mining to pro-mining, to commitments to distinct ways of governing mining. Associated with each of these positions were distinct views on what

---

[10]MYSA has stated that in the future it may once again exercise this right.

constituted adequately sustainable rural resource use. In this sense, while the movement channels grievances it has not channeled any coherent, alternative proposal for a particular form of regional or livelihood sustainability, not least because the actors who make up the movement have quite different positions on whether mining should proceed in the region, and if so, how.

The existence of these internal differences has not meant that the movement has had no effect on the relationship between mining, livelihoods, and rural resources in Cajamarca. Indeed, the mine has changed some of its practices as a result of these mobilizations and protests. Furthermore, it appears to have been more responsive since the movement "urbanized"— viewing such urbanized protest as ultimately more threatening than purely peasant protests. Thus, between 1999 and 2004 MYSA's investments in environmental remediation almost tripled, while those in social responsibility increased almost ninefold (Morel 2005).[11] These programs have been shown to increase the financial and human capital asset bases of household livelihoods, while weakening their social capital (Bury 2004). Protest has also forced some rethinking of expansion plans, as evidenced in the mine's withdrawal from Quilish. The mine has not, though, broken its tendency to combine social responsibility programs with strategies of intimidation against activists and others who appear to stand in its way, nor has it stopped its overall expansion. This expansion, land and water hungry, continues to transform livelihood options in the areas directly affected, primarily through the effects on natural capital assets.[12] Furthermore, it has served as a sort of nucleus around which a range of other mining projects have developed, producing a mining district and in some senses, a concessioned department.

## Piura: Movements and the Search for Strong Sustainability

Though Piura is often thought of as having a dominantly agricultural economy, extractive industry has played an important part in its modern economic history, in the form of both hydrocarbons and fisheries. This experience has been less than encouraging in the eyes of some, who argue that Piura's is a history in which natural resource extraction has been controlled by external actors, and that the bulk of both resources and profits has been taken out of the region to be consumed and invested elsewhere. In

---

[11]However, MYSA profits also grew significantly over the same period.

[12]Meanwhile, and perhaps more important, the money spent by MYSA in local contracting and purchasing increased almost sevenfold over the same period (1999–2004), a direct response to urban criticisms that the mine operated too much as an enclave. This response increases greatly the urban stake in the continued activities of the mine.

comparison with that experience, such commentators view (post–land re-form) agriculture as producing forms of development that involve a larger portion of the population, that allow resource-use decisions to be made much closer to that population, and that generate income and products that are more likely to be reinvested and consumed within Piura.

Some therefore see agricultural land use as more inclusive than the forms of land use produced by extractive industry. However, the performance of the agricultural economy does not suggest (at least under current conditions) that such land use alone can serve as the basis of Piura's development. Thus, be-tween 1970 and 2004, Piura's agricultural sector grew at 1.18 percent per an-num, while departmental GDP grew by 1.51 percent;[13] and while agriculture employs some 37 percent of the economically active population, it accounts for only 11 percent or so of GDP. Agricultural exports do not exceed $100 mil-lion a year. One set of factors constraining agriculture growth in Piura relates to water management. Not only could water be managed far more produc-tively at a farm level, it could be managed far more strategically at a regional level. Currently, only 140,000 hectares are irrigated, while 200,000 could be irrigated with current resources. But, more important, if investment were to go ahead in three long planned irrigation projects, a further 150,000 hectares could be irrigated. This would allow agricultural exports to grow to between $600 and $1,500 million per annum, estimates Humberto Correa.

Water is therefore central to any expansion, productivity growth, and en-hanced export orientation of Piura's agricultural sector. But water is also scarce, and an expansion of the irrigated frontier requires public investment. Furthermore, there are multiple demands for (and potential threats to) this water. One of these is badly managed urban growth and waste management; another is the fact that some 33 percent of Piura's land surface is currently concessioned for potential extractive industry use—primarily for hydrocar-bon, phosphate, and copper extraction. This makes the strategic, planned management of water resources an essential part of Piura's future develop-ment. This would seem to have two implications. First, that land use zoning and planning should guide development, serving as the basis for strategic planning of synergies between different sectors of the department's economy; and second, that it makes no strategic sense for extractive industry projects to be decided upon on a project-by-project basis. Such an approach (which cur-rently exists in Peru) allows no scope for strategic planning of resource (espe-cially land and water) use and development.

---

[13]These and the following data are supplied by Humberto Correa, professor of economics at the Universidad Nacional de Piura and advisor to the regional government.

The need to make land use planning functional and legally binding is an urgent issue because Piura is one of two or three new frontiers for mining expansion in Peru. As rates of growth in other parts of Peru slow down, the mining sector needs to open new frontiers to sustain its rate of growth. The pressure to use land for mineral extraction in a region with no significant history of mining has brought those actors fostering such land use conversion into direct conflict with actors who argue that land should be used to produce agricultural landscapes (on the grounds that they are socially and economically more inclusive) and water (on the grounds that water is needed to dynamize the use of these agricultural landscapes).[14]

In the confrontation between these two agendas for land use, the first conflict—one that has had resonance across Latin America—occurred in the town of Tambogrande, where a Canadian junior company, Manhattan Minerals Corporation, sought to bring a gold mine to approval in the late 1990s and early 2000s. Manhattan's exploration operations led to a period of sustained conflict between local populations and the company between the years 1998 and 2003, until the company finally withdrew (Portugal Menodoza 2005). The conflict was made especially acute because it pitched mining directly against human settlement and export agriculture. The mine would have required resettlement of much of the town and would have done potential damage to a zone of successful, export-oriented, high-value irrigated agriculture that had been made possible, inter alia, by earlier World Bank investments in water management. The case thus lent itself to clear dichotomies: a private investment undermining an earlier successful public investment; a mineral development landscape undermining an export-oriented landscape that appeared both more economically valuable and more inclusive in employment terms; and a mine site displacing people from their houses.

The conflict escalated quickly and became violent. The main leader of the opposition to the mine was murdered, and further escalation was apparently avoided only through the implementation of a local referendum to determine the future of mining in the area. This referendum, organized by the local government and supported by national and international nongovernmental organizations (and in some sense indirectly by the National Peruvian Electoral Office, ONPE), enjoyed a turnout of some 27,015 people, roughly 73 percent of eligible voters.[15] The result was that 93.85 percent voted against mining activity in Tambogrande, and 1.98 percent voted in favor (the balance

---

[14]Although Piura has no significant history of mining, it does have experience with other extractive industries that have left little behind in terms of development.

[15]ONPE did not formally assist in the implementation of the referendum, but did supply electoral registers.

being abstentions, spoiled ballots, etc.). This model—of the public referendum on mining—has since been proposed and used by social movements and activists in Argentina and Guatemala as part of their efforts to halt mining projects.

The fact that contemporary land use in Tambogrande is still dominated by agriculture and the prior urban settlement grid, and not by an expanding mining sector, can only be explained by the emergence of a social movement that culminated in this public consultation. But how did this movement emerge and achieve what it did? At the core of the success of this movement was the fact that it grew from, and succeeded in building bridges between, a number of distinct social groups in the region. In particular, it built bridges between rural and urban groups (as both populations had much to lose), and between small and quite large export-oriented farmers (again, as each perceived it had much to lose). In the process it also brought local government into the movement, an involvement that was critical, as it was this government that had the power to convene the referendum. Just as important, though, this movement built links with actors in Lima and beyond. As the process unfolded, activists in Tambogrande gained the support of a group of Lima-based advisors (organizations and individuals) who operated as a technical committee to Tambogrande's social movement. The committee provided information; helped with the studies that argued that Tambogrande would be more economically productive as an agrarian landscape than as a mining one; helped with legal issues; and, crucially, helped with the referendum. It also played important roles in making links to international actors in North America and Europe, not only for advice but also for financial support—and in particular to fund the referendum. Absent any one of these groups, and Tambogrande's current landscape would likely be an emerging mineral landscape.

This experience in Tambogrande has forever marked conflicts over mining in Piura (as well as in Peru more generally). This is reflected in our second example from Piura. Just as the referendum in Tambogrande was being conducted, exploration was beginning to expand in another part of Piura—in a project known as Rio Blanco, located in the highland provinces of Ayabaca and Huancabamba (Bebbington et al. 2007). To the extent that the conflict in Tambogrande was not only over Manhattan's project, but also over the general expansion of mining in Piura, the rise of exploration in Rio Blanco suggested to activists that while they might have won the battle in Tambogrande, the larger war was still waging—just as it suggested to the mining sector and the government that even if it had lost a battle, the war was still there to be won. To those in Rio Blanco doubtful of mining's benefits, the Tambogrande experience provided an antecedent that helped instill what Alejandro

Diez (2006, 434) calls "skepticism in Huancabamba and open opposition in Ayabaca." Also, the group of organizations and individuals who gave technical support to activists in Tambogrande has now morphed into a group supporting local authorities and activists critical of the way the Rio Blanco project is evolving.

In a very real way, then, the conflicts surrounding the Rio Blanco project constitute a replay of the Tambogrande case—the next battle in the same war. Thus, while part of this conflict constitutes real, specific concerns about the potential effects of a mining project in its area of influence, another part of the conflict constitutes an argument over (1) whether there will be and should be mining in Piura; (2) the conditions under which decisions about such mineral development should be made; and (3) who should participate in those decisions. In this larger conflict, the mining sector (both the industry and the Ministry of Energy and Mines) lines up on one side in favor of mineral expansion in the north of Peru. On the other side is an activist sector combining much the same cast of actors as were present in Tambogrande's mobilizations: mayors, community leaders, NGOs, parts of the Roman Catholic church, and other rural and urban organizations coupled with international organizations providing moral, political, financial, and some technical support.

This conflict continues to the present, although it has been deeply marked by a referendum that was held on September 16, 2007, in which 93 percent of those who voted said they did not want mining in the area.[16] The referendum—modeled again on the Tambogrande experience—has served to deepen the conflict around the mine and turn it far more explicitly into a national issue. The central government, wholeheartedly committed to mining expansion in Peru, declared (from the offices of the president and the prime minister) that the referendum was illegal and responded to it with a barrage of criticism, both of individual actors as well as the process as a whole. Beyond the hubris of government denominating local Jesuits as "red priests" and President Alan Garcia's declarations on October 28, 2007, that environmentalists concerned about mining were no more than repackaged communists from a century ago, more significant is the fact that the referendum elicited a range of legal and political responses, making it evident that the central government will allow no mineral project to suffer the same fate as Tambogrande, blocked by local protest. Shortly after the referendum the president's office sponsored legislation declaring 20 mining projects (including Rio Blanco) to be in the "national interest" in an effort

---

[16]For more information on the referendum, see the addendum by Burneo and Bebbington to Bebbington (2008).

to ease their approval and continued expansion, and more generally Rio Blanco and its referendum became a topic of heated debate in the national media and in Congress. While this debate has many undercurrents, one of the themes at its core has been an argument over the type of development that Peru ought to pursue, how far local concerns should influence decisions about these development trajectories, and whether in fact rural people really have the capacity to make an informed choice on such issues. Whatever the prejudices about this—be they from Lima or the pages of *The Economist*—local activists and peasant organizations have stood their ground, and at the time of this writing, the prime minister's office is chairing a dialogue process with activists and other regional players over what to do. That having been said, however, the rest of the government's actions suggest that while it speaks of dialogue, it will not accept a future in which the use of land in the Rio Blanco area revolves around the sustenance of water sources and agrarian cultural landscapes rather than around mineral extraction.

## The Social Dimensions of Rural Resource Sustainability

Conflicts around extractive industries bring to the surface a series of issues relevant to a reflection on the social dimensions of rural resource sustainability and the future roles of land in society. One theme—perhaps not so novel—is that to analyze what happens to a given resource it is important to understand it in relation to the other resources on which both regional economies and livelihoods are built. Actors make decisions on how to use a resource in terms of other resources and on how the use of that resource may affect the other resources at their disposal. Actors—whether farmers, mining company managers, ministers of energy and mining, or NGOs—always view resources in terms of their substitutability for other resources. As they do so, though, they operate with (sometimes spoken, sometimes unspoken) notions of how much substitution is acceptable. In that sense, they operate with notions of the sustainability of resource (asset) portfolios, not the sustainability of individual resources.

A second theme is that resources can be politically contentious. This is particularly so for resources that have acquired special significance for one or another actor. One clear domain in which their control is a contentious issue is that of livelihoods, and when the resource bases of livelihoods are threatened, it is likely (though not automatic) that social and political responses will ensue—responses that can often involve social mobilization and the emergence of social movements. This triggers a broader process of conflict whose final outcomes have great affect on subsequent resource use.

A third theme is that for significant parts of the world, the use of resources in rural areas is influenced not only by local social movements and the actors who are the proximate source of the discontent that triggers these movements. It is also affected by networks among people and organizations that are anything but rural, and that bring in actors from all around the globe. The cases described here demonstrate this for mining. But if our interest was in regions affected by protected areas, things would look similar (Chapin 2004; Khare and Bray 2004). Likewise, if we were interested in regions caught up in supermarket commodity chains (Reardon and Berdegué 2002), textile chains, or other forms of export agriculture, we would find networks of consumer activists, supermarket purchasers, environmentalists, investors, NGOs, and more, all active and all having something to say about how land should be used, and by implication how livelihoods should be structured, in particular places.

It is no longer sufficient to remark on such phenomena and merely note that they reflect the ways localities are now transnationalized and globalized. This is not simply because local processes and local histories still matter a great deal in determining patterns of resource management (as Piura and Cajamarca each show). It is also because we need to say much more about *how* and *in what ways* this transnationalization affects resources and livelihoods. Of the many themes that need to be deepened in this regard, one is that these different networks do not merely help convert rural *things* into rural *resources* with national and international meaning. They are also domains in which the very meanings that give purpose to these resources are defined and argued over.

For the purposes of this chapter I have suggested that these networks are domains in which different ideas about sustainability and about the role of land are debated and contested. I have also suggested that, ultimately, the ideas of sustainability and land that become dominant help fix—in a political and policy sense—a *common sense* about acceptable trade-offs between different forms of capital in any process of development. This common sense then makes some forms of rural resource use and governance more possible and others less possible. Likewise, they are spheres in which ideas of livelihood are debated and ultimately fixed.

Though not discussed above, among actors within mining development networks in the Andes there is a recurrent effort to fix the ideas that mining is the only livelihood option for areas over 3,500 meters above sea level, and that any other livelihood option is unviable and commits rural populations to a continued existence that is primitive and ultimately miserable. For lower-altitude (typically forested) zones, actors in the same networks aim to make the case that farming does more environmental damage than mining does. For their part, activist networks aim to make other ideas about mining and resource use common sense. The cases above suggest that in Cajamarca they have not succeeded in this regard, whereas in Piura they have (so far), largely because of the greater similarity of vision among activists involved in these networks.

These are therefore *struggles over ideas* in which participants have as their goal the fixing of a certain notion of sustainability and of land use over and above another one. At this point, mining networks have more or less defined dominant commonsense ideas about appropriate trade-offs, livelihoods, and rural resource management in Cajamarca; while activist networks have done this in Tambogrande. To go back to the second section, it has been through these networks that the terms of exchange among capitals and the "meanings" of livelihood, land, and development have been defined for these two spaces. These struggles over ideas and meaning are not merely of abstract academic interest—a topic to help post-structuralists and ethnographers while away their idle hours. Their outcomes have enormous impacts in the landscape and in the use of rural resources.

This notion of struggle also places another theme at the center of any reflection over the social dimensions of rural resource sustainability. This is that any reflection on social dimensions must also be a reflection on power and conflict, and that the outcome of power relations goes a long way in determining how resources are used. Understanding the workings of this power is hardly straightforward, and requires getting inside these different organizations and networks. In the examples above, getting inside the networks that touch ground in Cajamarca and Piura helped explain why activist networks have had so much more power to influence debates and resource use there than they have in Cajamarca. Furthermore, it suggested that power differences within networks are as important as the differences between mining and activist networks in determining whose ideas about sustainability and whose resource management practices ultimately influence what happens to rural resources.

These cases also help us think about land. In both Cajamarca and Piura it is evident that land is much more than simply land, and that different actors and networks give land a range of distinct meanings. Thus, it is not simply that the meaning of land has changed over time (see chapter 10); it is also that these different meanings coexist and can come into conflict with each other at a point in time. The same piece of land can be expendable or sacred, depending on who is viewing it—something to protect or something to dig up in order to access what lies below. In the cases discussed here, some actors view land as something to be mined in order to produce mineral wealth—as a productive asset tout court. Some view land as something to be farmed, also as a productive asset, but as one that allows more culturally resonant and socially inclusive forms of production. Others argue that land (or at least certain areas of land) ought to be viewed (and valued) primarily in terms of the ecosystem services it provides (in these cases, primarily water provision). And still others, though fewer and more implicitly perhaps, see land also as territory, a space that *of necessity* brings with it certain cultural and governance implications. Thus, part of what is going on in the struggles between (and within) the networks discussed here is an effort to fix the meaning of land — of what land is, what it is for, and which sets of values and functions should ultimately determine its use. Which meanings become dominant will have important material effects, putting into motion particular bodies of legislation, and thus particular sets of possible ways in which this land can be governed, owned, and used.

## CONCLUSIONS

Perhaps the most important *social* dimension of sustainability is that sustainability is itself *socially defined.* Such a statement can sound either banal or hopelessly constructivist, depending on one's standpoint. Yet the statement has important implications for our discussion here, for it focuses attention on the processes through which this social definition of sustainability is arrived at. Many of these processes happen far away from the point at which rural resources are used. They happen in boardrooms, in policy-making processes (on and off camera), in the classroom, and in the press. They happen both in the public sphere and in distinct, more private spheres — spheres in which views are formed about precisely what is to be sustained, about the nature of the trade-offs to be made among different forms of capital, and about the distribution of the costs and benefits associated with these trade-offs.

Different societies and social groups form different views about what is to be sustained and what is to be traded off. Thus it is that Costa Rica, as a country, has decided not to allow mineral development, but instead to use rural resources as part of a tourist and bioscience-led road to rural development, while Peru (as a government, at least) has decided to base a large part of its macroeconomic strategy on the extraction of minerals and hydrocarbons, even when this occurs in areas of hydrological sensitivity, high biodiversity, and even noncontact indigenous groups. One message of this chapter is that it is vital to understand how and why different societies form these different views of what to sustain.

The Peru–Costa Rica comparison also occurs within countries. We have noted the cases of Tambogrande and Rio Blanco, experiences in which populations in particular territories appear to have formed one view on what they feel development should sustain, while national institutions (in the spheres of state, market, *and* society) tend toward other, quite distinct views. Part of the argument between these different actors—local populations on one hand, national elites on the other—is about the *scale* at which sustainability criteria should be decided. Should territorially based rural resource use be determined by the populations living in those territories, or should it be a function of what other social processes have come to define as national priorities for sustainable development?

These, of course, are simultaneous arguments over *who* should form the views on sustainability that ultimately guide policy and national development processes. Again, as we have seen, these are contentious and difficult discussions. Within a nation there are real issues—rarely voiced—over who is more of a citizen, and who less; who has more say, and who less. These discussions are not only shot through with the classic argument over the relative roles of technocratic and popular knowledge—indeed, that is the easier discussion, because it is one whose name can be spoken. The harder themes are those that are not spoken—about which ethnic groups, social classes, genders, and racial groups will ultimately have more or less say in these discussions; and about the extent to which, and reasons why, international actors of varying hues have a voice in national discussions on sustainability.

While observations such as these typically open up a reflection on participation, discussions of participation rarely do justice to the issues at stake. The examples discussed in the chapter suggest that if there were to be real conversations on what to sustain in Andean societies (at least), far larger questions would have to be opened up at the same time. These questions would address, inter alia: the macroeconomic models and overall models of sustainability that Andean societies want to move toward; the relationships between state, race, ethnicity, and space; the relationships between resources, land, and territory; and the relationships between citizenship and livelihood and the rights that different social groups are able to exercise in determining their livelihoods.

This makes land a terribly political issue, and, of course, it is. Indeed, it was suggested by one commentator on this chapter that the cases discussed were really about political struggles and had nothing to do with sustainability. But surely this is to have an excessively technical view of what constitutes sustainable development. The meaning of sustainable development, the strategies for achieving it, and the place of land in this process are themes of deep disagreement in society (back to the Peruvian election). The only reason that these deep disagreements do not spill over into visible conflicts more often (and so make us aware, every day, that sustainability and land are inherently political) is because certain actors are far more powerful than others, and so are able to fix taken-for-granted meanings, contain public debate, and contain the deeper frustrations of those with less power to determine dominant ideas about land and development. The examples discussed here—and the broader reflection on social movements—suggest the conditions under which, at certain moments, these asymmetries of power might begin to change, at least somewhat, and under which taken-for-granted ideas might begin to be challenged and public debate made more vigorous. International linkages and solidarities are an important element of such conditions, as is the presence of local activists able to weave powerful alliances against the odds.

Will debates on land in 2015 be more open, more vigorous, more participatory, and more indicative of the multiple, subaltern visions of land that coexist with the hegemonic ones that dominate so much policy debate? While some of us can only hope so, others would probably prefer not, hoping that such competing visions can be simply "compensated" out of existence.[17] If subaltern visions do become more vocal and powerful, they will bring challenges to land use planning, to theories of land, and to land information systems. They will challenge planning to open its doors yet more widely to still disenfranchised publics—and there are many more of these across the world than an optimistic reading of planning processes in North America might have us believe. They will also challenge theories of land to deal with the multiple, at times noncommensurate meanings and values that land can have for different actors. These theories also ought to destabilize ideas about compensation, for they suggest that compensation mediates not between what different groups are willing to pay, but between what they believe. And they will challenge land information systems to register not just the geography of formally recognized rights in land, but also the geographies of the many overlapping functions of land and the many still unrecognized rights in land. Indeed, it is not just that sustainability is socially defined; it is that land policy studies are also socially defined. Studies too often convey to the balance of power in society what it is that these powers need and want to know. If that balance of power were to change, the study of land would also change.

## REFERENCES

Appadurai, A. 2004. The capacity to aspire: Culture and the terms of recognition. In *Culture and public action: A cross-disciplinary dialogue on development policy.* V. Rao and M. Walton, eds., 59–84. Stanford, CA: Stanford University Press.

---

[17]This is the optimistic view. The other option for those resisting a democratization of debates on land would be simply to repress dissent.

Bebbington, A. 1996. Organizations and intensifications: Small farmer federations, rural livelihoods and agricultural technology in the Andes and Amazonia. *World Development* 24(7):1161–1178.

———. 1997. Social capital and rural intensification: Local organizations and islands of sustainability in the rural Andes. *Geographical Journal* 163(2):189–197.

———. 1999. Capitals and capabilities: A framework for analysing peasant viability, rural livelihoods and poverty. *World Development* 27(12):2021–2044.

———. 2004. Livelihood transitions, place transformations: Grounding globalization and modernity. In *Latin America transformed: Globalization and modernity*, 2nd ed. R. Gwynne and C. Kay, eds., 173–192. London: Arnold.

———. 2008. La sostenibilidad social de los recursos rurales: Apreciaciones a partir de los conflictos mineros en Latinoamérica. *Debate Agrario* 42:31–78

Bebbington, A., M. Connarty, W. Coxshall, H. O'Shaugnessy, and M. Williams. 2007. *Mining and development in Peru with special reference to the Rio Blanco project*. London: Peru Support Group.

Bebbington, A., S. Guggenheim, E. Olson, and M. Woolcock. 2004. Exploring social capital debates at the World Bank. *Journal of Development Studies* 40(5):33–64.

Bridge, G. 2004. Mapping the bonanza: Geographies of mining investment in an era of neoliberal reform. *Professional Geographer* 56(3):406–421.

Bromley, R. 1994. Informality, de Soto style: From concept to policy. In *Contrapunto: The informal sector debate in Latin America*. C. A. Rakowski, ed., 131–152. Albany, NY: SUNY Press.

Bromley, R., and C. Gerry, eds. 1979. *Casual work and poverty in third world cities*. New York: Wiley.

Bury, J. 2004. Livelihoods in transition: Transnational gold mining operations and local change in Cajamarca, Peru. *Geographic Journal* 170(1):78–91.

———. 2005. Mining mountains: Neoliberalism, land tenure, livelihoods and the new Peruvian mining industry in Cajamarca. *Environment and Planning A* 37(2):221–239.

Carney, D., ed. 1998. *Sustainable rural livelihooods: What contribution can we make?* London: Department for International Development.

Chambers, R. 1987. Sustainable livelihoods, environment and development: Putting poor rural people first. Discussion Paper 240. Brighton, U.K.: Institute of Development Studies.

Chambers, R., and G. Conway. 1992. Sustainable rural livelihoods: Practical concepts for the 21st century. Discussion Paper 296. Brighton, U.K.: Institute of Development Studies.

Chapin, M. 2004. A challenge to conservationists. *World Watch Magazine* (November/December):17–31.

Daly, H., and K. Townsend. 1993. *Valuing the earth: Economics, ecology, ethics*. Cambridge, MA: MIT Press.

de Janvry, A. 1981. *The agrarian question and reformism in Latin America*. Baltimore: Johns Hopkins University Press.

de Soto, H. 1989. *The other path: The invisible revolution in the third world.* New York: Harper and Row. (Orig. pub. in Peru in Spanish, 1986.)

Diez, A. 2006. Ronderos y alcaldes en el conflicto minero de Rio Blanco en Piura, Perú. In *Movimientos sociales y desarrollo territorial rural en América Latina.* J. Bengoa, ed., 432–443. Santiago, Chile: Editorial Catalonia.

Escobál, J. 2001. The determinants of nonfarm income diversification in rural Peru. *World Development* 29(3):497–508.

Escobar, A. 1995. *Encountering development: The making and unmaking of the third world.* Princeton, NJ: Princeton University Press.

Fox, J., and D. Brown, eds. 1998. *The struggle for accountability: The World Bank, NGOs and grassroots movements.* Cambridge, MA: MIT Press.

Harvey, D. 2003. *The new imperialism.* Oxford: Oxford University Press.

Hickey, S., and S. Bracking. 2005. Exploring the politics of chronic poverty: From representation to a politics of justice? *World Development* 33(6):851–865.

Keck, M., and K. Sikkink. 1998. *Activists beyond borders: Advocacy networks in international politics.* Ithaca, NY: Cornell University Press.

Khare, A., and D. Bray. 2004. Study of critical new forest conservation issues in the global south. Final report submitted to the Ford Foundation (June).

López, R. 1995. *Determinants of rural poverty: A quantitative analysis for Chile.* Washington, DC: World Bank, Technical Department, Rural Poverty and Natural Resources, Latin America.

Morel, R. 2005. *Quién es responsable de la responsabilidad social?* Mimeo. Cajamarca, Peru: Minera Yanacocha (September).

Moser, C. 1998. The asset vulnerability framework: Reassessing urban poverty reduction strategies. *World Development* 26(1):1–19.

Ormachea Choque, I. 2005. *Report to the Defensoría del Pueblo, Perú.* Lima: Defensoría del Pueblo.

Perreault, T. 2006. From the guerra del agua to the guerra del gas: Resource governance, neoliberalism and popular protest in Bolivia. *Antipode* 38(1):150–172.

Portugal Menodoza, C. 2005. *Gobernanza en el acceso de la actividad minera a los recursos naturales locales: El caso Tambogrande.* Santiago, Chile: Grupo Chorlavi.

Putnam, R. 1993. *Making democracy work: Civic traditions in modern Italy.* Princeton, NJ: Princeton University Press.

Reardon, T., and J. Berdegué, eds. 2002. Supermarkets and agrifood systems: Latin American challenges. *Development Policy Review* 20(4).

Reardon, T., J. Berdegué, and G. Escobar. 2001. Rural nonfarm employment and incomes in Latin America: Overview and policy implications. *World Development* 29(3):395–410.

Schejtman, A., and J. Berdegué. 2003. *Desarrollo territorial rural.* Washington, DC: Banco Interamericano de Desarrollo y Fondo Internacional de Desarrollo Agrícola.

Scoones, I. 1998. Sustainable rural livelihoods: A framework for analysis. Working Paper 72. Brighton, U.K.: Institute of Development Studies.

Serageldin, I. 1996. *Sustainability and the wealth of nations: First steps in an ongoing journey.* Washington, DC: World Bank.

Serageldin, I., and A. Steer, eds. 1994. Making development sustainable: From concepts to action. Environmentally Sustainable Development Occasional Paper Series No. 2. Washington, DC: World Bank.

Smith, G. 1989. *Livelihood and resistance.* Berkeley: University of California Press.

Starn, O. 1999. *Nightwatch: The politics of protest in the Andes.* Durham, NC: Duke University Press.

Tendler, J. 1997. *Good government in the tropics.* Baltimore: Johns Hopkins University Press.

Tsing, A. 2004. *Friction: An ethnography of global connections.* Princeton, NJ: Princeton University Press.

Zoomers, A. 1999. *Linking livelihood strategies to development: Experiences from the Bolivian Andes.* Amsterdam: Royal Tropical Institute/Center for Latin American Research and Documentation.

# 12

# Future Challenges of Sustainable Land Use in Taiwan

## Kuo-Ching Lin

W hen we talk about issues related to sustainable environments, there are two important questions to consider: (1) What is a sustainable environment? and (2) What is the purpose of having a sustainable environment? The purpose of achieving a sustainable environment is not just achieving it per se.

I propose that the purpose of having a sustainable environment is the enhancement of human welfare. We could talk about a sustainable environment that includes everything in the biosphere and also the natural environment, but if we leave out the central role of human beings, sustainability issues will lose their solid grounding. Without the value judgments of human beings, Mother Nature plays by her own set of rules. The whole system will evolve by its own natural laws and will stay on its own developmental course.

The survival of the fittest and adaptive processes will self-select which species will survive and which ones will disappear. In this process, defining a sustainable environment is difficult. If we believe that this natural process is not sustainable because some species will disappear, then this again is based on the value judgments of human beings. And when humans take certain measures to rectify this natural process, this also reflects our value judgments. In a general sense, the purpose of our intervention in the natural

This chapter was presented as a keynote address at a conference cosponsored by the Lincoln Institute of Land Policy and the International Center for Land Policy Studies and Training in Taiwan in October 2006.

process to save some species from extinction is, in fact, to increase the welfare of human beings.

From this perspective, I would argue that a sustainable environment is a necessary condition for sustainable development. Without developmental concerns, sustainability issues will lose their importance. The reason we are concerned about creating a sustainable environment, therefore, is because of our concern for the sustainable development of human welfare.

What is sustainable development? The answer to this depends on what is included in the measurement of development (i.e., what elements are included in the developmental concerns and how the developmental progress is measured) and what the objective of development is. In abstract terms, the objective can be expressed as maintenance of the capacity to enhance social welfare over the long term. We then have to examine what is included in the social welfare. Does biodiversity carry its own value, or is the value generated through human beings' judgments? I believe it is the latter.

## LAND USE IN TAIWAN

The purpose of land use policy in Taiwan is to promote the sustainable development of social welfare. To achieve that goal, the Taiwanese government must help nurture the environment. Every nation defines its institutional framework, such as a set of institutions and rules under which each player tries to maximize its own welfare. In that institutional framework, two elements are important: One is the assignment and enforcement of property rights, and the other is the market mechanism. Different nations and different societies have their own unique institutional frameworks and market systems, which to some extent reflect the content of a sustainable environment. So the environment we are going to talk about later is the institutional environment, which will affect the natural environment. We will treat our natural environment as a given and as a constraint, under which the people of Taiwan try to maximize their social welfare and create an environment conducive to sustainable development.

First, some basic facts about Taiwan will lay the groundwork for understanding the later discussion. Taiwan is a small island of 36,000 square kilometers, approximately two-thirds of which are mountainous. The highest altitude is close to 4,000 meters. Since the distance between the mountains and the coast is short, rainfall flows into the ocean quite rapidly. The total population is about 23 million, and the total area of cultivated land is about 830,000 hectares. Among countries with populations of more than 1 million, Taiwan has the third-highest population density in the world, after Bangladesh and Singapore.

Agricultural land prices in Taiwan are among the highest in the world. The average price per hectare is more than 10 million New Taiwanese (NT) dollars, about US$300,000. The average farm size is about one hectare per farm; it has been around that level for the past 40 years. The average rental rate per hectare is only about NT$40,000. The production rate of return on farmland is therefore very low. The gross revenue of rice farming per hectare is about NT$100,000, with net profit only around NT$20,000. Only about 18 percent of farmers farm full time.

The per capita GDP in Taiwan was around US$15,000 in 2005. The percent of agricultural GDP to total GDP was 1.8 percent. Farmers generate their income mostly from nonfarming activities. Less than 20 percent of a farmer's income is generated from farming activities; the ratio of farm income to nonfarm income is less than 80 percent. Since trade liberalization started in 1996, the agricultural sector has been adversely affected, and farmers' income has stagnated. Taiwan became a member of the World Trade Organization (WTO) on January 1, 2002.

Taiwan held its first democratic presidential elections in 1996 and is in the process of becoming a more experienced democratic society. Taiwan is not a member of the United Nations, although the country has been applying to become a member for 12 years. Taiwan is situated near China, which proclaims that Taiwan is part of China and opposes Taiwan's UN membership application. Currently, more than 800 Chinese missiles are directed at Taiwan across the Taiwan Strait. Thus, Taiwan has been spending a large amount of its resources on national defense. Security concerns play an important role in the policy formation process. After all, without survival, talking about sustainability is a luxury.

In terms of the social environment, Taiwan is in the process of consolidating its national identity. Taiwan is unique in many ways, and the problems it faces in achieving and maintaining a sustainable environment are thus different from those of many other countries. I would also argue that the definition of a sustainable environment carries different meanings for different societies. Even within Taiwan, the concept of a sustainable environment for the people living in the mountains is quite different from that for those living in the plains.

The high agricultural land prices in Taiwan are not conducive to agricultural development. The major reason behind the high prices is that nonagricultural land prices are also very high, so the expected gains from land conversion are high. What is the optimal mechanism for agricultural land conversion? How do we decide how much land should be converted and at what location? Should the government make conversions more difficult?

In order to improve the quality of life and enhance the general welfare of the whole society, farmland cannot be locked in the agricultural sector. There will always be competition for the use of farmland. So the question is how to set up a system to harmonize the competition and create an efficient and fair use of farmland. Do we have a serious conflict in land use in Taiwan? How do we resolve that conflict?

Agricultural policy makers in Taiwan have difficult decisions to make. On one hand, Taiwan's farm income is well below nonfarm income. Farmers are asking for more direct income support and are demanding continuous government protection from foreign competition. On the other hand, Taiwan is under international pressure to liberalize its agricultural trade. Thus, the government has to find solutions to the adverse impacts of agricultural trade liberalization on the farming sector while maintaining farmers' incomes at satisfactory levels.

To modernize the farming sector and maintain farmers' incomes at a politically acceptable level, some kind of government assistance is unavoidable. However, expanding subsidies and increasing government spending has historically failed to raise farmers' incomes to a satisfactory level. A better solution has to be formulated that not only effectively improves the competitiveness of the farming sector but also maintains a viable rural community.

In a context of very small land size and high population density, continuous rapid economic growth is one of the main factors that have nurtured the farmland price increases. With the stagnation of farmland rentals and high expectations for capital gains, incentives for holding land for productive purposes have decreased over time, while the incentives to hold on to land as an important means of preserving existing wealth, as well as for speculation, have increased immensely. Due to an efficient transport network and job opportunities in the rural areas, farmland owners who decide to stay in rural areas can find nonfarming employment nearby and remain as part-time farmers. The number of part-time farmers has thus increased rapidly, while full-time farmers are finding it more difficult to enlarge their farms.

Another factor adversely affecting farming efficiency is that the average farm size is small, and farms are also divided into many plots scattered in different places. Even where farmers have decided to enlarge their operation, the amount of rent they can afford to pay tends to be low due to high transaction costs and low economies of scale. Moreover, with the combination of efficient rice marketing and price-support systems, standardized and highly mechanized rice farming operations, and only seasonal labor requirements, part-time farmers have found rice growing to be a flexible, profitable, and relatively low-risk operation. They can manage full-time nonfarming jobs while remaining in the rice growing business. The continuous improvements in farmers' health conditions and farming mechanization have enabled old farmers to prolong their farming careers. Consequently, the numbers of farmers and farms are decreasing very slowly.

There are also continuous calls from the nonfarming sector to allow more agricultural land to be converted into nonfarming uses. Although the expected nonagricultural rent of some farmland is already much higher than its current agricultural rent, to safeguard self-sufficiency of important food items government policy restricts conversion of the land. This type of zoning restriction creates resentment among landowners, especially when the expected gains from conversion are enormous. Unless the government's decision-making process to allow some land to be legally converted is transparent and coherent, and no huge amount of windfall gains or losses is involved in conversion decisions, resentment will continue.

The expected windfall gains involved in rezoning will certainly invite rent seeking and speculative activities. This issue will continue to be of serious concern to the general public and to land use policy makers. This problem is especially acute in suburban areas where agricultural zoning is in serious conflict with the welfare of residents and with urban development. Some would argue that unreasonable agricultural zoning in suburban areas of big cities is the main culprit in causing high land and housing prices, thereby providing fertile ground for speculative and rent seeking activities, attracting illegal conversions, and stifling industrial development by making industrial sites much more expensive.

Hence, the formulation of agricultural land use policy must go beyond the scope of agriculture and take nonagricultural interests into account. The main issue is how to formulate a policy that harmonizes with the needs of national economic development and promotes the efficient use of national land resources.

## AGRICULTURAL ZONING

Those lands classified as farmland under regional planning acts and nonurban land use control regulations are not allowed to be converted to nonagricultural uses. The conversion is legal only when, after due process, farmland is reclassified into nonagricultural uses.

Under the Regional Planning Act enacted in 1974, the government started classifying nonurban land and putting it under land use control. Nonurban land is classified into nine different zones: special agricultural, general agricultural, rural developed, industrial, forestry, slope land preservation, scenery, national park, and land specifically designated for particular purposes. In each zone nonurban land is further classified into 16 different kinds of uses; by law land users have to follow the specified use restrictions under which the land is classified. The nonurban land zoning was implemented first in Pin Tong County in 1975, and the last county implemented it in 1986.

The main reason for agricultural zoning is to preserve farmland for food security. Almost all prime farmland, especially paddy fields, without consideration of its location advantage, was included in the special agricultural zone and legally put under tight control. Once land was classified into the special agricultural zone, obtaining permission to rezone and legally convert its use became almost impossible for private landowners. Rezoning is possible, however, through a comprehensive city planning review. This comprehensive review has become a serious loophole that allows insiders to achieve huge windfall gains and outsiders to engage in speculative activities.

Since the original zoning was carried out on short notice, no comprehensive planning was conducted beforehand. The most convenient and least controversial way to conduct zoning without planning is to zone according to existing land uses. That method has created serious land use control problems in the past. The problems included intense pressure to make illegal conversions, which led to large areas of illegal conversions, inefficient land use, and high land prices.

In response to those problems, the government has conducted a review and allowed a partial zoning adjustment. In light of the many remaining problems, however, including changes in the social and natural environments, a comprehensive review of the existing zoning system is still needed before an overall solution can be found. The future review and readjustment of agricultural zoning should consider the location of farmland and establish equitable treatment of landowners; it should also encourage the involvement of citizens in bringing together the many different interests.

## AGRICULTURAL LAND TAXATION

To reduce the farmer's tax burden, increase the farmer's income, and increase farm size, farmland is exempted from the land property tax, the land transaction levy, and the value increment tax. In the past few decades, however, speculative activities on farmland have been gaining momentum and generating widespread concern. The call for repealing the tax exemption status of farmland is slowly gaining supporters in the government. Since so many vested interests are beneficiaries of the tax-exempt policy, however, it will be difficult to reform.

## SET-ASIDE LAND

Taiwan's high population density and high agricultural land prices make land-based agriculture less competitive, and since entering the WTO, Taiwan's agriculture has encountered more competition. Under WTO rules, Taiwan has started to import rice. To keep the domestic rice market stable and maintain a satisfactory income for rice farmers, current government policy is to reduce domestic rice production and shift some agricultural land to uses such as rural tourism, forestation, set-aside agricultural land, and other nonagricultural uses.

Although the agricultural land is precious, as evidenced by the high prices, the set-aside land area has ironically increased over time to an alarming level. The total set-aside land area in 2004 was 239,724 hectares, which marks the first time that the amount of set-aside land was larger than the total area of harvested rice, the most important crop in Taiwan. The harvested area of rice has been decreasing over time, while the set-aside area of paddy fields has been steadily increasing.

How to rectify this problem and to use agricultural land more efficiently has been a great challenge to policy makers. The new policies implemented in the past few years to use agricultural land more efficiently include afforestation of the plains area and installation of a high-tech agricultural scientific park. Currently, the government is formulating programs for using the set-aside land to plant new crops such as sunflowers and sweet potatoes that can be processed to produce diesel and ethanol for energy uses.

## AFFORESTATION IN THE PLAINS AREA

The policy of afforestation in the plains area was certified by the Executive Yuan on 31 August 2001 and enacted on 1 January 2002. The implementation of that policy will increase forest in the plains area and improve the ecological environment, as well as the greenery and scenic areas. If the greenery in the plains area can be increased, it will create a better environment for promoting agricultural tourism. A better rural environment will also improve the quality of life for farmers.

Providing guidance and assistance to farmers to reduce agricultural production and promote afforestation is a policy that conforms to the WTO green policy. It is generally believed that if such a policy can be properly implemented in Taiwan, it will effectively increase the demand for agricultural lands, reduce the set-aside and vacant land areas, and make agricultural land use more efficient. It could thereby relieve the pressure of oversupply of agricultural products and alleviate the marketing disequilibrium problem.

The concept of afforestation in the plains area is certainly not new or unique to Taiwan. It is widely accepted in Europe. In Germany, for example, forest used to occupy significant portions of territory, and in the 1990s the most noticeable trend in forest development was afforestation of agricultural land.

According to the plan for afforestation of Taiwan's plains area, the period of implementation was from 1 January 2002 to 31 December 2007. In principle, areas with low agricultural productivity—such as those areas that lack irrigation systems, lowland along the coast, set-aside sugarcane fields, polluted agricultural land, and agricultural land on both sides of railways—would have priority for being included in the program.

To decrease the adverse effects of fragmentation in the surrounding agricultural environment and to maximize the positive externality from economies of scale, there was a minimum size requirement for farmers to be eligible for the afforestation subsidy. To qualify for the plan, the area of afforestation had to be at least two hectares in a contiguous piece or at least five hectares within the same land district.

To promote the program, the government also decided to increase the reward amounts. Based on the experience of extending the afforestation policy in the sloping land area, and taking into consideration the opportunity costs and the production potential of agricultural land, as well as the willingness of farmers to participate in the program, the government decided to pay NT$530,000 per hectare for privately owned land to cover the cost of planting trees and managing the forest for the 20-year period.

The government also pays NT$54,000 per hectare per year of direct payment for 20 years to cover the opportunity costs of agricultural land. The current annual rental rate of agricultural land is about NT$40,000 per hectare. If the farmer decides to set aside his agricultural land, the current basic set-aside payment per hectare is NT$27,000. If there are two crops per year, the government includes that in its criteria to determine the amount of direct payment, which is then twice the basic set-aside payment per hectare. In total, the farmer will receive NT$1,610,000 for privately owned agricultural land for a 20-year period.

## NEW STRATEGY FOR SUSTAINABLE DEVELOPMENT

On 1 July 2004, tropical storm Mindulle hit Taiwan, bringing torrential rains that caused mudslides and heavy losses. The Taiwanese government subsequently tried to formulate new strategies to tackle these problems. The

National Land Restoration Act was approved by the Executive Yuan on 25 May 2005, and as of this writing it awaits approval by the Legislative Yuan. This act limits or outlaws development in mountainous, coastal, and flood-prone areas. It also forbids cultivating or otherwise developing steep slopes and fragile terrain or areas above a designated altitude. The government will offer incentives to residents living in such areas to encourage them to relocate and sell their land to the government.

Three farms operated by the Veterans Affairs Commission were asked to set an example of land conservation and ecological protection. As of 2007, Chingching, Wuling, and Fushoushan farms will cease all farming activities over the three-year period to allow the natural afforestation of the land. The government will not renew any leases on forestland currently used to grow fruit, vegetables, or flowers. The tenant farmers of those products have invested large sums of money in their businesses, and the decision not to renew their leases put hundreds of people's livelihoods in jeopardy. To alleviate that problem, the government promised to ensure that implementation of the policy included job placement services and financial compensation for the displaced farmers. Based on past experience, it is widely believed that that would be a very difficult task to accomplish.

## THE ZONING ADJUSTMENT SCHEME

In order to improve the current zoning system, it is recommended that the agricultural zone be further divided into a development zone and a long-term agricultural zone. Those farmlands that have high potential for nonagricultural uses and are expected to be converted to nonagricultural uses in the near future should be considered for inclusion in the development zone. The farmlands within that zone would no longer be allowed to enjoy the favorable treatments extended to the farm sector. They also would no longer be tax exempt; the landowners would have to pay land property taxes and land value increment taxes when the land is sold.

## AGRICULTURAL LAND USE PLANNING

The guiding principle of agricultural land use planning should be reexamined, and the main emphasis on the physical productivity of farmland should be adjusted. Planning also has to take location factors into account. Moreover, it cannot be used to substitute for the market mechanism. The main purpose of planning should be to provide incentives for profitable agricultural production, to stimulate farmers' entrepreneurial spirit, to suf-ficiently use regional economies of scale in agricultural production, and to use the market mechanism efficiently.

Taiwan has made efforts to understand its land use problems in the past and has made some policy recommendations, but the problems have been stubborn and persistent. I doubt there are any easy answers to our problems; at least, the answers are not derived solely from academic exercises. Land and sustainable environment issues are so complicated that any institutional re-form must involve property rights reassignment and wealth reallocation, and these are certainly political issues. In the process of reforming, some people will be significantly affected—for some it is a matter of survival; for others, of lifestyle adjustment. Given such an unfavorable environment, in retrospect, the people of Taiwan have come a long way. Looking into the future, we be-lieve that we have to face these problems and try to communicate among our-selves the most proper and equitable ways to improve the situation. I believe the current institutional setup is not adequately equipped, however, at least not to tackle the serious agricultural environmental problems.

# 13

# Environmental Planning for a Sustainable Food Supply

## Robert E. Evenson

wo major scientific revolutions have affected food supply: the green revolution and the gene revolution. The green revolution, which began around 1975, was based on "conventional" breeding techniques entailing crosses between parent cultivars with subsequent selection of progeny through several generations. The gene revolution, by contrast, uses recombinant DNA techniques to achieve transgenic (genetically engineered) crop varieties. The green revolution was criticized first by Marxist-Leninists and then by environmental critics. The gene revolution has been subject to more extensive criticism, with many European critics recommending that developing countries consider the "precautionary principle" in regulatory policy.

## INVESTMENT IN THE GREEN REVOLUTION

Table 13.1 reports global expenditures for both public- and private-sector agricultural research in millions of 2001 U.S. dollars. It shows that public-sector expenditures are significant for all regions. Aggregate investment in public-sector agricultural research in developing countries increased more than fivefold from 1965 to 1995.

The table also shows that private-sector R&D in agriculture is high for the OECD developed countries (almost as high as public-sector spending), but that for developing countries private-sector R&D was only 5.5 percent of developed country spending in 1995.

**TABLE 13.1** Global Expenditures on Agricultural Research in 1995 (Millions of 2001 U.S. dollars)

| Research sector | 1965 | 1976 | 1985 | 1995 |
|---|---|---|---|---|
| Public sector | | | | |
|   Developed countries | 6,532 | 8,270 | 10,192 | 11,900 |
|   Developing countries | | | | |
|     China | 377 | 709 | 1,396 | 2,036 |
|     Other Asia | 441 | 1,321 | 2,453 | 4,619 |
|     Middle East–North Africa | 360 | 582 | 981 | 1,521 |
|     Latin America and the Caribbean | 562 | 1,087 | 1,583 | 1,947 |
|     Sub-Saharan Africa | 472 | 993 | 1,181 | 1,270 |
|     International agricultural research centers | 12 | 163 | 315 | 400 |
| Private sector | | | | |
|   Developed countries | | | | 10,829 |
|   Developing countries | | | | 672 |

*Sources*: Pardey and Beintema (2001); Boyce and Evenson (1975).

Table 13.2 reports public-sector research "intensities" in the form of expenditures as a share of agricultural GDP and expenditures per capita. Developed countries have much higher expenditures as a share of agricultural GDP and very much higher expenditures per capita than developing countries. (Data were unavailable for the Middle East–North Africa region.) Developed countries had similar expenditures as a share of agricultural GDP in 1976 except for sub-Saharan Africa, where a high proportion of expatriate agricultural scientists led to higher expenditures as a share of agricultural GDP. All regions increased spending as a share of agricultural GDP except sub-Saharan Africa, where it declined from 1985 to 1995 as expatriate scientists were replaced.

## THE GREEN REVOLUTION

More than 40 years ago, Theodore W. Schultz wrote an influential book called *Transforming Traditional Agriculture* (1964) in which he argued that "traditional" agricultural economies were "poor but efficient" and "efficient but poor." Traditional agriculture was defined as an agriculture in which the

**TABLE 13.2**  Public Agricultural Research Intensities

| Countries | Expenditures as a share of agricultural GDP | | | Expenditures per capita | | |
|---|---|---|---|---|---|---|
| | 1976 | 1985 | 1995 | 1976 | 1985 | 1995 |
| Developed countries | 1.53 | 2.13 | 2.64 | 9.6 | 11.0 | 12.0 |
| Developing countries | 0.44 | 0.53 | 0.62 | 1.5 | 2.0 | 2.5 |
| China | 0.41 | 0.42 | 0.43 | 0.7 | 1.3 | 1.7 |
| Other Asia | 0.31 | 0.44 | 0.63 | 1.1 | 1.7 | 2.6 |
| Latin America and the Caribbean | 0.55 | 0.72 | 0.98 | 3.4 | 4.0 | 4.6 |
| Sub-Saharan Africa | 0.91 | 0.95 | 0.85 | 3.5 | 3.0 | 2.0 |

*Sources*: Pardey and Beintema (2001); Evenson estimates for Sub-Saharan Africa.

development of improved technology in the form of improved crop varieties and improved animals was proceeding at a very slow pace. Implicit in that definition is the notion that agricultural technology has a high degree of "location specificity." Crop varieties, for example, require breeding programs in the regions served by the program.[1]

The Schultz argument implicitly suggests that agricultural extension programs cannot effectively "transform traditional agriculture," because traditional agriculture is already efficient. That statement assumes that the transaction costs associated with institutions will remain constant. Thus, markets may be inefficient with high levels of transaction costs, but given that, farmers are efficient largely because they have had time to experiment with technological improvements under conditions of slow delivery.

We now have an opportunity to reassess the Schultz argument in the context of the green revolution. Agricultural extension programs might not be effective in improving the efficiency of farmers in a setting where farmers are already efficient, but they could be successful in facilitating the transfer of technology from one country to another. Many countries have counted on this technology

---

[1]This was first noted in the study of hybrid maize (corn) by Zvi Griliches (1957, 1958). Griliches noted that farmers in Alabama did not have hybrid maize varieties until 20 years after farmers in Iowa had them. It was not until breeding programs were established in Alabama, selecting varieties for the farm conditions there, that farmers in Alabama had access to hybrid maize. Farmers in West Africa did not have hybrid maize until 75 years after farmers in Iowa had hybrid maize. Farmers in Central Africa still do not have access to hybrid maize.

transfer. In many sub-Saharan African countries the number of agricultural extension personnel far exceeds the number of agricultural scientists.[2]

Schultz believed that the technology transfer function of agricultural extension was not realized because of the inherent "localness" of agricultural extension programs. Ultimately, he indicated that only a "green revolution" could "transform" traditional agriculture, and a green revolution depends primarily on competently managed plant breeding programs in national agricultural research system (NARS) programs supported by international agricultural research centers (IARCs).

Table 13.3 lists 87 countries classified according to aggregate green revolution modern variety (GRMV) adoption rates in 2000. The 12 countries in the first column report negligible GRMV adoption in the year 2000. All other classes are based on area-weighted GRMV adoption rates for the 11 crops included in the GRMV study.[3]

Tables 13.4 and 13.5 list economic and social indicators, respectively, by green revolution cluster. The clusters can be roughly categorized as nonperforming (cluster 1), underperforming (clusters 2, 3, and 4), and performing (clusters 5, 6, 7, and 8).

The economic indicators in table 13.4 show the following:

- Crop value (in U.S. dollars) per hectare is very low for countries not realizing a green revolution and rises to high levels for countries realizing the highest levels of GRMV adoption.
- Fertilizer application per hectare is negligible for the first four clusters and significant for the highest GRMV clusters.
- Crop total factor productivity (TFP) growth is negligible for countries not realizing a green revolution and highest for countries with the highest levels of GRMV adoption.[4]
- Countries without a green revolution did have both agricultural scientists and extension workers. Scientists per million hectares of cropland rise with higher levels of GRMV adoption.
- Extension workers per million hectares of cropland are roughly 20 times as great as scientists per million hectares of cropland. The number of extension workers increased in every cluster. No correlation between extension workers per million hectares of cropland and GRMV adoption exists.

---

[2]Evenson and Kislev (1975) report relative price ratios of 20 to 1 for the cost of scientists compared to the cost of extension workers. This is partly related to the relative prices of extension personnel relative to the price of agricultural scientists.
[3]The 11 crops were rice, wheat, maize, sorghum, millet, barley, groundnuts, lentils, beans, potatoes, and cassava (Evenson and Gollin 2003).
[4]Crop TFP growth is reported in Avila and Evenson (2007).

**TABLE 13.3** Green Revolution Clusters by GRMV Adoption Level in 2000

| LT 2% | 2–10% | 10–20% | 20–30% | 30–40% | 40–50% | 50–65% | GT 65% |
|---|---|---|---|---|---|---|---|
| Afghanistan | Burkina Faso | Bolivia | Colombia | Cuba | Dominican Republic | Algeria | Argentina |
| Angola | Cambodia | Benin | Costa Rica | Egypt | Iran | Bangladesh | Chile |
| Burundi | Chad | Botswana | Ecuador | Mexico | Kenya | Brazil | China |
| Central African Republic | El Salvador | Cameroon | Ghana | Namibia | Morocco | Myanmar | India |
| Congo (B) | Gabon | Congo (Z) | Laos | Paraguay | Nepal | Tunisia | Indonesia |
| Gambia | Guatemala | Côte d'Ivoire | Madagascar | Peru | Thailand | | Malaysia |
| Guinea Bissau | Guinea | Ethiopia | Mali | Saudi Arabia | Turkey | | Pakistan |
| Mauritania | Haiti | Liberia | Sierra Leone | South Africa | | | Philippines |
| Mongolia | Jamaica | Honduras | | Syria | | | Sri Lanka |
| Niger | Libya | Mauritius | | | | | Vietnam |
| Somalia | Malawi | Nicaragua | | | | | |
| Yemen | Mozambique | Nigeria | | | | | |
| | Panama | Rwanda | | | | | |
| | Senegal | Sudan | | | | | |
| | Swaziland | Tanzania | | | | | |
| | Togo | Uruguay | | | | | |
| | Uganda | Venezuela | | | | | |
| | Zambia | Zimbabwe | | | | | |

**TABLE 13.4**  Green Revolution Economic Cluster Indicators

| Clusters by GRMV adoption | Crop value per hectare (dollars) | Fertilizer per hectare (kilograms) | Crop TFP growth (1961–2000) | Scientists per million hectares of cropland | | Extension work per million hectares | | Industrial competitiveness (UNIDO) | |
|---|---|---|---|---|---|---|---|---|---|
| | | | | 1960 | 2000 | 1960 | 2000 | 1985 | 1998 |
| LT 2% | 78 | 2 | .09 | .019 | .030 | .230 | .461 | .002 | .002 |
| 2–10% | 128 | 22 | .72 | .018 | .093 | .392 | .402 | .020 | .028 |
| 10–20% | 94 | 6 | 1.07 | .013 | .033 | .149 | .220 | .028 | .029 |
| 20–30% | 112 | 12 | .87 | .033 | .076 | .245 | .416 | .037 | .051 |
| 30–40% | 180 | 40 | 1.30 | .033 | .179 | .070 | .371 | .050 | .076 |
| 40–50% | 227 | 52 | .96 | .023 | .063 | .287 | .827 | .038 | .072 |
| 50–60% | 300 | 68 | 1.36 | .050 | .063 | .070 | .140 | .060 | .080 |
| GT 65% | 488 | 166 | 1.56 | .079 | .120 | .150 | .442 | .047 | .111 |

**TABLE 13.5**  Green Revolution Social Cluster Indicators

| Clusters by GRMV adoption | Countries in class | Population in 2000 (millions) | Population (millions) | | Birth rates (millions) | | Child mortality rates (millions) | | Dietary energy sufficiency | | GDP per capita | |
|---|---|---|---|---|---|---|---|---|---|---|---|---|
| | | | 1960 | 2000 | 1960 | 2000 | 1960 | 2000 | 1960 | 2000 | 1960 | 2000 |
| LT 2% | 12 | 75 | 2.2 | 6.1 | 47 | 41 | 293 | 160 | 2,029 | 2,192 | 361 | 388 |
| 2–10% | 18 | 153 | 3.1 | 8.5 | 45 | 36 | 236 | 118 | 2,074 | 2,387 | 815 | 1,291 |
| 10–20% | 18 | 385 | 7.0 | 21.4 | 44 | 36 | 214 | 134 | 1,983 | 2,282 | 866 | 1,295 |
| 20–30% | 8 | 115 | 9.0 | 14.3 | 46 | 32 | 238 | 124 | 2,070 | 2,384 | 695 | 1,156 |
| 30–40% | 9 | 337 | 14.3 | 37.4 | 42 | 26 | 156 | 27 | 2,050 | 2,574 | 1,169 | 3,514 |
| 40–50% | 2 | 284 | 15.5 | 40.3 | 46 | 26 | 221 | 61 | 2,084 | 2,506 | 805 | 1,660 |
| 50–60% | 5 | 385 | 34.9 | 76.7 | 46 | 23 | 240 | 50 | 2,038 | 2,391 | 1,096 | 2,153 |
| GT 65% | 10 | 2,886 | 135.1 | 288.6 | 39 | 22 | 165 | 43 | 2,100 | 2,719 | 1,049 | 2,305 |

- None of the countries without a green revolution has industrial competitiveness. A UNIDO index of .05 or greater indicates industrial competitiveness. Only countries in the 30–40 percent GRMV clusters and above have industrial competitiveness. Improvement in industrial competitiveness is greatest for the highest GRMV clusters.[5]

The social indicators in table 13.5 show the following:

- Sixty-three percent of the 4.65 billion people living in developing countries are located in the 10 countries in the highest green revolution cluster; 84 percent live in performing clusters. Countries without a green revolution make up less than 2 percent of the population in developing countries.
- The average population of countries in 1960 and 2000 rises as GRMV adoption levels rise. This suggests a strong bias against small countries.
- In 1960, birth rates were similar across GRMV clusters. By 2000, birth rates had declined in all GRMV clusters, with highest declines in the highest GRMV clusters.
- Child mortality rates in 1960 were similar in most GRMV clusters. By 2000, they had declined in all GRMV clusters, with highest declines in the highest GRMV clusters. In the top two GRMV clusters, child mortality rates in 2000 were only 24 percent of their 1960 levels.
- Dietary energy sufficiency (DES) was similar for all GRMV clusters in 1960. By 2000, improvements were achieved in all clusters, with highest improvements in highest GRMV clusters. DES improvement is highly correlated with child mortality reduction.
- GDP per capita (using exchange rate conversion to dollars, Atlas method) was lowest in countries without a green revolution in 1960 and did not improve in 2000. GDP per capita for the next three GRMV clusters rose by 56 percent from 1960 to 2000. GDP per capita for the highest four GRMV clusters rose by 140 percent from 1960 to 2000.

NARS programs in specific countries bear the ultimate responsibility for failing to deliver GRMVs to their farmers. But IARC programs are not immune from criticism. There are three IARCs located in Africa — the International Centre for Research in Agroforestry (ICRAF) in Nairobi, Kenya; the International Livestock Research Institute (ILRI) in Ethiopia and Kenya; and the International Institute of Tropical Agriculture (IITA) in Nigeria. ICRAF has had little impact because agroforestry generates little income for farmers.

---

[5]None of the countries without a green revolution reported investing in R&D in 1970. The Central African Republic reported industrial R&D in 1990. Of the 18 countries in the 2–10 percent cluster, 5 reported industrial R&D in 1970, and 12 reported industrial R&D in 1990.

ILRI has also had little impact, although it does not deal with crops. IITA has had an impact only after developing breeding programs with the Centro Internacional de Mejoramiento de Maiz y Trigo (CIMMYT) for maize and with the Centro Internacional de Agricultura Tropical (CIAT) for cassava. Similarly, the International Crops Research Institute for the Semi-Arid Tropics (ICRISAT) had little impact until sorghum, millet, and groundnut breeding programs were developed in Africa.

Why did 12 countries fail to produce a green revolution? A closer examination suggests three explanations. The first is the "failed state" explanation. The second is the "small state" explanation. The third is the "civil conflict" explanation. Most or all of the countries failing to deliver a green revolution to their farmers are effectively failed states—they cannot manage to deliver the mail, much less produce a green revolution. They are also small states, with an average population of 2.5 million people in 1960 (Angola and Yemen had 5 million people in 1960). None have universities to train agricultural scientists. All have been in civil conflict for much of the past 40 years. Given low GDP per capita, limited taxing power, and civil conflict, it is not surprising that they did not produce a green revolution.

The countries in the second GRMV cluster did have a small green revolution, but they too are small (Mozambique and Uganda being the largest, with populations around 7 million in 1960). Most of these countries have also been in civil conflict. Few have universities to train agricultural scientists.

Figure 13.1 depicts "real" prices for the 1960 to 2000 period (a five-year moving average). The prices of rice, wheat, and maize in 2000 were approximately 45 percent of their 1960 levels (35 percent of their 1950 levels). The real prices of the world's major cereal grains have been declining by more than 1 percent per year for the past 50 years.

In the OECD developed countries, it is estimated that total factor productivity rates (a measure of cost reduction) in agriculture have been roughly 1 percent per year higher than in the rest of the economy. For developing countries, crop TFP growth rates have been high except for countries in the lowest GRMV clusters. A few of the industrially competitive countries have had industrial TFP growth rates higher than agricultural TFP growth rates.

Why then do we have hunger in a world awash with grain? For this we need only look at crop value per hectare in table 13.4. With low crop yields, crop value per hectare is low. The highest GRMV cluster produces more than six times as much crop value per hectare as the lowest cluster. At 1960 prices, farmers in sub-Saharan Africa with 1.2 hectares could earn $2 per day per capita. At 2000 prices with .8 hectares, farmers in sub-Saharan Africa can

**Figure 13.1:** World Grain Prices, 1960–2000

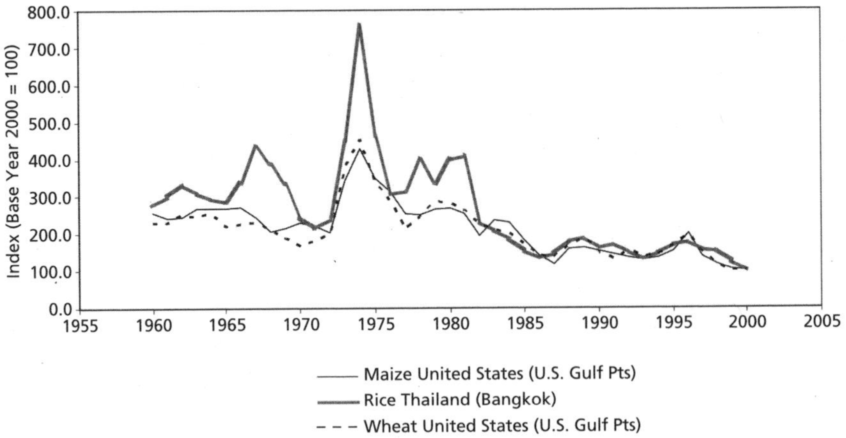

———— Maize United States (U.S. Gulf Pts)
———— Rice Thailand (Bangkok)
– – – Wheat United States (U.S. Gulf Pts)

*Source*: International Food Policy Research Institute.

earn only $1 per day per capita. Farmers in a number of countries have been delivered price declines without cost declines, and many have moved from mass poverty to extreme poverty.

## THE GENE REVOLUTION

In 1953 Watson and Crick reported the "double helix" structure of DNA and showed that DNA conveyed inheritance from one generation to another. In 1974 Boyer and Cohen achieved the first "transformation" by inserting alien DNA from a source organism into a host organism, and the field of genetic engineering was born.

The first genetically modified (GM) products (Ice Minus and the Flavor-Saver tomato) were not commercially successful. Monsanto introduced bovine somatotrophin hormone (BST) to dairy farmers in 1993. In 1995, several GM products were introduced to the market. One class of GM products provided herbicide tolerance, enabling farmers to control weeds and practice low tillage methods with conventional herbicides (e.g., Roundup, Liberty). A second class of products conveyed insect toxicity to plants (from *Bacillus thuringiensis*).[6]

---

[6]Seven multinational firms now dominate the GM product market. Three (Monsanto, Dupont, and Dow) are based in the United States, three (Bayer, BASF, and Syngenta) are based in Europe, and one (Savia) is based in Mexico. These firms now spend $3 billion per year on R&D.

Scientific reviews for food safety show no serious food safety issues for GM crops (or foods). Environmental studies show that environmental issues can be managed using existing management technology. Thus, existing GM products convey cost reduction advantages to farmers in countries where they are approved for sale. Because farmers using GM products increase their supply, world market prices are lower. This means that farmers in countries not approving GM crops for sale suffer a double penalty. They do not realize cost reductions, and they face lower prices.

The political economy of GM crops (foods) over recent years has resulted in a significant divergence between North America (the United States and Canada) and the European Union (EU, before expansion). North America advises developing countries to take advantage of cost-reducing opportunities. The EU countries urge developing countries to follow the precautionary principle in science policy.[7]

The European Union has little cost reduction potential because European countries do not produce significant quantities of cotton, soybeans, canola, or rice. Thus, EU countries have little at stake in terms of cost reduction potential. But they do have significant influence on developing countries because they threaten to ban GM crop imports.[8]

Nonetheless several developing countries—Mexico, Argentina, Brazil, Paraguay, Bolivia, Costa Rica, China, and India—have realized some cost reduction for GM crops. The potential for cost reduction in cotton-producing countries in Africa is large, but only South Africa has taken advantage of that potential. None of the countries without a green revolution has realized a gene revolution.[9]

Table 13.6 reports potential cost reduction gains from adopting GM crops and the gains realized as of 2004. As noted earlier, European countries produce little cotton, canola, soybeans, or rice. Even with 80 percent adoption of transgenic crops, European countries have little to gain. But several countries in sub-Saharan Africa (Mali, Benin, Burkina Faso, and Zimbabwe) have considerable potential gains (mostly because they produce cotton), but have not realized those gains because they do not have adequate food safety and environmental safety regulations in place.

---

[7]The precautionary principle is usually interpreted as requiring a high level of proof that food safety and environmental safety rules are being met. When applied to regulatory policies, this requirement is problematic. When applied to science, it effectively halts progress.
[8]Actually, most of the countries in sub-Saharan Africa export little or nothing to the European Union.
[9]It is unlikely that unimproved crop varieties benefit from genetic modifications.

**TABLE 13.6**  Potential and Realized (as of 2004) Cost Reduction Gains in Selected Countries

|  | Potential cost reduction (%) | Realized cost reduction, 2004 (%) |
|---|---|---|
| **Developed countries** | | |
| Canada | 5 | 2 |
| United States | 9 | 6 |
| Japan | 1.5 | 0 |
| European Union, northern | 0.6 | 0 |
| European Union, southern | 1.5 | 0.1 |
| Eastern Europe | 3 | 0.1 |
| Former Soviet Union | 4 | 0 |
| **Developing countries** | | |
| *Latin America* | | |
| Mexico | 3 | 0.5 |
| Argentina | 9 | 8 |
| Brazil | 7 | 2 |
| Paraguay | 9 | 2 |
| Bolivia | 7 | 1 |
| Costa Rica | 10 | 2 |
| Other | 4 | 0 |
| *Asia* | | |
| China | 4 | 1 |
| Southeast Asia | 4 | 0 |
| Bangladesh | 5 | 1 |
| India | 3 | 1 |
| Pakistan | 5 | 0 |
| *Africa* | | |
| Egypt | 3 | 0 |
| Kenya | 3 | 0 |
| Central Africa | 3 | 0 |
| Mali | 12 | 0 |
| Benin | 11 | 0 |
| Burkina Faso | 11 | 0 |
| Malawi | 4 | 0 |
| South Africa | 5 | 1 |
| Zimbabwe | 11 | 0 |

## RETURNS TO RESEARCH

Two sets of returns to agricultural research investments have been reported, the first in Evenson (2001) in volume 1A of the *Handbook of Agricultural Economics*. The methods for estimating returns to research range from project evaluation methods for cases where technology adoption rates are available to statistical methods utilizing research stock variables with time and spatial weights. Table 13.7 summarizes studies of returns to research as measured by internal rates of return (IRRs).[10] Pre-invention science IRRs are for basic research investments. Private-sector R&D programs do not reflect returns to R&D in the private companies but measure returns that spill in to the agricultural sector.

Table 13.8 reports IRRs and benefit-cost ratios for IARCs and NARS programs for the green revolution based on GRMV adoption rates. The low rates for sub-Saharan Africa reflect the fact that many sub-Saharan NARS have been spending significant funds for many years, often with few benefits.

## CRITICISM OF THE GREEN REVOLUTION

Early critics of the green revolution were from a Marxist-Leninist perspective. However, Marx and Lenin did not appreciate the distinctions between mechanical and biological (green revolution) technology because little biological technology had been realized when they were publishing. Biological technology is highly management intensive and is actually well suited to small farms. Many early critics have also failed to appreciate this distinction, along with the fact that pressure from population growth has effects on precapitalist institutions that are to some degree independent of the effects of biological technology. Ruttan (2004) notes that the original critics argued the following points:

- New technology is monopolized by large farmers and landlords.
- Financial constraints prevent small farms from purchasing fertilizer and chemicals.
- Large farms use profits to enlarge their holdings.
- Large farms realize scale economies and purchase machinery to reduce labor costs.

---

[10]Internal rates of return are the rates for which the present value of benefits equals the present value of costs.

**TABLE 13.7** Returns to Agricultural Research

| | Number of IRRs reported | Percent distribution | | | | | | Approximate median IRR |
|---|---|---|---|---|---|---|---|---|
| | | 0–20 | 21–40 | 41–60 | 61–80 | 81–100 | 100+ | |
| **Applied research** | | | | | | | | |
| Project evaluation | 121 | .25 | .31 | .14 | .18 | .06 | .07 | 39 |
| Statistical | 254 | .14 | .20 | .23 | .12 | .10 | .20 | 45 |
| Aggregate programs | 126 | .16 | .27 | .29 | .10 | .09 | .09 | 40 |
| **Commodity programs** | | | | | | | | |
| Wheat | 30 | .30 | .13 | .17 | .10 | .13 | .17 | 50 |
| Rice | 48 | .08 | .23 | .19 | .27 | .08 | .14 | 58 |
| Maize | 25 | .12 | .28 | .12 | .16 | .08 | .24 | 55 |
| Other cereals | 27 | .26 | .15 | .30 | .11 | .07 | .11 | 45 |
| Fruits and vegetables | 34 | .18 | .18 | .09 | .15 | .09 | .32 | 60 |
| All crops | 207 | .19 | .19 | .14 | .16 | .10 | .21 | 52 |
| Forest products | 13 | .23 | .31 | .68 | .16 | 0 | .23 | 35 |
| Livestock | 32 | .21 | .31 | .25 | .09 | .03 | .09 | 30 |

| By region | | | | | | | |
|---|---|---|---|---|---|---|---|
| OECD | 146 | .15 | .35 | .21 | .10 | .07 | .11 | 35 |
| Asia | 120 | .08 | .18 | .21 | .15 | .11 | .26 | 60 |
| Latin America | 80 | .15 | .29 | .29 | .15 | .07 | .06 | 45 |
| Africa | 44 | .27 | .27 | .18 | .11 | .11 | .05 | 35 |
| **All applied research** | 375 | .18 | .23 | .20 | .14 | .08 | .16 | 45 |
| Pre-technology science | 12 | 0 | .17 | .33 | .17 | .17 | .17 | 50 |
| Private-sector R&D | 11 | .18 | .09 | .45 | .09 | .18 | 0 | 45 |
| *Ex ante* research | 83 | .11 | .36 | .16 | .07 | .01 | .05 | 40 |

**TABLE 13.8**  Estimated Benefit-Cost Ratios and Internal Rates of Return from Green Revolution Contributions

| Region | NARS B/C | NARS IRRs | IARC B/C | IARC IRRs |
|--------|----------|-----------|----------|-----------|
| Latin America | 56 | 31 | 34 | 39 |
| Asia | 115 | 33 | 104 | 115 |
| West Asia–North Africa | 54 | 22 | 147 | 165 |
| Sub-Saharan Africa | 4 | 9 | 57 | 68 |

*Note:* B/C = benefit-cost.

To address these concerns, we can ask the following questions:

- Was farm size or tenancy a serious constraint to GRMV adoption?
- Did farm size change with the adoption of GRMVs?
- Did the adoption of GRMVs promote mechanization?
- Did the adoption of GRMVs reduce labor employment and wages?

Ruttan provides evidence on each question. He notes first that farm size differs by country. Most Asian farms are small. African farms are larger, and Latin American farms are much larger. But farms of all sizes have adopted GRMVs. Some large farms adopted them slightly earlier than smaller farms. Adoption was largely guided by whether the GRMVs were suited to the location.

As to the second question, farm size in Asia and Africa has actually declined over recent decades. In Latin America, farm sizes increased in some countries (Brazil and Argentina). But farm size is driven by population growth and by the wage-machine price ratio. Mechanization of farm operations is also driven mainly by the wage-machine price ratio. Mechanization does increase farm size, particularly in high-income countries (Huffman and Evenson 2006).

Did the adoption of GRMVs promote mechanization? There is some evidence that it did. Many farms in Asia adopted GRMVs and are not mechanized, but as countries like India begin to generate nonfarm employment opportunities and wages begin to rise, they are mechanizing rapidly. Mechanization is the consequence of a rising wage-machine price ratio. Finally, did the adoption of GRMVs promote a reduction in employment and wages? In

India, the regions adopting GRMVs first experienced an increase in wages. Ultimately, wages rise as economies generate nonfarm jobs, which is now occurring in India.

The criticisms listed above have an "old-fashioned" Marxist flavor. Most have been made by sociologists and anthropologists. Most economists, particularly empirical economists working in Asia and Africa, reach different conclusions.

The criticism that GRMVs have been "fertilizer-using" is accepted as valid. It is also accepted as rational. The price of nitrogen fertilizer has declined in real terms since the Haber process was introduced for the production of ammonia. Before 1965, traditional crop varieties were not fertilizer-using. But by then every developed country had taken advantage of low-cost nitrogen fertilizer, the reduced cost having been achieved through breeding. Developing countries followed the lead of the developed countries.

The criticism that GRMVs are linked to more insecticide use was true for the first generation of GRMVs. Again, this was a matter of developing countries following the path of developed countries.

The argument that GRMVs were herbicide-using does not hold up well. All farmers know that if you don't control weeds, you are not a competent farmer. In Asia, most weed control is done by hand. Many African countries have poor levels of weed control, but do not use herbicides. Only in some Latin American countries are herbicides used. For the most part, the developing countries have not followed the lead of the developed countries in this case.

Does the use of herbicides produce chemical residue problems in GRMVs? Yes. Are they manageable? They are at least as manageable in developing countries as they are in developed countries, where fertilizer and chemical use is much higher.

The critiques regarding mechanization have some validity in Latin America but little in Asia. Many countries are being rapidly mechanized today, but mechanization appears not to be having the effects on farm size observed in North America and Europe. Harvesting equipment is also being adopted, but at a slower rate. We do not see the same harvesting equipment in Asia that we see in the United States. Africa, particularly sub-Saharan Africa, has relatively low levels of mechanization, and we see some in Latin America. Many countries have not even fully adopted animal power yet. The poorest farmers in Africa use a simple planting technology (a dibble stick) and achieve very low yields.

## EVIDENCE ON ENVIRONMENTAL EFFECTS

### The Green Revolution and the Environment

Curiously, the green revolution was criticized not for its uneven delivery but for an increase in resource intensity. Most, but not all, crops subject to the green revolution experienced an increase in fertilizer use. However, although all countries with major green revolutions have increased fertilizer use, table 13.4 shows that many countries have very low rates of fertilizer use per hectare. Prior to the green revolution (i.e., in 1960), fertilizer use rates were low because both wheat and rice "lodged" (fell over) when high rates of fertilizer were applied. The lodging problem was eventually overcome by the judicious use of "semi-dwarfing" genes in breeding programs. The increased use of fertilizer was thus consistent with the breeding objectives of the green revolution. It was also consistent with the "induced innovation" model of productivity change, which indicates that when the price of an input (e.g., urea) continues to fall over time, that signals inventors that they should exploit that advantage.

Has increased fertilizer use had environmental effects? It is, of course, possible that "runoff" problems might exist, but it should be noted that even the maximum rates of fertilizer use in developing countries are well below the OECD levels of fertilizer use (The Netherlands applies roughly 700 kg of fertilizer per hectare), and OECD countries manage to control runoff problems effectively.

The broad-scale use of insecticides and herbicides is also an environmental concern (see the discussion of the gene revolution below). There is little question that insecticide use increased during the green revolution. Many farmers increased spraying to very high levels, partly in response to lower-cost insecticides. As integrated pest management (IPM) techniques were developed and breeding objectives were further developed, insecticide use was reduced, however.[11] It is not always appreciated that green revolution plant breeders found that the first generation of GRMVs was susceptible to insect damage. As breeders responded to that susceptibility, they developed varieties with insect resistance, which helped reduce insecticide use.

### The Gene Revolution and the Environment

Until the gene revolution, most developing countries used relatively small amounts of herbicides. The first crop of GM products, introduced in 1995,

---

[11]Some of the "gains" from IPM programs are overstated because a major objective of second-generation GRMVs is insect resistance.

included herbicide-tolerant products and insect-toxic products. Today approximately 60 percent or more of the soybeans and canola produced in the world are herbicide tolerant. The most widely used herbicide in the world is Roundup, produced by Monsanto, and most of the world's soybeans are now "Roundup Ready." As a result, most soybeans are now produced under "minimum tillage" conditions. A single spraying with Roundup is usually sufficient to control weeds, and herbicide use has probably declined as a result.

The insect-toxic products (based on a protein from *Bacillus thuringiensis*) have dramatically reduced insecticide use. These products are now available for cotton, rice, maize, sorghum, and millet. Yields of cotton, in particular, are higher because of these products, whose net effect is certainly to reduce insecticide use and to have minimal effects on herbicide use.

## THE U.S. AGENCY FOR INTERNATIONAL DEVELOPMENT

In 1985 the U.S. Agency for International Development (USAID) provided roughly $2.5 billion in aid to farmers. Almost all of that aid was provided to small family farms; some was also for research and extension programs, and some was for agricultural credit programs. In 2005 USAID provided only $400 million in aid to farmers. The USAID response to sustainable development was to eliminate aid to farmers; in addition, support for Ph.D. training was effectively eliminated.

The Millennium Challenge Account (MCA) policy strategy of the U.S. State Department argues that aid is ineffective in countries below a certain institutional or governance threshold. The first MCA grant went to Madagascar (see table 13.3). Most countries with lower levels of institutional development than Madagascar are ineligible for MCA grants.

Table 13.4 shows that there is a sectoral sequence to development. In the 1960s only 25 or so of the developing countries in table 13.3 could be considered industrialized. After 1960, virtually all countries in table 13.3 realized productivity gains in the agricultural sector before they realized productivity gains in the industrial sector. The abandonment of the agricultural sector by USAID and, to a lesser extent by the World Bank, is thus a serious matter.

The decline in aid effectiveness and in aid support is related to the end of the cold war. Prior to the early 1990s, both the west and the east (i.e., the Soviet Union) vied for influence in developing countries. Many developing countries initiated Marxist-style revolutions before the economic model underlying those revolutions, the "centrally planned economy," collapsed in both the Soviet Union and China.

## SUMMARY

In summarizing the literature on economic growth, Jones (2002) points out that the "steady state" equilibrium in early models shows that product per worker is constant without invention and innovation. He also reports a Malthusian extension of growth models showing that although the rate of population growth does slow growth in product per worker, it can be tripled by growth in technology. Many developing countries experienced a tripling of population from 1950 to 2000.

The more recent growth models treat R&D as a variable endogenously determined by incentive structures, particularly regarding intellectual property rights. These endogenous growth models treat population growth as a positive inducement to invention and innovation. The reasoning is that invention and innovation are proportional to population size and produce externalities that benefit all members of the population. Data on patents granted certainly do not bear that out. The number of patents granted to inventors in sub-Saharan Africa and even in South Asia is negligible. Inventions are not proportional to population.

Because of the green revolution, Dietary Energy Sufficiency (reported by FAO, a measure of calories consumed per capita) increased in virtually all developing countries.

Have the green and gene revolutions damaged the environment? The answer to that question is in part affected by one's perception. As mentioned previously, countries in the European Union (before expansion) advise developing countries to follow the precautionary principle in regulatory policy (and indirectly in science policy). That advice can be defended for regulatory policy, but not for science policy. There simply is no possible rationale for allowing the precautionary principle to dominate science policy.

Does the production of "transgenic" crop varieties harm the environment? The development of herbicide-tolerant soybean, canola, and maize varieties may possibly have increased herbicide use, but the herbicides in question are quite benign.

There is little question regarding the insect-toxic products for cotton, rice, and wheat. They reduce insecticide use and associated insecticide spillovers.

## REFERENCES

Avila, A. F. D., and R. E. Evenson. 2007. Total factor productivity growth in agriculture: The role of technogical capital. In *Handbook of agricultural economics*, vol. 4. R. E. Evenson and P. Pingali, eds., chap. 73. Amsterdam: Elsevier–North Holland.

Boyce, J. K., and R. E. Evenson. 1975. *Agricultural research and extension programs*. New York: Agricultural Development Council.

Evenson, R. E. 2001. Economic impacts of agricultural research and extension. In *Handbook of agricultural economics*, vol. 1A. B. L. Gardner and G. C. Rausser, eds., 573–628. Amsterdam: Elsevier.

Evenson, R. E., and D. Gollin, eds. 2003. *Crop variety improvement and its effect on productivity: The impact of international agricultural research*. Wallingford, U.K.: CAB International.

Evenson, R. E., and Y. Kislev. 1975. *Agricultural research and productivity*. New Haven, CT: Yale University Press.

Griliches, Z. 1957. Hybrid corn: An exploration in the economics of technological change. *Econometrica* 25(4):501–522.

———. 1958. Research costs and social returns: Hybrid corn and related innovations. *Journal of Political Economy* 66:419–431.

Huffman, W. E., and R. E. Evenson. 2006. *Science for agriculture: A long-term perspective*, 2nd ed. Ames, IA: Blackwell.

Jones, C. I. 2002. *Introduction to economic growth*. New York: Norton.

Pardey, P. G., and N. M. Beintema. 2001. Slow magic: Agricultural R&D a century after Mendel. Food Policy Report No. 36. Washington, DC: International Food Policy Research Institute.

Ruttan, V. 2004. Controversy about agricultural technology lessons from the green revolution. *International Journal of Biotechnology* 6(1):43–54.

Schultz, T. W. 1964. *Transforming traditional agriculture*. New Haven, CT: Yale University Press.

# 14

# Toward a 2015 Vision
# of Land

## Jim Riddell

T he previous chapters cover a range of topics that at first glance might appear only marginally related. There are chapters on urban sprawl, land taxes, the economics of genetically modified crops, land law, the dynamics of what constitutes land and natural resources, and the future of spatial data analysis. Rather than being a potpourri of papers collected at random from a conference, however, this volume compiles the work of authors (and their selected topics) who were carefully recruited by the International Center for Land Policy Studies and Training (ICLPST) and the Lincoln Institute of Land Policy to explore a vision of land in 2015, the target date that the members of the United Nations agreed to for achieving real progress in meeting the Millennium Goals.[1] The achievement of these goals will, quite naturally, involve new and innovative uses of land.

This chapter has the task of braiding together these seemingly diverse visions into the coherent message we first set out to create. We hope our efforts will go beyond the temptation to predict the future of land policy and administration. Such predictions are almost always wrong and provide little more than humorous examples of speculative thinking for future generations.

---

[1]The Millennium Summit was held 6–8 September 2000 at the United Nations headquarters in New York. "The Millennium Development Goals (MDGs) are the world's time-bound and quantified targets for addressing extreme poverty in its many dimensions—income poverty, hunger, disease, lack of adequate shelter, and exclusion—while promoting gender equality, education, and environmental sustainability. They are also basic human rights—the rights of each person on the planet to health, education, shelter, and security" (www.un.org/ millenniumgoals).

As our time horizon is fairly close, we hope to provide less of a prediction and more of a prescriptive essay.

It takes no crystal ball to see clearly that we are in the midst of a series of fundamental processes that are changing forever the nature of the human-land equation. In this volume we have focused on public finance, local economic development, institutional reform, and the impact of technology on land administration. Cutting across all these issues is the need to find the institutional means to manage the competition for local resources that is becoming more global every day. As chapters 10 and 11 make clear, the competing demands for the use of land causes us to see the earth and its resources in new ways. Thus, as "land" is an ever-changing concept, land and resource tenure is our unit of analysis, not land per se. The fundamental policy question that faces us is how are decisions to be made regarding who has the rights to how much, for how long, and for what purposes.

## GLOBALIZATION OF ESSENTIAL RESOURCES

During the rapid economic growth that has characterized the early years of the present decade, our attention has focused on a globalization of the marketplace. Many of the products that used to be made in Japan, Italy, Taiwan, and the United States are now made in China, Malaysia, Honduras, and places many consumers would have difficulty finding on a world map. That is, however, just the tip of the iceberg. Much more important for the person interested in land is the globalizing trend in natural resource use and control on the one hand and the transactions in those resources on the other.

First, we already know that essential resources such as water and air are parts of global natural systems. The earth's water system cannot be defined by any national boundaries. It involves oceans, rainfall that respects no human-defined boundary, and rivers that can only be marginally controlled. In the last century we built on the very elegant water and riparian rights regimes that had been elaborated over the centuries as a special branch of land tenure. Perhaps the biggest development was to shift our analysis of water systems to examinations of whole water basins. That led to the realization that water law would have to be much more attuned to transboundary issues, as there was hardly a major river basin system in the world that did not involve two or more national as well as multiple subnational jurisdictions. The last quarter century has witnessed rapid progress in water registries and water rights markets by global firms.

The globalization of transactions in resources like water that have traditionally been viewed as free goods (e.g., belonging to God in all major schools of Islamic law) will become the norm in this century. Thus, it is not surprising that many land administration specialists are working on various approaches to water markets, water user fees, and taxation systems for allocation, affluent discharges, and so forth. These market mechanisms have become well established almost under the radar of most citizens. There is also growing awareness that the oceans that make up three-quarters of the globe are no longer sustainable as an open resource. Ocean resource cadastres, registries, and similar innovations are becoming an exciting area of research, as well as legal and land administration institutional development.[2]

We all know that water is one of the resources that are sure to cause transboundary and international conflict in the coming decades if we are not successful in finding institutional means of allocation. The global warming debate addresses the same transboundary nature of the atmosphere. The air we breathe, the emissions we discharge, and the shared threat and responsibility for these resources will exist long after 2015. The point I wish to emphasize here is that land and natural resource administration is already becoming global, to date primarily through scientific debate, arms-length negotiations on treaty agreements, and open markets.

## DEMOGRAPHIC CONCENTRATION AND AN URBAN WORLD

Demographers at the United Nations have declared that there are now more people living in urban centers than in rural communities. This reversal of the historic demographic relationship between rural and urban is accompanied by the equally dramatic dominance of urban culture and its values. There is hardly a village so rural that it does not have some member who has moved to an urban setting. Everywhere rural populations are demanding inclusion in those institutions that until recently were urban based. The youth in rural households know the same music as their urban cousins, try to wear the same clothes, and share the same values. Rural songs are reworked in urban centers

---

[2]The massive effort to get international agreement in 1982 for the wording of the Convention on the Law of the Seas (UNCLOS III) was a significant achievement of the twentieth century. The convention had enough signatories to come into force in 1994, and what had hitherto been subject to "gunboat" diplomacy was then placed in an institutional framework of arm's-length negotiations, the final result having the force of international law. From a land administration perspective, a major achievement was to establish the rights of states to the sea up to the continental shelf. The land administration responsibilities of a country like New Zealand, for example, grew twentyfold upon the law's accession in 1996. Since UNCLOS III set the convention for the passage of ships and aircraft over the seas bordering member nations, it is hard to see how a global economy would have been possible without it.

and emerge on the radios, iPods, and party nights in villages that have no historical connection to their place of origin.

Along with the acceptance of urban cultural values by rural residents, we are witnessing the declining relative importance of the rural economy. When ICLPST offered its first Regular Session program[3] in 1969, the world was predominately rural, both in terms of population and culture. Indeed, the early collaborations between the Lincoln Institute and ICLPST were primarily concerned with land reform because agriculture was widely recognized as the "engine of growth." Kuo-Ching Lin has outlined in chapter 12 how Taiwanese agriculture has gone from its prime position to a relatively small component in terms of national GDP. This phenomenon is evident almost everywhere today. Furthermore, in Taiwan nowadays—as in the United States, the European Union, Japan, and many other OECD countries—close to 80 percent or more of the income of existing farm families comes from off-farm sources. The engine of growth today is clearly the city, not the agricultural sector.

The really serious problem for twenty-first-century policy makers is how to make any kind of rural economy work. All the rich nations outside the CAIRNS Group[4] have had to resort to subsidies and other interventions just to keep people in agriculture. There seems to be little agreement, theoretical or practical, on how to create a viable rural economy in the present age. Yet Robert Evenson (chapter 13) demonstrates that there is no bypassing sound agricultural development. Those countries that have most neglected basic research on food crops, and have missed out on the green and genetic revolutions, are also those with the poorest and most food-deficit populations. It has been popular in some circles to attribute evil intentions to the efforts of plant scientists to improve our basic food and material crops. But, as Evenson makes clear, it is not how you "feel" about something that is important; it is what you "know" about it that counts. He points out that, since the first green revolution, even with its shortcomings, food prices worldwide have been falling at about 1 percent per year. In addition, the cost of production has been falling by a slightly greater amount due to improved technologies.

Policy makers who have been convinced of the prudence of taking a wait-and-see attitude to adopting the genetic revolution in the agriculture of food and fiber have consigned their rural producers to a lose-lose state of affairs: they lose the savings in lower production costs while suffering the continuing

---

[3]ICLPST courses that are developed through cooperation with the Lincoln Institute are called "Regular Sessions."

[4]The CAIRNS Group is a coalition of nineteen agricultural exporting countries that work together for the elimination of commercial displacement in food aid and the elimination of export subsidies. More information can be found at www.cairnsgroup.org.

downward trend in farm-gate prices. In addition, it has become an urban legend in all OECD countries that genetically modified crops are a major threat to biodiversity, as they potentially will outperform and outbreed existing varieties. For example, in 1900 there were more than a thousand varieties of rice being cultivated in Taiwan; today there is only a handful.[5] The reality is, however, much more positive in regard to maintaining biodiversity in the world's major food and commercial crops.

Evenson emphasizes that one has to distinguish between the first faltering steps of the green revolution and subsequent modification, as lessons learned resulted in new and better science. The same is true of the genetic revolution in agriculture. In the first phase, much focus was placed on finding exogenous genetic material that could be inserted into the DNA of existing high-performing varieties of common crops. Today genetic "engineering" focuses on attributes within the genetic makeup of a plant's entire genus.

This new approach is the result of the falling cost of genetic sequencing. It is now more economical to look at all the myriad varieties of wheat or rice, for example, for the attributes that one would want for a crop in a given location, or for a target set of customers (e.g., wheat products for sufferers of celiac diseases). This means that the efforts by organizations such as the United Nations Food and Agricultural Organization (FAO) to preserve genetic material from all of the world's food crops move from being the avocation of a few scientists to a major new resource.

Indeed, rediscovering the diversity in genetic material is one of the bright spots in the world's food economy, and people everywhere are voting with their stomachs. In OECD countries, organic food is the fastest-growing segment of consumer expenditures on groceries. It may come as a surprise to many food activists, but the green and genetic revolutions are compatible with family-run organic farms. High-value natural food production requires a density of management that is not cost effective for large industrial farms. Finding ways to grow a greater variety of foods, even staples like wheat and rice, caters to what appears to be an ever-elastic market for food-conscious consumers. No longer satisfied with just white rice, growing numbers of food-aware shoppers are opting for red rice, spelt wheat breads, and other foods largely unknown to their parents but perhaps recognizable to their great-grandparents.

---

[5]Remarks by Professor Ming-Chien Chen, dean of the College of Management, Hsuan Chuang University, Taiwan. A conference was organized by ICLPST in Taipei in October 2006 to bring all of the chapter authors together. In order to facilitate discussion, Professor Cheng-Min Feng, a leading expert in the subject matter, was asked to prepare a presentation on what were considered the most salient points. In referring to some of the points made in this and other excellent presentations, they are hereafter referred to as "comments prepared for the ICLPST 2006 conference."

The green and genetic revolutions that produced the large factory farms have also made possible a closer fit between the economy of agricultural production and the urban market for diverse products produced through intensive agriculture on family farms.

To make things even more interesting, the future shape of urban growth is in flux. We can note, on one hand, the huge literature that has grown up around the "centrifugal" growth represented in urban sprawl, and the rise of megacities. UN Habitat, in its ongoing Global Land Tool Network, estimates that the world's slums are growing by at least 50,000 persons each day and will house roughly one billion of the earth's inhabitants in the year 2008 (www.gltn.net). On the other hand, the resulting costs of congestion, energy, commuting time, and delivery of basic services have resulted in "centripetal" policy forces calling for denser living arrangements. From the land tenure policy perspective, we have no clearer long-term answers for the growing urban half of humanity than for the shrinking rural half.

Gerrit-Jan Knaap makes the case for a planning discourse in addition to efforts to get prices right. This is essentially a counterargument to the position of one school of economic thought that holds that the market and pricing can optimize urban growth if distortions are removed. For example, (1) underpricing of undeveloped land; (2) underpricing of automobile travel; (3) public infrastructure is underpriced, and we can use impact fees that equal the marginal cost in each case. Knaap's argument is that if urban expansion or falling density is the problem, there is no theoretical reason why pricing is necessarily a superior approach to direct control.

Knaap takes a social welfare approach to urban sprawl, stating that "many of the attributes that define urban form—besides density—have impacts on household utility and thus social welfare" (p. 73). Much of urban growth is shaped by public investments in roads, sewers, and parks, for example, which are largely unaffected by price systems. Pricing is important, but not sufficient. Also, it is not so easy to get prices right for all the attributes. In addition, networked parks, greenways, and natural areas are becoming increasingly important to the decision of where to reside in the United States. Something more than pricing is at play in land use policy formation in a modern democracy. In comments on Knaap's chapter that were prepared for the ICLPST 2006 conference, Professor Cheng-Min Feng, from the Institute of Traffic and Transportation, National Chiao Tung University in Taiwan, summarized it thus: "A comprehensive approach to urban sprawl should include both pricing and nonpricing measures."[6]

---

[6]Remarks by Professor Cheng-Min Feng, Institute of Traffic and Transportation, National Chiao Tung University, Taiwan, in comments prepared for the ICLPST 2006 conference.

Knaap's argument is amplified by John Chien-Yuan Lin, who explores in chapter 5 how to create more density of use in existing urban environments. This is a desirable goal not only to prevent sprawl effects, but also due to the extremely high land prices in Taiwan. Lin suggests that there will be greater reliance on a redevelopment methodology, as an outgrowth of the work on urban regeneration. The Taiwan situation makes the driving force of that tactic optimizing social and economic costs through two types of conservation—cultural conservation and nature conservation—by improving existing land uses. There are certain problem areas to overcome, however. First, it is usually more expensive to rebuild than to finance new construction; and second, there is uncertainty in the market response. After all, regeneration, as its name implies, is investment in a declining-value area. Old facilities are less compatible with current demands for access, parking, and convenience.

Thus, Lin argues that increasing the density of use and investment in decaying urban centers, brownfields, and environmentally fragile areas will not take place unless government offers an incentive to balance out the additional costs. While it is not discussed explicitly in this book, the reader can readily appreciate the relevance of this argument to the lives of the billion humans living in the world's slums. Current UN data indicate that even before 2015 fully one-third of city dwellers will be living in inadequate housing with no, or only partial, basic services.[7]

The predisposition in developed democracies is that government will be called upon by the voting public to play a more assertive role in confronting the negative effects of urban growth. This is associated with a demand for increased participation by voters in the decision-making process. Michael Luger in chapter 6 analyzes the growing trend for local government to take an active role in trying to attract new business through incentives, as well as strategic investments in education. As he points out using data from the United States, to be competitive in the twenty-first century, state and local government must achieve a certain level (critical mass) in research and development centers (top universities and so forth) and provide a high level of those factors that constitute people's perception of a good quality of life.

However, this trend of local government's proactive efforts to enhance its competitive position vis-à-vis other localities in attracting knowledge-based industry is much more complex when we examine it against a larger background. Yu-Hung Hong of the Lincoln Institute looked at the same U.S. data in his comments prepared for the ICLPST 2006 conference. His interpretation of the data is that while people are voting for proactive development

---

[7]Ulrik Westman, UN Habitat, personal communication (www.gltn.net).

strategies by local and state government, the actual proportion of R&D investments by all levels of government (national, state, and local) has actually fallen during the first half decade of this century. What has taken up the slack is a rapid increase in research and development financed by the private sector. Hong says, "These data imply that if municipalities want to promote R&D, the cooperation from the private sector is imperative."[8] Given their limited financial capacity, communities compete with each other in terms of incentives such as tax abatements and land grants, as also discussed by Lin.

Hong raises an even bigger issue in regard to land use and administration in the early decades of the present century. What is the role of these scattered local initiatives in the context of a global economy? For instance, the United States accounts for around 38 percent of the world's total R&D, but around half of that is devoted to "defense" research that may or may not ever have any civilian applications. Furthermore, in the United States, government investment in R&D is overwhelmingly devoted to biomedical research. And as Hong suggests, it is not very likely that every competing municipality can become a major player in the biomedical field. Finally, total R&D investment as a share of GDP in the United States is flat; it is rising in countries such as China, Japan, and South Korea.

Consequently, policy makers at the local level are faced with very hard choices. On one hand, voters want better urban environments, yet businesses, especially knowledge-based enterprises, tend to locate where urban quality of life is already well established. On the other hand, achieving improvements in metropolitan design requires local government to make expensive "lumpy" investments, whether through regeneration and smart urban planning or by finding a way to harness the private sector. These so-called lumpy investments require large initial outlays for such projects as upgrading and expanding municipal sewage systems; developing traffic corridors; and providing incentives for the private sector to participate in science parks, urban renewal, and conservation projects. Thus, we have the planning dilemma that is part and parcel of an urban world. The voters want their parks and bicycle paths, as well as preservation of a surrounding countryside, and municipalities that have them are more attractive to investment; yet the same voters rebel against the increased taxation needed for the initial investments to prime the pump.

A major source of local government's funding comes from property taxation. The first part of this book devotes considerable space to discussing the innovation foreseen in public financing, valuation, appraisal, and taxing real

---

[8] Remarks by Yu-Hung Hong, Lincoln Institute of Land Policy, in comments prepared for the ICLPST 2006 conference.

property. Here our concern is with the method in the use of data on land and its role in policy making. The foundation of almost all our current records on land is taxation. The physical dimensions of real property were recorded in ancient times and preserved in such records as the *capitatio terreno* of Rome and the *katastikhon* of the Byzantine empire. The Venetian Republic borrowed that name for its *catastico* (property register).

Originally, therefore, cadastral and other records of rights in real property were seen basically as fiscal instruments. Land registration as an institution of recording transactions concerning registered parcels evolved in tandem with the development of private rights at the end of Europe's feudal age. I will later address the fact that so much of our current development effort in land administration in countries in transitional and developing economies has to do with institutions that responded to changes in one of the world's many cultural traditions. At this juncture, however, I would like to direct the reader's attention to the issue of what is happening to land tenure data and the new uses to which it is being put.

Almost all of the data on "what is where and where is what" was, by the nature of its technology and maintenance, largely hidden from public view in all but a handful of jurisdictions until the beginning of this century. Property records in a land registry were consulted by professionals only when a major transaction occurred, when a legal action was initiated, or in regard to inheritance. Otherwise, they largely took up space, in the off chance they were needed. Property maps used for taxation purposes were kept in another database, normally under the control of a different agency. In spite of the tremendous expense that society invested in these official property records, their accuracy was never tested.

Indeed, it has long been known in the land administration profession that the best data on property and resident identity is in the records of the utility companies. Furthermore, data on natural resources are found in numerous other data sets that are scattered among various agencies and private-sector enterprises (maps on water quality, maps on soil types, forestry maps, fisheries maps, mineral maps, and so forth). Once again, most of these data were not available to citizens when they were asked to vote on land administration and land use issues.

What changed was both the technology and the way we look at land administration data. The computation power of modern graphic systems supported the development of GIS technologies that allowed the integration of diverse spatial data sets. Suddenly, projected urban expansion could be mapped onto any number of environmental data sets. The spatial databases of the built-up environment could be contained in the same database that was used for nature conservancy and land conservation.

Ian Williamson has long been one of the leaders of this revolution. He argues in chapter 8 that sustainable development objectives cannot be achieved unless natural and built environmental data are integrated. This development in spatial data infrastructures has been paralleled by an effort to revitalize democracy by more intimately connecting citizens to their government through e-government. Therefore, it was only natural that the mostly "dead" paper in the land registry and cadastre office be included in transparent government. Williamson asks us to go beyond e-government, and he introduces the concept of iLand and its use in a global economy. iLand is a vision of integrated, spatially enabled land information available on the Internet that makes possible the "where" in government policies and information. For instance, he asks how land administrators and policy makers in a given jurisdiction can see the international context of land information and its importance to their national government in its competition for private sector investments. iLand can be that tool. It is seen as an integral part (I suspect he would say it is the missing part) of future e-governance. This kind of accessible data will be a key resource and will revolutionize voter participation in debates on urban planning because voters will be able to access relevant information. In concluding his chapter, Williamson states, "Unfortunately, unless [land administration systems] are refocused on delivering transparent and vital land information and enabling platforms, modern economies will have difficulty meeting sustainable development objectives and achieving their economic potential" (p. 186). He puts his finger on an important relationship between globalization in trade and the need to be able to undertake transactions in diverse jurisdictions. Therefore, in light of these new needs, it is not surprising that the land registries of the leading players in the global economy are beginning to look very much alike. Those jurisdictions in which the land administration institutions are the most transparent and the most secure are also those that tend to attract the most investment. For example, in his comments on Williamson's paper during the ICLPST 2006 conference, Professor Tien-Yin Chou was able to point to how many of the ideas proposed for iLand were being implemented in Taiwan.[9]

An even more fundamental change is taking place as land information is rapidly becoming part of the new economy. Information like that contained in most land information systems (LIS) of the past quarter century has been viewed as a necessary expense, borne by the taxpayer for the benefit of all. We are used to seeing land survey teams with total stations and GPS receivers at

---

[9]Professor Chou is Director, GIS Research Center, Feng Chia University, Taiwan. He can be contacted at www.gis.fcu.edu.tw.

the side of the highway, out in the nature preserves, strung along rivers, and so forth. Where the data went, who used it, and for what purposes were something of a mystery to anyone outside the specific project. Only graduate student researchers, tax watchers, and land investors had the tenacity and resources to find out. The data have traditionally been locked away in surveyors' field books, planning maps, and proposals for land use change. The proposed new use of the land has always been considered to have all the value and has attracted the investment; the data collection was just a necessary expense.

Today the information itself is rapidly becoming the more valuable commodity. Its value, however, depends on coverage and completeness. The more complete the LIS, the more users we will have of that data; the more users of the data, the more value the data have in the new economy. Once companies like Google, Microsoft, and others began offering the capacity to focus from a satellite image to any place on the face of the globe, new data uses and revenue streams were created. So far, this has turned out to be a virtuous circle. The more transparent the data and the market, the more participants are attracted, and hence the economic value keeps growing.[10]

So, in moving toward 2015, is it to the land tenure institutions that we need to look for development models, or the land information data sets? The chapters by John Bruce, Daniel Bromley, and Anthony Bebbington make clear that simply importing property law and institutions from Europe, North America, or one of the Asian Tigers is not necessarily conducive to economic development.

In his analysis of the role of the multilateral development banks in directing the change in the legal foundations of land administration, Bruce (chapter 9) sees these efforts much stimulated by Hernando de Soto's work, especially his book *The Mystery of Capital* and his concept of vitalizing "dead capital." Bruce effectively argues that de Soto's line of reasoning is an oversimplification. We have found that it is much more complex than simply taking a land registry design that works in Australia or Austria and implementing it in another country for the very reasons set forth in chapter 10. What "land" and "property" mean in a particular jurisdiction is conditioned

---

[10]Land registries and cadastres are expensive public undertakings. Dale and McLaughlin (2000, chapter 5) argue that a complete modern cadastre costs several hundred million U.S. dollars to create from scratch. Thus, a very relevant part of "normal" land registration planning was to look for ways to recover costs through filing fees and so forth. When the Dutch cadastre and the Austrian cadastre went public, they found that the demand for data was so great that nominal fees for data access by mortgage banks, notaries, and real estate agents, in addition to property owners curious about their property, more than paid for state-of-the-art systems. Such an open cadastre has value only to the degree to which it is complete and accurate.

not only by local culture, but also by the institutional history. The track record of successfully creating modern land registries and cadastres in developing countries has been spotty at best.

An example of where good intentions but lack of understanding of the local reality led to bad policy in a legal reform and natural resource project is illustrated by the case of Mongolia, where the 2003 Land Law undid the community access commons of the 1994 law and in effect returned pastureland to the status of an open access resource. There is still much work to be done in getting customary rights recognized and integrated into land administration. As Professor Shih-Jung Hsu pointed out in his comments prepared for the ICLPST 2006 conference, in the case of Taiwan the imposition of a land registry by the Japanese from 1900 to 1945 was not evolutionary, but revolutionary. It required a complete paradigm shift in the way people see and use land.[11] As Hsu said, it was a political process, in that it was imposed as part of a way of controlling the native Taiwanese and taking land for Japanese colonial enterprises. It was anything but a response to the felt needs of the Taiwanese land users. Indeed, land rights issues have never been fully resolved in Taiwan; the government has established a ministry to address the land claims of the descendants of the pre-Han inhabitants of the island.

Projects by influential agents such as the multilateral development banks can be an essential catalyst in legal reform because most countries now have up-to-date laws on the books somewhere. The problem is that layer upon layer of law and legislation also reflects every development fad from earlier historical eras. A housecleaning is needed, but is often resisted by those (often lawyers and notaries, but also players in inter-ministry turf conflicts) who make a living off the confusion. Bruce stresses that the legal foundations for sustainable use of land need much care and reassessment to get actual ownership by a country and its institutions.

In chapter 10, Bromley helps make clear why this is the case. He argues that there can never be a single concept or idea of land. Following the philosopher Charles Sanders Peirce, he postulates that "land is nothing but the effects that land has on us—and the implications that land holds for us" (p. 220). On the surface this can sound like a "just so" statement, but Bromley develops the concept as an extremely powerful tool for understanding why land issues will require complex analysis in the future.

We are currently in an intellectual state of mind in regard to land, such that the answers seem to be in hand before any data is collected. The vast

---

[11]Professor Shih-Jung Hsu, Department of Land Economics, National Chengchi University, Taiwan. He can be reached at srshiu@nccu.edu.tw.

amount of research that led to the Washington Consensus clearly brought the importance of "getting institutions right" back into the spotlight.[12] Since there are no rich countries with badly working land tenure institutions (e.g., land registries and cadastres), and there are no poor countries with good systems, it seems obvious—we only need to duplicate the good institutions found in OECD countries. This conclusion, however, accepts that a concept of land that gave rise to those institutions must be, in essence, the correct one from a development perspective.

Unfortunately, this "easy" answer falls short on at least two counts. The first and most obvious is that land tenure reform following the given formula of registration of private rights in real property has fallen on barren ground in much of the world, for the reasons given by Bruce. The second is that a globalized competition for natural resources changes the way we see land. The answer to the question of what is the best use of a given area is not the same as it was in Ricardo's day, nor is it the same as it was just a decade ago.

Gregory Ingram agrees that although land in the postindustrial United States is perhaps becoming valued as a consumption asset (as a provider of environmental and ecological services), the actual distribution of land use has remained remarkably stable over the past half century.[13] As the data cited by Ingram show, although the land converted to urban uses had quadrupled in area, in 2002 it was still a very modest 2.7 percent of all land. Also consistent with the idea of land as a consumptive asset is the fact that the area devoted to parks and wildlife has tripled to 13.1 percent (figure 14.1). What Ingram takes from these data is that the "change is indeed evolutionary, and it proceeds by introducing more 'asset classes' in the land portfolio and not by replacing them." What has changed dramatically, however, is the market value of different categories of land during this same period. In comparing the monetary value of urban residential land relative to farmland and land devoted to commercial (nonresidential) uses, we see that these three categories were about the same in 1975. By 2005, the market value of residential property accounted for approximately 75 percent of the total market value of all three categories.[14]

---

[12]I am using Washington Consensus in the nonpejorative sense to refer to the development literature after the collapse of the Soviet Union in 1989 that has emphasized the need to protect property rights and enhance markets and trade, as well as tax and fiscal reform. The emphasis here is on the importance of legal security of property rights.

[13]Comment by Gregory Ingram on Daniel Bromley's "Land and Economic Development: New Institutional Arrangements," in Ingram's comments prepared for the ICLPST 2006 conference.

[14]Case (2006).

**Figure 14.1:** Land Use in the United States

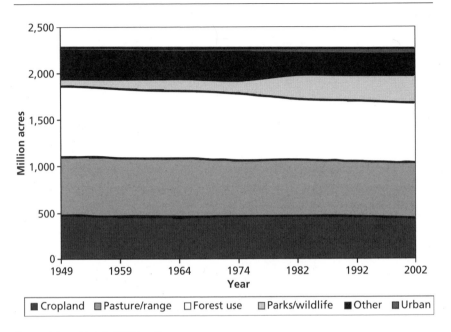

*Source:* Lubowski et al. (2006), p. 3.

That change in market value is another way of expressing Bromley's point. Land resources can remain more or less proportionally the same, but the value people place on them can change dramatically. This is certainly to be expected as publics in democracies absorb and debate scientific studies on earth resource sustainability. National parks were created to preserve natural beauty and to provide recreation. However, as the costs of nonsustainable natural resource uses are being felt by a greater proportion of humanity, we can foresee the day when the role of forests, coastal ecosystems, and glaciers in the local and global economy can be priced like petroleum, minerals, fish catches, and lumber.

The implications of this line of reasoning are really quite profound because we are talking about choices at the core of the future of modern society and how they will be made. For example, it is not too difficult to imagine in the near future a decision about whether the value of a forest as a reservoir of green water, as a sump in carbon sequestration, or as an air purifier is greater than its traditional economic uses.[15] That is, the incremental change in the

---

[15]Green Water is water that is held in the ground and in plant life; it constitutes somewhere between 60 and 70 percent of all precipitation. This concept of water is contrasted with that of "blue water," which is found in our oceans, rivers, and lakes (United Nations Food and Agricultural Organization 1996; Fourth World Water Forum 2006).

perception of land, water, and other resources leads eventually to a societal redefinition of land tenure. Society imposes new rules on who has the rights to use which resources for what purpose and for how long. Since such decisions take place at the supra-individual level, they become political. This brings us full circle to the arguments of the Knaap and Luger chapters that no matter what our theories of pricing tell us, as participants in the political process, citizens will insist on a role in deciding the new tenure rules of natural resource allocation and use.

That phenomenon is well illustrated in chapter 11 by Bebbington, who suggests that large-scale international investments offer to change forever the existing land tenure relationships, and hence the very meaning of the land on which people live. Ultimately, the residents, national policy makers, and international interest groups will all have to face the fact that there are many competing definitions of what "land" means in a specific place and time. Through Bebbington's case studies the reader is introduced to the complexity of how a piece of land is conceptualized. Is it the resource that lies under the soil that determines the "best" value? Or, indeed, is it as an environmental resource in an age of global warming that land is more valuable? Or is it something else that will affect our "conception of the object," to use Peirce's words?[16]

Bebbington's chapter is especially important because it analyzes the manner in which a carefully studied group of land users are changing how they look at land and what it means to them. His analysis allows us to begin to understand the complex interplay of multiple processes that are taking place simultaneously. How land is used has a direct bearing on all kinds of social relationships, which are quite different when we contrast those of the boardroom of the mining company with the professional activities of the geologists and engineers who draw up the design for the mine; the policy makers in the capital responding to pressures from many fronts on a global scale; and, last but not least, the people living in the area where land as a resource is being redefined with or without their participation. This short list leaves out all the new kinds of social relationships that never existed before the technology of the information age. Key to our understanding of the processes of change taking place is the fact that today the social capital of the residents in the affected area may include nongovernmental organizations, environmental advocates, and numerous experts who live in other places and have very different livelihoods.

---

[16]The whole quote, from chapter 10, is "Consider what effects, that might conceivably have practical bearings, we conceive the object of our conception to have. Then, our conception of these effects is the whole of our conception of the object" (Peirce 1934, 1).

## CONCLUSION

Unfortunately, this century has not gotten off to a good start, and there is less agreement on how to go about resolving fundamental resource allocation decisions than there was at the end of the previous century. The number of major players in our globalized economy continues to grow. Both China and India are predicted to overtake the United States as the most prolific users of natural resources during this decade. While public attention will in the short term be focused on petroleum and other scarce commodities of the day, the long-term land tenure policy choices will surely concern those natural resources that are vital to human life and are also part of the global system. No society is in complete control of its water and air or can protect itself completely from environmental contamination, pandemics, global warming, and other forces as science uncovers new dangers (as well as opportunities). The residents of an island city-state like Singapore, which is a model of good land administration, are just as vulnerable to the misinformed land use practices of the slash-and-burn farmers of Sumatra, if not more so, than the policy makers in Jakarta are.

That the authors who contributed to this volume met in Taiwan to share their ideas is significant. Taiwan has benefited greatly from a strong reliance on the market to inform policy discourse. In light of what is going on in other parts of the world, it seems clear that if the meeting had been held in Latin America, there would have been a much larger debate on the role of market pricing in the formation of land tenure and land administration policy. In 2000 the idea that "neoliberal" private property models were a necessary foundation for development had nearly universal acceptance in the development literature; the last five elections in Latin America show that that consensus no longer holds, however.

During the brief interval of years before 2015, our target date, it will be interesting to see how great a bifurcation transpires in policy debates between proponents of some new social property model and the informed consensus that has guided the arguments presented here. The fall of the Berlin Wall in 1989 is at a sufficient distance in time that a whole new generation of scholars will soon arrive on the scene who never experienced the socialist models of the last century.

Demographers tell us that we now live in a world where more people live in cities than in the vast countryside. Yet we also learn that one in three of those urban residents lacks access to adequate water, waste disposal, and hygiene and lives in deplorable physical conditions. The profound irony is that as bad as the slums are, they are considered preferable to life in the rural economy. Yet any improvement in the lot of the vast majority of human beings rests with the land policy decisions made concerning the sustainable use of rural resources. The nonbuilt-up areas are where cities, farmers, and miners get their water, air, food, and natural resources. It is over those rural resources that great policy debates will have to be resolved. On one hand, it is rather depressing to have arrived at this stage and find that the way we lived in the twentieth century is not sustainable in any conceivable mid- to long-term time horizon. On the other hand, it is an exciting time for the student of land tenure. We must get back to basic research and collect data on what the real situation is, rather than relying on answers that evolved out of conceptions of land no longer in tune with our awareness.

## REFERENCES

Case, K. 2006. The value of land in the United States: 1975–2005. Paper presented at Land Policies for Urban Development conference, Lincoln Institute of Land Policy, Cambridge, MA, June 5–6. Also published in *Land policies and their outcomes*. G. K. Ingram and Y-H. Hong, eds. Cambridge, MA: Lincoln Institute of Land Policy, 2007.

Dale, P., and J. McLaughlin. 2000. *Land administration*. London: Oxford University Press.

Fourth World Water Forum. 2006. *Final report*. Marseille, France: World Water Council. Also available at www.worldwaterforum4.org.

Lubowski, R. N., M. Vesterby, S. Bucholtz, A. Baez, and M. J. Roberts. 2006. Major uses of land in the United States. Economic Information Bulletin No. EIB-14 (May). Washington, DC: U.S. Department of Agriculture.

Peirce, C. S. 1934. *Collected papers*, vol. 5. Cambridge, MA: Harvard University Press.

United Nations Food and Agricultural Organization. 1996. *The critical role of water in agriculture*. Background study for the World Food Summit, November 13–17. Rome: Food and Agricultural Organization of the United Nations.

# Contributors

## Editors

GARY C. CORNIA
Marriott School of
Management
Brigham Young University
Provo, Utah

JIM RIDDELL
Course Coordinator
International Center for Land
Policy Studies and Training
Edina, Minnesota

## Authors

ROY BAHL
Andrew Young School of
Policy Studies
Georgia State University
Atlanta

ANTHONY BEBBINGTON
Institute for Development
Policy and Management
School of Environment and
Development
University of Manchester
United Kingdom

DANIEL W. BROMLEY
Department of Agricultural and
Applied Economics
University of Wisconsin–Madison

JOHN W. BRUCE
Land and Development Solutions
International, Inc.
Vienna, Virginia

PETER F. COLWELL
Department of Finance
University of Illinois at
Urbana–Champaign

ROBERT E. EVENSON
Department of Economics
Yale University
New Haven, Connecticut

GERRIT-JAN KNAAP
National Center for Smart
Growth Research and
Education
University of Maryland
College Park

CHI-MEI LIN
International Center
for Land Policy Studies
and Training
Taoyuan, Taiwan

JOHN CHIEN-YUAN LIN
Graduate Institute of Building
and Planning
National Taiwan University
Taipei

KUO-CHING LIN
Department of Agricultural
Economics
National Taiwan University
Taipei

MICHAEL I. LUGER
Manchester Business School
University of Manchester
United Kingdom

JORGE MARTINEZ-VAZQUEZ
Andrew Young School of
Policy Studies
Georgia State University
Atlanta

JOSEPH W. TREFZGER
Department of Finance, Insurance
and Law
Illinois State University
Normal

SALLY WALLACE
Andrew Young School of
Policy Studies
Georgia State University
Atlanta

IAN WILLIAMSON
Department of Geomatics
Centre for Spatial Data Infrastructures
and Land Administration
University of Melbourne
Parkville, Australia

# Index